Born for Liberty

Born for Liberty

A History of Women in America

Sara M. Evans

THE FREE PRESS
A Division of Macmillan, Inc.
NEW YORK

Maxwell Macmillan Canada
TORONTO

Maxwell Macmillan International
NEW YORK   OXFORD   SINGAPORE   SYDNEY

The Free Press
A Division of Macmillan, Inc.
866 Third Avenue, New York, N.Y. 10022

Maxwell Macmillan Canada, Inc.
1200 Eglinton Avenue East
Suite 200
Don Mills, Ontario M3C 3N1

Macmillan, Inc. is part of the Maxwell Communication Group of Companies.

First Free Press Paperback Edition 1991

Printed in the United States of America

printing number

   4 5 6 7 8 9 10

Library of Congress Cataloging-in-Publication Data

Evans, Sara M. (Sara Margaret)
  Born for liberty.

  Bibliography: p.
  Includes index.
  1. Women—United States—History. 2. Women—United States—Social conditions. 3. Women in politics—United States—History. I. Title.
HQ1410.E83 1989   305.4'0973   88-33544
ISBN 0-02-903090-0

In memory of my grandmothers,
Sallie Baker Everett
and
Mary Ligon Evans

Born for liberty, disdaining to bear the irons of a tyrannic Government. . . . Our ambition is kindled by the fame of those heroines of antiquity, who have rendered their sex illustrious, and have proved to the universe, that, if the weakness of our Constitutions, if opinion and manners did not forbid us to march to glory by the same paths as the Men, we should at least equal, and sometimes surpass them in our love for the public good.

—*Sentiments of an American Woman*
PHILADELPHIA, 1780

Contents

Acknowledgments   xi

Introduction   1

1. The First American Women   7

2. The Women Who Came to North America,
1607–1770   21

3. "But What Have I to Do with Politicks?":
The Revolutionary Era   45

4. The Age of Association: 1820–1845   67

5. A Time of Division: 1845–1865   93

6. "Maternal Commonwealth" in the Gilded Age:
1865–1890   119

7. Women and Modernity: 1890–1920   145

8. Flappers, Freudians, and All That Jazz   175

9. Surviving the Great Depression   197

10. Women at War: The 1940s   219

11. The Cold War and the "Feminine Mystique"   243

12. Decade of Discovery: "The Personal Is Political"   263

13. The Politicization of Personal Life:
Women Versus Women   287

Notes   315

Further Reading   367

Index   373

Acknowledgments

Fifteen years ago, when I began to teach women's history, the field had only a handful of books. No standard text gave women more than a few lines (usually about suffragists) and maybe an illustration or two. Since 1974 I have watched the eagerness of students for whom women's history is a constant revelation, generating simultaneous pride and anger. And each year the resources available have become richer. Without the impressive body of scholarship on women produced in the last two decades I could not have written *Born for Liberty*. Standing on the shoulders of so many colleagues I admire, I am humbled by the debt while also aware that many will disagree with some or all of what I have done with this material. It is an honor simply to participate in the conversation.

In five years of work, I have accumulated many more specific debts as well. I am grateful to my editor, Joyce Seltzer, for encouraging me to begin and to persevere undaunted by the grandiosity of the project. Carol Berkin also urged me to take it on and generously shared her work. Throughout these years I have relied on the steady concern and critical feedback of several friends and colleagues. Their interdisciplinary perspectives and willingness to read.multiple drafts have inhanced this book immeasureably. Elaine May, Riv-Ellen Prell, Cheri Register, and Amy Kaminsky were unfailingly generous with their honesty, their knowledge, and their friendship.

Nancy Cott, Suzanne Lebsock, and Anne Firor Scott read the entire manuscript, made numerous helpful suggestions, and caught errors which would have been embarrassing. I have accepted some of their ideas and rejected others, but in either case, the process has been a clarifying one. Any errors which remain are of course my own responsibility. Graduate students at the University of Minnesota have helped me in numerous ways. In part, the experience of teaching graduate seminars provided a forum for the conversations I pursued in these pages. More specifically, Liz Faue and Rosalind Moss gave me helpful readings of chapters on which they had particular expertise. Angel Kwolek-Folland and Colette Hyman found photographs for me while pursuing their own dissertation research. Susan Cahn worked as a research assistant tracking down wayward footnotes and in the process offered incisive comments on virtually every chapter. Laurel Haycock, John Davidann, and Deborah Kitchen also contributed important research assistance.

In the search for specific details, I found that friends were always willing to help out. Linda Kerber provided an obscure citation. Joyce Lyon and Linda Brooks thought with me about pictures for the cover, and Linda gave me the run of her photographic library. Jill Petzall and Lisa Sedaris gave me the benefit of their professional responses to my pile of photographs. Jacqueline Peterson, Janet Spector, and Melissa Meyer offered invaluable bibliographic assistance for sources on Indian women, as did Dennis Valdez on Chicanas. And Barbara Nelson, herself an important role model of someone who works on several projects at once, never complained when I withdrew periodically from our joint project on comparable worth to devote myself to this one.

In the early stages of this project, several families gathered under the aegis of the W. K. Kellogg Foundation to discuss the stresses and benefits of balancing professional and family lives. I am especially glad to have had the advice and ongoing support of Kellogg Fellows Helen Kivnick, Cheryl Mabey, and Holly Wilson. My family was not simply part of a balancing act, however; it also shaped and facilitated my work. My parents, Claude and Maxilla Evans, were, as always, interested and enthusiastic. My children, Craig and Rachel, anchored me in the realities of daily life and kept the pressures of work in their proper perspective. And Harry C. Boyte's criticisms and suggestions were conceptually central just as his willingness to shift the burdens of parental and domestic responsibilities were practically central to the writing. *Born for Liberty* continues an ongoing conversation about the meaning of public and private life which we have pursued for more than two decades.

Introduction

*I*n the last two decades there have been dramatic changes in women's visibility at every level of American life—politics, the labor force, popular culture—accompanied by important shifts in women's perceptions of their own potential. This new visibility sparked a reconsideration of the history they had been told. Women wanted to know about their past. Indeed, they found it difficult to envision future changes without some grounding in a history that included their experience. Yet the only images available consisted of brief references to suffragists or mythic but relatively inconsequential figures like Betsy Ross. Most women still know very little of the female experience in the past, remaining spectators in popular versions of both past and present. Yet the stories they demanded are being unearthed in ever-greater numbers. There has never been a better time for American women to claim the possibilities for full democratic participation in political and social life that their history reveals. To do so, however, requires a retelling of their history that explores women's hardships as well as their achievements and places their stories within the broader context of our nation's history.

The virtual invisibility of women to historians was no oversight. When history is conceived as a narrative of public (primarily political) action, its arena is a stage from which women have traditionally been excluded. The ideological power of that exclusion in turn fostered a double standard; women were ignored regardless of their political importance. The new social history of the last two decades has introduced an amazing pluralism into traditionally defined history by exploring the experiences of women, blacks,

1

family life, factory workers, and immigrants. Now we have many histories, and the historian's task is to integrate these experiences into the dominant narrative of the American past, the main story we tell ourselves about who we have been as a nation.[1]

That story is characterized by a set of ideas perceived by many as a unique gift of American political culture. These ideas include a deep belief in popular sovereignty, in an active and "virtuous" citizenry, and in the importance of "independence" based on having enough property to allow one to look beyond narrow self-interest to the common good. Rooted in English political history and in the classical republicanism of ancient Greece and Rome, and brought to life by the debates over independence, the themes of popular sovereignty, civic virtue, and personal autonomy took dramatic hold in North America in a way different from the rest of the industrializing world. The pluralism of American society required republican principles to expand and adapt to new circumstances and institutions. As classical republicanism mingled with evangelical Protestantism and Enlightenment liberalism, it brought forth a new formulation of active public life blending unique and indigenous elements with traditions shared with Western Europe.

The rhetoric surrounding the American Revolution, rooted in classical Greek assumptions, presumed a sharp dichotomy between public and private. According to philosopher Hannah Arendt, the public was the realm of politics, where citizens who commanded independent resources and private households gathered as peers to debate the future of the community. This political realm was also the exclusive locus of freedom, an arena for action through which individuals made themselves visible using persuasive speech and seeking public recognition of their achievements. Also essential to an active, vital "public" was a strong sense of "virtue," the responsibility of being concerned about community affairs. By contrast, the private domain was not concerned with the issues of constructing a common world but rather with maintaining life, with necessity and species survival (producing food and bearing children). Precisely because women and slaves devoted themselves to the necessities of life, male heads of households had the freedom to engage in politics.[2] According to political philosopher Jean Bethke Elstain, "The flip side of a coin that features the public-spirited visage of the male citizen and dutiful father is the profile

2

of the loving, virtuous, chaste, selfless wife. . . . Without someone to tend the hearth, the legislative halls would grow silent and empty, or become noisily corrupt."[3]

Although initially outside the public arena where politics and citizenship had meaning and specificity, American women effectively reshaped the boundaries of that arena in ways that have not been explored. In doing so they changed the meaning of public life itself. American women did this over a long period of time while simultaneously shaping and adapting their own private sphere, the family, to changing times. By pioneering in the creation of new public spaces—voluntary associations located *between* the public world of politics and work and the private intimacy of family—women made possible a new vision of active citizenship unlike the original vision based on the worlds of small farmers and artisans. Women's vision is an integral part of our nation's distinctive democratic political culture.

The story of women's struggle to situate themselves in the public and civic life of American society is filled with ironies. It forces us to think hard about the slippery definitions of "public" and "private," "male" and "female" over the course of four centuries. During the colonial period, for example, a participatory public life had begun to emerge in the practices of self-government, as town meetings and colonial assemblies developed in small settlements along the Atlantic coast. There were sharp rhetorical distinctions between that narrowly defined "public," from which women were excluded, and the privacy of familial domesticity. The realities of seventeenth-century life, however, allocated to the family many activities and responsibilities—such as education, business activities, and health and welfare—that we now associated with public life and institutions. As a result, political and religious activities remained highly personalized, more like kinship than the impersonal relationships associated with twentieth-century public life, because people knew one another in multiple ways in small communities. For example, the tanner from whom one bought leather could also be a cousin, neighbor, elder in the church, and colonial assembly member. Thus, even though women were excluded from most formal public roles, they had access to private sources of social control over public action. The most powerful example were Iroquois women who, unlike their colonial counterparts, could act as a group to nominate council elders and veto appointments of chiefs. The most extreme example is the women of Salem, Massachusetts; as accused witches, accusers, and witnesses, these women held an entire colony in thrall for months.

The Revolution gave new political meaning to domestic life, raising the role of women to a problematic status in the new political order—a status that has persisted to the present. Public life was the formal realm of "freedom," the arena in which achievement and excellence could receive recognition. Shut out as this realm expanded dramatically in the nineteenth century, women responded by creating a different form of public life. In different ways and to different degrees, virtually every group of women— middle class, immigrant, black, and working class—used voluntary associations to express their interests and to organize for public activity. This allowed public expression of private perspectives and values often at odds with those of a male, upper-class elite. It also sustained and gave political power to certain moral values like compassion and fairness that were eroding in the dominant political culture.

From their earliest roles as helpmates in family economies, to the republican motherhood of the revolutionary era, to the female politics of nineteenth-century reform, to contemporary struggles to define women's public roles and the meaning of gender equality, American women have continually challenged and redefined the boundaries of public and private life. They have demanded public attention and action on issues that arise first in the domestic arena—issues such as health, education, and poverty. They have entered public work by laboring for wages outside the home even though by the nineteenth century being a wage earner had become an integral part of the cultural definitions of both "public" and "manliness." Women created female professions such as teaching, nursing, and social work, making public roles which originated in domesticity. They developed a distinctively American form of public life through voluntary associations that made the vision of active citizenship a sustainable one even as economic individualism on the one hand, and massive bureaucracies on the other, eroded the original Jeffersonian dream of an independent and virtuous yeomanry.

Such an achievement cannot be underestimated, as it holds the possibility for a continual reworking of the democratic dream in the face of the stark realities of great inequality of wealth and power. Since the early nineteenth century, both female and male voluntary associations have been a fundamental aspect of American life. Through them women brought concerns rooted in domesticity into the public arena, forcing changes in the definition of the state with ironic consequences. As the welfare state assumed responsibilities previously relegated to the family, it also reduced the arenas for active citizenship and enforced traditional gender roles in an often intrusive and impersonal way.[4] Yet women's voluntary activities which shaped this development also honed an essential tool for regenerating civic participation, one used over and over by groups outside the mainstream of American life. The powerful, if little recognized, consequences of this development make more poignant the traditional relegation of women to the invisibility of the private realm. Recognizing the crucial importance of active civic participation clarifies the costs of exclusion both for women themselves and for society.

The unexamined nature of this problem can be traced in part to the failure of feminist theorists and historians to confront the distinctive nature of public life and the meaning of citizenship.[5] Feminist historians have devoted themselves primarily to tracing out the dimensions of women's worlds—the work they did, the organizations they built with other women, and changing ideologies about gender. With a few key exceptions, these historians have avoided the study of politics, accepting the cultural definition of politics as male, or they have seen women's political action in instrumental terms, as means to other ends, not as a distinctive activity in its own right.[6] Similarly feminist theorists have tended to sideline any consideration of the nature of public life and female citizenship in favor of a focus on "female values" rooted in the private realm and in reproduction. Thus, although much of the evidence we need has been gathered, the broader patterns remain to be sketched out.

Historian Mary Beard, writing in the 1940s, called women a "force in history." To understand the force of women's experience, we need to transform the traditional stage of public life and history by taking as central what was previously understood to be a backdrop or an unnoticed stage prop. We must adjust our vision so that we can see the world not only through the major male figures in the foreground but also through the eyes of female figures: a Puritan goodwife, an African slave, an Iroquois matron, a westering woman, a female immigrant, a settlement house worker, a secretary. We need to see the household and daily work of middle-class women and migrant workers, of domestics and factory hands; the changing experiences of labor and childbirth; the statistical realities of fertility and mortality; and the female spaces of clubs, benevolent associations, and settlement houses. Then, and only then, can we understand how these stories, so diverse among themselves, affected and transformed the dynamic interplay of public and private life in our past and how the experience of women in America actively shaped the broader history that we, women and men, all claim as our own. Only then can we begin to imagine what it will really mean for women to be *citizens*, full participants in the decision-making process that shapes our future.

1

The First American Women

A ccording to the Iroquois, the creation of the earth began when a woman came from heaven and fluttered above the sea, unable to find a resting place for her feet. The fish and animals of the sea, having compassion on her, debated in council about which of them should help her. The tortoise offered his back, which became the land, and the woman made her home there. A spirit noticed her loneliness and with her begot three children to provide her company. The quarrels of her two sons can still be heard in the thunder. But her daughter became the mother of the great nations of the Iroquois.[1]

Women appear frequently at the cosmic center of native-American myths and legends, tales that are undoubtedly very ancient. The history of women on the North American continent began 20,000 years ago with the migration of people from the Asian continent across the land bridge that now is the Bering Strait. These early ancestors of contemporary native Americans gradually created a great diversity of cultures as they adapted to varied environmental circumstances and conditions over time. The archaeological record indicates that 2,000 years ago some North American cultures lived nomadically, hunting and gathering plants and animals. Others settled in villages and subsisted on domesticated plants as well as wild resources. Still others built complex, hierarchically organized societies centered in relatively large cities or towns. In these latter groups, archaeological remains reveal widespread trade relations and religious systems uniting people over vast areas of the continent. When the first Europeans reached North America in the fifteenth and sixteenth centuries, there

7

were some 2,000 native American languages in use, a cultural diversity that made Europe look homogeneous.[2]

Gatherers and Nurturers, Traders and Shamans

Among the peoples of North America whose tribes lived in the woods, along the rivers, and on the edges of the plains, women were essential to group survival. In a subsistence economy, daily life revolved around finding food for the next meal or, at the most, the next season. Women's work as gatherers and processors of food and as nurturers of small children was not only visible to the whole community, but it also shaped ritual life and processes of community decision making.

Women's activities were sharply divided from those of men in most Indian societies. Women gathered seeds, roots, fruits, and other wild plants. And in horticultural groups they cultivated crops such as corn, beans, and squash. Women were also typically responsible for cooking, preserving foods, and making household utensils and furnishings. In addition, they built and maintained dwellings, such as earth or bark lodges and tepees, and associated household facilities like storage pits, benches, mats, wooden racks, and scaffolds. In groups that moved on a seasonal basis, women were often responsible for transporting all household goods from one location to the next.

Male activities in many groups centered on hunting and warfare. After the hunts, Indian women played an important role in processing the hides of deer or buffalo into clothing, blankets, floor coverings, tepees, or trade goods; preserving the meat; and manufacturing a variety of bone implements from the remains of the animals.

Indian societies differed in their definitions of which tasks were appropriate for women or men and in their degree of flexibility or rigidity. In some groups people would be ridiculed and shamed for engaging in tasks inappropriate for their gender, while other groups were more tolerant. Sometimes men and women performed separate, but complementary tasks. Among the Iroquois, for example, men cleared the fields so women could plant them. In other cases men and women performed the same tasks but the work was still segregated on the basis of sex. For example, many Plains Indian tribes divided the task of tanning hides according to the animal, some being assigned exclusively to women, others to men.

8

These differences shaped the relationships among women and between women and men. Societies with a clear sexual division of labor and cooperative modes of production, for example, encouraged gender solidarity. The Pawnee, a Plains society, lived in lodges large enough for several families, or about fifty people. Women shared cooking responsibilities among themselves, alternating between those on the north and those on the south sides of the lodge. Among the Hidatsa, another Plains group, female labor was organized by the household of female kin while male activities, ranging from individual vision quests to sporadic hunting parties, were organized by age and by village. Groups of female kin built and maintained their homes, gathered seeds and edible plants, raised crops, and processed the meat and skins of animals killed by the men.[3]

In Iroquois society, where men were frequently away for prolonged periods of time, women farmed in a highly organized way. A white woman adopted in 1758 by the Seneca (one of the five tribes of the Iroquois Confederacy) described their work:

In the summer season, we planted, tended, and harvested our corn, and generally had all of our children with us; but had no master to oversee or drive us, so that we could work as leisurely as we pleased. . . . We pursued our farming business according to the general custom of Indian women, which is as follows: In order to expedite their business, and at the same time enjoy each other's company, they all work together in one field, or at whatever job they may have on hand. In the spring, they choose an old active squaw to be their driver and overseer, when at labor, for the ensuing year. She accepts the honor, and they consider themselves bound to obey her.

When the time for planting arrives, and the soil is prepared, the squaws are assembled in the morning, and conducted into a field where each plants one row. They then go into the next field and plant once across, and so on till they have gone through the tribe.[4]

As they gathered, cultivated, and produced food, tools, and housing, some women also actively participated in trade. Algonkian women on the Atlantic coast traded with whites from the earliest days. In 1609 John Juet, Henry Hudson's first mate, recorded an incident in New York Harbor: "There came eight and twentie Canoes full of men, women and children to betray us: but we saw their intent, and suffered none of them to come aboord us. . . . They brought with them Oysters and Beanes, whereof we bought some."[5] In later years many observers noted both transactions with women and the high proportion of trade goods that were particularly interesting to women. Far to the northwest, on the Alaskan coast, the Tlingit built their economy on fishing for plentiful salmon and on trading with neighboring groups. Tlingit women not only dried and processed the salmon but they were also entrusted with managing and dispensing the family wealth. White traders were continually struck by the skill and sophistication of these women, who frequently stepped in to cancel unwise deals made by their husbands. These shrewd dealings paid off in that society where status could be gained by impressive displays of gift-giving.[6]

Religious myths and rituals offered women additional sources of power and status in their villages and tribes as they reflected in a symbolic realm the relations between people and nature.[7] In most North American Indian creation myths, females played critical roles as mediators between supernatural powers and earth. Many horticultural societies ritually celebrated the seasonal powers of Earth Mother—whose body produced the sacred foods of corn, beans, and squash. Groups primarily oriented to hunting more frequently conceptualized sacred powers as male, but in some cases the Keeper of the Game appeared as a woman. She observed humans' failures to address proper ritual prayers to the spirits of the animals and to treat the animal world on which they depended with proper respect; she could also inflict punishments of disease and famine.

American Indians perceived their world as sacred and alive. Power and mystery infused all living things, inspiring awe and fear. Women, like men, sought spiritual understanding and power by engaging in individual quests for visions. Quests involved a period of seclusion, fasting, and performance of prescribed rituals. Women's quests drew on the fasting and seclusion accompanying menstruation.

In most societies menstruating women were believed to be dangerously powerful, capable of harming crops or hunts and draining the spiritual powers of men. To avoid such harm they withdrew to menstrual huts outside the villages. Did women interpret this experience in terms of pollution and taboo, seeing it as a banishment, as many observers assumed? More likely they welcomed the occasional respite from daily responsibilities as an opportunity for meditation, spiritual growth, and the company of other women. The power that visions conferred allowed some women to serve as herbalists, midwives, medicine women, and shamans.

10

Marriage practices in some societies granted women considerable control in choosing their partners. In others, marriages were arranged by elders (often women) as a means of building economic alliances through kinship. Divorce, on the other hand, was common and easy to accomplish. A woman could simply leave her husband or, if the house was hers, she could order him out on grounds of sterility, adultery, laziness, cruelty, or bad temper. Women's autonomy often had a further sexual dimension: Although the male-dominated groups prized female chastity, most Indian groups encouraged sexual expressiveness and did not enforce strict monogamy. Female power in marital and sexual relations could also be shaped by the proximity of a woman to her own kin.

Women's political power was rooted in kinship relations and economics. The scale of clan and village life meant that people knew one another primarily through kinship designators (daughter, husband, mother's brother, grandmother), and in many cases the most important level of sociopolitical organization was the local kin group. It seems likely that female power was most salient at the level of the village group, where it would shape many facets of daily life. In many tribes, however, there were some (often transitory or temporary) public forums, such as a council of elders, where decisions could be made for the community as a whole. Women held proportionately few of these public roles, but a recent reevaluation of ethnographic evidence shows that despite most scholars' belief that women had no significant political roles, there were numerous female chiefs, shamans, and traders.[8]

Iroquois women represented the apex of female political power. The land was theirs; the women worked it cooperatively and controlled the distribution of all food whether originally procured by women or by men. This gave them essential control over the economic organization of their tribe; they could withhold food at any point—in the household, the council of elders, war parties, or religious celebrations.[9] The Iroquois institutionalized female power in the rights of matrons, or older women, to nominate council elders and to depose chiefs. As one missionary wrote: "They did not hesitate, when the occasion required, to 'knock off the horns' as it was technically called, from the head of a chief and send him back to the ranks of the warriors. The original nomination of the chiefs also always rested with them."[10] When the council met, the matrons would lobby with the elders to make their views known. Though women did not sit in formal or public positions of power, as heads of households they were empowered *as a group*. This, in turn, reflected their considerable autonomy within their households.[11]

Gender and Change: The Impact of European Contact

When Europeans began to invade the Americas in the 1500s, the most devastating assault on Indian life initially came from the unseen bacteria and viruses Europeans brought with them. Within a century raging epidemics of typhoid, diphtheria, influenza, measles, chicken pox, whooping cough, tuberculosis, smallpox, scarlet fever, strep, and yellow fever reduced the population of Mexico to only 5 to 10 percent of its former level of 25 million. The population of the northern areas which later became the United States suffered similar fates.[12]

As cultural, economic, and military contacts grew, the differences between women and men in each group began to change. In some cases women appropriated new sources of wealth and power; in others they lost both skills and autonomy. These various changes were shaped by the sexual division of labor in indigenous cultures, the demographic composition of European colonizers, and the nature of the economic relations between Indians and Europeans.

For example, when the Aztec empire fell before the superior military technology of the Spanish, women were booty in the military victory. The demographic facts of a dense Indian population and Spanish conquerors who were almost exclusively male shaped a continuing sexual interaction between Spanish men and Indian women. Seeking stability, the Spanish soon began to encourage marriages with Christianized Indian women. These Indian mothers of the mestizo (mixed-bloods) were historically stigmatized both by a racial caste system and by association with illegitimacy. Nevertheless, they fashioned for their children a new culture blending Christianity and the Spanish language with cultural concepts and practices from their Indian heritage. Contemporary Mexican culture is the result of their creative survival.[13]

On the Atlantic coast of North America, by contrast, English colonizers emigrated in family groups, and sexual liaisons with Indians were rare. Algonkian Indian women quickly seized the opportunity to trade for European goods such as metal kettles, tools, and needles and put them to use in their daily work. Although quick to appropriate European technology, they and their

12

people actively resisted European domination. They fought back militarily, politically, and culturally. One key form of resistance was the Indian insistence on continuing women's prominent roles in politics, religious ritual, and trade despite the inability of Englishmen to recognize or deal with them.[14]

The impact of Europeans was more indirect for inland Indians. The European market for furs represented an opportunity for tribes eager to procure European trade goods. In all likelihood the men's increased emphasis on hunting and warfare sharpened the separation of men's and women's lives. The Iroquois, for example, quickly became dependent on trade goods and lost traditional crafts such as making pottery, stone axes, knives, and arrowheads. Yet by the 1640s they had depleted the beaver supply and had to compete with neighboring tribes for hunting grounds. One result of their longer and longer hunting expeditions was that the village itself became a female space. As hunters, traders, and fighters, men had to travel most of the year while women stayed at home, maintaining villages and cornfields generation after generation.[15] One consequence, then, of the fur trade in the first two centuries after contact was increased power for Iroquois women as they controlled local resources and local affairs.

Lacking a similar strong base in highly productive local agriculture, however, women in other tribes did not gain the power and influence that Iroquois women did. Among the Montagnais-Naskapi in the upper St. Lawrence valley, the fur trade gradually shifted the economic balance toward dependence on income provided by the men's trap lines or wages.[16] In some tribes, polygamy increased when a single hunter could provide more carcasses than a single woman could process.[17]

One group of Indian women—those who married fur traders—created an altogether new cultural and economic pattern. European fur traders, principally the French and later the English and Dutch, were almost exclusively male. As they traveled thousands of miles inland, traders depended on the Indians for their immediate survival and for long-term trade relations; thus, they began to marry Indian women. Indeed, Indian women provided the knowledge, skills, and labor that made it possible for many traders to survive in an unfamiliar environment. On the basis of such relationships, over the course of two centuries a fur trade society emerged, bound together by economics, kinship, rituals, and religion.[18]

Essentially traders adopted an indigenous way of life. Indian

13

women prepared hides, made clothing and moccasins; manufactured snowshoes; prepared and preserved foods such as pemmican—a buffalo meat and fat mixture that could be carried on long trips; caught and dried fish; and gathered local fruits and vegetables such as wild rice, maple sugar, and berries. Stories abound of trading posts saved from starvation by the fishing or gathering or snaring skills of Indian women.

Indian women's ability to dress furs, build canoes, and travel in the wilderness rendered them invaluable to traders. A Chipewyan guide argued that the Hudson's Bay Company's failed expeditions were caused by a lack of women:

> in case they meet with success in hunting, who is to carry the produce of their labour? Women . . . also pitch our tents, make and mend our clothing, keep us warm at night; and, in fact, there is no such thing as travelling any considerable distance, or for any length of time, in this country, without their assistance.[19]

Indian women were active participants in the trade itself: They served as interpreters on whose linguistic and diplomatic abilities much depended. They trapped small animals and sold their pelts, as did many of their sisters who remained in traditional Indian society.

There is considerable evidence that some marriages between Indian women and fur traders resulted in long-lasting and apparently caring alliances. William McNeil, ship captain for the Hudson's Bay Company, mourned the loss of his wife Haida in childbirth: "The deceased has been a good and faithful partner for me for twenty years and we had twelve children together . . . [she] was a most kind mother to her children, and no Woman could have done her duty better, although an Indian."[20]

Despite their importance, many Indian women involved in the fur trade were exploited. As guides or as wives, they lived in a social and economic structure organized around the needs of male European traders.[21] When they decided to return to Europe, traders were notorious for abandoning wives of many years, sometimes simply passing them on to their successors. Such practices contributed to the increased reluctance of Indian women to have any relations with white men. According to observers in the early nineteenth century, the fertility of traders' wives, who commonly had eight to twelve children, was sharply higher than that of traditional Indian women, who bore only four children on average.

Traders did not observe traditional practices that restricted fertility, such as lengthy hunting expeditions and ritually prescribed abstinence. And unlike their traditional sisters who had virtual control over their offspring, traders' wives experienced the assertion of patriarchal authority most painfully when their children—especially their sons—were sent away to receive a "civilized education."[22]

The daughters of such marriages eventually replaced Indian women as the wives of traders. Their mothers' training in language and domestic skills and their ongoing relations with Indian kin fitted them to continue the role of "women-in-between" and their marriages settled into more permanent, lifelong patterns. At the same time, these mixed-blood, or metis, daughters lacked many of the sources of power and autonomy of their Indian mothers. They were less likely to choose their marriage partners and they married at a much younger age. Also, they did not have strong kinship networks to which to escape if their marriages proved unhappy or abusive. The absorption of European norms meant a far more polarized notion of men's public and women's private spheres along with the explicit subordination of women in both. The ultimate burden for the Indian wives of European traders came with the arrival of increased numbers of white women to the wilderness in the nineteenth century. Indian and mixed-blood wives experienced a growing racial prejudice that was not abated by even the highest degree of acculturation.[23]

The fur trade collapsed in the middle of the nineteenth century, as did the society that had grown up around it. Sizable towns in the Great Lakes region were populated by metis people who spoke a common language used in trade, shared the Catholic religion, and grounded their lives in the economics of the fur trade. The disappearance of the fur trade and the emergence of reservation policies in the United States forcing persons of Indian descent to register as Indians defined out of existence a people whose unique culture was built on the lives and activities of Indian "women-in-between."

By contrast, in the sixteenth and seventeenth centuries a very different set of circumstances strengthened the influence of women in some tribes on the Great Plains while marginalizing their power in others. These changes were less a product of trading relationships than of new technologies and economic possibilities inadvertently introduced by Europeans. Navaho women, for example, owned and managed livestock, enabling them to develop broad social and economic powers and a position of high prestige based on their economic independence. Sheep and goats, originally introduced by Spanish explorers, rapidly became the principal livestock, greatly expanding women's resources.[24]

Farther north, the introduction of horses in the early 1700s transformed the technology of hunting and, therefore, the Indians' way of life on the Plains.[25] Nomadic tribes previously had traveled slowly, depending principally on women's gathering for subsistence and engaging in highly organized collective hunts that often failed. Early in the eighteenth century, however, Plains tribes gained access to horses descended from those brought by early Spanish explorers. Horses enabled bands of hunters to range over a far wider territory and transformed buffalo hunting. An individual hunter could ride into a herd, choose as prey the largest rather than the weakest animals, and shoot his arrows at point-blank range. The consequence for the material life of Plains people was sudden, unprecedented wealth: more meat protein than they could consume, with plentiful hides for tepees, clothing, and finally, for trade.

More individualized hunting styles placed a premium on skill and prowess while encouraging the accumulation of wealth. The fact that a single hunter could easily supply several women with hides to dress and meat to cure encouraged polygamy. And the chronic shortage of horses led to institutionalized raiding and continuous intertribal warfare. The life-style that emerged under such circumstances has become in some respects the center of American mythology about the Indian. Mythical images of warlike braves galloping across the Plains in full headdress or engaging in rituals like the famed sundance leave little place for Indian women except as passive squaws waiting in the background.

The myths themselves reflect the heightened emphasis on male domination and concurrent loss of female power that accompanied the social and economic revolution brought by the use of horses. Certainly men's and women's life experiences diverged substantially. Frequently women traveled with hunting parties, charged with the care of tepees, children, food preparation, and clothing manufacture, as well as the processing of the huge carcasses. Though the women continued to do the bulk of the work, the romance and daring of war and hunting dominated the ritual life of the group. Male bonding grew with such ritual occasions and the development of military societies.[26]

By the nineteenth century the Lakota culture had incorporated an emphasis on sexual differences into all aspects of daily life. Cultural symbols sharply emphasized the distinction between aggressive maleness and passive femaleness. The sexual division of labor defined these differences concretely.[27] Extreme distinctions in demeanor, personality, and even language flowed from this rigid division. Men went on vision quests, directed religious rituals, and served as shamans and medicine men. Though women were economically dependent, their work remained essential to group survival, and their importance found ritual expression in female societies and in some women's individual visions that gave them access to sacred powers. The most important female society was made up of quill and beadwork specialists devoted to the mythic Double Woman Dreamer. The Lakota believed that dreams of the Double Woman caused women to behave in aggressive masculine ways: "They possessed the power to cast spells on men and seduce them. They were said to be very promiscuous, to live alone, and on occasion to perform the Double Woman Dreamer ceremony publically."[28]

The Double Woman Dreamer enabled the Lakota and other Plains Indians to incorporate specific social roles for women whose behavior violated feminine norms. Another was the widespread role of a "warrior woman" or "manly hearted woman" who acted as a man in both hunting and warfare. The manly hearted woman is a parallel role to the male "berdache," a man who could assume the dress and roles of a woman and was presumed to have special powers. Thus, although women lost both economic and cultural power as Plains tribes began using horses to hunt, to some degree women and men could move outside the boundaries of strictly defined feminine and masculine roles.

This fluidity allowed a few women quite literally to live the lives of men. In some societies manly hearted women were noticed very young and raised with extreme favoritism and license. In others the shift in gender roles received validation at a later age through dreams or visions. A trader on the Upper Missouri River told the story of one such woman, a member of the Gros Ventres captured at the age of 12.

> Already exhibiting manly interests, her adopted father encouraged these inclinations and trained her in a wide variety of male occupational skills. Although she dressed as a woman throughout her life, she pursued the role of a male in her adult years. She was a proficient hunter and chased big game on horseback and on foot. She was a

17

skilled warrior, leading many successful war parties. In time, she sat on the council and ranked as the third leading warrior in a band of 160 lodges. After achieving success in manly pursuits, she took four wives whose hide-processing work brought considerable wealth to her lodge.[29]

What the Europeans Thought They Saw

At the time of the American Revolution, the existence of Indian societies, and in particular the highly democratic Iroquois Confederacy, provided for white Americans a living proof of the possibility of self-rule. Their virtues furnished a useful contrast to the corruption and tyranny against which Americans saw themselves struggling. For example, Thomas Jefferson wrote that the Europeans "have divided their nations into two classes, wolves and sheep." But for the Indians, "controls are in their manners and their moral sense of right and wrong." As a result, Indians "enjoy . . . an infinitely greater degree of happiness than those who live under European governments."[30]

What the founding fathers did not explore, however, was that the Iroquois model included considerably more political and economic power for women than any Europeans considered possible. Many white observers overlooked the cultural complexity of Indian societies and the great range of women's economic, social, and religious roles. From the sixteenth to the nineteenth century both male and female writers persisted in describing Indian women— if they described them at all—as slaves, degraded and abused. A sixteenth-century Jesuit outlined the many tasks of Montagnais-Naskapi women, contrasted them with the observation that "the men concern themselves with nothing but the more laborious hunting and waging of war," and concluded that "their wives are regarded and treated as slaves."[31] An English fur trader, exploring the Canadian forests in the 1690s, described the status of Cree women: "Now as for a woman they do not so much mind her for they reckon she is like a Slead dog or Bitch when she is living & when she dies they think she departs to Eternity but a man they think departs to another world & lives again."[32]

Similarly, Europeans failed to comprehend women's political power. Early contacts with the coastal Algonkians, for example, produced elaborate descriptions of villages, tribes, and occasional confederacies headed by "chiefs" or "kings." Because Europeans looked for social organizations similar to the cities and states they

18

knew, they could not imagine that the most significant political and economic unit of these people was the matrilineal-matrilocal clan in which women had considerable power and autonomy.[33]

What these observers saw was a division of labor in which women performed many tasks that European culture assigned to men. They were especially outraged to see women chopping wood, building houses, carrying heavy loads, and engaging in agriculture—jobs that in their view constituted the very definition of manly work. Missionaries, for example, persistently defined their goal as civilizing the Indians, by which they meant not only urging them to accept Christian doctrine and sacraments but also to adopt a way of life based on female domesticity and male-dominated, settled agriculture. Not surprisingly, their ideas met sharp resistance.

Iroquois women by the late eighteenth century, for example, were eager to obtain information about the agricultural practices of Quaker missionaries, but they wanted to use it themselves. When Quakers insisted on teaching men, the women ridiculed them as transvestites. "If a Man took hold of a Hoe to use it the Women would get down his gun by way of derision & would laugh & say such a warrior is a timid woman."[34]

In the long run, the Iroquois example held deep implications not only for self-rule but also for an inclusive democracy that sanctioned female participation. The latter, however, was something that revolutionary founding fathers could not fathom. Their definitions of "public" and "private," "masculine" and "feminine" did not allow them to see the more fluid, democratic, and simply *different* realities of Indian life. Yet over the course of American history, an understanding of public, political life built on an inclusive definition of citizenship proved to be a powerful idea, one capable of subverting even the ancient hierarchies of gender.

To understand whites' obliviousness to realities of gender in Indian societies and the alternatives they represented, we must examine the lives of the white women who came to North America in the seventeenth and eighteenth centuries by consent and the black women who came by force. The new possibilities created by these immigrants and their descendants, as well as the boundaries within which they lived, in turn set the terms for the long struggle over female citizenship.

2

The Women Who Came
to North America, 1607–1770

*T*oward the end of her 91 years (1665–1754) in Ipswich, Massa-chusetts, Elizabeth Rogers Appleton drew up the following stark account: "Hear is an account of all my posterity. 6 sons and 3 daughters, 20 grand son and 20 grand daughters, 58 in all." Only five of her nine children had lived to adulthood, however, and less than half of her grandchildren survived. "I often look over this list with sorrow," she continued, but she took comfort in her faith that "I shall mett them all att Christ's rit hand among his sheep and lambs." Concerned about the spiritual health of her descendents and convinced of her own right to direct their lives, this good Puritan also admonished her survivors to "remember their creator in the days of thire youth, and fear God betimes."[1]

In the years since her birth, the Massachusetts colony had grown into a thriving commercial community. From the outset the constant cycle of pregnancy, birth, and death shaped the lives of women like Elizabeth Appleton. And yet, the inner meanings of those webs of kinship and the kinds of power women could exercise would be different for Appleton's granddaughters than they had been for her. On the one hand, family life was growing more emotionally expressive and religious experience more inward, one could say even more "feminine." On the other hand, women's informal power to control behavior through networks of communication and gossip was in decline by the 1750s as men's and women's work began to occupy increasingly different spaces and a new public life emerged from which women were excluded.

21

From the beginning the gendered world of the North American colonies was infused with strong notions about women and men. European immigrants explicitly believed in female inferiority. Even Protestants, in revolt against a male Catholic hierarchy and convinced of the equality of souls before God, nevertheless insisted on women's proper subordination within the family. As John Calvin asserted: "Let the woman be satisfied with her state of subjection, and not take it amiss that she is made inferior to the more distinguished sex."[2] While still aboard the *Arabella* when he described the Puritan mission in the New World, John Winthrop began with an assertion of divinely ordained hierarchy: "God Almightie in his most holy and wise providence hath soe disposed of the condition of mankinde, as in all times some must be rich some poore, some highe and eminent in power and dignitie; others meane and in subjection." John Milton's famous line in *Paradise Lost*—"he for God only, she for God in him"—explained how the subjection of woman to man paralleled that of man to God. Thus the subjection of wife to husband, like that of man to God, could function metaphorically to describe a range of hierarchical social relationships within the broader political and social order.[3]

Women were inferior not only religiously but also legally. Under English common law a married woman was "covered" by her husband. The name given to her status was *feme covert* and as such she had no independent legal standing. She could neither own property nor sign contracts; she did not even own the wages she might earn. Her legal existence merged into that of her husband. Only single women over the age of twenty-one, and widows, with a status known as *feme sole*, had legal rights to make contracts and hold property in their own names. Widows in particular exercised considerable legal rights as the agents of their deceased husbands.[4]

At the same time, images and myths of female power were very much in the minds of seventeenth-century Europeans. They knew, for example, that it was possible for women of the aristocracy to control nations and armies. The reign of Queen Elizabeth I over England remained in living memory. Although ordinary women could never aspire to such positions, they had other powers unique to their sex: Women were disorderly, sexual, and lusty. Their cold and wet humors (in contrast to the hot and dry humors of men) made them deceptive. A woman's womb, without sufficient sexual and reproductive activity, might leave its moorings and wander about the female body producing hysteria. With woman's intellect at the mercy of her lower nature, she would be prone to the evil powers of witchcraft. Her very sensual and disruptive power, in fact, dictated the necessity of her subordination within marriage.[5]

In real communities women could and did exercise considerable social power through informal channels. Working together, sharing childbirths and funerals, selling and buying milk, butter, or thread, they knew intimate details about most people in the community. Privacy was virtually nonexistent and social control of matters from sexuality to economic transactions remained primarily external—often in the hands of neighborhood women whose gossip could create or destroy reputations. Sometimes even the overt power of male-dominated governmental and religious institutions paled before the informal powers of female voluntary association and gossip.[6]

The Migrations of European and African Women

Women were an integral part of the massive migrations into North America beginning in the seventeenth century. Once the purpose of travel shifted from male-dominated exploration and fortune-seeking to permanent settlement, women joined in large numbers. Like men, women came from a variety of backgrounds and for very different reasons. With hope, and sometimes out of desperation, English Puritans and Quakers, Irish Catholics, Dutch farmers, and Scottish Presbyterians came for religious freedom and economic opportunity.[7] Women's roots in the Old World shaped not only their expectations but also the repertoire of female responses with which they coped in a New World.

A combination of religious disorder and socioeconomic change in England and Europe drove settlers to set out on small, unstable sailboats for the three-month voyage across the Atlantic. Women, like men, came because they saw the New World as an opportunity for a better life or because they had little other choice. In New England and the middle colonies they usually arrived with their families. In the southern colonies they more often came alone as indentured servants and prospective wives for male settlers.

Whether women migrated in families or alone, by choice or by force, they arrived in a wilderness whose climate and terrain was unknown except to the native peoples whom they rapidly

23

displaced. Its chief attribute, in contrast to crowded Europe, was space. The land seemed endless. For Puritans this meant an opportunity to create a godly society that could serve as a beacon to the rest of the world. For Quakers in New Jersey and Pennsylvania it meant an escape from persecution. For leaders in every colony it meant financial opportunity. In these wide spaces women's lives were shaped by the demographic imbalance between women and men, by high fertility and mortality, by a social world in which the boundaries between family and community, private and public spheres remained highly permeable, and by a culture that prescribed specific tasks and subordinate status to women.

Anne Dudley spent her British childhood on the lush estates of the Earl of Lincoln, where her father served as a steward, managing the property and household. Private tutors and access to the earl's extensive library fed her eager mind through her fifteenth year. She absorbed the strong beliefs of Nonconformist Protestants who increasingly believed that the Church of England had become corrupt and heretical. At sixteen she married twenty-five-year-old Simon Bradstreet; two years later, in 1630, she embarked with her husband and parents on the *Arabella* with a company of Puritans determined to create a godly community in the New World. Boston—a few muddy roads and makeshift houses clinging to the edge of the harbor—shocked the eighteen-year-old wife. Her "heart rose" within her. "But after I was convinced it was the way of God, I submitted to it and joined to the church at Boston."[8] For the rest of her life she was an active and devout member of her community, bearing and raising eight children. Although her life in many ways followed the pattern of most Puritan women, the fact that Anne Dudley Bradstreet wrote poems sets her apart. Her poetry offers us a glimpse of the daily trials and inner life of a Puritan woman. Suffused with an abiding faith in God, she wrote of her warm love for her husband, her sorrow at the deaths of children, and fears of death in childbirth. The night her house burned down she traced out her loss as a map of the familiar artifacts of daily life:

> Here stood that Trunk, and there that chest;
> There lay that store I counted best:
> My pleasant things in ashes lye,
> And them behold no more shall I.
> Under thy roof no guest shall sitt,
> Nor at thy Table eat a bitt.[9]

Four years after Anne Dudley Bradstreet arrived in Boston, an older Puritan woman disembarked with her family. Forty-three-year-old Anne Hutchinson came with her husband and twelve children as followers of Puritan minister John Cotton, who had been hounded from his pulpit in England. Although Anne Bradstreet traveled as a daughter and wife, making the best of her life once she arrived, Anne Hutchinson and her husband clearly made a joint decision to emigrate on religious grounds. She immediately immersed herself in the religious life of the Boston community, discussing theology with the women she served as a nurse and midwife and holding meetings in her home to interpret the sermons of her mentor, Reverend John Cotton.

In the middle colonies of New York, New Jersey, and Pennsylvania, women arrived with their families as had Anne Bradstreet and Anne Hutchinson, though some also came individually as indentured servants or slaves. From Holland, Sweden, Germany, Scotland, Ireland, France, and Switzerland they came primarily seeking economic opportunity. Quakers, Mennonites, and French Huguenots sought freedom from religious persecution and an opportunity to live a godly life as they understood it. During the seventeenth century they tended to live in scattered agricultural settlements where the contacts with Indians often prevented starvation.[10] However, colonial women observed that European diseases were even more devastating to Indian people than firearms in the ongoing conflict over land. Mary Smith, a Pennsylvania Quaker, wrote in the early eighteenth century that "God's providence made room for us in a wonderful manner, in taking away the Indians. There came a distemper among them so mortal that they could not bury all the dead. Others went away, leaving their town."[11]

Further south in the region around the Chesapeake Bay colonies of Virginia and Maryland, women rarely immigrated in family groups. Instead of tight-knit self-governing communities, southern colonies were money-making enterprises focused on staple crops such as tobacco in the Chesapeake region and, later, rice in Carolina. Women, like men, emigrated primarily as indentured servants, obliged to work for four or five years to repay the cost of their travel. The opportunity these women sought was not religious freedom but a chance to marry and, therefore, ensure their economic survival.

Few of these women were literate and even fewer wrote about

their experiences. In the eighteenth-century a young servant's lament to her father described conditions similar to those in the previous century: "What we unfortunat English People suffer here is beyond the probibility of you in England to conceive." She went on to enumerate her woes, "toiling almost Day and Night" while her master yelled "you Bitch you do not [do] halfe enough . . . tied up and whipp'd . . . scarce any thing but Indian Corn and Salt to eat . . . almost naked no shoes nor stockings to wear . . . what rest we can get is to rap ourselves up in a Blanket and ly upon the Ground, this is the deplorable Conditions your poor Betty endures."[12]

Women who worked on tobacco farms scattered along the bay and rivers of the Chesapeake region faced harsh conditions of labor and new diseases: malaria, influenza, dysentery. Men died young, most by the age of forty-three; women, even younger. But three men immigrated for every woman. If women survived their indentures, they invariably married.

The demographic and environmental setting in the Chesapeake region contrasted sharply with women's experiences in England; the New World was harsh and more precarious.[13] Uprooted from family and community, they worked in households and tobacco fields and once their indentures were finished they chose their marriage partners without parental supervision. Once married, they began bearing children relatively late. Unsupervised by close neighbors and vulnerable to sexually abusive masters, one in five female servants wound up in court, pregnant before her term of servitude was up. If she or her lover could not buy out her term, she could be sentenced to pay a fine, receive a whipping, and serve one to two additional years for breach of contract. Furthermore, her child could be taken from her by the court and bound out to another family. If women exercised new prerogatives in their choice of husbands or their management of estates, they did so in a context of high mortality and social isolation. One in four children died before the age of one, and nearly half died before reaching adulthood. Women were also likely to experience widowhood as the odds for marriages lasting as long as ten years were only one in three. Even though they often outlived their husbands, they were usually left with two or three children.[14]

Another group of uprooted women also began to arrive in the colonies in the late seventeenth century, but the conditions

26

of their emigration from Africa involved no elements of choice or of future hopes. African slavery had begun in the Caribbean. It spread in the southern colonies, where labor-intensive cash crops such as tobacco created an intense demand for a highly controlled labor force.

Snatched from their homes in what are now Nigeria, Angola, and Biafra, African women who survived the forced march to the coast were herded onto slave ships for the infamous "middle passage" from Africa to the New World. Surrounded by strangers, naked, prone in the dark and crowded hold of the ship (or on the deck, exposed to weather and sexual assault), up to a fifth of them died on the trip. Others died soon after landing, whether in the sugar-producing colonies of the West Indies or the mainland colonies. Slave ships carried women and men in a ratio of about one to two. On arrival, any friendships formed en route were sundered as Africans marched one by one to the auction block where strange-looking people stared at them, spoke unintelligible words, poked their bodies, inspected their teeth and the women's breasts, and bought them. At her master's home, a new slave would be lucky to discover that the plantation was large enough to employ several slaves and even luckier if some of them spoke her native language. With them she would live in the slave quarters and work in the fields. African women began an African-American community and culture as they taught their American-born children the memories of their homeland.[15]

Work and Family in the Seventeenth Century

To capture the rhythm of a colonial woman's daily work, it helps to envision the environment in which she accomplished her tasks. Imagine a large room, fifteen by twenty feet, dominated by a cavernous seven-foot-wide fireplace on one wall. Along the walls are a bed or two, a table, perhaps a chair, and several chests. In the earliest years, houses consisted entirely of this single room. Over time the loft reached by a ladder might become sleeping as well as storage space, or a second large room could be built with a fireplace sharing the original chimney. Out back would be a lean-to shed providing more storage and smaller buildings for washing, storing milk, keeping hens, or brewing cider and beer. The main room or "hall," however, continued to be the center of household activity. The lack of differentiation in this

space reflected the unity of the family economy within which
tasks were clearly allocated by gender.[16]

Building and maintaining the fire and processing and preparing
food for the household were endless tasks for Euro-American
women just as for American Indian women. Throughout the day
the housewife would find herself banking the fire, coaxing a blaze,
setting dough to rise, baking bread, and boiling meat. In between
she turned to the most pressing tasks that varied by season: dairy-
ing (milking and making cheese and butter), gathering eggs and
feeding chickens, brewing cider or beer, slaughtering, smoking
bacon, or managing her vegetable garden. She sewed clothes and
quilts for the family though she relied on others to spin thread,
weave cloth, and grind wheat. In turn, she might sell surplus
cheese, eggs, or butter in the village. The resulting networks of
trade among women played a critical role in village life. Because
such networks were local and personal and transactions tended
to be oral, not written, these economic activities remain largely
undocumented.[17]

In cities housewives drew even more heavily on trade to provide
for their families. They became experts at procuring the items
they needed rather than personally manufacturing or processing
them, yet their households retained the undifferentiated quality
of more rural farmhouses. If their husbands were artisans or
shopkeepers, women managed the family business whenever necessary. Like their rural counterparts, city women spent hours boiling laundry and later ironing clothes with heavy irons heated
on the fire. Wealthy women had servants to help with such chores,
and in southern cities like Charlestown, S.C., they supervised the
labor of slaves. Though household manufacture was less critical
in urban areas, some women occupied themselves and their children with spinning to bring in additional money.

Few colonial women received any formal education, though
in New England it was common to bind young girls out as apprentices and servants to other families who promised to teach them
reading as well as household tasks. Beginning at about the age
of six, these children learned the basic skills of housewifery and
sometimes the rudiments of reading from their mothers. Their
brothers were far more likely to be literate as well as to receive
training in a variety of artisanal crafts. Women's skills were acquired in the daily rounds of activities in the household, the family
business, and the marketplace.

Women on the outer edges of white settlement most closely approximated the image of the self-sufficient colonial housewives who—with their husbands—produced and manufactured virtually everything their families used. Distance and poverty gave them little choice and their manufacturing was often of a crude sort. When Magdalen Wear's husband died in York, Maine, he left her and their six children with an estate of 7£ in household goods: "some old pewter, a pot, two bedsteads, bedding, one chest, and a box."[18]

On hardscrabble farms in both the north and south, women worked in the fields as well. On the southern frontier women pounded and ground corn, gardened, milked cows and made butter and cheese, sewed and laundered clothes. Few spun or wove cloth until later in the century, nor did many manufacture items such as candles. Larger planters' emphasis on cash crops and the constancy of trade with England and the Indies made such items available except when the tobacco economy experienced a recession. The necessity of female labor, and the clearly understood divisions of tasks, appeared in contracts such as one signed by a tenant farmer specifying that he would work the land with one servant and that his wife would "Dresse the Victualls milk the cowes wash for the servants and doe allthings necessary for a woman to doe upon the s[ai]d plantation."[19]

Slave women, on the other hand, primarily worked in the fields cultivating tobacco, rice, and, later, indigo. A few moved into household work gradually as the pressing need for field laborers abated. Within the slave quarters, where huts often were built on an African model, they processed food for their households late at night and early in the morning. When possible they supplemented their diets with produce from small garden plots as well. It may well be that South Carolina planters learned to cultivate rice successfully from West Africans familiar with rice culture, especially those from Sierra Leone. These women knew the basic methods of raising and harvesting rice, and their ancient mortar-and-pestle technique for separating the grains from the husks became the standard procedure in South Carolina after Europeans failed to devise another means.[20] In the Chesapeake region African women labored in the tobacco fields and barns, hoeing, picking, stripping, and drying.[21]

As women pursued their daily rounds, they were likely to be pregnant or nursing. Although the first generation of southern women—both black and white—married late, they immediately began a cycle of pregnancy, birth, and breast-feeding that recurred every two to three years. Their daughters, in turn, married much younger—often as young as sixteen—and bore children at the same rate until their forties if they lived that long. Similarly, women in New England bore an average of eight children.[22]

Childbirth, in a village or town, was a female ritual. The expectant mother would lay in a store of "groaning cakes" and "groaning beer" for the women who would gather when labor began. Midwife, neighbors, and kin stayed with her through her travail and for several days afterward, while her husband for once remained on the periphery in his own house. Women knew that they faced death with each birth. Ministers reminded them that this was the price for the sin of Eve. The presence of others who had also suffered and survived was a deep comfort.[23] Imagine then the fears of women on isolated farms and frontier settlements where childbirth was less communal. Wherever possible, however, women were attended by other women, and midwives like Anne Hutchinson held an honored position in the community. Indeed, with their knowledge of herbal medicines, they served as doctors as well.

Children, born with such frequency, were highly vulnerable to disease and accidents in their early years. Motherhood involved loss and grief. In seventeenth-century Maryland 25 percent of infants died before their first birthdays and 40 to 55 percent died before the age of twenty.[24] Huge fireplaces, pots of boiling meat or laundry, agricultural tools and implements lying about, open wells—all awaited the hapless child who wandered momentarily out of sight. With so many children and a life of constant physical labor, motherhood itself had a different emotional quality. Many documents testify to women's love for their children and grief at their deaths, but the intensive time and emotional investment in individual children that would characterize relationships in the nineteenth-century middle classes was simply not possible for most colonial women.[25]

Women who bore children outside the bonds of marriage faced additional burdens. They could be hauled before the courts by neighbors (themselves frequently female) and tried for fornication or adultery. In most cases, extended family networks appear to have provided some support, perhaps even forcing the legitimating marriage. The continuing presence of infanticide, however, indicates that for a variety of reasons such support was sometimes inadequate or absent. The reasons for infanticide varied from the shame and terror of a lonely young woman fearing community condemnation to episodes of temporary (or permanent) insanity. Based on British precedent, the law ruled infanticide murder; prior to 1730, those convicted were invariably put to death. Puritan ministers railed against the "uncleanness," "whore mongers," and "mothers of bastards" for whom the "fire of lust" led to the "fire of hell."[26]

Colonial courts were filled with cases involving accusations against women ranging from infanticide to adultery, "lewd carriage," heresy, and witchcraft. The presence of women as both the accusers and the accused indicates not only the extent of women's informal role as guardians of communal morality but also the absence of any formal power in both church and state courts, where women could be witnesses but never judges, lawyers, or prosecutors. Two prominent New England cases of social and political conflict in the seventeenth century revolved around women, and they illustrate the strains introduced by the Protestant emphasis on spiritual equality in a society based on female subordination.

The first occurred between 1636 and 1638 when the Massachusetts settlement was still new and many future colonies had yet to be settled by Europeans. Anne Hutchinson, mother of fifteen (three of whom died in England and the last born since her arrival), midwife, and follower of John Cotton, drew large numbers of women, and later men as well, to her home where she expounded on the doctrine of "grace." Extending Cotton's teachings, she charged that most Puritan ministers failed to espouse the true gospel by advocating a "covenant of works" emphasizing outward signs of salvation such as good works and worldly success. In contrast, she emphasized the inner experience of God's grace, which could in no way be "earned" by works.

The tension between good works and grace runs through Puritan theology, and settlers in Massachusetts were familiar with the heretical possibilities of each. In Hutchinson's hands, however, the radical potential of the doctrine of grace for women became compelling even as it undermined clerical authority. The inner experience of grace offered women divine sanction for voicing their own religious experience and rejecting the judgments of earthly authorities. This liberating possibility for women no doubt

31

contributed to Hutchinson's large female following, even though she also drew influential men as well.

In a religiously based community the boundary between theological and political difference hardly exists. Both clerical and civil authorities found Hutchinson's activities alarming and they set out to silence her. In the course of her trials Hutchinson was effectively isolated from her supporters including, finally, John Cotton. Governor John Winthrop and a series of clerics engaged her in a brilliant defense in which she responded to them Biblical citation for Biblical citation. Winthrop, however, was mortified to be intellectually embattled with a woman. "We do not mean to discourse with those of your sex," he admonished this most "disorderly" woman.[27] Another interrogator, Hugh Peter, charged "you have stept out of your place, you have rather bine a Husband than a Wife and a preacher than a Hearer; and a Magistrate than a Subject."[28] Her rebellion, in other words, threatened all hierarchies: familial, religious, and political. Hutchinson's accusers were unable to win the argument conclusively until she announced that she had received a direct revelation from God. With that, she was excommunicated, and she left with her family to join a small settlement in Rhode Island. Following her husband's death in 1642 she moved with her six youngest children to a Dutch colony near Long Island Sound where, in 1643, she and five children were killed in an Indian raid.

The second crisis was the famous Salem witchcraft trial in 1692, when fourteen women and six men were executed as witches. Witchcraft was thought to be widespread in the seventeenth century. Virtually everyone believed in it and knew many of the signs proving allegiance to the devil. Outbreaks of witchcraft accusation punctuated the seventeenth century.[29] The Salem episode, however, was both the largest and the last of these. The events in Salem mirrored many of the social tensions that existed elsewhere in the colonial world.

The Salem terror began when several young women in the Putnam household asked the West Indian servant, Tituba, to divine their futures. Soon the girls began to claim that they were bewitched and tortured and to accuse women on the margins of Salem society: older, cantankerous women known for squabbles with neighbors; Tituba, a West Indian; a scandalous woman known for her red bodice and rowdy parties. But they also accused Sarah Nurse, elderly and deaf, with her husband a newcomer to Salem.

The accused were brought to trial where the testimony of hysterical girls convinced observers that the devil was at work in their community. The trials ended abruptly when the charges shifted toward increasingly prominent and powerful individuals, seeming wild even to firm believers, and several of the young women confessed that the whole thing had been a fabrication.

The association between witchcraft and women was pervasive, and most accused witches were seen to threaten the established order in some way. Some were women who inherited money directly because they lacked brothers or sons, thus upsetting the orderly transmission of property through the male line. Others were older women whose aggressive and contentious behavior (itself not so unusual) was interpreted by their neighbors as an unwillingness to accept their proper place. Still others were newcomers who had not yet found a familiar niche in the order of things. Women were often convenient scapegoats for vague anxieties about economic uncertainty and underlying fears of female power and unruliness.[30]

The young Putnam women who accused their mothers' generation of abnormal powers embodied some of the social and economic tensions of seventeenth-century life. In contrast to their mothers' experience, for example, this younger generation faced a shortage of marriageable suitors as young men migrated to the frontier rendering the young women's futures less secure.[31] Their accusations also exposed political and economic conflicts between those related to the accusers, the powerful Putnam family, and those who were accused, many of whom like the Nurses were encroaching on the Putnams' land. Young women in the Putnam household knew who the family's enemies were. They also knew very well the powers of the supernaturally possessed, and in this case they used them to act out broader social conflicts. In seeing visions and becoming possessed, for a moment young women placed themselves outside the hierarchies of age, gender, and clerical authority. "The possessed could command their minister, speak in the church, and comment on the sermon as no other child, servant, or female adult could have done."[32]

More than half a century before the Salem witch trials, Anne Hutchinson demonstrated the enormous influence of female networks by using them as a channel for her religiously and politically threatening ideas. The Salem witch trials illustrated again the potentials and the limits of women's informal power. As accusers, accused, and witnesses, women were central to this major social upheaval, and yet they remained outsiders to the formal power of male political and religious elites. They remained economically dependent and vulnerable.

Class and Commerce in the Eighteenth Century

Economically the colonies proved to be a great success as the boom in trade across the Atlantic by the late seventeenth century fostered the growth of cities, merchant elites in northern and middle colonies, and slave-based planter elites in the tobacco- and rice-growing south. The evolution of class in the eighteenth century meant greater and greater social differentiation for both women and men. As some grew wealthy, increasing numbers of people, especially in the cities, owned no property at all.

As commerce reshaped colonial economies, demographic changes, in particular the emergence of a majority born in North America, transformed colonial populations. The Puritan emigration to New England had stopped abruptly in 1640, but other colonies continued to receive large numbers of immigrants for many decades. Gradually, however, the populations of most colonies came to be composed predominantly of the native born rather than of immigrants. This was accomplished not only by a slowed rate of new arrivals but also by extremely high fertility rates among Euro-Americans. The exception to this demographic pattern in the early eighteenth century was the population of African slaves. African-Americans were overwhelmed by new arrivals in several decades of the first half of the eighteenth century as the tobacco boom generated an insatiable demand for slave labor. Only after 1740 or 1750 did births consistently outnumber recent immigrants.

The emergence of a native-born population gradually transformed the sexual imbalance of the immigrant population. By the eighteenth century there were about the same numbers of women as of men, and indeed as younger men pushed out into the frontier seeking new land some communities experienced as much as a 15 percent surplus of women. The result was gradually rising marriage ages and a declining rate of remarriage for widows. As young men moved to the frontier and young women married at more mature ages, parents found that they could not control their children's decisions as tightly as they once had. Even though young women had more say-so about their choices of marriage partners, they had few real means of controlling their economic fortunes. External controls were weakening, but the consequences for women were mixed. In terms of sexual behavior, for example, the greater freedom of young people can be documented in the number of premarital pregnancies that rose with each decade of the eighteenth century. Women's futures, as the young women in Salem Village may have sensed, were no longer so secure.[33]

By the early eighteenth century, as second and third generation settlers constructed a more permanent life-style, household inventories indicated an increasing number of homes with the accoutrements of gentility: table linens, forks, chairs, and looking glasses.[34] Whether merchants' wives in Philadelphia or planters' wives in Virginia, the women who managed such households found their duties changed, multiplied, and somewhat narrowed at the same time. Consumer goods required their own care. Gentility meant a leisured social life, taking tea with friends or in the south entertaining large numbers of friends or relatives who might arrive at any time and stay for a week or two. It meant cultivation of decorative skills such as fine needlework and acquaintance with more refined social rituals associated with eating and entertaining.

The emergence of the "pretty gentlewoman" in the eighteenth century marked a differentiation in life-styles between the well-to-do city woman whose energies were focused on the upkeep of her home and family and her rural or lower-class sisters who continued to assume more diverse social and economic roles. The gentlewoman was less likely to know about, or assist in, the management of her husband's affairs or to be involved in trade or business of any sort. Her servants were members of a different class, not the daughters of peers training in the skills of housewifery, and she was less enmeshed in that tight world of gossip and mutual support that surrounded networks of female trade and barter.[35]

At the same time, an increase in single women—spinsters and widows—accounted for increasing numbers of women who had to support themselves in cities. Commercial growth provided employment opportunities for a few though their existence remained precarious. Single women most likely entered domestic servitude or entered a traditional female trade like millinery. Some widows continued the artisanal trades of their husbands. Others ran taverns and inns such as the Plume of Feathers, the Blue Anchor, or the Rose and Crown in Philadelphia or opened "dame schools" in hopes of attracting a few young scholars. An impressive number of women operated printing presses. And in commercial districts retail goods were often sold by "she-merchants," especially when the goods were clothes, hats, and other items consumed by women.[36] One such group of shopkeepers wrote to the New York *Journal* in 1733:

> Mr. Zenger, We, the widdows of this city, have had a Meeting, and as our case is something Deplorable, we beg you will give it Place in your Weekly Journal, that we may be relieved, it is as follows.
> We are House keepers, Pay our taxes, carry on Trade, and most of us are she Merchants, and as we in some measure contribute to the Support of Government, we ought to be Intitled to some of the Sweets of it; but we find ourselves entirely neglected, while the Husbands that live in our Neighborhood are daily invited to Dine at Court; we have the Vanity to think we can be full as Entertaining, and make as brave a Defense in Case of an Invasion and perhaps not turn Taile so Soon as some of them.[37]

Beneath the ironic, jesting tone of their letter lay an implied battle of the sexes. Such women could rib men about masculine pretensions, but they were also acutely aware, and resentful, of their own secondary status.

Commercial opportunities also changed the lives of rural women. In the Brandywine valley, a Quaker-dominated area near Philadelphia, farm women shifted their work from spinning and weaving to the production of butter. First they sold their surplus to exporters trading with the West Indies. Then as Philadelphia grew into a major city, they found a ready urban market. The income from women's butter production brought a new affluence to "middling" farm families, allowing women to buy goods they had previously produced themselves and sustaining the family economy in the face of rising costs.[38]

Southern plantation mistresses also presided over households growing in size and complexity, but the sources of their wealth in staple crop, slave-based agriculture shaped a very different environment for their activities. Early in the eighteenth century the emerging Virginia gentry began to construct palatial houses to demonstrate their status and growing dominance over a violent and unruly society. The towering "great house" emphasized patriarchal power flanked by subordinated wings, smaller out buildings, and, at some distance, the slave quarters. Public spaces—stores, taverns, and courthouses—were for men only. Even in church people sat by rank and by gender: After the women and poorer men were seated in ranked family pews, the gentlemen tromped into church "in a Body" as the service began and left "in the same manner," as if everyone else was simply an audience for their display.[39] Within the great house specialized uses of space—dining rooms, parlors, and libraries—marked a shift away from the crowded, undifferentiated homes of smaller farms and increasing separation of male and female spheres of activity.

Despite the increasing segregation of women and their work, in at least one remarkable case the combination of wealth and southern frontier conditions provided an arena for female assertion and creativity. As a teenager in the 1740s, Eliza Lucas moved with her family from the West Indies to a plantation on Wappoo Creek in South Carolina. Educated in England, she was unusually literate and well-read in the classics. With her father away serving as governor of Antigua and her mother in ill health, energetic Eliza found herself managing several plantations alone. She loved growing things and she had a good eye for economic advantage. After experimenting with new crops, in 1744 she succeeded in producing the first successful crop of indigo in the colonies and devised a workable method for extracting the bright blue dye. By 1747 the colony was exporting 100,000 pounds of indigo per year, and it rapidly became the agricultural base of the South Carolina economy until the Revolution.

While Eliza Lucas's indigo experiments were under way, she rejected numerous suitors, finding most men boring. Of one suitor whom her father urged on her she wrote, "the riches of Peru and Chili if he had them put together could not purchase a sufficient esteem for him to make him my husband."[40] Later she fell in love with Charles Pinckney, a Charleston widower twenty years her senior, who encouraged her intellectual pursuits. Following their marriage in 1745, Eliza Lucas Pinckney bore four children, raising the three that survived infancy with intense attention to their educations. She also continued to exercise administrative responsibility for her father's plantations and, widowed at thirty-five, took over the responsibility for her husband's property. Her scientific and administrative achievements were unique for her time, but the setting in which they occurred—a southern plantation—was one that shaped the lives of many thousands of women, most of them black.

To shift one's perspective from the woman in the elegant great house to the women in the slave quarters requires an imaginative

37

leap. The contrast between the two environments could hardly have been greater. In the slave quarters, huts were clustered together communally, housing a variety of familial arrangements, two- and one-parent households with children or various combinations of unrelated people who treated one another as if they were related. Domestic activity in the early mornings, evenings, and holidays involved beating or grinding corn into meal, cultivating small plots of corn, cooking over an open fire in rude pots and pans furnished by the master, laundering clothes, carrying water from a well for cooking and laundry, and maintaining a small household furnished with straw beds and barrels for seats.[41] As the eighteenth-century economy grew more diverse and prosperous, owners on larger plantations began to assign a few tasks specifically to male or female slaves. Some men learned artisanal skills. Some women went to work in the "big kitchen," but most men and women worked side-by-side in the fields.

African-American mothers provided the first link in a chain of kinship around which an Afro-American community began to develop. Male slaves frequently lived on plantations separated from their wives and children. Women were less likely than men to lose their children through sale, though that remained a constant possibility. Wherever large numbers of slaves lived together for a significant period of time and where the black population grew more from natural increase than from the importation of Africans, communities began to grow. They were marked by extensive webs of kinship in which siblings, cousins, aunts and uncles, grandparents, and even great-grandparents lived on the same or adjacent plantations. In these networks, daily survival grew into shared language, values, and ritual despite the cruel harshness of the slave system.[42] The power of kinship as a source of definition for community and mutual obligation was reflected in the development of numerous "fictive kin" relationships modeled on kinship and treated as if they were kinship relations. Calling one another "auntie," "uncle," "cousin," or "sister," for example, and assuming the obligations of kinship that go with such titles are common examples of fictive kinship relations which have continued within Afro-American culture.

For a time there were probably many Afro-American cultures, just as the setting of each colony harbored a distinctive European-based culture. The weaving together of various African traditions and European patterns shows up in distinctive patterns of sociability, especially singing and dancing, the persistence of some African religious and magical practices even among Christian converts, marital patterns that prohibited first-cousin marriage (a common practice among the white upper classes), and marriage and funeral ceremonies. In the constricted spaces of slave quarters and the networks of roads and paths that bound one plantation to another, Afro-Americans claimed autonomy and built a community about which their masters knew very little.[43]

The patriarchs of the plantation system, however, feared the resentment and possible revolt of their slaves. Slavery had to be constantly enforced with violence. White owners perceived their slaves not only as dangerous but also as strangely "other."[44] Blackness in Elizabethan England had symbolized evil and sin while whiteness represented good, beauty, and purity; the moral judgment implicit in that association was deeply rooted. Africans were seen as heathens, potentially dangerous and decidedly immoral. As such, their passions and sexuality were exotic and forbidden, arousing desire in the very people who debated their humanity. From the beginning, sexual danger and appeal wove through the racist attitudes and violent acts of slave traders and slave owners.

Sexual domination of African women reenacted white men's power, just as rape has historically served conquering armies. One group of men demonstrates their control over another by forced sexual access to their women. Where the proportion of slaves was extremely high and the numbers of white women very low, as in the West Indies and in South Carolina, liaisons between white men and black women were common and occasionally even consensual. This was publicly acknowledged especially in humor. In 1732 the *South Carolina Gazette*, for example, published a verse speculating on the consequences of a chameleon's changing to the color of whatever it touched:

> No Wonder then, that the *Amours* of *such*
> Whose *Taste* betrays them to a close Embrace
> With the *dark* Beauties of the *Sable* Race
> (Stain'd with the Tincture of the *Sooty* Sin)
> Imbibe the *Blackness* of their *Charmer's* Skin.[45]

For most English slaveholders in North America, however, sexual relationships with Africans also threatened to undermine their own sense of identity as civilized, Christian—that is, white—people.

White males engaged in these sexual relationships while publicly denying and condemning such behavior.

White women, however, could not do the same. For one thing, their relationships with African men carried the terrifying implication of black male dominance, if only momentarily, over white women; this undermined white patriarchy. For another, the products of such unions were far harder for a woman to deny. White women who gave birth to mulatto children received harsh physical punishments, and the black men involved might face death. Black women who bore mulatto children, on the other hand, simply provided more slaves, as the child's status followed that of the mother. The denial of any "in-between" status to mulatto children marked the extreme degree to which Euro-Americans divided their world into black and white. For African-American women, sexual violence added immeasurably to the pain and humiliation of enslavement.

With the initial differentiation of women's work and space from men's as the economy flourished in the eighteenth century, a new construct of ideal roles emerged. The idea of the "pretty gentlewoman" in the north and the "lady" in the south each drew intellectual substance from publications in England and the older definitions of the upper-class woman. Such images commanded attention, however, because they made sense of changing realities in the upper and middling classes.

Economic success separated women's and men's religious as well as economic activities during the eighteenth century. With each generation Euro-American men had become less religious and more attentive to economic opportunity. Laments about the decline in church membership began among Puritans in the mid-seventeenth century; in fact, the decline took place primarily among men. By the late seventeenth century women outnumbered male church members by a ratio of three to two. Loss of male piety also meant loss of power for the male clergy.

Thus, women became a majority of church goers just as churches moved from the center to the margins of colonial political life. The goals of religion—to create a godly society—often conflicted with the goals of commerce and commerce generally won, but not without creating considerable anxiety. Many colonials, men and women alike, found the clash of values troublesome. They resolved it for a time by placing the burdens of religious responsibility on women under the leadership of male ministers, making the passive female a symbol of Christian virtues, and associating men and manliness with the materialistic and competitive world of trade.[46]

Female passivity had been the product of the earlier rigorous suppression of dissent and lay activism among women like Anne Hutchinson in the seventeenth century. The eighteenth century association of women and spirituality, however, shifted theological ground away from earlier Protestant understandings of spiritual equality—Eve was Adam's "helpmeet," made like him in the "image of God"; both had sinned, though Eve's was the more grievous. Now, as in the widely praised and influential work of English poet John Milton, Eve became a ravishing beauty, object of Adam's adoration. The detectable shift "from a harmony built upon sameness to a harmony built upon difference" echoed in verses and essays throughout the eighteenth-century colonies and established women's body and soul as a distinct and different creation of God.[47]

The Great Awakening, a religious revival movement starting in England and sweeping up and down the colonial coast in the 1730s and 1740s, offered women and ministers, in their different ways, an opportunity to reassert their influence and win men back to the church. In the beginning most converts were males whose female relatives—wives, mothers, and sisters—were church members. As revivals spread, female converts also came forward in roughly equal numbers.[48]

For both women and men the Great Awakening offered an opportunity to challenge clerical authority by following itinerant preachers and to begin to forge a more inward-looking religious mode. Although women's and men's conversion experiences followed essentially the same pattern, in either case it involved an emotional expressiveness and a submission to God's will and grace that white colonial culture increasingly defined as "feminine." Female conversion was often precipitated by the confrontation with death that childbearing women experienced every two to three years. One woman described her conversion after several years of "consideration about my soul" that "would wear off again 'till the time of my first Lying in; and then I was in my own apprehension brought to the very brink of eternity; and that night I received comfort."[49]

The association of women with spirituality and of spiritual experience with emotion meshed with increasing emotional expressiveness within families. Female emotionality, regarded as a source of disorder in the seventeenth century, could in a sentimentalized version be considered a source of order. Affection, nurture, and piety represented the emotions that provided social glue rather than social disruption. Greater solicitude for mothers and maternal sentiment, for example, made judges and juries more willing to consider evidence of stillbirth or accidental death even when an illegitimate pregnancy had been concealed. As a result, after 1730 convictions for infanticide declined markedly.[50]

Emotional expressiveness similarly changed expectations of marriage relations. Mutual attraction and love replaced parental choice in marriage arrangements, and a new rhetoric emphasizing partnership and companionship in marriage influenced a rising number of divorce cases as well. In 1766 for the first time divorce cases appeared in which "alienation of affection" was one of the charges.[51] For some at least, rising expectations of affection within marriage met with bitter disappointment.[52]

Most women in the years preceding the American Revolution continued to experience their lives as their mothers and grandmothers had, shaped most powerfully by the constantly recurring cycles of birth and pregnancy and by the arduous physical labor of housewifery. Even though literacy increased, women lagged far behind men. Most of the new schools were closed to them. Some legal rights established in the seventeenth century in part because of the extreme scarcity of women—dower rights, the ability of some women to sign contracts or to be consulted regarding the sale of property—continued, though in the context of a burgeoning commercial economy and increased emphasis on individual rights they had less and less meaning. Women in the wealthiest families, for example, had less and less family business knowledge with which to exercise such rights.[53] The social and political power that flowed through women's informal networks also appeared strong, but the conditions supporting it were undergoing rapid change. Martha Air's story illustrates both the force of women's judgment and intimations of the new world that was beginning to emerge.

Mary Angel and her friend Abigail Galloway took a walk together in Boston, Massachusetts, in 1773. As they strolled past an open window they spied a neighbor, Adam Air, "in the act of copulation" with Pamela Brichford. Knowing that Air was a married man, they intervened without a second thought. As Mary later told the Boston court when Martha Air sued for divorce:

> on Seeing this we went into the House, & stood behind them as they lay on the Floor, and after observing them some time, the said Abigail Galloway spoke, & asked him if he was not Ashamed to act so when he had a Wife at home, he got up & answered, one Woman was as good to him as another he then put up his nakedness before our faces, & went away, and she on his getting off her, jumped up & ran away into another part of the House.[54]

Colonial Americans, including New England Puritans, were hardly repressed about sexuality. They watched and reported on one another with avid interest. Social control remained primarily external—often in the hands of neighborhood women—and privacy was virtually nonexistent. That Martha Air could sue for divorce, however, marked a dramatic change from the previous century and from European practice, but her chances of success for the charge of adultery alone remained dim. Her divorce required other grounds. The law appeared evenhanded, yet a double standard decreed that it would not be in practice.[55]

By the time of the Revolution, even the informal powers of gossip and neighborly oversight had begun to change in towns and cities as expanding trade disrupted rooted communities, undermining social networks, separating women's and men's activities, and shaping a new family life. The bustling commercial worlds of eighteenth-century cities and plantations were a long way from the muddy little colony that Anne Bradstreet had joined in the previous century. Private and domestic concerns seemed increasingly separate, marginal to the rough and tumble of transatlantic commerce or colonial political affairs. The evolution of colonial society offered men new arenas for activity. Colonial men began the creation of a public arena distinctly separate from the domestic realm, as county courts met in regular session, town meetings grew, and colonial legislatures held elections and heated debates. Such places became the locus of community decision making as well as schools for participants in the practices and skills of public life. In an earlier time, though different and unequal, women and men inhabited similar worlds. Though personal concerns remained subject to communal supervision, everyone knew that *politics* was the province of men alone. Yet, the upheaval of the Revolution generated debate about the proper place of women in public life and gave a new, political meaning to domesticity.

3

"But What Have I to Do with Politicks?"
The Revolutionary Era

*I*n November 1776 Edmund Burke, addressing the British House of Commons, voiced his frustration with the rebellious colonies of North America. "[S]till is not that continent conquered," he raged. "[W]itness the behaviour of one miserable woman, who with her single arm did that, which an army of a hundred thousand men could not do—arrested your progress, in the moment of your success." He accused the unnamed woman of starting the Great Fire in New York City, and thus slowing the advance of invading British troops.

> This miserable being was found in a cellar, with her visage besmeared and smutted over, with every mark of rage, despair, resolution, and the most exalted heroism, buried in combustibles, in order to fire New-York, and perish in its ashes;—she was brought forth, and knowing that she would be condemned to die, upon being asked her purpose, said, "to fire the city!" and was determined to omit no opportunity of doing what her country called for. Her train was laid and fired; and it is worthy of your attention, how Providence was pleased to make use of those humble means to serve the American cause, when open force was used in vain.[1]

At a time when North Americans proclaimed liberty and political participation as their birthright, women remained separate from the institutions of political life. Individual heroic acts, such as that of the zealous arsonist, broke the rules and astonished leaders like Edmund Burke precisely because the public arena where political conflict and activity occurred was presumed to belong to men. Courthouse meeting days, taverns, and gatherings of the local militia provided opportunities for male—not female— socializing and the communication of political ideas and information. Even when women had access to such public places or to political writings and pamphlets, their lower literacy rates ensured that few could read or fully understand them. Yet despite their general exclusion from daily political life, women were stirred by the same revolutionary zeal. Like men, some supported the crown while others proclaimed that they were "born for liberty."

From the Stamp Act crowds in the 1760s, to consumer boycotts in the 1770s, to the military conflict between 1776 and 1781, women were inescapably caught up in the revolutionary ferment regardless of whether they were patriots or loyalists, urban or rural, slave, free, or Indian. At first, the only tradition of female activism was associated with the "lower sort" and particularly with "mobs" as their opponents would call them; these crowds had regularly protested economic injustices throughout the eighteenth century in Europe and America. When merchants charged more than the accepted "just price," especially for food or household goods, women commonly joined or led food riots to seize the goods they and their families needed.[2] The New York arsonist as well as women participants in various revolutionary crowds certainly reflected these rather established practices. A more fundamental shift in perspective emerged as women's experience in the revolutionary era helped shape a new consciousness of women's political worth and capacities; this made their official exclusion increasingly problematic.

Politics, Domesticity, and War

The decades preceding the Revolution were rife with passionate ideas about political liberty. An outpouring of political pamphlets, newspapers, and sermons explored the history and meaning of political rights and freedoms and of just and legitimate government. Political writers charged that the imperial government threatened to destroy the true liberties of Englishmen [sic] in the last stronghold of political virtue, North America. One nervous observer wrote that political writings seemed to flow from "ALMOST EVERY AMERICAN PEN."[3]

Slogans in defense of liberty and virtue, however, rang differently in the ears of women than of men. The rhetoric and imagery of the Revolution was strongly gendered in its explorations of legitimate and illegitimate power. America was a pure and innocent child; Britain a corrupt and evil mother. "O Britannia!" cried an angry colonist in 1767. "Can a Woman forget her sucking Child, that she should not have Compassion on the Son of her Womb? Yes they may forget—But, when this is the case, 'such mothers Monsters prove,' . . . They Forfeit the Character of True Mothers." In such terms, the Revolution was the struggle of an adolescent male for the manhood embodied in the rights of English*men*.[4] Male political rights were the goal and their value was reinforced by rhetoric used to describe the corruption of an effeminate Europe. John Adams worried about the triple danger of "Elegance, Luxury and Effeminacy." Luxuries stripped men of their vigor. As "dissipation and extravagance" undermined American virtue, "Venality, Servility and Prostitution, eat and spread like a cancer."[5]

The oppositions blended the language of economics, class, and gender: wealth versus frugality; aristocracy versus yeoman farmers; "silks and lace" versus simplicity; sloth and "voluptuousness" versus industry; effeminacy versus manliness. A true republic, in John Adams's view, would be suffused with "all great, manly, and warlike virtues."[6] A true republican government required of its people a spirit of manly self-sacrifice and public spiritedness, what eighteenth-century people called "public virtue."[7]

The very language of the Revolution reinforced the view that political activities and aims were male. The arena for politics was the public (the *polis* according to Aristotle), separated from the privacy of the household associated with women.[8] Public virtues were male, manly, even martial. Femininity and depravity seemed to be effective symbols for the forces that could undermine such virtue. These were, in fact, common themes in American culture. Evangelists in the Great Awakening, the Protestant revival movement of the mid-eighteenth century, for decades had presumed that female sexuality was a source of corruption, preaching against "immodest" female dress and attention to fashion.[9]

The coexistence of contradictory images of women in the Revolution could not be more stark. The image of the corrupting whore coexisted with notions of virginal female purity as the seventeenth-century emphasis on the darker, powerful side of female nature had begun to yield in the eighteenth century to a more idealized, sentimentalized notion of femininity. While some described the true republic as "manly," others depicted the principles of liberty and virtue as feminine, sources of inspiration rather than corruption, and therefore, "continual victims of the lust for domination that was natural to men."[10]

People in general did not experience this contrast as problematic, however, because neither image questioned the centrality of women's domestic responsibilities and because the widely shared vocabulary of gendered imagery (like the virgin and the whore) had resonances—Biblical, literary, and political—that were so deeply imbedded in the culture as to appear to be common sense. Yet, the difficulty of defining citizenship and the place of women in a republic made the contradictions more and more apparent during the course of the Revolution.

Political crisis and warfare politicized women and the domestic arena in ways popular rhetoric could not encompass. Women who perceived themselves as uninterested in politics were quickly caught up in political thought and conversation. In the midst of political protests in the 1760s a New York newspaper observed that even "peasants and *their housewives*" (emphasis added) had started "to dispute on politics and positively to determine upon our liberties."[11]

Letters and diaries of literate women in the 1760s began to refer to political matters. The deep cultural divide between the female sphere and the more public political sphere, however, led them again and again to apologize for their temerity. Sarah Jay interrupted her sharp political criticisms in a family letter to note that she could hardly suppress the observations prompted by her lively curiosity and intense commitments: "I've transgress'd the line that I proposed to observe in my correspondence by slipping into politicks, but my country and my friends possess so entirely my thoughts that you must not wonder if my pen runs beyond the dictates of prudence." In an earlier letter praising the freedom and justice of America she paused, "But whither, my pen, are you hurrying me? What have I to do with politicks? Am I not myself a woman, and writing to Ladies? Come then, the fashions to my assistance."[12] Many women found it impossible to "impose a silence" on themselves regarding topics that were on everyone's lips. As another woman put it, "[T]ho a female I was born a patriot and cant help it If I would."[13]

As the conflict escalated, whole families, not just men, were forced to declare their political allegiance. In the 1760s and 1770s, consumer boycotts of British goods, especially the famous tea boycott, required that women exercise political judgment in the purchase of household goods. One strategist in 1769, pondering the problems associated with resisting the sale of British goods, proposed that "the *greatest difficulty* of all we have to encounter . . . is, to persuade our wives to give us their assistance, without which 'tis impossible to succeed." In his view women remained outside the audience of political actors, a kind of shadowy back-drop—"wives"—which nevertheless with proper persuasion could be activated. "Only let their husbands . . . convince them, that it is the only thing that can save them and their children, from distresses, slavery, and disgrace."[14]

Women themselves, however, did not cling to such a narrow view. Boycotts politicized their daily activities of shopping and home manufacture, and those who cooperated did so with a broader vision. In Boston, Ipswich, Long Island, Providence, and other cities women organized mass spinning bees to revive the art of homespun. Poems and essays by women urged patriotism and political principle. In 1768 a poem addressed to the Daughters of Liberty mocked the Sons of Liberty, "Supinely asleep, and depriv'd of their Sight/ Are strip'd of their Freedom, and rob'd of their Right." The author's solution was to

> Let the Daughters of Liberty, nobly arise,
> And tho' we've no Voice, but a negative here,
> The use of the Taxables, let us forbear.
> Stand firmly resolved and bid Grenville to see
> That rather than Freedom, we'll part with our Tea.

In exercising their ingenuity to replace British goods with home-made items, women could not only foil the plans of Lord Grenville but "Thus acting—we point out their Duty to Men."[15]

Groups of women signed public pledges to abstain from tea, a political act shocking some observers. When fifty-one women in Edenton, North Carolina, met to endorse the Nonimportation Association resolves of 1774 with a petition that stated their inability to "be indifferent on any occasion that appears nearly to affect the peace and happiness of our country," they met ridicule and satire. A British cartoonist portrayed the "Edenton Ladies' Tea Party" as a grotesque gathering. And Arthur Iredell, an Englishman whose relatives had participated, wrote in mock alarm, "Is there a Female Congress at Edenton too? I hope not, for we

Englishmen are afraid of the Male Congress, but . . . the Ladies
. . . have ever, since the Amazonian Era, been esteemd the most
formidable Enemies."[16]

Yet in spite of ridicule, women who refused to buy British
goods, who made herbal teas, spun and wove their own cloth,
and insisted on "buying American" were engaging in defiant political acts in the course of their domestic responsibilities. That some
enacted their intentions in more public and formal ways through
meetings and petitions demonstrates not only the reality of their
political commitments but also a new level of self-perception as
political actors.

In 1780 Philadelphia women proposed to create a national wom-
en's organization to raise money for the troops. In a broadside
entitled "Sentiments of an American Woman," they claimed the
mantle of patriotism for women "born for liberty, distaining to
bear the irons of a tyrannic Government." Women's loyalty and
courage would be more visible "if the weakness of our constitutions,
if opinions and manners did not forbid us to march to glory by
the same paths as the men." The time had come, they urged,
"to display the same sentiments which animated us at the beginning
of the Revolution, when we renounced the use of teas . . . when
our republican and laborious hands spun the flax, prepared the
linen intended for the use of our soldiers; when exiles and fugitives,
we supported with courage all the evils which are the concomitants
of war." Women in Philadelphia and later in New Jersey, Maryland,
and Virginia raised substantial sums by going door to door. When
General George Washington refused Philadelphia women's stipu-
lation that the money go directly to the troops, they bought linen
fearing that cash would be ill-spent. After making shirts, they
inscribed each with the name of the woman who made it to emphasize their personal gesture of support and solidarity as well as
their intention to contribute on their own terms.[17] Their spirit
and sentiment reflected a newfound sense of political awareness
and engagement born of the times but having deeper implications.

The pressing realities of military conflict that began in 1774
with the famous skirmishes at Lexington and Concord brought
increased pressure to declare allegiance to either Britain or to
the revolutionary republic as it shattered the rhythms of daily
life. Like civilians in any civil war, women coped with economic
and demographic disruption as well as the horrors of war itself.
One observer noted that women "surpassed the Men for Eagerness

& Spirit in the Defence of Liberty by Arms." Along the road from Cambridge to Boston he watched "at every house Women & Children making Cartridges, running Bullets, making Wallets, baking Biscuit, crying & bemoaning & at the same time animating their Husbands & Sons to fight for their Liberties."[18] Battles in backyards began with skirmishes in New England where the occupation of northern cities soon followed. In the later years of conflict, southerners experienced prolonged and bloody warfare on their home ground.

When enemy troops were nearby and when farms or city blocks became battlefields, women and children predominated among the refugees forced to flee their homes. Because the presence of troops brought diseases such as smallpox and dysentery and the danger of rape, women and children fled from the army's shadow. Extreme cases heightened women's sense of vulnerability. In the fall and winter of 1776 British troops in New Jersey and on Staten Island systematically and brutally attacked women. Such events expressed British frustration over a conflict they expected to win handily but which had turned into a prolonged war. As in other wars, women's bodies became another field on which the politics of conquest were enacted.[19]

Occupying armies not only forced civilians to quarter soldiers and prisoners but also seized provisions from nearby farms. On Long Island Lydia Mintern Post described how she was forced to quarter Hessian soldiers who "take the fence rails to burn, so that the fields are all left open, and the cattle stray away and are often lost." When soldiers were issued their monthly ration of rum, "we have trying and grievous scenes to go through; fighting, brawls, drumming and fifing, and dancing the night long; card and dice playing, and every abomination going on under our very roofs."[20]

While some women faced military troops with dread, another group of women were active in the military itself. Crowds of camp followers, mostly the wives and families of soldiers, followed American troops about the country to the distress of General Washington who considered them a great hindrance. Yet his army had almost none of the support staff that accompanies a modern military force, and so they were an essential auxillary. For basic tasks like cooking and laundry, troops depended on the women who came with them and shared their ragged and uncomfortable situation. They provided service and solace, considerably improving the soldiers' morale. Some women found work as nurses doing the most subordinate, low-level tasks in military hospitals. And a few served as spies, couriers, and even soldiers.[21] Several women disguised themselves as men and fought in the army. Deborah Sampson, the most famous of these, fought for two and a half years before being discovered while ill with a fever. In later years Congress granted her husband a pension as the widower of a revolutionary soldier.[22]

For camp followers, civilians, and female soldiers alike the fact that the revolutionary war was fought on American soil forced them to declare a *political* allegiance. Some, like Deborah Sampson, welcomed the opportunity and challenged the restrictions on female behavior. Others may well have preferred to have their lives continue uninterrupted, relatively untouched by political conflict, but they had no choice.

For enslaved Afro-Americans, the war against England at first represented an ironic inversion of the colonists' themes of independence, liberty, and self-government. Slaves initially found in the presence of *British* troops a possible instrument of freedom. In November 1775 Lord Dunmore, the Royal Governor of Virginia, offered liberation to any slaves who fled to join the British army. In the resulting flood of runaways, the high number of women with children contrasts sharply with statistics from before and after the Revolution when very few women with children escaped. Once some women were persuaded that the presence of British redcoats and the general disruptions of the war made it possible to run away without abandoning their families, they eagerly seized the opportunity. For many others, however, fear, danger, and the loss of ties with widespread kinship networks remained powerful incentives to stay. Indeed, many who fled were returned to their owners; others found freedom in Britain, Canada, or Africa.[23]

Perhaps the most important consequence of the Revolution for black Americans was the growth of a free black community throughout the south; it offered a living example of the idea of freedom in sight of many slaves. Growing numbers of escaped slaves not only enlarged the free black community but also darkened the complexion of what had previously been largely a mulatto community, making the community itself a safer place for new members to blend into, undetected. In a brief period when revolutionary ideology caused many to question slavery and the disturbances of war diverted attention, free blacks had room to maneuver as they began to embody and institutionalize their Afro-American culture in black schools and churches. The opportunity to buy the freedom of kin, which occurred predominantly in the north and the upper south during the Revolution, further strengthened family life. In Washington, D.C., for example, Aletha Tanner bought her own freedom and subsequently that of twenty-two friends and relatives.[24] Wartime conditions enabled many slaves to acquire new liberties. Future wars would see a similar pattern of liberty gained in exchange for loyalty or service.

The attention given to a precocious young slave in Boston provided evidence for those who would argue that educated Africans could equal the intellectual achievements of Europeans. Phyllis Wheatley, purchased from a slave boat in 1761 when about seven years old, exhibited such facility with words that she was raised more as a daughter than as a slave in the Wheatley household. Her poetry and her personal magnetism received widespread notice in America and in England for a brief period. George Washington was even said to have conferred with her in the midst of the war. Though she died in obscurity in 1784, Wheatley offered future generations of black women a powerful symbol of possibility.[25]

In contrast to many whites and blacks, Indian women in coastal tribes found no real sources of hope or transformation in the Revolution through alignment with either the colonial or British cause. Warfare touched them when both sides competed for Indian loyalties. For women it meant increased mobility, traditional war preparations, and the loss of husbands and sons. Most tribes supported the British as a way of resisting the pressure of white settlement in the west. More acculturated tribes like the Cherokee joined the patriots, along with two members of the Iroquois federation. At the end of the war, however, the British signed the Treaty of Paris (1783) giving the newly constituted United States government full control of western lands and of relations with Indian tribes. Whatever their prior allegiances, both former allies and former enemies among the Indians were forced in subsequent years to cede most of their territory to whites.[26] The resultant struggles and losses were to indelibly mark the lives and existences of American Indian women.

With the men away at war, women of all classes and races had to assume a range of tasks traditionally allocated to men. Women ran farms and businesses, often with great trepidation at the outset.

Sally Logan Fisher, whose Quaker husband was forced into exile in 1777 when she was eight months pregnant, lamented: "I feel forlorn & desolate, & the World appears like a dreary Desart, almost without any visible protecting Hand to guard us from the ravenous Wolves & Lions that prowl about for prey." In the ensuing months, however, she found herself "enabled to bear up thr' every triall & difficulty far beyond what I could have expected." Loyalist women, who had remained true to the British flag, had a particularly difficult time because they were cut off from the support of family and community. Trying to hold their lives and loyalties together against a growing tide of revolution left them isolated. Patriot women, however, experienced growing pride and self-respect as they learned to manage financial decisions and to act autonomously while their husbands fought the enemy. Lucy Flucker Knox wrote to her husband in 1777 that after the war she wanted to continue to exercise her own judgment and participate in handling their affairs. "I hope you will not consider yourself as commander in chief of your own house—but be convinced . . . that there is such a thing as equal command."[27]

Struggling to provide for their families in the face of wartime scarcity and extreme inflation, women banded together to demonstrate their demands and dissatisfactions. They attacked merchants, especially those with loyalist leanings who were suspected of hoarding, and demanded goods at a "just price." When they met resistance, they seized the goods, sometimes leaving the amount of money they felt was proper. Abigail Adams described one incident in 1778 in which "a Number of Females, some say a hundred, some say more assembled with a cart and trucks, marched down to the Ware House" belonging to "one eminent, wealthy, stingy Merchant." They wanted the coffee they believed he was hoarding and when he withheld the keys "one of them seazd him by his Neck and tossed him into the cart." Once in possession of the keys they "opened the Warehouse. Hoisted out the Coffee themselves, put it into trucks and drove off. . . . A large concourse of Men stood amazed silent Spectators."[28] Because the war had given political overtones to domestic consumption, it offered increased opportunities for women to act politically and aggressively from within their role as housewives.

At the same time that domestic production and consumption assumed a political cast, the political theories of the Revolution raised new questions about women. Enlightenment thinkers in

Europe offered a powerful critique of aristocratic society premised on the subordination of one class to another. Articulating a world-view rooted in the rising commercial middle classes, they emphasized the infinite perfectibility of the individual. Through education, people could abandon the superstition and irrationality of tradition. Educated citizens became the foundation of a rational and just republican social order.[29]

Revolutionary political theorists drew on Enlightenment thought to create a distinctive mix of premodern and modern theories about the nature of legitimate government. Rejecting notions of rights rooted in inherited wealth or position and believing in individual capacities and merit, they turned to ancient theories of the republic, the state whose legitimacy rests on the consent of the governed. That, in turn, led them to elaborate the duties and rights of the citizen and the belief that sovereignty rests in the popular will. "All power is derived from the people," said one federalist. "Liberty is everyone's birthright. Since all cannot govern or deliberate individually, it is just that they should elect their representatives. That everyone should possess, indirectly, and through the medium of his representatives, a voice in the public councils, and should yield to no will but that of an actual or virtual majority." Governments not based on the will of the people, therefore, should be abolished, a justification for revolution receiving one of its most powerful expressions in the Declaration of Independence.[30]

The future of a government established on such principles clearly lay with the "virtue" of its citizens, which could only be expressed and renewed by constant participation in the life of the community. Yet the founding fathers shared a restricted vision of "the citizen." In their view, women, slaves, and propertyless men, along with children and the mentally ill, lacked the capacity for independent and rational judgment for the general good. The ringing declaration that "All men are created equal" used the word "men" quite literally. John Adams, in May 1776, noted what he viewed as the logical but absurd possibilities inherent in an egalitarian commitment to actual representation: "Shall we say that every individual of the community, old and young, male and female, as well as rich and poor, must consent, expressly, to every act of legislation?"[31]

Indeed every statement of republican principles implicitly assumed that women were exceptions. Jean-Jacques Rousseau, the

French theorist of democracy who provided inspiration for popular democratic groups during the Revolution and afterwards, presumed that the citizen was necessarily a male head of a household, a husband-father. His definition of the "public" and the ideal polity of male citizens presumed the existence of a private female world that sustained the "softer" domestic values. Women's participation in civic life, then, could destroy this essential balance between the (male) public and the (female) private. "Without someone to tend the hearth, the legislative halls would grow silent and empty, or become noisily corrupt." In turn, the woman who participated in politics violated her nature. As Rousseau put it, "A witty [i.e., articulate] woman is a scourge to her husband, to her children, to her friends, her servants, and to all the world. Elated by the sublimity of her genius, she scorns to stoop to the duties of a woman and is sure to commence a man."[32]

Yet even though the revolutionary conflict was cast as a battle for American manhood, white women in the propertied classes did present a problem for the new nation. If they were not citizens, what was their relation to the state? A few educated women at the time noted the logical contradictions. In 1776 Abigail Adams wrote her husband, John, that the new laws should curb the "unlimited power" of husbands over wives and threatened that "if particular care and attention is not paid to the ladies, we are determined to foment a rebellion and will not hold ourselves bound by any laws in which we have no voice, or representation." In this famous exchange, Abigail Adams adopted revolutionary rhetoric, charging men with a form of tyranny, but John Adams simply replied with a joking dismissal. Only in a letter to a male acquaintance did he develop the theoretical position that women and children, like men without property, were lacking in independent judgment and "their delicacy renders them unfit for practice and experience in the great businesses of life."[33]

As part of a great unleashing of sentiment and emotion, the Great Awakening began to redefine the meaning of familial relationships. Because it encouraged women's participation, it opened the door for new female public activities paralleling the greater political activism of women in the revolutionary era. With the disestablishment of state-supported churches in the mid-1780s, all churches became voluntary associations and had to sustain themselves through the active involvement of members, reinforcement of loyalty, and constant recruitment. By the 1780s, women

56

had begun to organize their own voluntary associations within churches such as sewing circles and charitable organizations.[34]

The ideas of evangelical religion provided further fuel to the gathering debate on women's place. The intensely emotional experience of conversion found expression in a supportive community sharply contrasting with the formality and external display of traditional upper-class Anglicanism.[35] Egalitarian, rooted in the lower classes, evangelical religion challenged traditional notions of authority. Men and women, whites and blacks, literate and illiterate often participated fully and together in revival and congregational activities. Women on occasion spoke and exhorted during meetings, voted in congregational decisions, organized prayer groups among themselves, and even initiated revivals.[36] As evangelicals sought solace in Christian community rather than in individualistic exploits, they at the same time personalized and individualized religion itself with an emphasis on emotion and subjective experience. Puritans had always understood conversion metaphorically as a feminine experience in which the convert, male or female, became a "bride of Christ." The Great Awakening amplified this with its positive evaluation of female emotionalism.[37]

The dilemma posed by women's public activities and republican theories relegating women to the hearth and home found an apparently simple resolution. The problem of female citizenship was solved by endowing domesticity itself with political meaning. The result was the idea and image of the republican mother. Her patriotic duty to educate her sons to be moral and virtuous citizens linked her to the state and gave her some degree of power over its future.[38] The responsibility of raising republican citizens offered women a political role which went well beyond common-law assumptions subsuming women's legal identities into those of husbands or fathers. Now women had a civic role and identity distinct from men, a role essential to the state's welfare. Although it did not challenge the primacy of domesticity for females or women's exclusion from the public, it solved a riddle that plagued the founding fathers: How was the virtue of future citizens to be ensured? They understood that public virtue—the willingness to sacrifice individual advantage for the common good—depended entirely on the private virtue of individuals, and it was to women they entrusted the nurturance of these virtues.[39]

Republican motherhood directed women's newfound political consciousness back into the home. Its ideology endowed motherhood with civic purpose helping to spawn the sentimentalization of domestic duties. At the same time, once enhanced by evangelical religion, the moral and civic responsibilities of women provided an impetus to community participation that, though not formally political, might well have political implications. Perhaps most important, in the 1780s the idea of republican motherhood stimulated a debate on women's education and provoked the founding of female academies, the first institutional settings in which young women could receive serious academic training.

The debate on women's education counterposed traditional hostility to female learning based on the assumption of an inferior nature and capacity to the Enlightenment belief in human malleability and the individual's potential for reason and justice. Emboldened by the optimism of the Enlightenment, women like Mercy Otis Warren, author of a three-volume history of the American Revolution, and writer Judith Sargent Murray argued that women's only disability lay in their lack of education. In an article "On the Equality of the Sexes" published in 1790, Murray pondered whether men were, in fact, mentally superior to women. Finding signs of reason, imagination, memory, and judgment among women, she proposed that women's deficiencies were due to their limited knowledge. "We can only reason from what we know, and if opportunity of acquiring knowledge hath been denied us, the inferiority of our sex cannot fairly be deduced from thence." She went on to assert that even in the book of Genesis, Eve's sin was the more admirable impelled as she was by "a thirst for knowledge." By contrast, Adam "was influenced by no other motive than a bare pusillanimous attachment to a woman."[40]

These sharp words, only partially blunted by humor, reflected Murray's awareness of the frequently expressed views that learning would unsex women and make them mannish. Advocates of women's education such as Judith Sargent Murray and Benjamin Rush argued strenuously that the purpose was not to make women like men but rather to enable them properly to fulfill their domestic functions in the new republic. According to Rush, "The equal share that every citizen has in the liberty and the possible share he may have in the government of our country make it necessary that our ladies should be qualified to a certain degree by a peculiar and suitable education, *to concur in instructing their sons in the principles of liberty and government.*"[41]

Murray's incipient feminism was directed toward the transformation rather than the elimination of women's traditional roles.

Republican motherhood was not an ideology simply imposed from the outside by a romantic male imagination, but rather one that women themselves crafted by weaving together familial commitments with their newly discovered sense of civic duty and individual possibility.[42] Fraught with explicit and well-defined limitations on women's participation as it was, republican motherhood afforded women a framework within which to express their political yearnings and to expand their civic roles. It held unforeseen possibilities for the reworking of the very definitions of "politics" and "public life."

Aftermath of War: The Changing Mission of Republican Motherhood

From the strengthened and occasionally freed families of black slaves, to educated republican mothers, to Indian families forced from their traditional lands, women entered the 1790s on an altered trajectory. The disruptions of the revolutionary war had changed women's realities greatly. They had boycotted tea and other British goods, concocting substitutes from their gardens and spinning wheels. They had assumed control of farms and businesses while husbands and fathers fought at the front. As camp followers, they had fed and clothed armies. And they had expressed political opinions in numerous ways, from rioting crowds to personal letters. In the intense atmosphere of the Revolution women were inevitably politicized, and they imbibed powerful ideas about human rights and liberties. White women, as republican mothers, gained a new status that was both political and domestic, filled with contradiction and possibility. In the postwar era, as thousands moved west and a new industrial order began to take shape, women found new roles and opportunities that accelerated changes begun in the Revolution.

Even as women experienced the ferment of revolution, in the 1780s and 1790s many of them joined the explosive movement of population across the mountains and into western lands. Such mobility by whites was facilitated by a series of treaties according Indian tribes "nationhood" in dealings with the federal government and driving them out of lands east of the Mississippi. Indian women's lives east of the Mississippi increasingly resembled that of Coocoochee, a Mohawk medicine woman who moved with her family five times and hundreds of miles from Montreal to the Ohio and Kentucky country. Her husband died in 1790 in one of many wars with whites. Living among the Shawnee, she was respected for her spiritual powers. In her later years Coocoochee told her grandchildren stories of their Mohawk ancestors, fearful in her sadder moments that she and they were the only survivors of her people.[43]

In the northern and western territories, young white men and families sought to settle and begin small farms. To the south and west, planters hoping to take advantage of a newly profitable cash crop, cotton, bought large numbers of slaves and established great plantations. White women on the frontier continued to live much as their colonial predecessors had lived, though they brought with them both republican and evangelical notions at odds with a prerevolutionary life-style. Even in rustic cabins many women understood their duties in the terms of republican motherhood and sought out other women who shared their sense of purpose. Many black slave women experienced the sharp pain of family separation as eastern planters sold slaves to others moving west, and they began to learn the arduous labor of planting, hoeing, and picking cotton. Mobility, desired and undesired, became the experience of many women, and ideas born in coastal communities began to spread across the continent.

Women participated in changing the face of the continent though none could know at the time the broader patterns they were creating.[44] Increasingly differentiated by class, women experienced new patterns in every dimension of their daily lives as they laid the groundwork for new life-styles that appeared full blown after 1820. In the bustling commercial cities and towns, economic changes undermined relatively homogeneous communities with opportunities for some, poverty for others, and disruption to all. Family-centered artisanal production began to shift to outside management as high demand prompted greater centralization. The "putting-out" system allowed a central dealer to provide materials to workers who would perform one or two tasks in the process of production in their homes. For example, this enabled women to take on some of the final tasks in finishing shoes previously produced completely within one shop by a male artisan.[45]

Women found growing markets for a variety of goods and services. Home-produced textiles grew dramatically even as the factory system made its beginning. In 1809 women at home produced 230,000 yards against only 65,000 yards produced in factories.

"She-merchants," still a small but important minority of retailers, found their opportunities for sales increased, while midwives and nurses also hired out services that in smaller communities might have been rendered free. The earliest factories, which simply brought together in one large room the traditional tasks of spinning and weaving, frequently hired women or even entire families. The introduction of water-powered machines in the 1790s, the spinning jenny in 1807, and the power loom in 1813 heralded the industrial era; even so, the predominance of women among textile workers continued. In 1816 according to one report, the cotton textile industry employed 66,000 women, 24,000 boys, and 10,000 adult men.[46]

Income-earning opportunities for more middle-class young women developed in response to the increased demand for education. Previously, older women had occasionally run "dame schools," where they taught only the barest rudiments of reading and writing. Literacy grew as young women began to teach summer session schools for girls and young children while boys were engaged in fieldwork. Very slowly such sessions evolved into full-fledged public grammar schools for boys and girls, and with them grew an increased willingness to hire women—at wages well below those of men.[47] A Massachusetts law in 1789 mentioned schoolmistresses as well as schoolmasters for the first time.[48]

Wealth generated in commercial centers facilitated a consumption-oriented upper-class life-style in which women occupied themselves increasingly with visiting and shopping. By contrast, women also constituted a high proportion of the very poor who no longer could rely on networks of extended kin for support. Some of them pursued income-earning possibilities, but many, widowed or deserted, found themselves in need of public relief. Thousands of dependent poor, a majority of them women, crowded into newly created almshouses or onto relief rolls. On the presumption that the poor lacked industry and that idleness should be avoided, women were given traditional tasks in almshouses like New York's Bellevue: spinning, sewing, cooking, cleaning, and nursing.[49] A growing number also took to the streets to sell another commodity: their bodies. In New York City alone there were between twelve hundred and seven thousand prostitutes in the early-nineteenth century.[50]

The new opportunities and difficulties women experienced outside their homes resulted from the growing separation of activity into spheres of home and work and the increased complexity of public life in urban areas. Yet, at the level of ideas, this separation was usually presented as if women's activities were located exclusively in the private sphere (home) while men occupied the public arena. Sentimental discussions of republican motherhood, therefore, overlooked the realities of many women by setting up an opposition of home and work, private and public, female and male. The fact remained that although public virtue was reserved for men, only women of the "middling" and "better" sort could afford a version of domesticity separated from family income production. The boundaries between work and home remained highly permeable.

Nevertheless, for the middling and the better sort the home itself provides evidence of the changing private life-styles that undergirded the perceived separation of domesticity from work and the public sphere. By the second half of the eighteenth century, homes had begun to change from places for work, sleep, and prayer to places of leisure and recreation. Meals evolved into more elaborate affairs as indicated by the presence of forks, knives, glass and chinaware, and tea and coffee serving equipment. Tea, associated with home consumption, "became one of those consumer goods that people connected with a change of lifestyle. They linked it with a mass consumer market in nonessentials, with leisure-time sociability in the home, and with women."[51] This perhaps explains the added symbolic importance of boycotting tea as a form of politicized domesticity. As a symbol, tea evoked the emerging patterns that were altering domestic labor toward consumption and sociability within the upper and middling classes. Urban women increasingly shifted away from primary production—carding and spinning, for example—to final processes such as sewing or to a greater investment of time in child rearing. The substitution of market-produced commodities for those produced in the home reduced some of the most arduous and time-consuming labor and opened the possibility for a more emotionally intense family life.

In the postrevolutionary era, as marriage was less and less conceived to be primarily an economic partnership and as parental control over adult children diminished, parents increasingly allowed their children to choose their own marriage partners. This new freedom reinforced the home as a center of sociability and sentiment and defined a new understanding of marriage. Such marriages with their emphasis on emotion and companionship were more egalitarian as illustrated by Judith Sargent Murray's ideal of a Philadelphia couple said to live in "perfect equality . . . as two friends, unusually well matched in understanding, taste, and knowledge." The republican ideal of marriage was mutuality, in Murray's words, "Mutual esteem, mutual friendship, mutual confidence, *begirt about by mutual forbearance.*"[52]

The influence of Enlightenment and republican thinking shifted perspectives on family authority from a patriarchal view linking father, king, and God to a republican emphasis on contract, duty, and consent.[53] Books and magazines carried articles arguing for continued patriarchal authority, but the more egalitarian voice, virtually unheard before the Revolution, rang eloquently as well. With the title, "Matrimonial Republican" in July 1792 one woman wrote in *Lady's Magazine: "I object to the word 'obey' in the marriage service because it is a general word, without limitations or definition. . . . The obedience between man and wife, I conceive, is, or ought to be mutual. Marriage ought never to be considered as a contract between a superior and an inferior, but a reciprocal union of interest, an implied partnership of interests, where all differences are accommodated by conference."*[54]

In letters and diaries literate women expressed their preference for romantic love rather than economics as the proper motive for marriage. Mary Orne Tucker wrote on April 17, 1802: *"Souls must be kindred to make the bands silken, all other I call unions of hands, not hearts,—I rejoice that the knot which binds me was not tied with any mercenary feelings, and that my heart is under the same sweet subjection as my hand."*[55] Here we find the roots of what would later be called the companionate marriage.

Further evidence of an increasingly contractual view of marriage and rising expectations within it can be gleaned from divorce records. In those New England states permitting divorce, rates rose in the postrevolutionary era along with petitions indicating growing expectations of love and affection within marriage. Courts remained reluctant to grant divorce, but began to recognize male as well as female adultery as a valid complaint.[56]

Among some sectors of the population, birthrates had also begun to fall, perhaps another consequence of mutuality and the increased value placed on individual children. Although initially a smaller birthrate may have been due to rising marriage ages, by the early nineteenth century it continued to fall in a manner that indicated deliberate family planning. One careful study of a Quaker population during the American Revolution found evidence of family planning in the delayed births of last-born children. Whether the means of contraception were abstinence, coitus interruptus, or prolonged breast-feeding, the conscious reduction of fertility certainly required mutuality if not equality.[57]

Rhetoric about mutuality and rising expectations notwithstanding, women's legal position following the Revolution did not reflect the republican ethos. Married women remained *femes coverts*, legally subsumed into the identity of their husbands and lacking independent rights to own or control property. The equity court system that had offered women an alternative to the common law went into a slow decline in the postrevolutionary era, though studies in South Carolina and Pennsylvania have shown that equity courts responded with increased flexibility to premarital agreements reserving to women or their trustees control of the property they brought into the marriage. In some cases there was a shift toward joint control by husband and wife, a pattern of "mutuality" congruent with republican marital ideals. Yet in South Carolina only 1–2 percent of marriages were accompanied by separate estates for women.[58]

Most married women, then, remained under the limits and protections of common law coverture, unable to own or control property in their own names. The primary protection which coverture offered, however, women's dower right to one-third of her husband's property, appears to have eroded significantly in the postwar era. A law in North Carolina changed inheritance patterns to force a widow with more than two children to share the inheritance equally, "she being entitled to a child's part." The stated purpose of the law was "to promote that equality of property which is of the spirit and principle of a genuine republic." In other states, widows found that the courts no longer protected their claims against their husbands' creditors. "By inhibiting the independent manipulation of property, coverture reinforced political weakness" of women.[59]

Though politically weak, women in the postrevolutionary era began to build on the idea and image of republican motherhood a sense of purpose and mission *as women;* for a century this would reshape their political consciousness and the terrain of politics itself. The beginnings, however, were small. The republican mother had an awesome responsibility for children who, in the Enlightenment view, were no longer seen as stamped with willfulness and sin but rather as possessing reason and the possibility of perfection. They should be taught rationally and carefully, preferably by example, and it was the mother's role to do so successfully.[60]

The movement for women's education in the name of republican motherhood evolved from female academies, founded in the 1780s by men, to female seminaries around the turn of the century. Founded and run by women, the seminaries offered curricula paralleling the studies offered by schools for boys with the omission of classical languages. They produced a new generation of literate women with a very different sense of their own capabilities. That sense of self represented an amalgam of the inward-looking individuality fostered when written culture replaces oral culture and a strong sense of identity with other women. Because women's education emphasized the primacy of gender, it increased women's awareness of themselves as a group. Within these schools women not only discovered themselves as intelligent but they also experienced an intense community of women suffused with the ideas of women's difference and special mission.[61]

That sense of special mission was further shaped by the religious sensibilities of a second wave of religious revivals between 1798 and 1826. From the beginning, the second Great Awakening involved even larger numbers of women than the first Great Awakening in the eighteenth century. Female converts outnumbered males by a ratio of three to two.[62] As Reverend Joseph Buckminster told a Boston women's organization, it was not "surprising, that the most fond and faithful votaries of . . . religion should be found among a sex, destined by their very constitution, to the exercise of the passive, the quiet, the secret, the gentle and humble virtues."[63]

In the years after 1800, emboldened by their gendered sense of religious and national mission, women built on their early organizing attempts during the Revolution to form a wide variety of associations and institutions. Prayer groups, missionary societies, and mother's clubs allowed women to begin to explore the dimensions of their emerging perspective. Associations and institutions, like the Female Orphan Asylum in Petersburg, Virginia, founded in 1813, gave it concrete shape.[64] Women used religion "to define self and find community."[65] To carry out the mission of republican motherhood, women needed support and advice from one another in ways that moved beyond kinship networks and into public organization. In the process they began to create a female culture and to redefine the meaning of public life itself.

4

🏴

The Age of Association
1820–1845

"It is woman's appropriate duty and particular privilege to
. . . implant in the juvenile breast the first seed of virtue,
the love of God, and their country, with all the other virtues
that shall prepare them to shine as statesmen, soldiers, philoso-
phers and christians."[1] Hannah Mather Crocker, writing in 1818
on the "real rights of women," expressed in full-blown form the
revolutionary ideology of republican motherhood. Those ideas
would soon find an altered form, however, as changes generated
in the revolutionary era reshaped American life. Between 1820
and 1845 women and men created voluntary associations on a
new scale, carving out a public space located between the private
sphere of the home and public life of formal institutions of government. In these spaces women gave new content to republican
motherhood that transformed the boundaries of domesticity even
as domesticity itself was being cloaked in Victorian images of submissiveness and purity.

The surge in association building occurred primarily within
the families of merchants, ministers, and doctors—respectable people of middling means and substantial education in the north
and midwest cities and towns. Women and men in this new middle
class, in the struggle to define themselves and their world, organized themselves in new ways. Through the 1820s and 1830s
Americans formed voluntary associations by the hundreds. French
observer Alexis de Tocqueville, traveling the United States in
1831, expressed amazement that "Americans of all ages, all conditions, and all dispositions, constantly form associations. They have
not only commercial and manufacturing companies, in which all

67

take part, but associations of a thousand other kinds, religious, moral, serious, futile, general or restricted, enormous or diminutive."[2] This new public space, however, also reflected the growing separation of men's and women's lives. The tasks they took on in defining themselves in relation to their communities were infused with powerful notions about gender. Voluntary associations became arenas in which women and men claimed and reshaped the definitions of public and private, male and female.

Ideas about Public and Private in the Victorian Era

Slowly and inexorably the growth of commerce and industry was separating "work" from home. For middle-class women this meant that marriage was no longer understood primarily as an economic partnership. The increasingly child-centered middle-class family—locus of companionship, emotion, and consumption—depended on a male wage. According to the popular literature of the nineteenth century, women and men occupied separate spheres of home (private) and work (public). "St. Paul knew what was best for women when he advised them to be domestic," according to Mrs. John Sandford. "There is composure at home; there is something sedative in the duties which home involves. It affords security not only from the world, but from delusions and errors of every kind."[3] Maleness and femaleness came to symbolize a series of oppositions characterizing these spheres. Work, as defined by men, meant the competitive, changing world of wage labor and entrepreneurship. Women's efforts in the home, though physically arduous, were no longer "work" both because women were unpaid and because of their increasing invisibility from the perspective of men.

The separation of women and domesticity from public life also facilitated the emergence of an entrepreneurial version of republicanism. Rather than emphasizing the virtues of citizenship and the importance of the common good, entrepreneurs stressed the right of the individual (man) to own and use property as the most basic liberty. Communal responsibility and virtue were subordinated to the pursuit of individual interest.

Women, then, came to embody the virtues that the new order threatened to destroy. If men were competitive, women exemplified cooperation; if men could reason, women were emotional and irrational; if men were building an increasingly secular and amoral political and economic order, women sustained piety and morality; if men sought dominance, women would submit; if men occupied the public sphere, women ruled in their own private, domestic realm, the home. Pious, pure, domestic, and submissive— the "true woman" portrayed in sentimental novels and the new women's magazines would have abjured public activity as unbecoming, even unthinkable. "Let her not look away from her own little family circle for the means of producing moral and social reforms," wrote T. S. Arthur in *The Lady at Home*, "but begin at home."[4]

The popular image of women reflected in part the anxieties of men whose world was being redefined by commerce, industry, and rising individualism. Opportunities coexisted with exploitation; competition undermined older understandings of honest and proper business relations. Women along with the family and religion moved to the periphery, charged with preserving old values and a safe and stable haven against change. In a series of lectures on *The Sphere and Duties of Woman* George Burnap portrayed marriage as "that sphere for which woman was originally intended, and to which she is so exactly fitted to adorn and bless, as the wife, the mistress of a home, the solace, the aid and the counsellor of that ONE, for whose sake alone the world is of any consequence to her."[5]

Although marriage represented emotional safety for men, its dangers for women only increased. For the urban middle classes, marriage was supposed to be a free choice based on romantic love (indeed—the attraction of opposites). Thus women gained increased control over their choice of husbands, a fateful moment after which they would be economically and legally dependent, charged with bearing and raising children, but with little recourse in the event things went wrong. Romantic love was the stuff of melodrama, and novels and stories spelled out the ideal. A character in Catharine Sedgwick's novel *Clarence* exclaimed: "I have always said I would never marry any man that I was not willing to die for."[6] But many young women in the 1820s and 1830s experienced a marriage trauma in which they withdrew emotionally from this decision. Some simply declared themselves "destined to lead a single life." Others, like Lavinia Kelly in New Hampshire, accepted their suitors with minimal expectations: "It was a serious business," she wrote in her diary, "but I had the approbation of my parents and I felt that I could love him as well as woman ought to love a husband."[7]

As norms of affection emerged within the still unequal setting of marriage, however, equally powerful bonds among women developed within their separate sphere. Grounded in daily lives which brought circles of female kin and neighbors together for rituals of birth and death, close relations among women found further expression in the institutions of church and school. Such institutions nourished a female culture where women could act, both privately and publicly, on a value system increasingly at odds with those of dominant males. A study of women's deeds and wills in Petersburg, Virginia, reflected this value system, one with a persistent emphasis on the particular individual, on the interests of other women, and on Christian benevolence rather than on abstract notions of rights and justice.[8]

Feminizing Public Spaces

Following on the heels of the female academies established in the revolutionary era, a new and more rigorous generation of schools emerged in the 1820s and 1830s. Their founders, women such as Emma Willard, Catharine Beecher, and Mary Lyon, wanted to train women to exercise their influence over children not only as republican mothers but also as enlightened teachers. Thus, the teaching profession enlarged women's public activities in the name of their domestic and moral responsibilities.

The growing availability of educated young women coincided with a massive demand across the country for teachers in communities that needed the skills of a literate citizenry. Because women teachers were an economical means of satisfying the nation's growing educational needs, the teaching profession became increasingly female. School boards and school directors felt from the start that women could be paid one-half or even one-third the salaries of men. By 1830 one Massachusetts school district employed three women for every two men. And by the end of the 1830s one out of every five native-born white women in Massachusetts had done some school teaching during her lifetime![9]

One of the crucial seedbeds for this new development started in 1821 when Troy, New York, offered Emma Willard a building and a committee of women overseers if she would establish a female seminary there. Willard was already a key advocate for women's education on the grounds that female character—effectively developed only through proper education—held the key to the success of the new republic. She added to the image of

70

the republican mother raising virtuous sons, however, a vision of female teachers instructing virtuous students of both sexes. Between 1821 and 1872 over twelve thousand women attended Willard's Troy Seminary. The alumnae created and sustained a women's network that stretched from New England to the deep south. Many set up their own female academies. Caroline Livy was typical. After graduation from the Troy academy she married a minister and settled with him in Rome, Georgia. Here, she became the principal of the local female academy, where over many years five thousand girls studied science, language, and moral philosophy as Emma Willard would have wished them to do.[10]

Even more than Emma Willard, Catharine Beecher stressed the close connection between domesticity and education. She believed in womanhood as a primary identity that cut across all class, regional, and religious lines—a natural sisterhood. Convinced of women's moral superiority, she believed that the salvation of the nation in a time of social disruption rested with educated women's influence as mothers and as teachers. In effect, she argued against egalitarian efforts to provide women with access to political and economic rights and offered instead a politicized domesticity.

Catharine Beecher was the daughter of a minister and the sister of an evangelical preacher. Thus, in applying the oldest Christian paradox of ultimate transcendence through immediate surrender of the will to the relationship of the sexes, she insisted on the power that resided in women's submission.

> Let every woman become so cultivated and refined in intellect that her taste and judgment will be respected; so benevolent in feeling and action, that her motives will be reverenced; so unassuming and unambitious, that collision and competition will be banished; so "gentle and easy to be entreated," that every heart will repose in her presence; then, the fathers, the husbands, and the sons, will find an influence thrown around them, to which they will yield not only willingly but proudly.[11]

Beecher's insistence on women's moral superiority and on women's moral mission in a democratic society extended women's sphere beyond the private home and thrust it into the public sphere. For Beecher, there was no contradiction, just as there was no contradiction between her advocacy of domesticity and her own refusal to marry, her glorification of mothering and her

71

own childlessness, her insistence on an unassuming nature in women and her own ambitious, energetic, outspoken career as the founder of schools and author of numerous books. The close identification of moral issues with her own sex made any setting a domestic one and any action womanly if its end was the virtue of society.

Mary Lyon, founder of Mount Holyoke Seminary, drew on women's religious and gender solidarity to build a new base for funding schools for teachers. She proposed a school for girls, "based entirely on Christian principles" and intended for "those who are in the middle walks of life." In appealing to women for funds, she argued that "this work of supplying teachers is a great work, and it must be done, or our country is lost, and the world will remain unconverted." Lucy Stone, a prominent abolitionist and supporter of women's rights, recalled that the women in her sewing circle responded to Lyon's plea with immediate action. "Those who had sewed and spent time, strength and money to help educate young men, dropped the needle and toil and said 'Let these men with broader shoulders and stronger arms earn their own education, while we use our scantier opportunities to educate ourselves.' "[12]

Willard, Beecher, and Lyon built on the educational revolution of their day. More women, and more men, were receiving some form of schooling in the nineteenth century than ever before. By 1840, 38 percent of all white Americans between the ages of five and twenty attended school. By 1850 most white women were literate, a sharp contrast to the eighteenth century when about half the women could not even sign their names and an even sharper contrast to southern slaves who were forbidden by law from learning to read. As a consequence, more women acquired the tools to analyze and to debate their place and their role in society.

The confidence with which women asserted their moral mission to teach and to engage in social reform outside the home was rooted in their participation in a powerful religious revival known as the second Great Awakening. This movement reached its apex in the 1820s in towns along upper New York state's Erie Canal, an area so frequented with fiery revivals that people called it the "burned over district." From the beginning, women converted in greater numbers than men, and the theological emphasis of revival preaching increasingly reflected female concerns and attitudes.

72

In hindsight, it appears that the revivals can be understood as a response to the increased marginalization of both women and religion within American political and economic life. As the growing commercial economy surged to meet new demands and opportunities, older, artisanal ways of living and working were slowly crushed. The boom and bust of capitalist expansion sidelined both home and religion which had previously been at the center of political and economic life. In alliance with ministers, middle-class women resisted this process and reasserted moral values through the process of conversion. Revivals themselves encouraged active female participation, including by the 1820s public praying in "promiscuous" (i.e., mixed male and female) audiences. Not that this went without challenge. One group of concerned clergy, including Lyman Beecher, Catharine's father, passed a resolution "that in social meetings of men and women for religious worship, females are not to pray."[13] Such objections, however, carried little weight. For many women public praying was just the first step in acting on their beliefs without the approval of male authorities. Like all converts, women felt impelled to express their new faith in good works, seeking the conversion of others. Not only did female converts outnumber men three to two, but also most male converts were the husbands and sons of converted women. By 1830 the country was thoroughly evangelized and the energy generated flowed into numerous reform movements and utopian experiments.

The second Great Awakening presented a distinctly feminized religion to its followers. Highly individualistic and emotional in style, revivalists preached universal salvation rather than predestination. Anyone could be saved if they experienced conversion, not just the elect. Preachers like Catharine Beecher's father stressed the idea that salvation was available to anyone who by a simple act of will rejected sin and accepted the grace of God. The idea of infant damnation, which had added guilt to the burdens of grieving mothers, gradually disappeared. Christ appeared as the epitome of feminine virtue: loving, forgiving, suffering, and sacrificing for others.[14] The Shakers—a sect founded by Mother Ann Lee—went so far as to assert that God had a dual nature, both male and female. Christ appeared first as a male, but in the Second Coming as a female, namely Mother Ann Lee herself.[15]

Thus, the notion of female moral superiority received further reinforcement as the ideals of femininity and of Christianity appeared to coalesce. Women's conversion experiences differed from those of men, evincing a sharper sense of guilt, anger, and power-lessness. Indeed, the female moral mission put women at odds with a world in which immorality seemed to lurk at every corner.[16]

If women found an outlet in religion for suppressed anger and anxiety, they also used religious and moral commitment to create new public spaces and female solidarity in the name of Christian duty. Female missionary societies and Sunday schools formed to reach out beyond the home and even the immediate community. Maternal Associations within churches met to provide support and education in the duties and responsibilities of Christian motherhood. In pioneering more nurturing methods of child rearing, Maternal Associations shifted the focus of childhood decisively from patriarchal authority to maternal affection.[17] By the mid-1820s wide-flung, sophisticated networks of women had become skilled at raising funds, building charitable institutions such as orphan asylums, orchestrating revivals, and pursuing courses of action as women outside the purview of men.[18]

Armed with a sense of religious mission, gender solidarity, and experience in the process of organization building, women took their new organizational skills and their zeal for changing the world into more secular and even political avenues when the fervor of revivalism began to wane in the 1830s. The language of reform remained, however, and the methods of organization retained the stamp of both evangelical religion and the search for moral perfection. Reform movements also permitted a public critique of men and male society from the perspective of female, personalist, evangelical values.

In May 1834 a small group of women met at the Third Presbyterian Church in New York City to create a national women's organization against prostitution, the double standard, and other forms of (presumably male) licentiousness.[19] Within a decade there were more than 400 chapters of the American Female Moral Reform Society.

The goal of the New York Moral Reform Society was to eradicate prostitution as a threat to the moral fabric of society and to vulnerable womanhood. Such a crusade clearly responded to an actual increase in prostitution in large cities; it also spoke in symbolic terms to broader concerns about the corrosive effects of the cash nexus on personal relations, particularly those between women and men. Their targets were the licentious men who sustained prostitution, not the prostitutes themselves. In the war against prostitution, the women of the Moral Reform Society fully developed the latent assumption of women's superior nature. In their newspaper, the *Advocate,* they exposed the "predatory nature of the American male": "reckless," "bold," and "drenched in sin" whose sexual appetite caused the downfall of innocent women. And they reestablished the connection between adultery and the moral security of the home by embracing the prostitutes as sisters, lost to their proper calling as wives and mothers. So closely were women linked to virtue in this argument that the ruin of any single woman was a threat to virtue's survival.[20]

In Utica, New York, the Female Moral Reform Association set out to change the norms of sexual behavior by enforcing premarital chastity. As mothers, they feared for the purity of their sons and daughters: "Even our small children are infested by it. Who among us have not had our hearts pained by the obscenity of little children [who bring home language they have heard in the streets]; who among us does not tremble lest some who are dear to us should be led away by the thousand snares of the destroyer" and lose their purity (virginity).[21] Through formal and informal channels women and their evangelical male allies clearly had an effect on behavioral norms if not on prostitution. Illegitimacy rates fell dramatically in the early decades of the nineteenth century.[22]

The temperance movement, against alcohol abuse, represented a similar attempt to control male behavior.[23] But the most overtly political of all reforms was abolition, a movement against the "sin of slavery"; it sprang to life in the early 1830s using the themes and methods of evangelical religion. In 1833 a Female Anti-Slavery Society formed in Philadelphia. Members joined their male counterparts in circulating petitions to Congress demanding an immediate and unconditional end to slavery in the District of Columbia over which Congress had jurisdiction. They also communicated through existing female networks to encourage the formation of additional female societies. By 1837 a national convention of antislavery women met in New York reflecting the extensive system of female antislavery societies. Through petition campaigns, thousands of women exercised their one political right. As they did so they learned the mechanics of the political system and methods of political discourse and persuasion. Vaults in the National Archives still hold the hundreds of thousands of signatures that women collected between 1834 and 1843 as testimony to their convictions and their actions.[24]

Religious reform activities strengthened women's sense of sister-hood and common purpose. Within them women developed many essential political skills: writing constitutions, electing officers, running meetings, raising money, recruiting members, voting, and planning and coordinating campaigns. Leaders claimed that female schools and reform associations simply extended women's traditional responsibilities for children and for morality into a larger sphere. But in so doing, women redefined that tradition and changed child-rearing practices and public definitions of morality.

In effect, middle-class women participated in the process of redefining the meaning of public and private life. Their activities indicated a growing tension between women and men as their lives pulled apart into separate spheres. Women used their associations to give new content to domesticity as well as to define a new public role for themselves, a domestic politics based on influence (benevolence) and on their moral mission as women. Their activism intersected and interacted with a similar impulse to association among middle-class men.

In the 1820s for the first time, white men—regardless of whether they owned property—gained the right to vote in most states. The sudden broadening of political participation in a time of rapid social and economic change offered men an arena for associational activity that was closed to women. Electoral campaigns rapidly became boisterous male rituals in which free-flowing liquor forged alliances among men across the boundaries of class.[25]

The very different public activities of women and men, and the tensions between women's activism and popular ideas of proper domesticity, generated a new debate about the "woman question" in the 1830s. Concerns about women's proper public roles were especially sharp and anxious in this period precisely because male roles themselves were undergoing changes as well. Legal changes, for example, regarding married women's property rights undermined traditional patriarchal prerogatives; the impetus behind them lay in the male-dominated market economy.

The competitive flow of goods and money that was creating new communities and new classes undermined older, personalized modes of dealing. Credit and debt became part of the lifeblood of the new economy along with a move to modernize legal conventions away from the feudal understandings imbedded in common law. Married women's inability to own or control property under

76

the common law posed several problems in this context. The fact that it violated widely held values about basic human rights (the rights of life, liberty, and property in John Locke's formulation) bothered very few because most men firmly believed in the relegation of women to dependent domesticity. But when the debt collector came to seize a man's assets, he seized the wife's as well, and the family could be left with nothing. As increasing numbers of widows found themselves destitute and forced to rely on public alms, their plight added further impetus to a movement to revise the law. Scenes such as the one recalled by Elizabeth Cady Stanton must have been enacted frequently by the 1820s.

Crouched outside her father's law office as she often did when her exasperated mother sent her away, Elizabeth Cady heard widow Flora Campbell inside pleading with Judge Cady, a man for whom she had worked for many years. Mrs. Campbell's husband had willed the small farm she bought from her own earnings to their son, whose reckless and drunken ways were sure to bring it to ruin. That farm was hers by rights, she said, and she wanted it back. Judge Cady gently explained that under the law all Mrs. Campbell's property and earnings had belonged to her husband, who had the right to dispose of it as he wished. He showed her the law in the book on his shelf. There was nothing to be done. As Mrs. Campbell left, weeping, Elizabeth resolved to cut out the offending pages from her father's law book. This first attempt to win women's rights ended in frustration when Judge Cady stopped her in the act, explaining that laws existed independently of the words in his books.

During the 1830s, however, the first married women's property acts guaranteed women the right to control property they brought into marriage as well as any money or goods they subsequently earned. Though not initially designed to rectify women's lack of citizenship rights, they fueled the growing debate on the woman question and perhaps in some eyes served as compensation in an era when the rights of men were undergoing significant expansion.[26]

At about the same time several utopian communities began to experiment with new forms of sexual relations which challenged the male/female, public/private dichotomy. Although utopians sought to demonstrate new models of cooperative human relationship, only a few took the additional step of challenging conventional gender roles in the name of their communitarian ideals.

Mother Ann Lee, founder of the Shakers, advocated celibacy to relieve women of the pain and danger of childbirth and the grief caused by infant deaths. Shakers believed that the end of the world was near, and Mother Ann Lee's followers interpreted her assertion that "it is not I that speak, it is Christ who dwells in me" to be the Second Coming of Christ. Women were twice as likely to join Shaker communities as men, and those women between the ages of twenty and forty-five, the childbearing years, were three to five times as willing to embrace Shakerism. By the 1830s there were eighteen Shaker communities, with over five thousand members, all proclaiming the dual sexuality of God and advocating an escape from female suffering through celibacy.[27]

John Noyes, who created the Oneida Community, condemned celibacy and rejected monogamy as well. At Oneida, Noyes and his supporters advocated birth control, specifically a form of prolonged intercourse that did not result in ejaculation; they established birth control as both a woman's goal and a man's duty. Noyes created a system of complex or multiple marriages that allowed both men and women the right to choose their own sexual partners, but forbade exclusive relationships. Next, Oneida devised a communal child-care system placing all children in a dormitory as soon as they were weaned. Infants went to the Children's House from 6 A.M. to 5 P.M., and then returned to their mothers; by three years of age all children spent the night in the Children's House dorm. Even though the responsibilities of child care fell to nurses selected by the community rather than individual parents, in general the sexual division of labor fell along traditional lines.

More radical yet was Fanny Wright, a young Scottish woman who set out to challenge the slave system as well as Victorian restrictions on female sexuality. Wright advocated "free love"—by which she meant the free and equal choice of sexual partners, monogamous but outside the legal restraints of marriage—and miscegenation as the solution to the race problem. After her own commune failed, she established a newspaper with another utopian, Robert Dale Owen. In 1828 Wright set out on a lecture tour in which she became the first woman in America to speak to large audiences of women and men. "However novel it may appear," she argued, "I shall venture the assertion, that, until women assume the place in society which good sense and good

78

feeling alike assign to them, human improvement must advance but feebly." Quickly she came under attack as "a bold blasphemer, and a voluptuous preacher of licentiousness." The editor of the *New York Commercial Advertiser* could hardly contain his horror: "Casting off all restraint, she would break down all the barriers to virtue, and reduce the world to one grand theater of vice and sensuality in its most loathsome form."[28]

Fanny Wright found herself a lone target when she broke a series of deeply held taboos all at once. Less than a decade later, however, the woman question reemerged in the context of evangelical reform movements that had a broader social base. Women posed a difficulty for male reformers who did not want their issues clouded with controversy about female participation, public speaking, and voting rights. For the most part, the woman problem was handled by the formation of separate female groups for temperance, moral reform, and abolition. Within the radical Garrisonian wing of the abolition movement, however, women received a full welcome.

The base for the Garrisonians in many communities lay with the Hicksite Quaker community, a radical group that split from their more orthodox colleagues in 1828 advocating a boycott of slave-produced goods and an egalitarian spiritual community. Like all Quakers, Hicksites allowed women to exercise leadership as ministers and to meet together in a women's meeting to oversee the spiritual life of female members. During the 1830s the women's meeting voiced increasing demands for equal participation, asking in 1837 at the Genesee Yearly Meeting that "the discipline be so alter'd that men and women shall stand on the same footing in all matters internal in which they are equally interested."[29] That same year, communities around the northeast were enveloped in controversy as two Quaker women traveled around to speak not only to women but also to mixed audiences about the "sin of slavery."

Sarah and Angelina Grimke had grown up in Charleston, South Carolina, in a prominent slave-owning family. Encouraged by William Lloyd Garrison to speak about their own experience and knowledge of the horrors of slavery, they began a tour of female antislavery societies in New England and New York in 1836–1837. The sensation they created, however, drew larger and larger audiences, sparking concern among ministers who felt that women should exercise their influence in the privacy of their homes, in "unostentatious prayers," and in "leading religious inquirers to the pastors for instruction." "The power of woman is her dependence, flowing from the consciousness of that weakness which God has given her for her protection. . . . But," they trumpeted in an alarmed *Pastoral Letter,* "when she assumes the place and tone of man as a public reformer . . . she yields the power which God has given her for her protection, and her character becomes unnatural."[30]

Neither Sarah nor Angelina Grimke, however, felt "unnatural." They spoke from deep moral conviction in the tradition of evangelical reform. And they sharpened the contradiction in the ideology of true womanhood: How could women discharge their moral duty while remaining silent on the fundamental moral dilemma of their time? In defense of their actions, the Grimke sisters asserted their kinship with female slaves, eloquently fusing the issues of race and gender: "They are our countrywomen—they are our sisters, and to us as women, they have a right to look for sympathy with their sorrows, and effort and prayer for their rescue. . . . Women ought to feel a peculiar sympathy in the colored man's wrong, for like him, she has been accused of mental inferiority, and denied the privileges of a liberal education." Schooled in a biblical idiom, accustomed to inspiring women to activity by drawing on strong female figures from the scriptures, they refused to cede any religious sanction for male domination. "I rejoice that they have called the attention of my sex to this subject," replied Sarah Grimke to the ministers' letter.

> No one can desire more earnestly than I do, that woman may move exactly in the sphere which her Creator has assigned her . . .
> The Lord Jesus defines the duties of his followers . . . I follow him through all his precepts, and find him giving the same directions to women as to men, never even referring to the distinction now so strenuously insisted upon between masculine and feminine virtues: this is one of the anti-Christian "traditions of men" which are taught instead of the "commandments of God." Men and women were CREATED EQUAL; they are both moral and accountable beings, and whatever is *right* for a man to do, is *right* for a woman to do.[31]

Their ringing words won many admirers among female antislavery activists though the abolition movement itself remained deeply divided on the issue of women. Most important, however, the antislavery movement provided women with both an ideological and a practical training ground in political activism for democratic and egalitarian change. The process by which a few women would begin to apply those lessons to their own condition, however, was necessarily long and slow.

Three years after the Grimke sisters' speaking tour, the American movement sent a delegation of men and women to the World Anti-Slavery Convention in London. Among them were Lucretia Mott, a Quaker minister and veteran of decades of reform activity, and a delegate's young wife on her honeymoon, Elizabeth Cady Stanton. Women's presence triggered a tumultuous debate after which the convention barred female delegates from participation and forced them to sit behind a curtain, hidden from view. In the evenings the women joined in debates with male delegates over boardinghouse supper tables. Stanton found herself drawn to Mott's serene and self-confident radicalism, and by the end of the convention the two of them agreed to initiate a women's rights convention in the United States. It took eight years, however, before they accomplished their task.[32]

Women in the Emerging Working Class

Even though middle-class women predominated in evangelical reform, the outpouring of association building in the 1830s crossed class lines. Elite women most often formed benevolent associations and moral reform societies; their sisters in the growing working class led in the formation of labor organizations.

The industrial revolution sparked changes transforming women's lives in sharply different ways according to their region and by class. The cotton gin and the power loom, for example, first revitalized southern slave agriculture by generating a strong demand for raw cotton to feed British mills. Slave sales boomed as the cotton culture spread into the southwest, rupturing families and introducing new forms of back-breaking field labor. In the north, cotton meant the first water-driven factories in which women labored as harbingers of a new, propertyless working class.

In the emerging working classes, opportunities for association, like virtually every other resource, were scarcer. In an age of economic expansion and apparent opportunity, working-class women suffered a decline in their standard of living. While Catharine Beecher and other writers of prescriptive literature were busy establishing the view that woman's place was in the home, "respectable" farmers' daughters began to enter the industrial labor force.

A unique group of women, for whom age, marital status, and geographic location were key factors in the revolution in their lives, became harbingers of a new workers' movement. They were young women from the New England countryside who had followed their traditional chores out of the home and into textile mills.

Throughout the colonial period, single daughters of rural white households had been assigned the tiring and tiresome tasks of spinning and weaving. By the 1820s manufactured cloth was cheap enough to make the daughters' work redundant. The American mills, however, needed laborers and concluded it was easier to attract single farm women than their still productive farm brothers or fathers. Almost without protest, traditional patterns of residence and work reversed as young men remained within the family circle and young women left the household for paid employment. By the 1830s the work force in the Lowell, Massachusetts, mills— the heart of America's textile production and of the industrial revolution itself—were almost exclusively young, native-born women.

Most of these workers saw their mill work as a way to reestablish their value to the family, either by relieving parents of the burden of their support, or by saving up wages to provide their own dowries, or by sending money home as a direct contribution to the family economy. Soon it was hard to separate their sense of duty from their sense of independence. Lucy Ann, a Massachusetts mill "girl," put it bluntly: "I have earned enough to school me awhile and have I not a right to do so, or must I go home, like a dutiful girl, place the money in father's hands, and then there goes all my hard earnings."[33]

The Lowell mill workers experienced a new sense of peer group solidarity and a new gender consciousness that was as important as their sense of economic independence. Almost three-fourths of the operatives at the Hamilton Manufacturing Company of Lowell lived in company-run female boardinghouses. Here they could be chaperoned and supervised by company employees who enforced strict hours and attendance at worship services—all designed to reassure families that their daughters would receive the same protection and cultivation as they did at home. At the mill itself, segregation by sex continued, for most female operatives worked in a large room with only one or two male supervisors and a few children to break the homogeneity of their sex and age group.

Mill production separated these women from their families. Mill organization separated them from men. Mill owners' housing policies separated them from the community. In this new space young women created a female culture that ordered their new lives. They established a cultural norm, consciously socializing all newcomers to that boardinghouse culture. Rural newcomers arrived with their "Yankee twangs" and their old-fashioned style of dress. Old-timers set to work on them at once, using the "severest discipline and ridicule" to school them in their own "way of speaking" and in their own distinctive fashions. Dress codes and speech codes were one form of indoctrination; moral codes were another. The mill workers were hedged round by rules and regulations governing their off-work hours, but they themselves forged these restrictions into a code of behavior and they alone enforced it by peer pressure. "A girl suspected of immoralities, or serious improprieties," wrote a local minister who observed the boarding-house patterns closely, "at once loses caste. Her fellow boarders will at once leave the house, if the keeper does not dismiss the offender. In self protection, therefore, the patron is obliged to put the offender away."[34]

The same solidarity that enforced moral norms, however, was also the basis for resistance against deteriorating wages and working conditions. When mill workers struck for higher pay and shorter hours, the heart of the strike was the boardinghouse cadres. When women "turned out" at the Hamilton Manufacturing Company in October 1836 over 95 percent of the strikers lived in boardinghouses. Women in the boardinghouses were over twice as likely to participate in such organized labor activities as women whose residence reinforced family rather than gender identification.

Although the strikes confirmed a class consciousness, many Lowell women also voiced an awareness that factory owners' paternalism was analogous to the paternalism of middle-class family ideology. "Bad as is the condition of so many women," Lowell workers wrote in an open letter to a state legislator who opposed a ten-hour workday law, "it would be much worse if they had nothing but [men's] boasted protection to rely upon." From their "bitter experience" they learned not to expect help from "those who style themselves their 'natural protectors' . . . but to the strong and resolute of their own sex."[35]

In the boardinghouses they had woven together a working-class female culture that could draw on the democratic and insurgent heritage of their "patriotic ancestors" in whose name they demanded their rights. With little experience or skill, they formed an association in 1836, aware that a more structured organization would be necessary to secure their rights. Growing discontent in subsequent years led them to more sophisticated, and even political, action. In 1844 when the Massachusetts legislature formed a committee to consider the ten-hour day, Sarah Bagley, a Lowell worker, founded the Lowell Female Labor Reform Association that quickly grew to several hundred members. The association presented petitions with more than two thousand signatures and several members testified before the legislature. After their defeat, the Lowell Association campaigned against a local legislator who had opposed them and succeeded in defeating him. Though their cause was lost for the time being, the women of Lowell had blazed a path in labor organization and political action.

Mill owners recognized the connection between solidarity and boardinghouse culture. By the 1840s any new construction of boardinghouses was forbidden. Newcomers to the mills were forced to find housing in privately run tenements or as boarders with families. Work and living were thus separated and could not reinforce the sense of collectivity that caused mill owners such trouble. This change, as much as the arrival of an Irish immigrant work force in the 1840s, diminished the power of action based on gender and class congruence.

Working-class women in cities, however, did not have the opportunities for collective action in this era that the "mill girls" had for a brief time. Until the 1830s, most urban artisan families lived in small, detached houses and kept small garden plots as well as a cow or some chickens or pigs. The garden and the livestock were not nostalgic reminders of rural life; the produce, meat, and eggs kept the family's diet varied and the family members healthy. During periods of economic depression or unemployment, the garden and livestock meant the difference between starvation and survival. Rapid urban changes, however, altered the physical setting for working-class families and the changes were not welcome.

Domestic Lives

Traditional women's work has always included processing food. These Taos Indian women (above) are winnowing grain, tossing it in the air so the wind can blow away the chaff. *(Library of Congress)* Indian women also constructed many of the basic tools and utensils needed to procure and process food, clothing, or housing. Ojibway women (below), shown making birchbark containers for maple sap in 1922, carry on the traditional skills of their ancestors. *(Minnesota Historical Society)*

European settlers in North America organized their household spaces according to the ancient division of labor between women and men associated with settled agriculture. More isolated into separate households than native Americans, European American women worked inside the home and in the nearby spaces of garden and barnyard. Care of chickens (above) and milking (below) were common female tasks from the colonial era to the twentieth century. *(Minnesota Historical Society)*

Above, enslaved African women, although responsible for the care of their families, were rarely allowed to remain within the boundaries of household and barnyard. Generations of Afro-American women worked with the hoe both in their own gardens and in their masters' fields. Below, black women were also central figures in the creation of slave families and Afro-American culture. This famous, and very rare, picture of a slave family in 1862, taken in Beaufort, South Carolina, portrays an image that evokes numerous portraits of *white* (and patriarchal) Victorian families. *(Library of Congress)*

Frontier conditions in the nineteenth century changed the meaning of domestic labor. Migrants to the western Plains, for example, experienced intense isolation. Beret Olesdater Hagebak and her husband built this 16- by 20-foot sod house in 1872. She was born in Norway in 1810 and immigrated to Minnesota in 1867. This picture was taken around 1896. *(Lac Qui Parle Historical Society)*

A few assertive and adventurous women seized the opportunity to pursue an independent rural life. In 1893 Ella Sly, seen here gathering buffalo or cow chips for fuel in Finney County, Kansas, filed a homestead claim to 160 acres on her own. *(Kansas Historical Society)*

For most women, domesticity has always included child care. The Victorian ideal of an intense, emotional bond between mother and child (above, left) masked other realities, however. *(H. Armstrong Roberts)* Clara and Mary Radintz (above, right), ages three and four, were not enfolded in domestic security. With an insane mother and a brutal father, they have just been admitted to the public school where they will be raised. *(Minnesota Historical Society)*

In upper-middle-class families, children frequently were cared for by immigrant or black domestic servants. The Walton family kept this picture of Dorothy and Audrey Walton in 1895, leaving the three young family servants nameless. *(Minnesota Historical Society)*

Household technology, mass production, and the rise of a new consumer culture dramatically reshaped women's household labor in the nineteenth and twentieth centuries. This 1930 advertisement for a "modern" washing machine contrasts the exhausting physical labor of old methods of hand washing with the leisure afforded by appliances. *(Library of Congress)*

Yet in the Great Depression women had to relearn older skills of household production with the help of public agencies. This woman, proudly displaying her canning in 1940, illustrated a Farm Security Administration program to promote farm self-sufficiency by teaching women to can, sew, garden, prepare nutritious meals, and make such household items as mattresses. *(Minnesota Historical Society)*

Sociability and neighborliness have always been important to women's domestic lives. The women and children above, chuckling at the off-camera antics of men in 1940, are twentieth-century homesteaders who migrated to New Mexico from farms in Texas and Oklahoma. In this picture their gritty lives are not sentimentalized, either with pity or with nostalgia. *(Photo by Russell Lee. Library of Congress)* Below, two women talk across their suburban backyard fences. *(H. Armstrong Roberts)*

In the twentieth century, household technology and declining family size have tended to isolate the middle-class woman within the home. Fewer domestic tasks take place in public spaces, as in the case of Taos women winnowing grain, and few require group effort. Here, Mrs. William Howe Smith stands, carefully posed, alone in her 1952 kitchen filled with modern conveniences. *(Minnesota Historical Society)*

As immigrants from Ireland and Germany and migrants from the American countryside swelled the population of cities like New York, landlords converted the small frame houses with their yards into wall-to-wall tenement flats. Working-class women now had to purchase all their food at the markets, placing a new strain on the family budget. Even when the traditional tactics for family survival were still possible, city governments made them illegal. City officials believed that livestock added to the already serious sanitation problems of the poorer neighborhoods and thus pushed through ordinances banning animals in congested areas of the city. The result was a deterioration in the working-class diet, with a decline in the variety, quantity, and quality of food a woman could place on her family's table.

Crowded tenements conjured up very different images of home than the spacious parlors and dining rooms of the prosperous classes. Home was no haven; working-class men, women, and children sought their camaraderie on the streets. Social life thus continued to be played out in public spaces rather than private ones. Wives, daughters, and widows as well as men could be seen at the theaters and in the dance halls.[36]

By the 1830s the social worlds occupied by the genteel and by the working classes were distinct and rarely overlapped. A lack of familiarity with one another's cultural patterns—and with the circumstances that explained them—quickly evolved into suspicion or contempt. Middle-class reformers often viewed the lower classes as a breed apart, and readily condemned their ideas of domestic comfort and standards of morals as far below their own.

Middle class critics were especially shocked by what they considered to be maternal neglect. For decades families had been shaped by the near idealization of the mother-child relationship. They had come to see the affection and devotion of the mother to the child as a natural instinct, independent of historical circumstances or the economic conditions in which a woman came to motherhood. Yet, many poorer women, especially unmarried domestic servants, continued to see motherhood as a condition of extreme jeopardy at worst, and extreme hardship at best. Accounts of abortions and infanticide, frequent in the newspapers and court records of the early nineteenth century, attest to the close relationship between notions of motherhood and real social conditions. Overwhelmingly, mothers brought to trial for infanticide were poor, unmarried, and homeless. The records of the New York courts in the 1810s and 1820s offer us a social portrait: "She has no regular place"; "she has 3 children now in the alms house;" "I am the mother of the baby I can't earn a living for myself and the baby four children I have besides this one."[37]

For working-class women the separation of the home and the world had little practical meaning. Many married women worked for wages in their homes. For them, economic productivity remained a vital part of their self-definition. Just as manufacturing and production moved out of the home for thousands of white Americans, urban manufacturing converted the homes of many working-class women into domestic factories. Hat and shoe manufacturing in New England and the garment industries of New York City were built on this new system called "outwork." Outwork usually assigned one step of the manufacturing process to women paid on a piecework basis. The advantages for the manufacturer were numerous: no equipment had to be bought or installed, no major source of power had to be harnessed to operate the machinery, and no staff was required to oversee production. Many married women believed outwork had advantages for them as well. They avoided the noise and dirt of the mill or factory. They worked, as traditionally they had done, without supervision. And they were able to attend to domestic duties as well as wage work tasks.

Outwork's disadvantages were less tangible, but no less real: It produced a mock privacy for these women, isolating them in their homes, in a parody of domesticity's retreat from the world. It reinforced working-class women's ties to their families rather than to their gender, for these women both lived and worked within their households and beside their children. It made their exploitation much easier, for they could not develop the collective consciousness and collective identity that allowed industrial workers to resist.

Most working-class women paid little heed to the canon of domesticity. It fit too little of their reality to prompt any desire for emulation or conformity to its tenets. Working-class men, however, frequently endorsed domesticity as a desirable goal. For them the domestic ideal became a barometer for the success of labor against capital: "If the productive laborer received his just due, and every man engaged in useful labor was properly remunerated, the female portion of their families would not need to leave their homes and domestic duties to earn their own subsistence."[38] Such statements subtly reduced women from active to passive roles in their working-class world, turning their lives into a reflection of men's success or failure in the world. Women who worked in the factories or mills, rather than in the isolation of their homes, firmly rejected this reasoning in favor of demands for higher wages and better working conditions for themselves as well as their husbands or fathers.

Race and Gender

Although cotton textiles generated commercial growth and embryonic industrialism in the north, the cultivation of cotton brought new life to the southern slave system. With the invention of the cotton gin in 1793, vast amounts of cotton could be processed profitably. The crop itself suited the long hot southern summers and its labor intensive cultivation matched the human resources of plantation slavery. Thus an institution and a social system that appeared to be waning in the revolutionary era not only rejuvenated but also began to spread rapidly. The old Virginia aristocracy discovered new wealth in their excess slaves while a new class of immensely wealthy cotton planters spread across the deep south and into the Mississippi delta.

Coming newly to life at a time when the northern states were suffused with democratic ferment, this southern upper class faced a need to define and justify its dominance. With the growth of northern commerce and industry, "free labor" (i.e., wage labor as opposed to slavery) had become a mark of manhood for northern workers. Thus, the southern ruling class faced a crisis of legitimacy, resolved through an elaborate defense of slavery and of the social order built on it. The idea of womanhood underwent significant change in the process, but southern white women had little or no collective part in generating these ideas. In cities they organized associations as their northern sisters had, sharing in the expansion of domesticity to include benevolence and moral concern. Evangelical reform, moreover, could not be tolerated because the slave masters brooked no criticism. Furthermore, the wives of the elite lived isolated lives on plantations, unable to develop a collective voice. To speak publicly against slavery the Grimke sisters had to leave the south, and once they did so, they could never return.

After 1820 when slavery had become a source of political conflict and tension between north and south and fears of slave rebellion grew, the southern elite solidified its position around a defense of the slave system. They condemned the legacy of the Enlightenment and the breakdown of deference in the north, proclaiming the superiority of their own "organic" hierarchy. The slave south was a patriarchy where fathers ruled over women, children, and slaves. Thus, conceptually the separation of public and private and male and female carried sharply different overtones in the south, for it was a product not of urban commerce but rather of intersecting gender and racial hierarchies.

In a political economy dominated by agriculture there was no separation of work and home. On rural plantations everyone worked regardless of class or gender. The plantation mistress oversaw garden; dairy; food processing, preservation, and preparation; the manufacture of clothing; and the health of blacks and whites alike. Despite images of the ethereal belle who brought civilization and refinement to men around her, the mistress performed arduous physical labor and shouldered substantial managerial responsibilities.[39] Without the assistance of slaves, poorer white farm women pursued a subsistence agriculture similar to that of their colonial ancestors.

In towns and cities middle-class southern women experienced a structural separation of home and work similar to their northern counterparts though the trajectory of self-organization and reform activity was not the same. Both white and black free women initiated organized benevolence and found within churches an environment in which they could organize themselves with relative autonomy.[40] But the middle classes were too small to be a significant force for change in the antebellum south, and the catalyst of social reform was suppressed.

Despite these differences, the romanticization of the family and of home reached even greater heights than in the north. White women's isolation in rural settings mirrored their ideological isolation, high on a pedestal. While northern women organized to enforce a single standard of sexual behavior on men, southern whites demonstrated a singular obsession with female chastity, especially before marriage. One planter observed in 1827 that "the only security a husband has is found in the purity of his wife's character before her marriage."[41] Such wives, whose lives could be ruined by the slightest implication of impropriety, lived with the knowledge that their husbands, fathers, and sons had constant sexual access to the black women they owned.

Without question, then, the ideology of separate spheres in the south was shaped by the bedrock of slavery on which the economy and society were built. White women were rigidly separated from public power and action. White men's guilt about their own sexual transgressions may have been one driving force, demanding obeisance to female purity. A toast in the 1830s praised "Woman . . . her spirit comes over us like the sweet South that breathes upon a bank of violets, stealing and giving ardor."[42] Such gallantry carried undertones of guilt and fear when it came from the lips of men whose sexual behavior violated standards of chastity as well as racial taboos. Guilt about their own actions and fear of the suppressed anger of slaves and white women fed the violence with which white men enforced their authority and defended their "honor." Violence against blacks redirected blame while it quelled resistance. The need to control white women was also fed by fear that female moral concern might indeed turn its attention to slavery.

Even though the authority of the planters depended on the clear and unambiguous subordination of white women as well as slaves, resistance to that authority never crossed racial lines. Racism and the slave system made solidarity among women impossible. Though northern elite and middle-class women could claim working women and prostitutes as sisters, southern white women found it inconceivable to respond to Angelina Grimke's plea to consider slave women similarly. Indeed, the evidence from slaves themselves indicates that mistresses could be extremely cruel, administering brutal whippings and degrading punishments with regularity.[43] Poor, non-slave-owning whites struggled to survive on the less productive lands. Bound by webs of kinship, their communal traditions remained strong, focused on religion and shared economic needs, and always in some tension with the dominant planter class. For women in such families, however, the daily life of the subsistence family farm discouraged voluntary association and racism undermined identification with black women whose life, on a material level, resembled their own.

Black women, nevertheless, from the depths of slavery had built a richly textured communal life rooted in family and religion in the slave quarters. The revival of the plantation economy in the first half of the nineteenth century threatened this slave culture by forcing the migration of thousands of slaves from coastal states into the deep south. When the slave trade ended in 1807, even as the demand for slaves was on the rise, reproduction became a major source of wealth for slave holders. Charges of slave breeding date from this period as owners pressed black women to bear as many children as possible and occasionally insisted on pairing them with specific male slaves. The importance of fertility led to some amelioration of working conditions for pregnant women, but the stability of family life, including mother-child relations, received a new and terrible challenge. Far worse than any threat of physical punishment now came the threat of being "sold down the river" for failure to obey. Women endured repeated sexual abuse rather than be torn from their children and sold off into the horror of frontier plantation life.

If the westward trek was harsh for whites, it was brutal for shackled slaves who walked for hundreds of miles. On frontier plantations, Afro-Americans came together with different dialects and religious practices, torn from communities that often had endured for several generations. There they used the metaphor of family to rebuild an Afro-American culture. Mutual obligation could be invoked through fictive kin relationships—referring to one another as "auntie," "uncle," "brother," or "sister."[44]

The lives of free black women demonstrated the limits of possibility imposed by the broader slave system. A study of Petersburg, Virginia, found signs of strength and autonomy among free black women. This independence was born of necessity with precious few resources. More than half the free black households in antebellum Petersburg were headed by females. Most free black women worked outside the home in the few ways open to them—domestic service, laundry, and tobacco factories—the worst-paid occupations in the city. Forced into independence on the edge of severe poverty, black women nevertheless managed to acquire and manage property in unusual numbers, and they demonstrated a marked reluctance to marry and thereby lose control of their own assets. Although their autonomy was real enough, it was usually "either a result of oppression or a form of punishment. Men were not present, or they were not free, or they did not make enough money." And furthermore, the wealth women controlled was extremely small.[45] In freedom as in slavery, black women exercised their creativity and ingenuity to support and sustain themselves and their families in an environment bounded by the sharp realities of race.

The forced movement of slaves into the south and west paralleled another forced migration of Indian peoples. Throughout the frontier, white land hunger ate into traditional Indian hunting grounds and living spaces. Then in the 1830s, in the administration of President Andrew Jackson, five southern tribes living on prime cotton land—the Creeks, Cherokees, Chickasaws, Choctaws, and Seminoles—were forced through trickery and military might to leave their homelands and move into Indian Territory (now Oklahoma) beyond the Mississippi. The Cherokees, most resistant and last to leave, followed a forced march they remember as the "trail of tears" during which thousands died.

As members of one of the Five Civilized Tribes, Cherokee women had already suffered dramatic changes in their social position. Following the Revolution, the federal government's "civilization program" encouraged tribal peoples to adopt Euro-American ways including language, religion, agriculture, political structures, and gender roles. Traditionally Cherokee women had "owned" the land and done the farming. Families lived in the mother's home (matrilocal) and traced descent through the female line (matrilineal). Cherokee women resisted civilization's assault on their prerogatives. In 1817 a Council of Women submitted a petition against additional land cessions to the Cherokee National Council. But prominent male leaders of the Cherokee assimilated quickly and began to demand that their women adhere to white norms of domesticity. Charles Hicks, later a principal chief, praised male leaders as "those who have kept their women & children at home & in comfortable circumstances."[46]

By the 1820s a new Cherokee political structure excluded women from political authority and participation. In the elections for an 1826 convention to devise a new tribal constitution "no person but a free male citizen who is full grown shall be entitled to vote."[47] Men had virtually taken over commercial farming, and the new tribal pattern enforced a patriarchal family structure that reckoned descent through men and prohibited polygamy. The bonds that women had shared in agricultural labor with female kin eroded as they found themselves newly isolated and domesticated. The opportunities for association among urban white women did not exist for Indians. For them, the cult of true womanhood represented loss and powerlessness even before the terrible trek to Oklahoma.[48]

Where racial oppression and gender intersected, Victorian womanhood maintained its most restrictive and oppressive face. Indian women lost traditional powers and sources of gender solidarity as southern tribes moved toward Anglo-American standards of civilization. And the southern slave system used the symbol of true (white) womanhood in its own justification, isolating upper-class women on rural plantations and denying slave women their most basic human rights.

In the north and west, however, between 1820 and 1845 the transformation of the American landscape accompanied a dramatic rise in voluntary associations through which white women and men acted to define themselves and change their world. For women this activity not only reflected the needs of the newly emerging urban middle classes but it also included women from artisanal families and the commercial elite. Voluntary associations made a powerful impact by redefining the meaning of public and private life, giving motherhood a new primacy and child rearing a gentler face. Working-class women in northern textile mills formed female associations for the purpose of demanding improved wages and working conditions. In so doing, they pioneered an organization that evolved into the modern labor union. This broad spectrum of women created a new public space, between the formal structures of government and the electoral system and the privacy of the home. In such spaces, women had a novel degree of independence with which to redefine their own identities and purposes and simultaneously raise pointed questions about—and sometimes challenges to—the larger structures of business and politics. They were able, in sum, to subvert the meaning of public life and tradition without appearing to challenge frontally Victorian notions of "true womanhood."

Inevitably, these developments combined to raise the dreaded woman question in the 1830s. Fanny Wright and the Grimke sisters generated intense debate on the propriety of female activism and public speaking. From a different angle, proposed legal changes raised the wisdom of traditional definitions of marriage and power relations within the patriarchal family. It would not be long before large numbers of women would use the skills and experience acquired in voluntary associations to demand liberty and citizenship as their birthright.

5

A Time of Division
1845–1865

We hold these truths to be self-evident, that all men and women are
created equal, that they are endowed by their creator with certain
inalienable rights, that among these are life, liberty, and the pursuit
of happiness.

—*Women's Rights Declaration*
Seneca Falls, N.Y., July 19–20, 1848

*E*lizabeth Cady Stanton held forth in Mary Ann McClintock's
kitchen in Waterloo, New York, on July 13, 1848, with an
eloquence that would soon become legendary. The last year of
managing three young boys and the drudgery of housework in
her new home in nearby Seneca Falls had undermined her merry
optimism and drawn her into a deep depression. Her marriage
provided little support—Henry Stanton's political career took him
on the road frequently, and he never really understood his wife's
radicalism or driving energy. Alone in a large and always dirty
home, tending sick children and chasing after naughty ones, and
far from the activity of New York and Boston she had loved so
much, Stanton found time to ponder the ideas she had first discussed with Lucretia Mott in 1840. For her, domesticity stripped
of opportunities for association and activism felt like a prison.
Now she had a sympathetic audience and the words poured out.[1]

A visit from Lucretia Mott and her sister Martha Wright provided the occasion for the gathering. They had just come from
the Genesee Yearly Meeting of radical Hicksite Quakers where
leading activists had precipitated a split over political action and

women's rights. Many Quakers found that their opposition to slavery made it impossible to avoid secular activity as the Hicksite community required. In addition, growing demands of women for equal participation had been postponed year after year. In June 1848 dissident Friends met in Waterloo, New York, to form a new society which would have no hierarchy, no rules about political activity, no restrictions on admission, and complete equality of race and sex.[2]

The issue of women's rights challenged the basic premise of domestic ideology, the separation of male and female spheres, by demanding equality of participation in public activities. Though the women who raised these issues did so initially from a political self-understanding rooted in women's domestic responsibilities, they found themselves quickly at odds with women whose identities and self-perceptions remained essentially private. One of the ironies of the subsequent generation, then, was the separate and parallel development of a woman suffrage movement that demanded equal citizenship rights and responsibilities for women, and a movement that defined political action for women as an extension of domesticity. The former emphasized similarities; the latter, differences.

In 1848 equity (or increased legal fairness) for women was on the agenda of many in New York who would never espouse equality. In April after more than a decade of debate the New York state legislature had passed a law granting married women sole control over property they brought into marriage or received afterwards. Indeed, forty-four women from Genesee and Wyoming counties (probably including some of the dissident Friends of the Genesee Yearly Meeting) had sent a strongly worded petition to the legislature in February. "Your Declaration of Independence declares, that governments derive their just powers from the consent of the governed," they charged. "And as women have never consented to, been represented in, or recognized by this government, it is evident that in justice no allegiance can be claimed for them." They demanded that legislators "abolish all laws which hold married women more accountable for their acts than *infants, idiots,* and *lunatics.*"[3]

The women in Mary McClintock's kitchen concluded that action was required and resolved to call a woman's rights convention the next week, July 19 and 20. On short notice, more than two hundred women and about forty men from the surrounding towns

94

and countryside came to the meeting in the Wesleyan Chapel at Seneca Falls. They must have known that such an event was radically new. Indeed, the leaders prevailed on James Mott to preside as they quailed before such a large, mixed audience. Yet the women at Seneca Falls brought with them a seventy-year-long tradition of female activity. Many had traveled the same route over and over to attend revivals, missionary meetings, and female gatherings in the name of temperance, moral reform, and abolition. Their mothers' generation had been the leading force in the Great Awakening two decades before. Their grandmothers and great-grandmothers boycotted tea, spun and wove for the army, and believed themselves "born for liberty." When the organizers of the convention started to write a statement for the body to debate, they returned to the legacy of their revolutionary foremothers: "We hold these truths to be self-evident," they wrote, "that all men and women are created equal."[4]

The Seneca Falls convention made this bold claim for full citizenship—including the right of suffrage—in a way that claimed republicanism for women not as mothers responsible for rearing good little citizens but as autonomous individuals deserving of that right. That was the essence of their radicalism: Women are citizens; their relationship to the state should be direct and unmediated by husband or children. Thus they directly challenged the doctrine of separate spheres at the heart of Victorian domesticity by asserting women's public rights as citizens.

The Power of Domesticity

Domesticity had emerged from the era of association as a much expanded version of republican motherhood. Women were responsible for children, the home, and morality, and the sentimentalized mother exercised her "gentle influence" in ways that constituted new, persuasive, rather than coercive modes of child rearing. The image of the female-centered Victorian home informed the efforts of middle-class reformers and missionaries (both male and female) who set out to change the behavior of virtually every group outside the white middle class to fit this domestic mold. And it shaped the hostile environment in which debate on the woman question grew in the 1850s into a full-fledged women's rights movement strongly allied with radical abolition.

Within the urban middle classes, domesticity had become fused with a broader worldview by the 1840s and 1850s. Catharine Beecher, one of its most prominent advocates, argued that the home could be a force for national unity in troubled and divided times. Women as nurturers and submissive wives could sustain the democratic social order. By redefining womanhood in middle-class terms and elevating the political importance of the home, Beecher envisioned women as agents of middle-class culture, of moral regeneration, and by implication of manifest destiny. "To American women, more than to any others on earth, is committed the exalted privilege of extending over the world those blessed influences, which are to renovate degraded man."[5]

"Influence," that was women's power. Beecher gave a more political twist to ideas that reached middle-class women in many ways, from pulpits and women's magazines like *Godey's Lady's Book* to innumerable sentimental novels published after 1840. Women, they all asserted, could be a force for good, not so much in their actions as in their being—beautiful, moral and pure, self-sacrificing.[6] Reverend Horace Bushnell, in a sermon on "Unconscious Influence" preached in 1846, argued that men "dislike to be swayed by direct, voluntary influence. They are jealous of such control, and are therefore best approached by conduct and feeling, and the authority of simple worth which seems to make no purposed onset." He went on to argue that this form of influence characterized the work of Christ as well.[7]

If domesticity granted women the indirect power of influence, it also nourished female community in the separate sphere of home, religion, and female association. The powerful meaning of that community is evident not only in deep and often lifelong friendships between women but also in women's anguished longings when isolated from other women. Women's letters and diaries written during the overland trek to the west—arduous trips that often took months—witness their distress at the loss of "home" and its symbols and especially the loss of female companionship. "I never recall that sad parting from my dear sister on the plains of Kansas without the tears flowing fast and free," Lavinia Porter recounted. "I stood alone on that wild prairie. Looking westward I saw my husband driving slowly over the plain; turning my face once more to the east, my dear sister's footsteps were fast widening the distance between us. For the time I knew not which way to go, nor whom to follow." Soon she "rallied [her] forces" and "overtook the slowly moving oxen who were bearing my husband and child over the green prairie . . . The unbidden tears would flow in spite of my brave resolve to be the courageous and valiant frontierswoman."[8]

Mary Ann Longley Riggs, a former student at Mary Lyon's school, trained as a schoolteacher and taught in Indiana. She and her husband, Reverend Stephen Riggs, shared an evangelical background that included temperance, peace, and abolition. They traveled to Minnesota in 1837 and spent the rest of their lives as missionaries to the Dakota Indians. Mary Riggs' detailed correspondence with her mother through the 1840s and 1850s frequently dwelled on her loneliness, anxiety, and longing for family and the company of other white women. During her six pregnancies she frequently expressed a wish to "step into your room and talk with my dear mother." When her sister sent her an album quilt in 1850 on which the woman who made each square had signed her name, Riggs' yearning for the community of women she had known in New England was palpable. Looking at the names, she wrote, "brings sister spirits into communion with my spirit and I feel that the same cause and the same Savior, induces you all to help me bear my burden."[9]

Dakota Indian women, by contrast, even if they converted and joined a female praying group, never satisfied this need. Mary Riggs understood Christian conversion to mean the adoption of a way of life that included male agricultural entrepreneurship and female domesticity; the missionary couple was supposed to model as well as to teach "civilized" ways. The sexual division of labor among the Dakota, however, differed fundamentally from middle-class ideals. Mary Riggs' loneliness reflected the cultural specificity of Victorian female community and its model of female behavior.

Dakota women not only performed domestic tasks but also were charged with agricultural and construction responsibilities that whites allocated to men. Thus work that white men considered "manly" had almost nothing in common with the tasks Dakota culture allocated to men. For each group of women, domestic work was performed in households with relatively undifferentiated spaces. Missionary women, in contrast to the Dakota, probably spent a much higher proportion of their time "inside." And their mental image of "inside" was more like an elaborate Victorian house collapsed into one room. Stephen Riggs described the one-room attic in which they lived for several years as a "study, workshop, kitchen, sitting and dining room, nursery, and ladies

97

parlor."[10] Dakota women, in the 1840s and 1850s, however, faced severe social and economic stresses. Missionaries were harbingers of a new order which threatened to obliterate their people. By the 1840s the fur trade had virtually collapsed due to overhunting, changed demand, and white pressure on Indian lands. In 1851 a few Dakota leaders signed away rights to most of their land in Minnesota following the patterns already set by tribes in Wisconsin and further east. Starvation was commonly reported, and Indian people became increasingly dependent on government payments promised for the land. Without good land, Indian men could not hunt, and Indian women could not cultivate crops. Without the hides they had traditionally manufactured into clothing and bedding, Dakota women turned to needlework taught by missionaries and brought traditional designs to crafts such as quilting.

Following a final military conflict in 1862, the Dakota people were forced out of Minnesota onto reservations in Nebraska and South Dakota. Their saga matched in many details the stories of other tribes in the west as white settlers flooded the land, preceded by soldiers and missionaries.[11] Like the Dakota, most western tribes were highly resistant to acculturation, conversion, and Victorian gender roles. Their own economies, however, and the sexual division of labor that had sustained them suffered irreparable damage. Once beyond the horrors of war and removal, Indian women and men had to struggle with what it meant to be a colonized people inside the United States. None of this did Mary Riggs understand.

In very different ways working-class families also presented a life-style at variance with middle-class domesticity. The "maternal influence" of women in artisanal families, for example, consisted largely in the practical training they offered their daughters in the basic skills of their craft. In Lynn, Massachusetts, women for generations had bound, or sewn, shoes made by their husbands and children; in the 1840s the "putting out" system had begun to break the craft apart. Under this system centralized dealers acquired raw materials and hired homeworkers to perform specific aspects of shoe production on a piecework basis. Nevertheless women continued to use traditional needle skills to bind shoes. Between 1849 and 1851 Sarah Trask described in her diary how she sometimes took her work to the home of friends where they could talk as they worked. A day's work generally consisted of binding four to five pairs of shoes. One day she counted up 719 stitches in a single size-five shoe.[12]

Although the putting out system had undermined the familial organization of the craft, changes in the 1850s and 1860s finally severed home and work for shoemakers. In the 1850s manufacturers set up stitching shops, where women could use newly invented machine stitchers. These quickly evolved into factories where all the processes of shoe manufacture came together under one roof and machines replaced the traditional shoemakers' skills.

The tensions of change, exacerbated by a depression, led shoemakers in Lynn to mobilize the legendary Great Strike in 1860, the largest labor uprising before the Civil War. More than twenty thousand workers throughout upper New England joined the strike, which was marked by rituals of community and artisanal life. Women organized their own associations and strike meetings and held a parade in which eight hundred female strikers marched with a banner reading: AMERICAN LADIES WILL NOT BE SLAVES! GIVE US A FAIR COMPENSATION AND WE LABOUR CHEERFULLY.[13] Married women found it difficult to balance the long hours away from home required by factory work with familial responsibilities even when wages were good. So it was not middle-class domestic ideals that kept married women out of factories, but the harsh realities of factory life itself.[14]

Domesticity, nevertheless, shaped the lives of working-class and poor women in critical ways. The presumption that women's true work was in the home (and unpaid) ensured that their factory labor would be undervalued—receiving wages often half those of men in similar work—and that they would be barred from the higher-paying, higher-skilled occupations.[15] If they should be poor, widowed, or ill and in need of assistance, domesticity also shaped the treatment they received at the hands of middle-class benevolence that consistently sought to make them conform to the Victorian model.

Cultural differences were especially sharp for immigrants from Ireland, Germany, and Scandinavia who swelled the ranks of working women and of the urban poor. Whether they accepted piecework, factory employment, or domestic service, they lived in crowded and dirty cities where opportunities for women were notably scarce. One measure of this was the high proportion of destitute immigrant women compared to men. Between 1845 and 1850 the Boston Society for Prevention of Pauperism received

14,000 applications from foreign women and 5,034 from foreign men.[16] Another measure of the plight of working women was the propensity of women to turn to prostitution. An 1859 survey of 2,000 imprisoned prostitutes in New York found that 25 percent of them were married women abandoned or abused by their husbands. Most of them had worked at other trades: a quarter in sewing and half as domestic servants. That one in four claimed to have freely chosen her work indicated both the extremely low income of available wage labor and a very different sensibility about domesticity and female "purity" than that of the middle classes.[17]

Indeed, the lives of urban poor women were anything but domestic. They and their children literally lived in streets crowded with people, cacophonous with the shouts of vendors, squeaking horse carts, and children's squeals, and reeking of rotting garbage. Children, sent out to scavenge, easily slid into petty thievery and prostitution. An 1850 newspaper item illustrated a common plight:

> Six poor women with their children, were discovered Tuesday night by some police officers, sleeping in the alleyway, in Avenue B, between 10th and 11th streets. When interrogated they said they had been compelled to spend their nights where ever they could obtain any shelter. They were in a starving condition, and without the slightest means of support.[18]

Middle-class reformers were horrified, not only by the visible poverty and human pain but also by the absence of "home" with all its domestic resonance.

Charities had changed by the 1850s, shaped in new ways by the domestic ideas forged in the age of association. Rather than provide outside help—bringing coal or food to the destitute— they preferred to bring the needy inside benevolent institutions. This more intrusive method accompanied a shift toward male leadership. In the eyes of men, poor women were not "fallen sisters" but "failed women." They bore the blame for dirty, ill-clad street children, because they did not remain at home, teaching their children the values and behaviors prescribed by Catharine Beecher. As a consequence, the New York Children's Aid Society had a policy of placing children in rural foster homes and, after 1854, of sending them by the train car full to the midwest. More than five thousand children—predominantly boys—had received such placements by 1860 with the expectation that middle-class homes in the west would serve as agents of regeneration.[19]

Politicized domesticity, which in the 1830s had given rise to a burst of women's voluntary activism with strong public overtones, fed a more quietist, deferential sensibility by the 1850s, at least among middle-class women, even though large areas of social activism remained. Thus, activities born in voluntary association had become institutionalized by the 1850s. Frequently this involved a shift from female to male control, sometimes with female auxiliaries. A historian of free women in Petersburg, Virginia, found symbolic shifts as well in the 1850s, such as newspaper references to women by their married names (Mrs. John Smith) rather than their own names (Elizabeth Smith). Together with structural changes these served as rituals of deference through which men reasserted, and women accepted, the hierarchy of gender.[20] Domesticity and female influence certainly claimed power for women, but only through subordination and indirection. Yet once set in motion the forces for change continued to work open new avenues for female action.

Women in the New York Children's Aid Society, for example, worked as volunteers, not staff like the men, reaching out to impoverished young girls to teach them proper domestic skills—needlework, cooking, and housecleaning. They urged their students' mothers to adopt the values of sobriety, neatness, and proper oversight of children. Their goal was not to remove children from working-class homes but to transform those homes themselves.[21] They did not identify with their clients as sisters in the way that moral reformers had done in the 1830s. The lines of class were more sharply drawn than that. Rather, like missionaries to the Indians or in foreign lands, they saw their task as one of cultural transformation, remaking the poor in their own image.

The Women's Rights Movement

Even though some women retreated into the redefined domestic sphere and others sought to extend its values and behaviors beyond the middle class, women in the Garrisonian wing of the abolitionist movement developed the woman question into a full-fledged feminist movement through the 1850s. Radical abolitionism provided organizing methods, constituency, and language for the conventions held virtually every year until the Civil War began. Attitudes inherited from the radical egalitarian Hicksite Quakers allowed women to assert their own deeply religious convictions and motivations while rejecting the authority of male-dominated

101

church hierarchies. Understanding themselves as a prophetic minority, emerging leaders honed their skills and hammered out an analysis and a program to guide them for several decades.

In essence, the antebellum women's rights movement demanded full participation in public and civic life for women, a challenge to the separation of spheres that met with intense hostility. Ministers argued from the "sin of Eve" and the masculinity of Jesus that female subordination was God-given. Newspapers questioned the femininity of women's rights advocates and the masculinity of their male allies. In 1852 the *New York Herald* asked, "Who are these women?", offering in answer a string of stereotypes that have pursued feminists to the present:

> Some of them are old maids, whose personal charms were never very attractive, and who have been sadly slighted by the masculine gender in general; some of them women who have been badly mated . . . and they are therefore down upon the whole of the opposite sex; some, having so much of the virago in their disposition, that nature appears to have made a mistake in their gender—mannish women, like hens that crow . . . there is [also] a class of wild enthusiasts and visionaries—very sincere, but very mad. . . .
>
> Of the male sex who attend these conventions for the purpose of taking part in them, the majority are hen-pecked husbands, and all of them ought to wear petticoats.[22]

Women's rights challenged the order of the middle-class world, threatening chaos in the view of opponents. The "strife, discord, anger, and division of the political" world would enter the family.[23] Indeed, male voluntary activity had shifted decisively in the 1840s and 1850s into the arena of formal politics where the themes of sectionalism, reform, and class tension erupted in a dizzying array of third parties and political factions: Whigs, the Liberty Party, Barnburner (antislavery) and Hunker Democrats, Antirenters, Know-Nothings, Free Soilers, and finally the Republican Party. But women's rights advocates persistently demanded admission to full citizenship rights as they had been granted to working and lower-class men. In making a claim on public rights, however, they never, despite the fears of their opponents, seriously questioned women's primary responsibility for the home and for children.

Married women's property laws provided a focus for their activism through the 1850s, an opportunity to use well-honed skills in petitioning and a growing capacity for public speech. Elizabeth

Cady Stanton had found her voice and her lifework in the new movement. She also found a partner in Susan B. Anthony, a former teacher and temperance-abolition activist, who with Stanton left the temperance movement in 1853 and turned her attention primarily to women's rights. In 1854 Stanton, Anthony, and Ernestine Rose presented petitions with ten thousand signatures for woman suffrage and married women's property rights to the New York legislature. Anthony was the organizer behind the petition drive; Stanton delivered the first major speech by a woman to the New York legislature, while both Anthony and Rose spoke to a variety of legislative committees. They set a pattern for action in New York through the rest of the decade winning a series of legal improvements in the process.[24]

The partnership between Stanton and Anthony brought together a brilliant organizer, Anthony, with a charismatic speaker and writer, Stanton. It allowed Stanton to continue her activism in the midst of a complex domestic life. Anthony, one of the few early women's rights leaders who never married, pressured Stanton to leave housework aside and attend to their cause. In 1856 she wrote for help in writing a speech: "So, for the love of me and for the saving of the reputation of womanhood, I beg you, with one baby on your knee and another at your feet and four boys whistling, buzzing, hallooing 'Ma, Ma,' set your self about the work." The next year Stanton, then forty-two years old, wrote: "Courage, Susan—this is my last baby, and she will be two years old in January. . . . You and I have the prospect of a good long life. We shall not be in our prime before fifty, and after that we shall be good for twenty years at least."[25]

Numerous other women's rights leaders emerged in these years including Lucy Stone, whose wedding in 1857 to Henry Blackwell was accompanied by a famous public protest in which they rejected the legal domination of husband over wife. Stone insisted on keeping her name in further rejection of coverture. Her sister-in-law and former Oberlin schoolmate, Antoinette Brown Blackwell, became in 1853 the first woman ordained in a mainstream denomination. Amelia Bloomer, assistant postmaster of Seneca Falls and editor of a temperance journal, *The Lily*, became famous for her advocacy of dress reform. The outfit she popularized in *The Lily* consisted of a shortened skirt over Turkish trousers or pantaloons. Other activists also praised the new style for it allowed freer movement and was less likely to accumulate dust and mud at the hem.

103

But public ridicule persisted until the dress reformers gave it up within a few years. Apparently the image of women wearing pants was symbolically too close to widespread fears about the implications of women's rights.

The leadership of black abolitionists in the women's rights movement gave further support for their more radical demands for political inclusion, and it exposed the underlying racism of domestic ideology. Frederick Douglass, an escaped slave, was Stanton's strongest supporter at Seneca Falls when the resolution for female suffrage proved particularly controversial. Another former slave, Sojourner Truth, majestically tall and regal in her bearing, electrified conventions with her eloquent insistence that womanhood should include black women.

In Akron, Ohio, in 1851, for example, the women's rights convention had been constantly interrupted by hostile ministers' tirades when Sojourner Truth rose and walked to the front. "Well, children," she began in a deep, resonant voice. "I think that twixt the niggers of the South and the women at the North, all talking about rights, the white men will be in a fix pretty soon." One observer recalled that she turned next to point to the objectors:

> "That man over there says that women need to be helped into carriages, and lifted over ditches. . . . Nobody ever helps me into carriages or over mud-puddles . . ." And raising herself to her full height, and her voice to a pitch like rolling thunder, she asked, "And ar'n't I a woman? Look at me! Look at my arm!" (And she bared her right arm to the shoulder, showing her tremendous muscular power). "I have ploughed, and planted, and gathered into barns, and no man could head me! And ar'n't I a woman? I have borne thirteen children, and seen 'em most all sold off to slavery, and when I cried out with my mother's grief, none but Jesus heard me! And ar'n't I a woman?"

One by one, she took on the objectors, demolishing their arguments with wisdom and logic to the great joy and gratitude of the crowd.[26] Few listeners could accept, however, the broad implications of Sojourner Truth's claim that took women's rights across the boundaries of race, class, and the bondage of slavery.

Stretching Boundaries: Female Professions and Frontier Life

The women's rights movement, though small, expressed broader currents of change that were likewise small but unsettling.

It fostered the growth of female professionals who began to create yet another female public space. Catharine Beecher, for example, though an ardent opponent of woman suffrage, argued strenuously that women should take up and dominate the profession of teaching so that they could influence ever larger numbers of children. For single women like herself it would also provide for women "a profession as honorable and as lucrative for [women] as the legal, medical and theological professions are for men."[27]

Beecher also joined health reform efforts, pointing out the high levels of illness and invalidism among middle-class women. We cannot be certain that Victorian women suffered more illnesses than their predecessors in part because the very definitions of "illness" were undergoing change. There is, however, plenty of evidence that middle-class women were preoccupied with their own health. Fashionable clothes with tight laces and pounds of petticoats distorted female bodies. Cloistered urban life may have reduced women's exercise. And the psychological pressures of maintaining the much-romanticized home may have made illness a socially validated escape from emotional responsibility.[28]

Health reformers, often overlapping with activists in other movements, advocated self-help in such forms as water cures, vegetarianism, and dress reform. They sharply criticized the medical profession, which frequently inflicted damage with its "heroic" cures such as bleeding, leeching, and amputation. Even though doctors had edged out midwives in the delivery of middle-class babies, entrepreneurial competition for students had held medical training to as little as a year with no clinical experience at all. And Victorian sensibilities further inhibited doctors and patients, leading to "examinations" with eyes averted or while the woman was fully clothed. It was only a matter of time until women interested in health sought entry into the medical profession. "The property of her nature which renders her the best of nurses," as one writer in *Godey's Lady's Book* put it, "with proper instruction, equally qualifies her to be the best of physicians. Above all is this the case with her own sex and her children."[29]

Elizabeth Blackwell entered Geneva Medical College in 1847 against the wishes of most faculty but with the support of many students. When she appeared, however, "A hush fell upon the class as if each member had been stricken with paralysis. A deathlike stillness prevailed during the lecture, and only the newly arrived student took notes." Geneva rejoined the tradition within a few years and barred further matriculation of female students. Through the 1850s and 1860s, then, supporters of women founded a series of schools: the Female Medical College of Pennsylvania in 1850, the New England Female Medical College in 1856, the Homeopathic New York Medical College for Women in 1863, and Elizabeth Blackwell's own Women's Medical College of the New York Infirmary in 1868.[30] These institutions themselves represented a new public female space, extending the efforts of female educators into new dimensions and offering access to a profession previously denied to women.

The changes pursued by educated women sometimes found fertile ground in the west, where female teachers, for example, were in great demand. But the west was a highly contradictory environment for women. Homesteaders sometimes lived in extreme isolation, cut off from any community. The work of midwestern farm families closely resembled that of colonial farmers. From the perspective of urban domesticity, "in the civilization of the latter half of the nineteenth century, a farmer's wife, as a general rule, is a laboring drudge," according to an 1862 report by the Department of Agriculture. The author, Dr. W. W. Hall, argued that "on three farms out of four the wife works harder, endures more, than any other on the place" and he recommended that men assist women in cutting firewood, hauling water, and washing and hanging winter laundry.[31]

On the Pacific coast and in western mining towns women were in short supply. Some exploited entrepreneurial opportunities, running saloons and providing cooking and laundry services. Most often, however, they found that prostitution was the most lucrative possibility. In many cases this was not a matter of choice. Thousands of Chinese women, for example, were kidnapped or sold in China and transported to California to work as prostitutes. The very first Chinese women to arrive, like the famous Ah Choi, may have worked independently, served wealthy clients, and amassed enough capital to develop businesses of their own. Very quickly, however, Chinese prostitution in California became an international business in which women were bought and sold like chattel. Many lived in tiny four-by-six-foot rooms with a bunk, a chair, and a washbowl. Those who escaped took great risks of being caught and beaten by their owners' thugs. Within the working-class Chinese community they were not considered "fallen" women, and those who married found acceptance.[32]

The west, then, provided spaces for intensified male domination as well as for female autonomy. An example of the former was the migration of thousands of Mormons in the 1840s and 1850s, fleeing religious persecution. Under the leadership of founder Joseph Smith, the Mormons were one of many religious sects born in the heat of revivals during the second Great Awakening. Smith urged middle-class virtues of hard work and frugality within a tight, clerically dominated, hierarchical community. Women and blacks were forbidden access to the priesthood.

Domesticity, with its emphasis on motherhood and household, defined Mormon women much as it did other Victorian women, but in a more controlled community with fewer opportunities for independent, female-dominated activity. A new and highly conflicted form of sisterhood developed, however, among a few Mormon women when Smith announced a revelation favoring polygamy in the 1840s: "We acted as nurses for each other during confinement," one Mormon woman recalled, "we were too poor to hire nurses. One suit or outfit for new babies and confinement did for us all, and when one piece wore out, it was supplied by another. For many years we lived thus, working together." Others, like Lucinda Lee Dalton, found plural marriage a trial: "Only for the sake of its expected joys in eternity, could I endure its trials through time." The practice of polygamy also heightened the antipathy of surrounding communities in Illinois and contributed to the decision to seek a new home in Utah.[33]

Southern Women

Victorian domesticity reigned in the south as well, and one can trace numerous similarities in southern women's lives and those of women in other regions. Over time urban middle-class women, like their counterparts in northern cities, had gained greater control of property and had successfully built numerous organizations and charitable institutions. Urban women in the small working class had entered factory work whose long hours and low wages paralleled factory jobs in the north. Wives of yeoman farmers probably resembled women on the agricultural frontier in the harsh work of subsistence farming. Isolated in the Appalachian mountains, communities woven together over many generations built a folk culture that has since infiltrated the mainstream primarily through music. In the rolling hill country, poor whites lived in communities that were always in tension with the planter elite and in which communal life was more developed than on the frontier. Most southern white women lived in non-slave-owning families, but we know less about their daily lives than we do about the elite slave-owning families.

Whatever the parallels for rural, middle-, and working-class women, however, southern domestic ideology continued to be framed by the needs and anxieties of the planter class and permeated with racist assumptions. The southern middle class remained weak; the association between abolitionism and women's rights in the north horrified southern ideologues, and the repression of political dissent on the slavery issue deprived southern women of the catalyst that had sparked women's rights activism in the north. And at the heart of the slave system—the plantation—the lives of women, white and black, diverged sharply from those in the north and west.

The booming plantation economy that fueled southern expansionism shaped the lives of most slaves. Clustered on large plantations, their lives revolved around the rhythms of a specific staple crop (most likely cotton, but also sugar, rice, or tobacco) and the dense community of the slave quarters. Most slaves were illiterate—by law—so we have very few written documents to tell us their stories. Despite this, the testimony of many former slaves, along with plantation records and oral tradition, has given a remarkably full picture of pre–Civil War slave life.

Afro-American culture developed religious institutions, family forms, and a gender system sharply at odds with those of the dominant white culture and largely invisible to slave owners. At the center of slave life was the family, and at the center of slave families were women. White owners tolerated and even encouraged family life among slaves because of their interest in high fertility and because slave families provided many daily needs—food grown in small gardens, food preparation, child care, laundry, and housekeeping. Economic considerations regularly interfered with family life, causing up to a third of slave couples to experience separation due to sale. And the harshness of slave life meant that an even higher proportion of slave families experienced the early death of one spouse.

Because mothers were less likely to be separated from young children than fathers, the mother/child bond became a critical link in sustaining family relations. Family ties, drawing on African

108

traditions and evolving to meet the harsh conditions of slavery, provided the key to survival of tradition and identity. The bonds between female kin were further cemented by work practices that allotted tasks to groups of women or men. One former slave recalled his mother's work as a head spinner who returned from the fields early to prepare the cotton and then oversaw the work of other women after supper. To encourage them to finish before darkness came, she sang "Keep yo' eye on de sun,/See how she run,/Don't let her catch you with your work undone."[34] In a setting which afforded them very little time to call their own, women used the bonds of kinship and work to allocate and reallocate the tasks of child rearing beyond the nuclear family. Family ties became the model for other relationships, teaching a respect for the wisdom and experiences of the old, and binding unrelated adults to one another.

Within slave families, women and men assumed complementary and roughly egalitarian roles. Women prepared food, managed the household, supervised children, manufactured clothing, and contributed food—sometimes from the master's kitchen, sometimes by fishing or gardening. Men supplemented the diet by hunting small animals, made furniture and tools, and cultivated small garden plots or cash crops.[35]

Sexual mores, marriage, and naming practices offer further evidence of a strong and internally coherent Afro-American culture. Slave women began childbearing early, often soon after puberty at fifteen or sixteen. Afro-American women appear to have been more sexually expressive than their peers in the Victorian middle class. Their community did not condemn them for premarital pregnancy, but it did insist on marriage soon thereafter and on fidelity after marriage, which was particularly remarkable because slave marriages had no legal status. Earthy and explicit songs, recorded in the early twentieth century, reflected this legacy of sexual expressiveness and explored the difficulties and the humor of sexual relations. White Victorian culture had suppressed all mention of physical sex in popular song, but a black woman could sing to her man, "If you go fishin', I'm a-goin' a-fishin' too,/You bet yo life yo sweet little wife can catch as many fish as you." At the same time, young slave women, especially household servants and mulattos, were always vulnerable to sexual abuse by whites, something from which no family could protect them. Former slaves recalled their horror and humiliation at seeing white men rape slave women and being unable to stop it. "My blood is bilin' now at the thoughts of dem times," was probably a common emotion even decades later.[36]

Most black women worked in the fields; even household workers did so in seasons of high demand. They planted, wielded heavy and awkward hoes, and harvested under the beating sun for fourteen hours a day. For months cotton pickers dragged bags behind them, up and down the rows, picking the required 150 to 200 pounds a day, receiving the lash if they failed. "I been so exhausted working, I was like an inchworm crawling along a roof. I worked til I thought another lick would kill me," remembered Hannah Davidson.[37] Women were excluded only from the heaviest labor such as clearing land and the skilled artisanal jobs requiring training. In the latter case, the gender assumptions and prejudices of whites were probably at work. Although they could put women to work like draft animals in the fields, they could not imagine a female, even a slave, as a carpenter, blacksmith, or tanner. Pregnant women generally left the fields a month before giving birth and returned a month after. But even a reduction in work load to "half-hand" was strenuous, and infant mortality was high. At night and on Sundays women met their families' needs as best they could.[38]

Even though powerful bonds of kinship proved central to the physical and cultural survival of Afro-Americans, they also provided owners with leverage that dampened protest. The threat of punishment of kin or sale to a distant plantation was a curb on insurgency. Delia Garlic, Virginia born and sold three times before the Civil War, recalled the hell of slavery:

> Babies was snatched from dere mother's breas' an' sold to speculators. Chilluns was separated from sisters an' brothers an' never saw each other ag'in. Course dey cry; you think dey not cry when dey was sold lak cattle? . . . It's bad to belong to folks dat own you soul an' body; dat can tie you up to a tree, wid yo' face to de tree an' yo' arms fastened tight aroun' it; who take a long curlin' whip an' cut de blood ever' lick. Folks a mile away could hear dem awful whippings. Dey was a turrible part of livin'.[39]

In contrast to the vulnerability of the family, slaves found in religious gatherings and language a space that was relatively free of planter control. Afro-Americans had blended the message of Christianity with their African past and found within scripture

resources for an alternative interpretation of the world. The story
of Moses and the liberation of the Israelites became a metaphor
for the hope and expectation of freedom. Spirituals such as "Steal
Away to Jesus" took on layers of meaning, serving as signals for
secret gatherings, warnings of trouble, and an outlet for deep
human longing. In a novel about her great-grandmother, Margaret Walker described the cook in the Big House. "When Aunt
Sally was deeply troubled she opened her mouth and raised a
real wailing song over her cooking

> I been buked and I been scorned,
> Lord, I been buked and I been scorned,
> Lord, I been buked and I been scorned,
> I been talked about sho's you bornd.
>
> But I ain't gwine a-lay my religion down
> Lord, I ain't gwine a-lay my religion down . . .
> Untell I wears a heavenly crown.[40]

Black churches nourished women's lives and created some opportunities for leadership in musical and highly emotional worship. Many women experienced a call to preach and minister,
despite resistance within both black and white communities.

Elizabeth, a preacher in Virginia and Maryland, described how the
people there would not believe that a colored woman could preach.
"And moreover . . . they strove to imprison me because I spoke against
slavery; and being brought up, they asked by what authority I spoke?
and if I had been ordained? I answered, not by the commission of
men's hands; If the Lord had ordained me, I needed nothing better."

Women in the independent African Methodist Episcopal Church
in the northern states demanded ordination, but after 1840 found
that the church hierarchy was increasingly resistant to formal
recognition of their ministry.[41] Female leaders, however, inevitably
found the sources of their courage and the language of freedom
in religion. The greatest of these women in slavery times were
Sojourner Truth, whose skill at biblical exegesis had thrilled wom-
en's rights conventions, and Harriet Tubman.

Harriet Tubman was a slave in the eastern shore of Maryland
in 1849 when she learned that the slaves of her deceased master
would be sold to another state. Alone, she escaped to Philadelphia
in safety; for more than a decade Tubman returned again and
again to guide slaves into freedom. She began with members of

her own family and made, perhaps, nineteen trips into Maryland to rescue others. Courageous, resourceful, she shepherded terrified people in the darkness, through forests and swamps, and into the friendly hands of abolitionists on the Underground Railroad who hid escaping slaves along their route to freedom. Deeply religious, certain that she acted by divine command, she exploited the symbols and coded communications religion afforded. A secret message signaling her arrival said: "[T]ell my brothers to be always watching unto prayer, and when the good old ship of Zion comes along, to be ready to step on board." By the late 1850s there was a $40,000 bounty on her head in Maryland, but nothing stopped her until the war.[42]

The Civil War

Three decades of female activism against the "sin of slavery" were woven into the growing political and economic tensions between northern and southern states that finally erupted in civil war. When the guns at Fort Sumter boomed on April 12, 1861, they signaled the beginning of a time of national trial that reshaped women's as well as men's lives—some for just a few years, others permanently. While northern and southern whites read of the war in bold headlines, word spread quickly among slaves who listened intently to guarded conversations among their masters. Soon they realized that their own liberation was at stake even in the midst of severe hunger or the bloody horror of nearby battlefields.

When a Union fleet of warships appeared off the coast of South Carolina in 1861, planters hurriedly gathered their families and a few belongings and fled the coastal islands to the mainland. For the most part their slaves refused to accompany them. Planter John Chaplin, in a frenzy to get his family to Charleston, sent for Moses Mitchell, the plantation carpenter, to man one of the flatboat oars. "You ain't gonna row no boat to Charleston," ordered Mitchell's wife, "you go out dat back door and keep a-going."[43] Others hid in the swamps and the fields, anticipating freedom. For most, the road to that promise was paved with heartache and hardship.

Black women felt the ambiguous impact of the war first in their family life. The proximity of Union troops or the disruption of the plantation's productivity meant a greater opportunity to flee toward freedom or try to rejoin relatives in other parts of the south. But the policies of the Confederate and the Union governments often worked to increase the chance of separation of black families. The Confederate government impressed male slaves throughout the war, using them as laborers to construct roads or move war materials—work that did not necessitate arming them. Impressment ran as high as 50 to 60 percent of all male slaves.

If the Confederacy's military strength separated slave men from their families, its military weakness did, too. When Union armies neared, planters fled deeper into the region or westward toward Texas. They took their slaves with them, keeping the faster moving and the more valuable male slaves at the head of this retreat and often abandoning the women and children along the way. Slave women not only lost track of husbands and sons this way, but they also faced the task of protecting their dependent children from hunger, illness, and Confederate raiders who might capture, rape, or kill them. Their only hope for safety lay behind Union lines, and so they began an odyssey that often returned them to the scene of their slavery. Union armies rarely applauded the black women's tenacity or ingenuity once they arrived safely in the refugee camps. Instead, Union officials complained of having to issue rations to "helpless" women and children.

Often a husband's valor in escaping slavery and enlisting with the Union army meant a wife's peril. Unable to punish the escaped slave, masters settled for beating his wife. Many slave women were forced off the plantation and out of their cabins by angry masters. When slave women made their bids for freedom they carried their domestic duties with them. Harriet Tubman recalled the women among the 700 slaves she helped to freedom during the Combahee River Raid of 1863:

> Here you'd see a young woman with a pail on her head, rice a-smoking in it just as she'd taken it from the fire, young one hanging on behind, one hand round her forehead to hold on, the other hand digging into the rice-pot, eating with all its might . . . hold of her dress, two or three more; down her back a bag with a pig in it.[44]

White women's activities were also affected by the realities of war. In both north and south the onset of war suddenly plunged them into public activity on a new scale. As during the revolutionary war, domestic activities also took on political meaning, but

113

the intervening three-quarters of a century had given women significant organizing experience allowing a new level of mobilization of female energies. This war was also more absorbing and draining than the Revolution. Before it was over, 620,000 men would die in battle, $20 billion would be spent to resolve the issue of union and secession, and the entire society would be mobilized in behalf of the war effort.

Two weeks after the war began women formed twenty thousand aid societies in the north and south, to supply the armies with clothing, food, medical supplies, and money. In the north, these societies, composed and led primarily by women, were coordinated by a central agency, the Sanitary Commission. In the south, the states' rights philosophy and the intense localism of the region produced independent local societies.

Through the Sanitary Commission women raised over $15 million worth of supplies during the war. Their member organizations staged everything from door-to-door fund-raising drives to county fairs, from musicales to lectures on the "Chemistry of Agriculture." New York City women financed the training of nurses; rural women provided fruit and vegetables grown in "Sanitary Potato Patches." In the south, the Society of Center Ridge, Alabama, was typical of women's efforts as unofficial quartermaster corps. In a single month, the group produced "422 shirts, 551 pairs of drawers, 80 pairs of socks, 3 pairs of gloves, 6 boxes and one bale of hospital supplies, 128 pounds of tapioca, and a donation of $18 for hospital use."[45]

Women also volunteered their services as doctors and nurses to their respective armies. Female doctors made little headway, but the demand for nurses overwhelmed the reluctance of those who recoiled at the image of "refined, modest ladies . . . caring for strange men and crude soldiers from all walks of life."[46] To avoid the specter of sexuality that authorities seemed to dread, Dorothea Dix, as superintendent of nurses for the Union Army, set out to hire only women over thirty and "plain in appearance." Thousands volunteered who were neither, drawn by patriotism, the chance for adventure, and most important, the salary of forty cents a day. Southern women likewise volunteered, for forty Confederate dollars a day (these were worth even less).

As in the Revolution, women assumed new economic responsibilities when men joined the military. They ran farms, plantations, and businesses in rural areas. In cities, they often sought employment where women had already found niches: in factories and in teaching. When the U.S. Treasury Department began to hire women to replace clerks who had gone to war, a new field of employment opened, if only slightly. Abraham Lincoln may have thought it a fine idea to hire women, especially war widows, but public opinion apparently did not. Office workers faced the same barrage from the press and other critics that nurses had faced. Their morals were called into question by some; others were willing to concede them their virtue, but argued that the "fair sex" were a distraction for male workers in the same office. The most vocal critics argued that women's nature made them a particularly poor choice for government offices. They would carry "the drawing room to the office . . . corrupting public morals."[47]

Most women who sought work, however, ended up in factories where conditions worsened throughout the war. Newspaper editors, even those not sympathetic to the working classes, openly marveled at how these women managed to survive. The price of room and board in New York City's working-class neighborhoods, they noted, was at least $2.25 a week. After a factory worker paid for washing and other necessities, she had no more than twenty-five to fifty cents left. Single women with no obligations might consider this a profit, but most women factory workers had entered the shops because they had mothers, brothers, sisters, or other family to support.

Married women with children avoided the factories and earned their wages through piecework at home. For them, falling wages and inflated living expenses spelled extreme want and deprivation. For example, tassel makers' wages had been six dollars a week in 1853 and fell to four in 1863; they still worked fifteen-hour days. The same year women and girls earned about seventeen cents for a twelve-hour day making underwear and twenty-four cents sewing shirts. Out of these wages came the cost of needles and thread. The decline in wages was due in part to the intervention of subcontractors who bid for government contracts and then hired female workers at extremely low wages, rarely paying on time, and finding numerous other methods of exploitation.[48]

By 1863 the sewing women had begun a petition campaign, modeled after the antislavery campaigns of the 1840s. In the hundreds of petitions laid before the president and Congress, these women called for an end to the subcontracting system. "We are unable to sustain life for the price offered by contractors who fatten on their contracts by grinding immense profits out of their operatives."[49] The same year, two other forms of less decorous protest likewise spelled out women's primary commitments to family and community. Bread riots and antidraft protests demonstrated women's willingness to engage in public, political activity—perhaps in the eighteenth-century sense of street politics—to defend their ability to function in their roles as parents and neighbors.

The south was in crisis by 1863. War had ravaged the countryside, filling cities with refugees. Scarcity, speculation, and hoarding drove prices for food to unimaginable heights, raising the specter of starvation for many. Bread riots erupted throughout the south as women demanded food at decent prices. In Richmond, Virginia, word of such activities in Alabama and North Carolina spread rapidly through the marketplace where female hucksters like Mary Jackson mingled and shared information with workers from the nearby munitions plant, soldiers' wives, and other refugees. At a meeting in the Belvidere Baptist Church more than three hundred women decided to take action; the next day their number had swollen to more than one thousand angry women led by Mary Jackson brandishing a six-chamber pistol and a bowie knife. For several hours the crowd broke into shops and food stores seizing bacon, flour, sugar, coffee, candles, cloth, shoes, and whatever else they could get.[50] When President Jefferson Davis pleaded for an end to the rioting, and offered to share "anything he had" with members of the crowd, the women ignored his requests and dismissed his offer as a gesture of empty hospitality. Only the city battalion's gunshots ended the rioting.[51]

By their acts of violence, protesters defended themselves against the encroachments of government policies that threatened their life-style. As ruinous inflation undermined the world of cooperation and mutuality they knew and wished to preserve, they refused to accept such a fate passively. White women in the rural south, whose lives depended on subsistence farming, wrote in desperation to soldier husbands to return. "My dear Edward," wrote his wife Mary, "I would not have you do anything wrong for the world, but before God, Edward, unless you come home we must die." Accepting the primacy of family obligations over those of the state, Edward deserted. Other women wrote to political leaders. "For the sake of suffering humanity," one woman begged Governor Zebulon Vance of North Carolina, "and especially for the

116

sake of suffering women and children try and stop this cruel war."[52]

Women of the Union also acted to protect family integrity on their terrain. In New York City, lower-class women demonstrated against the Draft Law of 1863. By that law, all white men between 20 and 45 were required to do military service. The government provided loopholes to this universal service, however. A man could "buy out" by paying the government $300, or he could hire another man to serve in his place. On Monday, July 13, 1863, only two days after the law was posted, poor Irish women joined their men in the streets, beginning a six-day demonstration and riot.

Initially the rioters' demands were posed in the political vocabulary of American egalitarianism. For instance, they called for an immediate end to all draft exemptions based on wealth, for these exemptions legitimated class inequality as a state policy. The rioters also spoke in the more basic vocabulary of men's primary responsibilities to family rather than to state when they demanded exemptions be added for all men with dependents. In addition, they exposed the deep fissure of race in the north as well as the south: Free blacks quickly became scapegoats for grievances about the war, as rioting crowds frequently terrorized and tortured free black women and men. Twelve hundred people were killed in the Draft Riots and several hundred women were arrested, convicted, and jailed. Here, at least, the growing primacy of the state was upheld.[53]

As rural and working-class women protested the intrusions of the state, women's rights advocates, who had spent a decade demanding a more direct relationship to the state, found themselves silenced. To continue protests and petitions would, they feared, brand women's rights as unpatriotic. Women's rights leaders organized the Women's National Loyal League to petition Congress for a thirteenth Amendment abolishing slavery. By 1865 they had collected 400,000 signatures. Like that of the Sanitary Commission, this mammoth effort brought thousands of women into public and political action, giving them organizational experience and new skills.

Hundreds of younger women seized the opportunity to serve as missionaries and teachers in the southern states wherever Union armies had captured territory. Like Mary Riggs among the Dakota, they wanted to spread Victorian values and mores. The black hunger for education, as well as food, made them welcome but they were unable to perceive or understand the Afro-American culture they sought to change. "At one of their prayer-meetings, which we attended last night, we saw a painful exhibition of their barbarism," Lucy Chase wrote to her family after her arrival in Craney Island, Virginia.[54] Eventually, the attempt to recreate southern black society in the image of the northern middle class failed in the face of a tightly woven (if invisible) cultural tapestry.

Women had thrown themselves into the Civil War effort with an energy and a level of organization never before seen in American public life. In the north, the work of the Sanitary Commission, women's petitions against slavery, and campaigns for working women introduced thousands to the complexities of civic activity. In the south white women gained new authority and a new public voice in the midst of wartime devastation while black women gained a freedom whose meaning and limitations were not yet clear. Many groups of women, then, in many different voices were prepared to claim new liberties in a postwar world whose politics had been reshaped by the war and whose economy was rapidly evolving into that of an industrial giant.

6

"Maternal Commonwealth" in the Gilded Age
1865–1890

"Law me, talk about crying and singing and crying some more, we sure done it." That was how Mary Armstrong remembered her reunion with her mother in Texas several years after the Civil War. She had searched for her since 1863 when she received her own freedom in Missouri at the age of seventeen.[1] Thousands like Armstrong sought out children, siblings, and spouses separated from them by the slave system, creating one of the greatest migrations in American history.

As newly freed black Americans sought to reconstitute their families and to begin to define a new place in society against intransigent and unrepentant white racism, their struggle placed the definition of citizenship on the national agenda. In the battles over the Fourteenth and Fifteenth amendments guaranteeing citizenship and voting rights to black men, suffrage became a central issue within the movement for women's rights as well. Female citizenship, in turn, began to take on new meanings in a world infused with racial and class conflict as well as tensions between women and men.

Aftermath of War: Reconstruction, Abolition, and Women's Rights

At the war's end, black Americans were slaves no longer. But freedom came to people with no property or income, whose families had been scattered by slavery and war. Most former slaves who set out to find family members never succeeded, but their

119

efforts testified to the strength of family ties as well as to black people's determination to define for themselves what freedom would mean. One mother announced as she reclaimed her child from the mistress who had raised her in the "big house": "You took her away from me and didn't pay no mind to my crying, so now I'm taking her back home. We's free now, Mis' Polly, we ain't gwine be slaves no more to nobody."[2]

Freedom—among other things it meant making one's own decisions, not taking orders from whites, sustaining an independent family life, and learning to read and write. In a vivid display of communal solidarity, southern blacks organized an array of associations immediately after emancipation. They withdrew from white churches en masse and formed their own churches, often joining up with the independent black denominations created earlier in the century among free blacks. Once secret and hidden under slavery, overnight black churches became the visible foundation of the black community. In Richmond, Virginia, three African Baptist churches alone had more than four and a half thousand members. In addition, blacks organized Republican party clubs, mutual aid and protective associations, fraternal societies, fire companies, and schools. Richmond alone had more than 400 such associations by the early 1870s.[3]

Under slavery blacks had learned the value of mutuality, of turning to the community for support. Individualistic competition had few rewards in that system, and the slave community developed many ways of enforcing its own norms. Knowing well the need for mutual aid and support, women played strong and visible roles both in their families and in associations. Ideas about the proper roles of women and men also surfaced, shaping different experiences according to gender. Women's abrupt withdrawal from field labor provided the first clear signal of this difference. Many women saw an opportunity for the first time to attend to the needs of their own families and expressed deep anger about the sacrifices they had been forced to make. Others withdrew at the request of husbands such as the one in Tennessee who announced, "When I married my wife I married her to wait on me and she has got all she can do right here for me and the children." Northern black leaders had urged for years that black women should be model housewives. They experienced a loss of manhood through enslavement and unemployment; and female subservience within a patriarchal family furnished one symbol of its reassertion. A white teacher on the Sea Islands in South Carolina reported that black leaders were urging men "to get the women into their proper place—never to tell them anything of their concerns."[4] Perhaps most important for women, black families moved away from the communal environment of the slave quarters to live scattered on separate plots of land. Although liberating and beneficial in most respects, it also privatized the labor of housework and child care with breathtaking swiftness.

Nevertheless, black women and men alike quickly found that without the productive and income-earning labor of women few families could survive. They owned no land, no cash, and few skills besides agricultural ones. Whites refused to hire former slaves for more skilled jobs or newly emerging industrial jobs. Tenancy and the crop lien system rapidly became a system of perpetual debt for black sharecroppers—almost a new slavery. Land owners provided seed, tools, and land on credit against the income of the future crop. That income, however, was rarely enough to erase the debt, so black families sank deeper and deeper each year. Blacks who managed to move toward economic independence despite these new economic pressures, or who showed signs of political activism, faced the terrorism of the Ku Klux Klan. Margaret Walker's novel *Jubilee* described her great-grandmother's struggle for survival in the early years after the Civil War: "We just had been from pillar to post. . . . First we was in the river bottom and we got flooded out when high water come the next spring, then we was sharecropping on a dirt farm for a year, and then we had us a brand-new house with windows from the mill and the Ku Kluxers burned us out. We lost everything excepten the clothes on our backs."[5]

The result was that women soon reentered fieldwork out of sheer necessity. According to one former slave, women "do double duty, a man's share in the field, and a woman's part at home. They do any kind of field work, even ploughing, and at home the cooking, washing, milking, and gardening."[6] Working in the hot sun hoeing or picking cotton and tobacco, frequently pregnant, sacrificing so that the next generation could be literate, southern black women lived their lives close to the bone. When such families moved into cities, women continued to work outside the home because even though their men were frequently unemployed, women could find work as domestics relatively easily.

Black women participated in the political mobilization of freed slaves during Reconstruction, much as white women had become caught up in the fervor of the Revolution. They attended rallies, joined parades, and even voted during mass political meetings. Reports from Yazoo County, Mississippi, during the 1868 presidential campaign indicated that black maids and cooks working in the homes of former Confederates defiantly wore buttons with the image of General Ulysses S. Grant.[7] The political centrality of black male suffrage that rapidly became the top priority of the Republican party and its abolitionist allies, however, heightened the difference between men's and women's experience during Reconstruction. Only the black vote would prevent the white Democrats from reclaiming control of southern states and thwarting the legislative goals of Republicans in Congress. Black leaders also knew that political power was their only hope against the continuing economic domination of the planter elite. Neither group saw the enfranchisement of women—black or white—as important. The Augusta, Georgia, *Colored American* editorialized that all people should have the vote with three exceptions: foreigners, children, and women whose "sphere is anywhere but in the arena of politics and government."[8]

Abolitionists, both black and white, found that their alliance with the Republican party forced a priority on black male suffrage. Women's rights advocates within the abolitionist movement such as Susan B. Anthony, Elizabeth Cady Stanton, and Sojourner Truth expressed horror at the inclusion of the word "male" in the Fourteenth Amendment to the Constitution; this amendment imposed penalties on states that denied the right to vote to male citizens over 21. Another group of women's rights activists led by Lucy Stone, Henry Blackwell, and Frederick Douglass agreed that "this hour belongs to the negro," fearing that debate about woman suffrage at the federal level would introduce additional controversy and endanger the passage of the Fourteenth and Fifteenth amendments. To this Elizabeth Cady Stanton hotly replied: "My question is this: Do you believe the African race is composed entirely of males?"[9] One consequence, then, of the battles over the political status of black Americans was a more focused women's rights movement which increasingly referred to itself as the "woman suffrage movement." This linguistic shift acknowledged the centrality of suffrage to women's demand for full citizenship. Suffrage provided a clear agenda around which the women's movement would organize and agitate for more than half a century.

The deep, bitter split between woman suffrage advocates in the 1860s fragmented the women's rights movement for more than two decades. In 1867 the state of Kansas sponsored referenda on both black male and woman suffrage. Stanton, Anthony, Stone, and Blackwell campaigned tirelessly for both, but found themselves attacked mercilessly by misogynist Republicans who ridiculed women's claim to full citizenship. In an attempt to taint her crusade with charges of immorality and illegality, one Republican spokesman accused Lucy Stone "and that seed-ward she carries around with her—called Blackwell" of practicing free love. As a result, Stanton and Anthony broke with Republican abolitionists whose first priority was black male suffrage and began to seek new alliances and constituencies. They were appalled that Stone and Blackwell would remain allied with men they considered woman-haters, sacrificing for the present what Stanton and Anthony saw as a golden opportunity to win universal suffrage. How could women's rights advocates not press their issues now that the definition of citizenship was on the political agenda, with strong political support for change, for the first time in many years? If this opportunity were lost, they believed, there might not be another for many decades. Stone and Blackwell, on the other hand, believed that although black male suffrage was politically popular, it should not be jeopardized by simultaneous consideration of woman suffrage. They were likewise outraged that Stanton and Anthony accepted financial support from racist Democrats like George Train who advocated white woman suffrage as a weapon against black political power (i.e., white women could outvote blacks).[10]

Out of this conflict came two woman suffrage organizations founded within months of each other in 1869. The National Woman Suffrage Association (NWSA), founded by Stanton and Anthony, refused to support the Fifteenth Amendment unless it enfranchised women, fearing that this would be their last opportunity. Strategically, they chose to work at the national level for an all-inclusive suffrage amendment, believing that state-by-state progress would be lengthy, arduous, and difficult to achieve. Cut off from most former abolitionists, they reached out to new groups of women who had not previously been touched by political struggle. Though attempts to build alliances with working-class women foundered on the deep differences of class, Stanton and Anthony discovered a new interest in women's rights among professionals such as teachers and journalists, women who had become active during the war through the Sanitary Commission, and others in the middle class who found the restrictions of domesticity increasingly confining.

The American Woman Suffrage Association (AWSA), by contrast, under the leadership of Stone and Blackwell, pledged support for the Fifteenth Amendment which enfranchised all males regardless of color and argued that woman suffrage was best achieved at the state level. Still convinced that the Republicans would support woman suffrage once blacks were enfranchised, they lobbied at the Republican convention, winning a brief mention of woman suffrage in the 1872 platform (known as a "splinter," not a plank). They were, however, proved wrong by subsequent events. The Republicans' neglect was so great that woman suffrage did not appear even as a splinter again until 1916.

The AWSA planned to devote itself primarily to woman suffrage and to a genteel and philanthropic concern for women's rights. As the masthead of its weekly newspaper, the *Woman's Journal*, announced, it was "Devoted to the Interests of Woman, to her Education, Industrial, Legal and Political Equality and especially her right to Suffrage." In contrast, the NWSA embarked on a wide-ranging exploration of women's condition making no concessions to gentility or to Victorian ideals. "It is a settled maxim with me," wrote Elizabeth Cady Stanton, "that the existing public sentiment on any subject is wrong." NWSA also preferred publicity-grabbing, activist tactics. In 1872 they backed the presidential campaign of Victoria Woodhull, a flamboyant advocate of free love who maintained that women were already enfranchised under the Fourteenth and Fifteenth amendments. Using this rationale, members of NWSA also tried to vote in several communities and, when refused, cast their ballots in a special box in protest. These two organizations with their very different styles but shared agenda kept the issue of woman suffrage alive for two decades before old animosities could be set aside and a new, joint organization formed.[11] In the meantime, however, the changing lives and activities of massive numbers of women provided new ground for the seeds of women's rights activism. With tragic irony, in those same years, the political rights of black men proved vulnerable to terror-

124

ism and the economic power of ruling whites. As Reconstruction ended in the 1870s, black men were once more being disenfranchised.

From the WCTU to Populism: Origins of Maternal Commonwealth

In the decades following the Civil War the rhythms of many women's lives became detached from the earth's seasons. Factory whistles sang out at the same time regardless of weather or changes in the sunrise or sunset. Train schedules imposed new "time zones" so that arrivals and departures could be predictable and synchronized. Machinery operated with an inhuman precision and monotonous repetition. "Family time" diverged increasingly from "industrial time" as industries rationalized and routinized their procedures.[12] Traditional family responsibilities did not yield easily to the new beat of urban industrial life, and women were often caught in the middle.

As time changed its meaning, so did space. The completion of the first intercontinental railroad in 1867 shortened coast-to-coast travel time from several months to several days, making east coast markets accessible to farmers in the west. At the same time, the social spaces of daily life of "home" and "work" became separate places for more and more people. The pace of change generated turbulent responses as women and men alike struggled to weave new patterns from older ways.

In the winter of 1873–74, women in small midwestern towns like Hillsboro, Ohio, and Adrian, Michigan, rose up in such numbers that they sent a shock wave through the nation. Temperance was their cause, a reform issue with roots in the antebellum era. Through temperance women not only expressed anxieties about the disruption of communities and families but also attacked a particular male behavior, the consumption of alcohol. The sudden eruption of the temperance issue in 1873 occurred in the midst of an economic depression. Ohio women devoted to temperance knew that the state legislature showed signs of yielding to pressure from saloon interests to loosen liquor laws. Many may well have felt that they had a stake in the outcome of a political process in which they had no say. Whatever the cause, suddenly the pent-up frustrations of decades poured out as more than sixty thousand women took to the streets, picking up the thread of temperance activism from the pre–Civil War years. Their goal was to close down the saloons; by the following summer they had indeed closed down more than a thousand of them.[13]

In Hillsboro, Ohio, eighty women had met in church the morning after a temperance lecture, signed pledges, prayed, and proceeded downtown double-file to sing and pray in the saloons until the owners agreed to close them. Morning after morning they pursued their task. One young customer told a visiting reporter from Cincinnati about how he and his friends had recently returned to town unaware of the crusade. They sauntered into the bar, ordered drinks, and pulled out their cigars when "the rustle of women's wear attracted their attention, and looking up they saw what they thought was a crowd of a thousand ladies entering." One young man spied his mother and sister, another two cousins, and a third was horror-struck to see his future mother-in-law in the crowd.[14]

Soon Hillsboro women were joined by sisters from Washington Court House, Ohio, whose crusade had already succeeded in closing saloons. As the local temperance men prayed in the church and rang the church bell, the women visited saloons with increasingly gratifying results. Throughout the midwest that winter, the streets literally ran with rum as saloon keepers "surrendered" to the women, signed temperance pledges, and rolled the casks of liquor into the street to be split open.

The crusade lacked the structure capable of sustaining a lasting movement and left some women feeling almost as if they had been on an exhilarating albeit temporary binge. Although the impact on the liquor industry was limited at best, the women's crusade created a cohort of women permanently changed by their new experience of power. As Frances Willard wrote:

> Perhaps the most significant outcome of this movement was the knowledge of their own power gained by the conservative women of the Churches. They had never even seen a "woman's rights convention," and had been held aloof from the "suffragists" by fears as to their orthodoxy; but now there were women prominent in all Church cares and duties eager to clasp hands for a more aggressive work than such women had ever before dreamed of undertaking.[15]

Similar to abolition, temperance was a secular reform with evangelical roots, couched in religious language. For middle-class women it became a vehicle for their accumulated grievances as women, much as moral reform had been for an earlier generation.

Protection of the home and family from the violence, financial irresponsibility, desertion, and immorality associated with drink and male abuse of alcohol became the keynote of the feminized temperance movement.

The national Woman's Christian Temperance Union (WCTU) emerged in 1874 as an organizational response to the midwestern women's crusade. Men were not allowed to join. Under the inspired and charismatic leadership of Frances Willard, president from 1879 to 1899, the WCTU was an open and democratic female environment—a free space within which women experimented and pushed their traditional self-definitions past the boundaries of domesticity and into the broadest demand for full political participation.

Willard's election to the presidency of the WCTU signaled the willingness of its membership to expand their concerns and their tactics. A leading educator and former dean of Evanston College for Ladies, Willard combined a passionate advocacy of Victorian womanhood—"Womanliness first—afterwards what you will" was a favorite slogan—with a call for female citizenship. She was best known as an advocate of the "Home Protection Ballot," a limited suffrage demand through which "the mothers and daughters of America" could participate in decisions about whether "the door of the rum shop is opened or shut beside their homes."[16] Such a demand epitomized the vision of a maternal commonwealth that fused public and private concerns, domesticity and politics, as well as the republican mother and the suffragist. Slogans such as "For God, Home, and Native Land" allowed restive, educated, and increasingly leisured middle-class women to redefine their spheres of interest and engagement without having to challenge them head-on. Willard used women's commitments to clubs and missionary societies and their social posture as moral guardians of the home to bring thousands into public, political activity for the first time.

The breadth of reform activity initiated by the WCTU, with autonomous choices for local chapters, made it possible for large numbers of women to work with the temperance movement on issues of immediate concern to themselves. This "Do-Everything" policy, passed at the 1882 WCTU national convention, encouraged local chapters to work on any and all issues they deemed important. This brilliant organizing strategy allowed more conservative chapters to avoid issues such as the "Home Protection Ballot" if they wished while unleashing the energy and creativity of militant activists. By 1889 Chicago WCTU activities included "two day nurseries, two Sunday schools, an industrial school, a mission that sheltered four thousand homeless or destitute women in a twelve-month period, a free medical dispensary that treated over 1,600 patients a year, a lodging house for men that had to date provided temporary housing for over fifty thousand men, and a low-cost restaurant."[17]

The sharply polarized gender roles of the mid-nineteenth-century middle class in which women were perceived as moral guardians provided the WCTU and other female reform groups with a vision of universal sisterhood, a sex-class whose "sacred claims," in the words of Julia Ward Howe, bound them to one another. This vision was exemplified in October 1873 by an incident at the first exclusively female prison in the United States. Mrs. Sallie Hubbard and her husband had murdered a family of seven. When she arrived as the first inmate, bowed down with manacles, Superintendent Sarah Smith ordered the men to "take off her shackles; she is my prisoner; not yours." She then "embraced her fallen sister, prayed for her, and showed her to a room decorated with bedspread, clothed table, curtains, a pot of flowers, a Bible, and a hymn book." In a similar spirit, the WCTU took up the cause of prison reform, agitating effectively for the presence of police matrons to deal with incoming prisoners of their own sex.[18]

The WCTU drew on and politicized familial tensions and strains between women and men in the middle classes. In cities and small towns alike, women's economic and social dependence on their husbands generated an undertow of anxiety and frustration. Anger at alcoholic men who failed to fulfill their familial responsibilities and provide for their wives and children thus grew into a broader challenge to the male mismanagement of the entire political/public arena, a criticism easy to sustain in the last quarter of the nineteenth century—the heyday of city bosses, robber barons, and corrupt legislatures.[19]

Willard consciously used domestic imagery, both verbal and visual, to encourage women's special sense of moral and political mission. She contrasted a national WCTU meeting with "any held by men: Its manner is not that of the street, the court, the mart, or office; it is the manner of the home." The first sign of this distinction lay in "the beauty of decoration. . . . [B]anners of silk, satin and velvet, usually made by the women themselves, adorn the wall . . . or the setting of a platform to present an interior as cozy and delightful as a parlor could afford." In addition, she argued, not only the setting but also the political methods employed in the "Do-Everything" policy were distinctively female: "Men take one line, and travel onward to success; with them discursiveness is at a discount. But women in the home must be mistresses, as well as maids of all work; they have learned well the lesson of unity in diversity; hence by inheritance and by environment, women are varied in their methods; they are born to be 'branchers-out.' "[20] By implication, womanliness could define a new political setting, bringing into the public women's moral concerns while insulating women from the corruption and immorality of male-defined politics.

The WCTU appealed to a broad range of women, small-town and rural as well as urban, western as well as eastern, wives of artisans and laborers as well as wives of businessmen and professionals. Its leadership, however, was predominantly upper-middle-class, educated, native-born white Protestant, a profile matching that of other female reform leaders. These women found in the WCTU an arena in which they could experiment with a new, more politically active role. The domesticity their mothers struggled to define was transformed in their hands into a demand that maternal values shape public behavior. Ultimately, however, the WCTU could not transcend the biases of its predominantly white, native-born base, with its increasing hostility to the lower classes, to immigrants, and to blacks. Willard's outreach to Catholics, for example, provoked internal dissension and a public protest against "the inroads which Romanists are making in our ranks, preventing freedom of speech and action."[21] She was never able to bring the WCTU as fully into electoral politics as she wished, nor to win a majority to her increasingly radical, socialist perspective.[22]

Nevertheless, the WCTU's radical legacy lived on in many guises. In the 1880s white and black farmers in the west and the south, trapped by fluctuating market prices and the credit manipulations of banks, railroads, and local landholders, developed a massive movement aimed at self-sufficiency. These populists, so-called for their emphasis on returning political and economic power to the people, founded cooperatives to free themselves from the crop-lien system and the threat of peonage. In camp meetings reminiscent of evangelical revivals, small farmers became visible to one another and their collective power emboldened them to envision a social order in which cooperation and human values would claim priority. They called it the "cooperative commonwealth".[23]

Only a few highly visible populist leaders were women, most notably Mary Elizabeth Lease, an Irish woman from Kansas and mother of four who was admitted to the Kansas bar in 1886. A gifted orator, she became famous for her admonition, "What you farmers need to do is to raise less corn and more *Hell.*" At the grass-roots level women participated actively, reflecting the laboring partnership that was the family farm. Populist women organized separately from men, using the technique of parlor meetings perfected by the WCTU, and they drew much of their membership from the WCTU ranks. Their commitment to woman suffrage, and its presence as an issue on the populist agenda, rested on the ideas and experience of the temperance movement—their version of the "cooperative commonwealth" constituted a variation on the "maternal commonwealth." When the farmers' revolt shifted from social and economic cooperatives to partisan politics, however, unenfranchised women had fewer roles in the movement. Campaigning for the Populist party in 1892, Mary Elizabeth Lease offered the populist version of maternal commonwealth or politicized domesticity: "Thank God we women are blameless for this political muddle you men have dragged us into. . . . Ours is a grand and holy mission . . . to place the mothers of this nation on an equality with the fathers."[24]

Immigrant and Working-Class Women in the Industrial City

Working-class women developed their own version of the maternal commonwealth in the 1880s in the context of a burgeoning labor movement. In some industrializing cities wage labor had become commonplace by the 1880s. Twenty-six percent of Philadelphia's workers were women, as were 34 percent in Fall River, Massachusetts, and 35 percent in Atlanta, Georgia. Where textiles, domestic service, and other female-dominated jobs were in short supply, as in Pittsburgh or Chicago, the numbers were far smaller.[25] Both the kinds of work and the composition of the working classes were undergoing dramatic change in the post–Civil War decades.

Beginning in the 1880s a new flood of immigrants from eastern and southern Europe joined the Irish, Germans, and Scandinavians who had dominated previous migrations. Whereas a substantial number of single Irish and Scandinavian women migrated alone, Slavic migration tended to be male-dominated. Many Eastern European and Italian men came to the United States intent on earning enough money to return to their homelands and build a better life. Wives and children came later if the men decided to stay. One Polish woman, finding peasant life extremely difficult without her husband, wrote to him: "The Wheelbarrow of life is too heavy for my shoulders . . . take me where you are . . . otherwise I shall perish."[26] Jewish immigrants from Russia and eastern Europe deviated from the dominant pattern and generally migrated in family groups, fleeing political persecution and discrimination, and the horrors of pogroms.[27]

For most newcomers, industrial American cities were strange places. Immigrants clustered in neighborhoods where they could be near kin and others from their homelands, but the sounds, sights, and smells of the slums in New York, Chicago, or Pittsburgh represented an abrupt change from the intimate and overlapping relationships of peasant villages. Families crowded into tenements that left little room for privacy. Basic services like potable water and sanitation were slow to come to poorer neighborhoods. Working-class women often had to carry water for cooking and laundry up several flights of stairs.

Peasant women were accustomed to productive work within the family economy, but what could they do in an urban, industrial context? Placing their highest priority on family needs, women stayed home whenever possible, shifting roles quickly according to familial necessity.[28] Taking in boarders, for example, solved the dilemmas of families caught between low wages in working-class jobs and high urban rents. It also met the housing needs of migrants from Europe or the American countryside who generally sought work and housing through the channels of kinship and ethnicity. Indeed, among urban immigrants, most people spent some part of their lives living with nonrelatives either as boarders when young and single or in families that took in boarders themselves. At any one time in the late nineteenth century between 25 and 50 percent of working-class families had others living with them.[29]

Caring for boarders was arduous work. Women cleaned, did laundry, shopped, and cooked for large numbers of people, often in very close quarters. One immigrant to New York described a household consisting of two parents, six children, and six boarders in a two-room apartment. On Saturday the apartment served as a synagogue. During the week it was also the workplace for one daughter who took in sewing and for a boarder who was a shoe-maker. "The cantor [who leads songs and chants in Jewish worship] rehearses, a train passes, the shoemaker bangs, ten brats run around like goats, the wife putters in her 'kosher restaurant.' At night we all try to get some sleep in the stifling roach-infested two rooms."[30]

Where possible, women took in home work, making garments or other items on a piecework basis, though as the century pro-gressed homework yielded to factory production except in the garment industry. Different cities offered different opportunities for domestic or factory work making such things as boxes, bread, or textiles. Whether or not women could add to their families' income, however, they learned the skills of consumers in order to stretch family resources as far as they could within a cash econ-omy. In Pittsburgh, for example, where women had few opportuni-ties to earn wages, they bore the burden of stretching the incomes of their husbands (and sometimes their children) to meet basic needs. Working-class neighborhoods had few amenities such as running water, indoor toilets, or washing machines, so women continued to cook, wash, and clean in the old-fashioned, labor-intensive way. They carried clean water in and dirty water out by hand in a constant battle with dirt and grime.[31]

Decisions about work were shaped primarily by economic need and opportunity, but ethnicity seems also to have influenced wom-en's work patterns. In Buffalo, New York, Italian and black women exhibited strikingly different patterns. Blacks placed a very high priority on the education of children, applied no stigma to married women working outside the home, and presumed that black men would face ongoing employment discrimination. As a result, mar-ried women frequently worked outside, especially if by doing so they could keep their children in school. Italians, on the other hand, strongly valued the continuous presence of the mother in the home. Thus, Italian women preferred to take in boarders or even to send their teen-aged sons and daughters to work in facto-ries rather than enter wage labor themselves.[32] Appalachian whites, in contrast, transferred a family economy in which every-one worked from the southern hills and mountains to mill towns in the 1880s. Owners paid wages designed to be sufficient only if several family members worked in the mills. Children as young as five and six worked in the lint-filled spinning mills. Their mothers rose early to bake bread and tend gardens and stayed up late to make garments after working their own twelve-hour shifts.[33]

A number of factors combined to increase the participation of young single women in the labor force quite dramatically in the second half of the nineteenth century. Until that time women in most groups married relatively late, often not until the age of twenty-five. Opportunities for employment not only grew rapidly in the cities but also provided many jobs stereotyped as women's work in such areas as domestic service, sewing, teaching, and nursing. Whether young women sought excitement and independence, or, more likely, to contribute to their families' subsistence and their own self-support, cultural and economic changes combined to create a new stage in the female life cycle. Young single women encountered a period of relative autonomy between childhood dependence and the adult roles of marriage and motherhood.[34]

Domestic work was the most common job available to young women, though by the late nineteenth century it had become an urban phenomenon and constituted a declining proportion of working women. The ratio of servants to families dropped as household production declined and job opportunities in manufacturing and sales increased. As a result, domestic work lost status and became more and more associated with groups considered to be socially inferior such as immigrants, blacks, and in the west, Chinese men.[35]

The supply of domestic workers was heavily weighted toward young immigrant women, especially the Irish and Scandinavians who brought with them a tradition of domestic service. The conditions in which they found themselves constantly emphasized their subordination in both material and symbolic ways: Typically, a young woman lived in her employer's home, in a small back or attic room. With perhaps one afternoon off a week, her hours were indefinite. She took her meals in the kitchen, after the family was finished, always ready to stop if beckoned. One young woman told an investigator that "it's hard to give up your whole life to somebody else's orders, and always feel as if you was looked at over a wall like." Another objected to being treated like a machine: "[My employer would] sit in her sitting-room on the second floor and ring for me twenty times a day to do little things, and she

133

wanted me up till eleven to answer the bell." Not only did she have no time for herself but also "I had no place but the kitchen to see my friends. I was thirty years old and as well born and well educated as she, and it didn't seem right." Young immigrant women also recognized quickly that the badges of servitude they wore at work followed them elsewhere: "A teacher or cashier, or anybody in a store, no matter if they have got common sense, don't want to associate with servants."[36]

Black women were the only group of married women to work extensively as domestics, largely because racial discrimination limited their options and black families needed two incomes. Because they had families and children of their own, they strenuously resisted employers' pressure to live in, setting a new pattern of day work that after 1900 became predominant. In 1883 an Alabama banker testified that black women "want to live at home, and very few of them, cooks or servants, will consent to sleep on the premises where they work. They seem to think it is something against their freedom if they sleep where they are employed."[37]

Young women who found factory employment ended up in a wide variety of low-skilled jobs. Machines increasingly broke work into smaller parts, diminishing skills and worker's control over their time. At a Boston meeting of working women in 1869, Aurora Phelps described the consequences for working women:

> When I was younger girls were taught full trades. They made pants, coats, overcoats and then they learned to cut. Now one stitches the seam, another makes the button-holes, and another puts the buttons on, and when the poor girl stitches up the seams and finds her work slack she goes from shop to shop, perhaps for weeks, before she can find the same kind of work.[38]

Even though immigrant women dominated the ranks of domestics and factory operatives, after 1870 new kinds of white-collar work emerged that employed primarily white, native-born young women. Most important among these were clerical and sales work. Neither field employed many women in 1870, but by 1900 women were more than one-third of all clerical workers and by 1920 they were in the majority.

Before the Civil War, clerks were typically young men who worked closely with their employers, aware that theirs was the first rung on the corporate ladder. As corporations grew in size and complexity, their record-keeping needs led to a proliferation of clerks and in the 1880s to the rapid adoption of newly introduced typing machines. E. Remington and Sons, a gun manufacturer had begun to produce the machines in 1873; by 1886 Remington was making 1,500 per month. In 1887 a business journal noted that "Five years ago the typewriter was simply a mechanical curiosity. Today its monotonous click can be heard in almost every well-regulated business establishment in the country. A great revolution is taking place, and the typewriter is at the bottom of it."[39] This revolution removed clerical jobs from the corporate career ladder as it gradually transformed them into women's work.

Postwar corporate expansion led to a great demand for literate workers, especially in the new jobs of stenographer and typewriter (the name of both the machine and the operator). Neither job had links to management careers. Similarly, retail sales in the newly created department stores demanded personnel who had basic arithmetic skills and were able to converse easily with predominately female customers. At the same time, rapid increases in educational opportunity had created a growing pool of literate women for whom there were few work opportunities outside of teaching. Almost immediately the new jobs were categorized as women's work. In 1875 E. Remington and Sons advertised their product as an excellent Christmas present by pointing out that "No invention has opened for women so broad and easy an avenue to profitable and suitable employment as the 'Type-Writer'." When the New York YWCA offered training for women typists in 1881, they soon had more requests than they could handle.[40]

Whether in factories, offices, or private homes, however, women's wages were about half those of men. In the late 1880s the average weekly wage for urban women was $5.24, adjusted for layoffs and illness. If they were fully self-supporting, their average weekly expenses were about $5.51. The government study providing this estimate cited specific examples like the bag maker in Philadelphia who earned $4.49 per week and spent $4.17 per week for basic expenses and the New York seamstress whose weekly earnings of $4.42 did not meet her expenses of $5.12.[41]

Poor working conditions and low wages certainly provided grounds for working women to join the emerging labor movement. Irish collar makers and laundry workers in Troy, New York, led two major strikes in 1863 and 1869 and then initiated a short-lived cooperative laundry.[42] Shoemakers in Lynn, Massachusetts, who remembered the time when their craft was a family affair, formed the first really effective workers' organizations: the Daughters of St. Crispin and the Knights of St. Crispin. They fought to keep their work in factories rather than allowing it to be done outside at cheap piecework rates. When members of the Daughters were fired in 1871, the Knights struck in sympathy and a national labor newspaper editorialized in their favor: "Have women the right to form protective associations? . . . It is her inalienable right, and in asserting it the American Daughter thus reiterates the spirit and independence of the Mother and Sire of '76."[43] Less than a year before, the same paper, appropriately named the *Workingman's Advocate* had asserted that "Man is and should be head of his own department, in the management of his business for the support of his family. Woman should be head in her own department, in the management of household affairs, and in the care and government of the children."[44]

The presence of women in factories provoked anxiety among male workers who feared competition for jobs and lowered wages; these men also viewed women's presence in the public arena as a violation of natural law. Most often they preferred to demand a "family wage" that allowed men to support their wives, and they actively excluded women from unions. In the 1860s only two national unions, the Cigarmakers and the Printers, opened their memberships to women.

In the meteoric rise and fall of the Knights of Labor in the 1880s, however, working-class women glimpsed an alternative possibility and began to formulate a maternal commonwealth rooted in their own perspectives and needs. The genius of the Knights was its ability to organize people not only through their workplace associations but also through family, fraternal and sororal, kinship and religious associations as well. This was particularly important for women as the Knights organized not only factory workers but also those who worked in the home, domestics, and housewives. For once, women were not forced to choose between work- and kinship-defined identities or loyalties. As a result, the Knights chartered approximately two hundred and seventy "ladies' locals" and another one hundred and thirty mixed locals of both women and men with a membership estimated in 1887 to include sixty-five thousand women.[45]

The Knights' emphasis on cooperatives as an alternative to the wage system appealed strongly to women who saw cooperation as an extension of domestic values. Cooperatives could also transform housework itself as when the Joan of Arc Assembly in Toledo created a baked-goods cooperative, or buying cooperatives in New York tenements reduced household food budgets by nearly 50 percent. "Why should there be as now in one block of dwellings from thirty to forty cooks with attending waste of materials and physical strength?"[46]

Similar to the WCTU, the Knights allowed a communal fusion of roles and groups in a way that simultaneously sustained difference and produced commonality. Just as the Knights of Labor was anticapitalist without being either anti-industrial or socialist, so it also espoused both the Victorian domestic ideal and the equal rights of working women. The Knights idealized housewives such as Elizabeth Rodgers who attended the 1886 Knights convention with her tenth child, a two-week-old daughter, as well as organizer Leonora Barry, a widow who came from a textile mill to work tirelessly for the movement, placing her two children with relatives and boarding schools to do so. Both of these women remained active not only in labor affairs but also in the temperance movement.[47]

The tension between domesticity and activism, however, existed within the Knights' social and political vision, which reinterpreted both republican and religious traditions to create a powerful alternative to the ravages of industrial capitalism. Vivid memories of an artisanal past and the self-sufficiency of the small farm became critical tools in describing the flaws in the lives of industrial workers and their loss of control over the processes and products of their work. Old images of the commonwealth fused with newer notions of cooperation required by larger operations of industry into a vision of a "cooperative commonwealth" that was anticapitalist without being anti-industrial.[48]

Women in the Knights blended this vision with the values of domesticity, using them to criticize the inhumanity of the public world of capitalism. Like suffragists and temperance advocates—which many of them were—the Knights believed that women, precisely because of their roots in home and family, could inspire and work for a more cooperative and moral public life—a maternal commonwealth.[49]

The explosive beginning of the Knights, however, was followed by an equally rapid decline. The flood of new members had outdistanced the organizational sophistication of its leaders, and then a series of violent and disastrous strikes for the eight-hour day crushed the newly raised hopes of tens of thousands. The demise of the Knights in the late 1880s left working women with few alternatives for organizing within a framework of ethnic and class solidarity.

Maternal Professions and Sororal Associations

While working-class women stretched their means to provide subsistence for themselves and their families, women in the growing urban middle classes shaped a more affluent pattern which nevertheless echoed some of the same themes of work outside the home, youthful autonomy, and maternal commonwealth. On the surface, however, the urban middle class appeared to be devoted primarily to the elaboration of a life-style focused on domesticity and motherhood.

The ideology of separate spheres could now be realized more fully than ever. Fertility had dropped dramatically, from seven or eight children on average in 1800 to four or five three-quarters of a century later. The availability in cities of bakeries, laundries, ready-made clothes, and canned foods removed much traditional labor from the home. Meanwhile, improved household technologies such as indoor plumbing, cooking stoves, and iceboxes reduced the amount of physical labor required for food preparation and the care of clothing. As a result of these changes, many more women's time and attention could be devoted to emotional nurture as well as physical care of children than ever before.[50]

Increasingly, elaborate houses displayed the Victorian obsession with privacy (a separate bedroom for each child and careful separation of family spaces from parlors where one might encounter the public) and the "professionalization" of the female sphere with a different room designated for every activity: sewing, music, breakfast, and dining, as well as sleeping. Such homes conveyed the expectation that much of the remaining physical labor would be performed by a domestic servant whose room was carefully concealed by a back stairway with direct access to the kitchen. From the perspective of those alert to new marketing opportunities, the complex management of such a household clearly offered possibilities. Women's magazines such as [Women's] Home Companion (1873), Women's Home Journal (1878), Ladies Home Journal (1883), and Good Housekeeping (1885) pursued a course laid out by Catharine Beecher in advising the modern housewife. To the perfection of her household and nurturing skills, however, they added enticements to increased consumption of household products.

The middle-class women's world was also filled with contradictions: If women were to become experts in their own arena, they needed more education than women's magazines could provide. With this claim, higher education for women flourished. Vassar College opened in the 1860s, Smith and Wellesley Colleges in the 1870s, and Radcliffe College in the 1890s. From the 1860s on state colleges and universities in the western states were coeducational. In the tradition of republican motherhood, colleges proclaimed their mission as the fulfillment of female destiny. As Sophia Smith, founder of Smith College, stated: "It is not my design to render my sex any the less Feminine, but to develop as fully as may be the powers of womanhood, and furnish women with the means of usefulness, happiness and honor, now withheld from them."[51]

In schools growing numbers of middle-class women also began to experience a period of autonomy between childhood and marriage. Their autonomy was not economic, as with domestic, clerical, or factory workers, but in the context of high schools and colleges, particularly boarding schools, they lived in an environment that emphasized their capacities and their solidarity as women. Scientists continued to proclaim that women's smaller brains could not withstand the rigors of higher education and that their reproductive capacities would be harmed by too much thinking.[52] Certainly college-educated women found that society had little use for their newly acquired capacities. Jane Addams floundered for years in a search for meaningful activity, "filled with shame that with all my apparent leisure I do nothing."[53]

Out of the discontent of middle-class women came a great wave of association building, more secular than its evangelical predecessors or the WCTU but similarly devoted to an increasingly politicized domesticity. The women's club movement began in 1868 with the formation of Sorosis by professional women angry that they could not attend a dinner for British author Charles Dickens at the New York Press Club. "We have proposed," they announced, "to enter our protest against an idle gossip, against all demoralizing waste of time, against the follies and tyrannies of fashion, in short, against everything that opposes the full development and use of the faculties conferred upon us by our Creator."[54] The structure they created, with smaller working groups focused on specific themes, attracted a broad audience and soon spread to many cities.

Women's clubs for the most part expressed the unmet needs of middle-class women both for intellectual stimulation and for mechanisms of upward mobility not totally controlled by their husbands. With fewer children, more material resources, and longer lives than earlier generations, they had a modest degree of leisure and enough education to generate ambition. Devoted to "self-culture," women's clubs often read and reported on "great literature" and provided cultural events. In their own way they were important training grounds for public activity. In them women learned to speak in public, to prepare and present reports, to raise and manage money. Clubs appealed to women who were too conservative for more radical reform groups, but whose new skills and drive to do something useful often led them to turn to civic and philanthropic work in the established traditions of female benevolence.[55]

Women college graduates founded the Association of Collegiate Alumnae (ACA) in 1882 to fill the personal and intellectual void many experienced after the intensity of sisterhood and intellectual life in colleges. The ACA provided both female community and an opportunity to "help raise the standards of female education." Most members were teachers, supporting themselves on very little pay. They worked to improve their own salaries, to counteract popular ideas that education went against female nature and to provide the first fellowships specifically for women who aspired to do graduate work abroad.[56]

Other associations worked to extend middle-class domestic ideals to the increasingly visible young working women. Boston's Young Women's Christian Association (YWCA) was founded in 1867 to help young, single women migrating to cities for work. "They generally come inexperienced, unacquainted with the difficulties which are before them, obliged to seek their homes where snares are spread on every side, with no kind hand to lead, or wise and judicious acquaintance to advise." The YWCA set out to meet "the temporal, moral, and religious welfare of young women who are dependent on their own exertions for support."[57] Their example led to the creation of many Travelers' Aid societies; by the 1880s Traveler's Aid workers handed out cards and notices in

140

many depots offering advice and referrals for housing and employment for young women.

Concern about the morality of boardinghouses led groups such as the YWCA to establish boarding homes for young women of "good character." In effect, they focused their concern on "white, native-born women dispossessed of their status by the need or desire to work." The rigid rules and constant oversight irritated factory operatives and domestics but some rural migrants or daughters of the "respectable" middle-class found comfort in this reinforcement of domestic values.[58]

Similarly in the 1870s and 1880s women began to organize in response to the growing female prison population. Like the WCTU, they advocated an ideology of gender solidarity in which middle-class women should work in behalf of their less fortunate "sisters," demanding separate prison facilities for women and the presence of prison matrons rather than male guards.[59] In prisons, boardinghouses, and colleges, separatism became a strategy supporting the creation of specifically female public institutions, a middle-class version of maternal commonwealth. Middle-class women believed in their mission as moral guardians and as nurturers. From this vantage point they were critical of public life in a rapidly changing, patriarchal world that endangered the lives and morals of poor, single women outside the protective embrace of middle-class families. And they created new institutions to safeguard other women's morality and domesticity.

Deeply believing in the special mission of women, and excluded from the professionalizing worlds of male, middle-class work, some women devoted themselves to creating female professions which for the first time permitted a life-style of economic independence for single middle-class women. By the 1870s Catharine Beecher's campaign to feminize teaching had fully succeeded. The demand for teachers, in turn, fueled the growth of women's education. Most states established schools for teacher training many of which evolved into women's colleges. In the south, black women such as Lucy Laney and Charlotte Hawkins Brown led in the establishment of educational institutions for black women.[60]

Other professions followed a similar pattern, building public acceptance largely on the grounds that the work itself was inherently domestic. Following the participation of women as nurses in the Civil War, in 1873 the first training schools for nurses opened at Bellevue Hospital in New York City, Massachusetts

General Hospital in Boston, and Connecticut Hospital in New Haven. By 1890 there were thirty-five such schools; their alumnae, still a distinct minority of nurses, had begun to organize associations and to work toward standardized training, examinations, and other professional credentials. With the discovery of the germ theory and antiseptic practices, nursing became more scientific. At the same time, the growing professional hegemony of physicians expanded the use of hospitals as centers of both research and treatment, creating a great demand for trained nurses.[61]

In many ways the relationship between physician and nurse replicated the domestic sexual division of labor, placing authority in the hands of the male doctor and subordinating the nurturing roles of women. Meanwhile, outside the purview of hospitals, thousands of midwives, many of them trained in Europe, functioned with almost complete autonomy in rural and ethnic working-class areas. Their implicit challenge to the emerging medical hierarchy did not last long into the twentieth century.

Other female professions were only embryonic before the 1890s. Librarians, social workers, music teachers—like teachers and nurses—were all understood to embody domestic virtues albeit in public roles. Like other working women they earned only half or less of what men in their own or comparable fields were paid. As a rule, women stayed in these jobs while single, leaving them for marriage and rarely returning. Many, however, devoted themselves to careers instead of marriage and wove a rich web of social relations with other women like themselves. Though the professional options were limited, for the first time, a lifetime of economic independence was a viable choice for unmarried women in the educated middle class.

Between 1865 and 1890 public life, if not the electoral arena, seemed to be filling with women. In a few western states women were even granted voting rights and began to run for office. For most, however, working girls' associations, women's clubs, missionary societies, and the Women's Christian Temperance Union made women publicly visible. "Woman's sphere" was evolving in new and internally contradictory ways.

On the one hand, republican motherhood had bifurcated into two women's movements: Republicanism fueled the demand for woman suffrage and full citizenship led by two different suffrage associations. Motherhood, as redefined in Victorian domesticity, fostered a vision of maternal commonwealth, an ideology about the public importance of domestic values surfacing in temperance, women's clubs, the YWCA, and the Knights of Labor.

On the other hand, expectations of domesticity had begun to change, and the cumulative impact of changing marital patterns along with women's increased public presence generated a backlash itself in the name of domesticity. After 1870, for example, the new wave of relatively liberal divorce laws came under severe attack. Horace Greeley predicted that "easy divorce" would destroy America "blasted by the mildew of unchaste mothers and dissolute homes."[62] Similarly, by the 1870s falling fertility rates, indicating deliberate family planning in middle-class families, led to the enactment of a series of laws against abortion and "obscenity," which was defined to include information about contraception.[63]

Clearly the terrain would be contested—in the context of a rapidly changing industrial and social order. After 1890 women would push ahead to perfect the politics of influence, to build organizations of working women, and to bring together the republican claim of female citizenship with the maternal commonwealth. But they would also find the very foundations of a distinctive politics of domesticity eroding as women discovered the expressive possibilities of modern individualism. Public life and women's conceptions of citizenship in the twentieth century were to evolve in dramatically different directions.

7

Women and Modernity
1890–1920

"Today we stand on the threshold of woman's era," proclaimed Frances Harper in 1893 to the World's Congress of Representative Women meeting in conjunction with the Chicago World's Columbian Exposition. "In her hand are possibilities whose use or abuse must tell upon the political life of the nation, and send their influence for good or evil across the track of unborn ages."[1]

Modern America—urban, industrial, bureaucratic—came of age between 1890 and 1920. American women shaped that new order with a profusion of new voluntary associations, institutions, and social movements. The collective power of women, which had been building throughout the nineteenth century, reached its apex in a massive push for political reform and woman suffrage. At the same time, new currents eroded female solidarity. The old divisions of race remained deep despite the emergence of black female activism. Frances Harper was one of a handful of black women and men to address the Congress of Representative Women at a time when racial terrorism was reaching new heights in the south. She knew that the reforming sensibilities of white women were deeply imbued with both racial and class bias. Even the solidarity of that white middle class was beginning to be undermined by the growth of modern capitalist economy which encouraged individual autonomy in the pursuit of pleasure and consumption and by the growth of larger and more distant institutions that increasingly dominated the politics and culture of America.

The 1890s marked the ascendance of urban, industrial lifeways over traditional small communities as the defining feature of American society. Women and men alike worked in larger, taller, and louder factories owned by massive, vertically integrated corporations. A new managerial class sought to control supply and demand of raw materials, finished goods, and workers and to rationalize the work process, breaking work into ever smaller components with new machines and technologies. Wives and daughters of the managerial and wealthy classes lived in new suburbs accessible by electric trolley, far from the huge, impoverished, and disease-ridden neighborhoods abandoned to the most recent immigrants. Farm women in the south and west watched their men plunge in desperation into electoral politics—an arena from which they themselves were excluded—hoping to stem the tide of debt after the banks and railroads destroyed their cooperatives.

Modern America had a violent birth, and although both perpetrators and victims of class and racial violence were predominantly male, women shared men's conflict-shaped environments and their ideas of race and class position. Severe depression, bloody labor disputes, racist terrorism, and the demise of populism punctuated the 1890s. It seems ironic that within these turbulent and violent times science—with its emphasis on rationality, methodical processes, and objectivity—should be in ascendancy. But there it was, the underpinning of new technologies as well as a new worldview. Science offered a vision of efficiency and order in the physical, chemical, and biological universe, order that could be harnessed and put to use. The germ theory, for example, suddenly made many infectious diseases understandable and preventable. Science meshed with the rational, secular worldview of the middle class and promised the capacity to restore order and rationality to their own highly disordered world. In the service of these middle-class values, science could be used to buttress traditional prejudices. Virtually anything could be classified and counted, whether it was the "depravities" of the poor, the brain sizes of racial minorities, the fertility of educated women, or varieties of sexual perversion.

Into this urbanizing, industrializing, conflict-filled context came the middle-class "new woman" and the working-class "working girl" each of whom enjoyed a measure of individuality and autonomy that frightened many of their contemporaries. Their interaction sparked a new "domestic politics" and a flowering of female voluntary associations. It brought into the middle classes some aspects of the maternal commonwealth. But the individuality of the new woman and the working girl also marked a shift away from communal domesticity, undermining Victorian culture with a new drive toward autonomy, pleasure, and consumption.

The New Woman

Perhaps the most striking evidence of change among women was the emergence of the college-educated, frequently unmarried, and self-supporting new woman. After the Civil War this first generation of such women had been formed in the intense world of women's colleges where they challenged conventional wisdom about women's intellectual capacities and developed deep and loving bonds with both teachers and sister students. By 1870 there were eleven thousand women students enrolled in higher education (21 percent of all students); a decade later there were forty thousand (32 percent of all students).[2] On graduation they faced a stark choice between the traditional domesticity of marriage and a career of paid work. Madeline Wallin, a graduate student at the University of Chicago, described the dilemma of women like herself: "They are just as much in earnest about their aims and career as they are about marriage. . . . They don't know which they want, and they are trying the first one that comes until they can decide. They don't make an ironclad resolution about either one."[3] Middle-class parents resisted any choice but domesticity. Mary Church's father, a black entrepreneur in Ohio, ordered her not to become a teacher, but like many of her cohorts, she did so anyway.[4]

Nearly half of all college-educated women in the late nineteenth century never married. Those who married did so later than most women and bore fewer children.[5] For a few years or for a lifetime these independent career women began to create a new life-style. Barred from traditional male fields, they moved into growing female professions such as teaching and nursing. By the 1890s this newly won, and still contested, independence began to show up in styles of dress as well. The fresh, athletic Gibson girl played tennis and golf and rode a bicycle despite her long skirts.

Career women created new ways of living outside the family. Stung by the accusation that they unnaturally refused motherhood, and by research purporting to show that too much education could harm the female reproductive system, they turned to the gender solidarity and reforming zeal of their mothers' generation,

147

honed in a host of female environments from missionary societies, to women's clubs, to the WCTU, and made a new public claim in the name of domesticity. While assuring their critics that educated women certainly would be superior mothers, they went on to argue that those who chose careers over marriage would unleash maternal skills and capacities on a needy world—schooling the young, tending to the poor, and improving the health of women and children.[6] The temporary success of this argument rested largely on the creation of new, female-dominated institutions that, alongside women's colleges, provided an autonomous base from which women could support each other in developing new ideas, experimenting with them, and launching political battles in their defense. Settlement houses and reform associations such as the National Consumers' League consolidated the collective power of female voluntary associations and furnished women a base of expertise from which to shape public policy for a generation.[7]

The settlement house movement began in 1889 when two young college graduates, Jane Addams and Ellen Gates Starr, established Hull House in a poor immigrant neighborhood of Chicago. Addams exemplified the crisis felt by many upper-middle-class women who found themselves with lots of education and little to do that felt "real" or significant. Following a prolonged period of illness and emotional turmoil, she conceived the idea of renting "a house in a part of the city where many primitive and actual needs are found, in which young women who had been given over too exclusively to study, might restore a balance of activity along traditional lines and learn of life from life itself."[8] Similarly, Vida Scudder felt "a biting curiosity about the way the Other Half lived, and a strange hunger for friendship with them. Were not the workers, the poor, nearer perhaps than we to the reality I was always seeking?"[9] And Mary McDowell described her pleasure at finding a commitment to living and working *with* the poor: "Here was something I had been looking for all my life, a chance to work with the least skilled workers in our greatest industry; not for them as a missionary, but with them as a neighbor and seeker after truth."[10] At the time, such women had no idea that they were inventing the modern profession of social work.

Settlement houses spread to most major cities; by 1900 there were nearly a hundred, the majority founded by women. For residents—most of whom were women—they provided a new family, a cross between the traditional home and the college dormitory.

The Emergence of Women in Public Spaces

From the earliest days of the Republic, women who intruded into the political arena challenged accepted definitions of femininity and masculinity. This cartoon ridicules the women in Edenton, North Carolina, who declared their patriotic intention in 1775 not to drink tea or to "promote ye wear of any Manufacture from England untill such time that all Acts which tend to enslave this our Native Country shall be Repealed." *(Library of Congress)*

THIRTY DOLLARS REWARD.

RANAWAY from the Subscriber yesterday morning, (June 17,) Negro Woman MARY, who has been bringing Milk to this Market for the last three years; she is of the common size, slender in form, and about thirty years of age. All persons are forbid harboring her.

JOHN W. L. BURTON.

Portsmouth, June 18, 1841.   3t*

The public spaces of newspapers recognized social and, occasionally, political activities of white women but noticed black women such as Mary (above) only for the purposes of sale or recapture. *(Minnesota Historical Society)*

Above, the image of the slave spurred working women and men in the North to claim their own rights to dignity and decent wages. Led by Lynn, Massachusetts, City Guards, in 1860, eight hundred women shoemakers marched ahead of four thousand workmen proclaiming their refusal to "be slaves." Such a public demonstration would have been considered highly indecent for middle-class Victorian women. *(Library of Congress)*

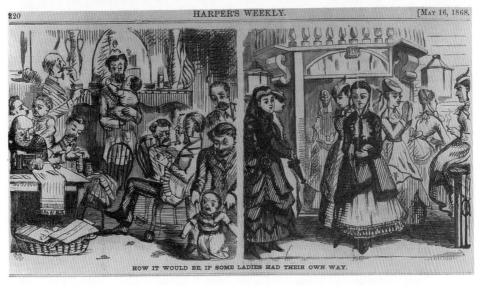

HOW IT WOULD BE, IF SOME LADIES HAD THEIR OWN WAY.

Middle-class women, with leaders like Susan B. Anthony (above), built a variety of reform movements—abolition, missionary and benevolent associations, temperance—in the nineteenth century. When they demanded the right of political participation, however, they met with ridicule that revealed underlying cultural anxieties about gender. Below, this 1868 cartoon from *Harper's Weekly* shows a topsy-turvey world in which women smoke in a saloon while men knit, sew, and handle babies awkwardly. *(Library of Congress)*

WOMANS HOLY WAR.
Grand Charge on the Enemy's Works.

The largest and most powerful women's association of the nineteenth century was the Women's Christian Temperance Movement. It grew from a spontaneous crusade in the 1870s in which bands of praying women shut down saloons in towns throughout the Midwest. The cultural force of their assault is captured in this 1874 cartoon. *(Library of Congress)*

The middle-class ideal of domestic womanhood shaped images of the proper appearance and treatment of all women. The cartoonist uses a sentimental image of female vulnerability and victimization to provoke indignation about the plight of immigrant sweatshop workers (above left). *(Library of Congress)* The portrait of Kansas City prostitute "Squirrel Tooth" Alice conveys romanticized beauty, even purity, thereby using the conventions of Victorian womanhood even though prostitutes in many ways represented their antithesis (above right). *(Kansas State Historical Society, Topeka)*

The role of missionary presented one of the few opportunities for middle-class women to escape the confines of domesticity. They devoted themselves, however, to teaching other women how to be properly domestic. Above, Episcopal missionaries teach Chippewa Indians to make lace on a Minnesota reservation. *(Minnesota Historical Society)*

"New women" in the late nineteenth and early twentieth centuries appeared in a variety of public spaces, both at work and at leisure. Above, art students prepare for an afternoon of sketching on the Mississippi in an idyllic scene of female companionship. *(Minnesota Historical Society)* Women's presence in offices, however, forced a rethinking of the design and the uses of this public space. What many men saw as the disruptive eroticism of the female presence is defused with humor in the picture (left). *(Library of Congress)*

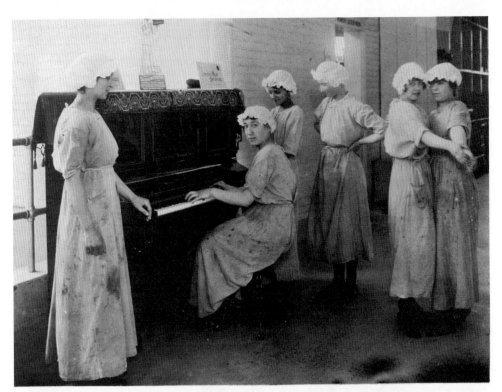

Because most work continued to be gender segregated, work environments could provide opportunities for female sociability. Above, young women employees enjoy "noon recreation" at Sanitary Foods, Inc., in about 1916. *(Minnesota Historical Society)* By World War I a few women, such as those below, were entering traditionally male blue-collar jobs. *(The Bettmann Archive)*

The suffrage movement culminated women's emergence into a variety of public roles in the nineteenth and early twentieth centuries. Militant feminists in the National Women's Party (above) dared to picket the White House in the midst of World War I *(Library of Congress)*, while the National Woman Suffrage Association built a massive, and highly respectable, grass-roots movement (left). *(The Bettmann Archive)* Together they mounted an irresistible claim to the rights of citizenship for one-half the population.

Some like Jane Addams found lifelong partners in other women who lived with them in the settlements. Others like Florence Kelley found in the settlement an escape from the bonds of a failed marriage, help in arranging care for her three children, and a base from which to launch a long and varied career in social reform.

Experiencing the terrible devastation of the 1893–94 depression that left thousands jobless, homeless, and utterly desperate from the heart of the poorest neighborhoods radicalized settlement house workers, as did association with working-class women. The neighborhoods in which they lived were filled with overcrowded tenements, whose tiny units averaged 300 square feet. Lacking kitchens and bathrooms, the large families cooked on a stove in the main room which also provided their heat, drew water at a sink or pump in the hallway, and used unsanitary privies in the basement.[11] An original belief that the introduction of art, music, and the humanities would lift the impoverished from their degradation gave way to more practical attempts to relieve suffering and provide alternatives.

Living in the slums and imbued with Victorian beliefs in the unified mission of women regardless of class, settlement house leaders soon moved into the vanguard of social and civic reform. Radicals, intellectuals, and socialists of all stripes held forth in the settlement house atmosphere that encouraged new ways of thinking and acting. Under the leadership of Florence Kelley, in 1892 Hull House joined with the Illinois Women's Alliance, an organization of working-class and middle-class women, to work for protective labor legislation for working women and children.[12] Leaders like Mary Kenney, a typesetter and union activist, supported unions and organized the Jane Club, a boardinghouse for young working women associated with Hull House.

Settlements allowed women to learn the intricacies of state, city, and ward-level politics. When Florence Kelley was appointed the first state factory inspector in Illinois, she remained a part of the Hull House community, and the lessons she learned became community lessons. Settlements became not only agents of change in themselves but also training grounds for leaders who appeared for several decades at the forefront of numerous social reforms. And for a generation of college-educated women, a summer's or a year's work in a settlement house became a jumping off point for social and political activism despite public concern about propriety. A Boston paper charged that "the falling of their young unsullied lives in this vicious dismal quarter seems like the falling of a lily in the mud."[13] Yet from such muddied lilies came skilled leadership in fights against child labor and for urban sanitation, improved working conditions, juvenile courts, maternal and child health, mother's pensions (forerunners of Aid to Dependent Children), improved public education, and union organization.

As the settlement house movement opened new avenues for reform, its leaders found important, if cautious, allies in the growing women's club movement. The General Federation of Women's Clubs (GFWC), founded in 1890, brought together 200 clubs representing 20,000 women. By 1900 it had 150,000 members and two decades later claimed to represent a million.[14] The generally middle-class constituency of the women's club movement demonstrated how once-radical ideas about female benevolence and civic action had become imbedded in a female subculture encompassing a very large and powerful segment of American women. Although many clubs continued to focus on self-development and literary activities, more and more entered a variety of benevolent activities in behalf of women and children. The Buffalo Union in 1890, for example, provided an extensive range of activities from art lectures for housewives to classes in typing, stenography, and bookkeeping for young working women. They also sponsored a "noon rest" downtown where women could come for lunch, an exchange and bake shop to sell handicrafts, a library, and a school for training domestics. In Chicago the Women's Club provided a forum and a powerful ally for the reform activities of settlement workers helping to found the Legal Aid Society, the Public Art Association, and the Protective Agency for Women and Children.[15] Women's clubs worked most actively on the broad agenda of "child-saving"—including reforms such as child labor laws and mothers' pensions. Their activism led many members to join other organizations as well and to openly proclaim the importance of women's civic participation.[16] As one member put it: "What college life is to the young woman, club life is to the woman of riper years, who amidst the responsibilities and cares of home life still wishes to keep abreast of the time, still longs for the companionship of those who, like herself, do not wish to cease to be students because they have left school."[17]

The zeal of clubwomen and settlement workers led to a proliferation of reform organizations. In 1890 the New York City Working

Women's Society called a mass meeting to talk about the low pay, long hours, and harsh working conditions of retail saleswomen. The resulting investigation sparked the interest of wealthy and influential department store patrons who set out to expose working conditions and then use their economic power to force changes. Consumers' Leagues, modeled on this first committee, soon formed in most major cities. They contacted store owners, publicized abuses (such as the fact that many stores required salesgirls to stand continuously for a ten-to-twelve-hour day), and encouraged shoppers to patronize the decent employers on their "white list." Formed under the leadership of Florence Kelley, the National Consumers' League (NCL) sponsored a "white label" campaign in which manufacturers who met their standards could use NCL labels on their clothes. The organization also lobbied for maximum hour and minimum wage laws.[18]

Though the league represented an alliance ranging across classes, and its leader, Kelley, was an avowed socialist, its success and lack of internal conflict rested in part on its domination by the highly educated and wealthy. Cultural as well as class differences clearly divided the women who sold from those who shopped in the new consumer emporiums that had emerged by the late-nineteenth century. Department stores offered shoppers the equivalent of a whole street full of small shops under one roof, a bright and attractive environment that invited impulse buying and promised shopping as an invigorating pleasure. As one trade journal put it in 1890, "almost unconsciously the [customer's] tired feeling drops away and a fresh interest awakens." Department stores also provided a setting in which working-class salesclerks dealt with middle- and upper-class customers on a daily basis. Store owners despaired of teaching their "girls" the proper decorum and dress so that they would not offend customers. Customers complained of overdressed employees whose clothes "do not accord with her position," and of "salespeople . . . so forward as to call customers 'Dearie.' The use of such terms is a liberty which the woman of finer sensibilities quickly resents."[19] The Consumers' League was never able fully to overcome the differences in experience and perception that divided young working women from their wealthy patrons.

Class had a different meaning, however, in the black community where professional women and middle-class housewives formed clubs similar to those of their white counterparts. From the outset their perspective, deeply shaped by the racism of American culture, gave them a more insurgent edge. As Mary Church Terrell, an Oberlin College graduate and prominent activist, put it: "Self-preservation demands that [Black women] go among the lowly, illiterate and even the vicious, to whom they are bound by ties of race and sex . . . to reclaim them."[20] Black women's clubs grew dramatically after one woman, Ida B. Wells-Barnett, galvanized the black community with her crusade against lynching in 1892.

Daughter of Mississippi slaves and a former teacher, Wells-Barnett edited her own newspaper in Memphis, Tennessee. In 1892 following a brutal lynching of three black businessmen, she undertook an investigation and exposé of the economic motives behind white violence. Resist, she urged the black community; demonstrate economic power with a boycott of white businesses; defend the honor of black womanhood and manhood by exposing the fraudulent cry of "rape" with which the white community justifies its terrorism. Driven from Memphis, her press destroyed, she started a national and international crusade against lynching and played a key founding role in a series of black women's clubs.

In 1896 the National Association of Colored Women (NACW) united more than three dozen such clubs in twelve states and Washington, D.C. Under the leadership of Mary Church Terrell the NACW provided a national network for black women's clubs analogous to the General Federation of Women's Clubs that refused to admit them. Emphasizing self-help and community responsibility, they set about the business of providing classes of all sorts, recreation, welfare institutions—kindergartens, orphanages, homes for the elderly and for working girls—and public health campaigns. In the process they trained new leadership within the black community and pushed male leaders, including the powerful Booker T. Washington, to fight for the rights and dignity of black women. Through organizations such as the Atlanta Neighborhood Union, founded in 1908 by wives of faculty members at Spelman and Morehouse colleges, the settlement house movement entered the black community.[21]

A Reunited Woman Suffrage Movement

Against the backdrop of a growing and highly organized middle class, the old animosities that had divided the woman suffrage movement for two decades no longer seemed salient to a new generation of leaders. Alice Stone Blackwell, daughter of Lucy Stone, initiated a process by which the two organizations agreed to merge. As a result, in 1890 the National American Woman Suffrage Association (NAWSA) was founded with Elizabeth Cady Stanton as its president. Susan B. Anthony succeeded Stanton in 1892 and remained a key leader until her death in 1906.* This united movement began to draw more and more heavily on the reform politics of the broader middle-class women's movement, but it remained internally divided over strategy. Even though Anthony preferred to work for a federal amendment to the Constitution, many others continued to advocate state level pressure for referenda and legislation. Those local campaigns had the virtue of involving and educating thousands of women, as well as a new generation, and building local alliances. As a strategy, however, experience proved state campaigns to be weak indeed. Between 1870 and 1910, four hundred and eighty campaigns produced only seventeen referenda, and only two of those resulted in a victory for woman suffrage.[22]

At the same time, suffragists added new arguments to those built on the Enlightenment tradition of individual rights. Increasingly they drew on the politicized domesticity of the women's reform tradition. No longer focused primarily on women's just claim to equal rights as citizens, they argued that the state needed women precisely because of their difference. On this ground by the 1890s the female reform tradition had developed a new and sophisticated notion of the role of the state, particularly in response to the massive urban problems of hunger, housing, sanitation, and education. Reverend Anna Garlin Spencer spoke to the NAWSA convention in 1898 on the "Fitness of Women to Become Citizens from the Standpoint of Moral Development." "So long as the State concerned itself with only the most external and mechanical of social interests," she argued, the presumption that men should rule was "inevitable, natural and beneficent. The 'instant, however, the State took upon itself any form of educative, charitable, or personally helpful work, it entered the area of distinctive feminine training and power, and therefore became in need of the service of woman."[23] Her view that the absence of women would harm the "mother-office of the State" anticipated Jane Ad-

* Anthony retired from the presidency of NAWSA in 1900 at the age of 80.

dams' assertion at the 1906 NAWSA convention that "city house-keeping has failed partly because women, the traditional house-keepers, have not been consulted as to its multiform activities."[24]

Suffragists not only asserted that women's nature suited them to the new social responsibilities of the state, they also claimed that female morality would clean up corruption. Indeed, "sweeping out the scoundrels" could be another form of civic housecleaning! Furthermore, because of their different life experiences, women needed the vote to protect their own special interests whether as mothers concerned for the education of their children, as working women subjected to exploitation without protection, or as the abused wives of drunkards. And finally, suffragists returned to the basic tenets of republican motherhood to argue that the vote would enhance women's capacity to carry out their traditional roles. Only a mother who exercised her own rights and responsibilities as a citizen could truly teach citizenship to her children, they said. Such a woman would also be a far more interesting wife and companion to her husband.

With these arguments, suffrage formed a crucial strand of the Progressive movement that viewed the feminization of government as a means of reform by proposing curbs on (male) competition and corruption and new, nurturing roles for the state. Suffragists challenged the perspective of opponents who argued that female voting undermined the separate spheres of men and women. According to former president Grover Cleveland, female voting threatened to disrupt "a natural equilibrium so nicely adjusted to the attributes and limitations of both [women and men] that it cannot be disturbed without social confusion and peril."[25] Female voting, suffragists replied, restored social order rather than threatening it. In effect, suffragists picked up the arguments that had evolved from the maternal commonwealth of the WCTU and the Knights of Labor to the "domestic politics" of middle-class Progressive reform. By the 1890s suffrage bore the stamp of the emergence of the new woman, who had appropriated the politicized language of domesticity into the more professionalized world of female reformers.

Women's rights advocates found a key theorist of "domestic politics" in Charlotte Perkins Gilman whose writings began to appear in the 1890s. Daughter of an old New England family, great-granddaughter of theologian Lyman Beecher, and great-

154

niece of Catharine Beecher and Harriet Beecher Stowe, Charlotte Perkins had experienced a deep depression following her marriage and the birth of her daughter in the 1880s. Though she remained friends with her first husband, an independent life in which she supported herself with lectures and writings clearly suited her temperament despite the criticism it evoked. Her second, happier marriage came later after her independence was well established. A socialist, Gilman argued that economic independence was the most fundamental necessity for women, an insight drawing directly on her own experience as well as that of a new generation of professional women. She advocated the professionalization of housework with collectivized cleaning, cooking, and child care and proposed that the key to future change lay in transforming the socialization of young children so that girls and boys would no longer be limited in their perception of their own capacities and life choices.[26] Her claims not only anticipated the emergence of modern feminism but they also recalled the idea of property as the foundation of civic virtue even as its more equitable distribution transforms the membership in public community.

As the growing middle-class base of the woman's rights movement shifted suffrage from the periphery of women's organized activities toward the mainstream, suffrage advocates increasingly espoused the class and race prejudices of the white middle class.[27] In response to critics who charged that female enfranchisement would increase the numbers of "undesirable" voters, the NAWSA responded at their 1893 convention:

> Without expressing any opinion on the proper qualifications for voting, we call attention to the significant facts that in every State there are more women who can read and write than the whole number of illiterate male voters; more white women who can read and write than all negro voters; more American women who can read and write than all foreign voters; so that the enfranchisement of such women would settle the vexed question of rule by illiteracy, whether of home-grown or foreign-born production.[28]

More bluntly, southern suffragist Belle Kearney proclaimed to the 1903 convention, "The enfranchisement of women would insure immediate and durable white supremacy, honestly attained."[29]

The presence of southern white suffragists, who had not been active until late in the nineteenth century, created an atmosphere

155

hostile to the participation of black women. Mary Church Terrell maintained a working relationship with Susan B. Anthony and addressed the 1898 NAWSA convention on "The Progress of Colored Women." Generally, however, black women found themselves unwelcome in many local suffrage groups and created their own suffrage organizations; by the early 1900s they had formed organizations in numerous cities including Tuskegee, St. Louis, Los Angeles, Memphis, Boston, Charleston, and New Orleans with seven state-level associations. Black women looked to the ballot as a defense against sexual exploitation as well as a guarantor of economic rights. And they, like white women, believed deeply that suffrage would empower their superior moral sensibilities for the benefit of their people as a whole. One woman argued that Afro-American women were "always sound and orthodox on questions affecting the well-being of the race. You do not find the colored woman selling her birthright for a mess of pottage."[30] In books and novels they advocated a transformed women's movement capable of addressing all forms of oppression, and they explored the ways white men used white women's bodies (with the charge of "rape") to deny the manhood of black men as well as the womanhood of black women.[31] It is tragically ironic, given the parallel growth in activism among black and white women, that broadening the movement for women's rights had accompanied a growing insensitivity on the part of many white middle-class women to the rights of others.

The Working Girl

While the college-educated new woman and the youthful Gibson girl captured media interest, growing numbers of working women in blue-collar, clerical, and service occupations also reshaped the parameters of female experience. By 1890, 19 percent of women over sixteen years old were in the labor force. Never-married women constituted 68 percent of working women and married women only 14 percent. The other 18 percent consisted of widows and divorcees. During this time, the proportion of married women in the labor force began to rise, reaching 23 percent by 1920, but by far the most visible workers were young, single immigrants.[32] Public recognition of the social importance of women's industrial work came through a series of government commissions and reports culminating in a nineteen-volume report on

Woman and Child Wage Earners commissioned by the U.S. Senate between 1910 and 1914.[33]

Though living standards had begun a slow rise, working conditions continued to be extremely dangerous, hours very long, and pay very low. As factories multiplied and new areas of work opened up in offices and department stores, a smaller and smaller proportion of women worked as domestics (from 50.1 percent of women working in 1870 to 29.4 percent in 1900 to 16.2 percent in 1920).[34] This decline was furthered by the construction of smaller urban, middle-class apartments with indoor plumbing and central heating; these homes no longer required servants to maintain them.[35] Black women, however, continued to represent an important exception to these patterns. Married black women worked in greater numbers than any other group (26 percent in 1900 compared to 3 percent of married white women).[36] Most black women in the late-nineteenth century were either agricultural laborers in the rural south or domestic workers, because factory work in both the north and south was generally closed to them.

Similar to their more privileged professional counterparts, female factory workers sought more control over their destinies. Unions, however, remained hostile. The American Federation of Labor (AFL), in particular, actively excluded women from many trades and expressed no interest in organizing the unskilled jobs in which women predominated. As a result, while working women continued numerous efforts to organize themselves and initiated spontaneous militant actions, they were not supported by the male unions. They turned increasingly to alliances with middle-class women reformers who viewed the plight of working women and children as critical obstacles to a more humane, maternal social order. Alliances between the two, however, remained difficult. The implied gender solidarity of "domestic politics" too often simply represented a middle-class worldview ignoring the realities of working-class women's lives where gender and class were always in tension.

Trade union women brought together thirty women's organizations in the Illinois Women's Alliance between 1888 and 1894. They worked for factory inspections by women "responsible to women's organizations," compulsory education and new schools, sweatshop regulation, abolition of child labor, and an end to police abuse of arrested women. Together with Hull House and the GFWC they succeeded in the 1892 passage of an eight-hour law for women and child workers and restrictions on the employment of children. The organization fell apart in the stress of the 1893–94 depression as differences in strategy and the perspective of working- and middle-class women grew.[37]

The obstacles to mutual understanding between working- and middle-class reformers in the early twentieth century rested on differences in experience and perspective. Middle-class new women took great pride in being self-supporting and found fulfillment in their work. In contrast, young immigrant women rarely lived independent lives; instead they contributed to the subsistence of their parents and siblings. Furthermore, work in textile mills, garment shops, and other industrial enterprises was hardly fulfilling. It exhausted the body and deadened the mind. Middle-class women's romanticized vision of sisterhood presumed a similarity of outlook and identity that simply did not fit the ethnic and economic particularities of working-class women's lives. Differences in circumstances and goals inevitably led to differences in means and strategies.

By the early twentieth century, however, a new generation of immigrants from eastern and southern Europe, many of them single young women imbued with a variety of radical traditions, made a more effective alliance with middle-class reformers possible if still difficult. They provided the suffrage movement with a new constituency, built a significant female presence in the Socialist party, and by their militant activism helped inaugurate a new unionism that eventually would challenge the craft-dominated AFL.[38] These were working-class new women who joined the second and third generation of college-educated new women after 1900 to generate an amazing diversity of female public activity.

The most effective alliance between middle-, upper-, and working-class women was the Women's Trade Union League (WTUL), founded in 1903. From the beginning the WTUL espoused the dual goal of organizing working women into the trade union movement and integrating working women's concerns into the women's rights movement. Wealthier members of the WTUL came from the institutions of female Progressive reform—settlements, the National Consumers' League, and the YWCA—while working-class women had ties to the trade union movement. The focus on trade union organizing shifted away from the maternalism of Progressive politics with its emphasis on state action such as protective legislation. It also created constant frustration as women activists struggled to win support and encouragement from an AFL deeply biased against women workers.[39]

For working-class women the hostility of men in the AFL and the class biases of middle-class allies framed an insoluble dilemma. When class solidarity foundered on traditional sexual attitudes of male unionists who believed women should stay at home, gender solidarity with middle-class women was an essential support. When middle-class allies dismissed trade unions as hopelessly prejudiced, class allegiance assumed a gut-wrenching primacy for women who felt their daily lives tied in a thousand ways with those of men in their workplaces and communities. A series of massive strikes, however, established the importance of both. The initial dominance of wealthy allies in the New York WTUL faded after 1909 in the wake of the "Uprising of the Thirty Thousand." This strike and leaders like Clara Lemlich made visible a new generation of working women, predominantly radical young Jewish immigrants in the garment industry.

Clara Lemlich fled the Russian pogroms with her family in 1903 at the age of fifteen. In New York she had to work making shirtwaists, foregoing her dream of schooling. Against her father's wishes, she had learned to read in Russia and was acquainted with radical literature. In 1906 she became a founding member of Local 25 of the International Ladies Garment Workers Union (ILGWU), after which she participated in numerous strikes and militant activities. In a series of walkouts in 1909 she was arrested seventeen times. Violence against strikers was so great that the WTUL began to send observers. On November 22, 1909, Lemlich joined several thousand other young women at Cooper Union meeting hall to discuss the possibility of a general strike. Union leaders droned on for more than two hours before the impatient crowd. Suddenly, Lemlich stood up and marched to the front of the hall. A hush fell over the crowd as the startled chairman yielded the floor to the young woman who proceeded, in eloquent Yiddish, to make the case for a general strike. A unanimous roar greeted her motion whereupon the chairman cried out, " 'Do you mean faith? Will you take the Jewish Oath?' and up came two thousand right hands, with the prayer, 'If I turn traitor to the cause I now pledge, may this hand wither from the arm I now raise.' "[40]

As thousands streamed out of their shops in subsequent days they felt like Natalya Urosova and her workmates who "hardly knew where to go—what to do next. But one of the American girls, who knew how to telephone, called up the Women's Trade Union League, and they told us all to come to a big hall a few blocks away." The WTUL, with assistance from Socialist party women and other groups, set up twenty strike halls where strikers could manage the daily complexities of picketing, speaking, strike support, and dealing with police brutality.[41] Ultimately, the solidarity of Jewish women could not easily be translated to Italian, native-born white, and black workers. Though the intransigence and power of the industry finally defeated the strike, the "Uprising of the Thirty Thousand" established the ILGWU as a major union. A year later the terrible Triangle Shirtwaist Fire killed 146 women in one of the shops that had refused to accept workers' demands for fire escapes and unlocked doors. Organized by industry, not by craft, the ILGWU and a similar union in the men's garment industry, the Amalgamated Clothing Workers, revived the industrial unionism that had allowed the Knights of Labor to organize working women successfully. Though their membership was largely female, the top leadership of both unions was virtually all male.

The Breakdown of Victorianism

Labor unions, women's clubs, and settlement houses all represented new public spaces for women, arenas in which they could experiment freely with new ideas and actions. Between 1900 and World War I the old Victorian code which prescribed strict segregation of the sexes in separate spheres crumbled. The womens' movement reached the apex of its political power, achieving new laws for pure food, protective legislation regulating wages and hours for working women and children, prison and court reforms, and the creation in 1912 of a Federal Children's Bureau headed by former Hull House resident Julia Lathrop. The older images of the pure and submissive Victorian woman and her benevolent patriarch began to soften around their rigid edges. As the twentieth century dawned, women and men alike began to appear in the public places oriented toward pleasure and consumption; dance halls, amusement parks, theaters, and movies drew increasing numbers of Americans out of their homes and into communal activities. In the cities younger men and women met frequently and easily outside the supervision of family, neighborhood, and ethnic community. Their activities emphasized the sensual, plea-

160

sure-seeking dimensions of the new century's culture and brought sexuality out from behind the euphemisms of the nineteenth century.

Young working-class women had long been known for their flamboyant dress and love of nightlife and dancing. After a ten-to-twelve-hour workday they flocked to dance halls where young men would treat them to drinks and join in the faddish "tough dancing." The raw sexuality of dances like the slow rag, turkey trot, bunny hug, grizzly bear, and "shaking the shimmy" horrified the middle classes. By 1910 slightly more decorous versions of these dances had become a new craze in middle-class cabarets. Such public eroticism shocked one magazine into announcing in 1913 that "sex o'clock" had struck.[42]

Women's appearance changed as well from the hourglass figure of the Gibson girl to a slender, smaller silhouette no longer weighted down with petticoats or restricted by corsets. The freedom of movement and greater exposure of extremities (like ankles) accented the flirtatious and active personalities of vaudeville and movie stars like Eva Tanguay, Mary Pickford, and Clara Bow. A few young women defied their parents and conventions of respectability to wear eyeshadow and rouge. And newspapers no longer referred to single working women as "women adrift," "homeless women," or even "spinsters" but rather called them "bachelor girls" who, like men, sought pleasure and autonomy.[43] The "working girl" now populated fiction and features in women's magazines while movies featured vamps whose sexuality, though dangerous, was hardly discreet. The flapper, so identified with the 1920s, was already a powerful image by 1913.

As single people, relatively economically autonomous and freed either by work or school from intense familial supervision, young women began to appropriate a more individualistic ethos for themselves. The breakdown of Victorian sexual norms was a gradual process, but in isolated pockets of American society newer ideas found environments in which they could flourish. Young working-class women danced their experiments with autonomy and sexuality, but when they found mates they withdrew again into the family circle and a life with little space for leisure or pleasure-seeking. The second and third generations of college-educated new women maturing after 1900, however, had both the economic and intellectual resources to seek a new life-style and a new ideology.

In the artistic and bohemian culture of New York's Greenwich

Village, for example, a community of "sex radicals" proclaimed women's right to sexual pleasure and experimentation. They read the new "scientific" findings of European sexologists like Havelock Ellis who affirmed the centrality of heterosexual sensual pleasures for women as well as men. And they flocked to hear flamboyant individuals like anarchist Emma Goldman denounce the chains of traditional marriage in the name of free love.

Where the settlement house had absorbed and educated an earlier generation of college graduates, focusing them on the power of female community and the reform agenda of politicized domesticity, this new generation of educated women used their growing autonomy to explore the possibilities of expressive individualism and the erotic within heterosexual community. Socialists and anarchists, they sought to challenge American society along every dimension. In a time when contraceptive information was considered pornographic and illegal, they followed the courageous lead of Emma Goldman and Margaret Sanger in proclaiming women's right to voluntary motherhood without sacrificing their sexuality.[44] And they explored alternatives to traditional domesticity in works such as Charlotte Perkins Gilman's *The Home* where she proposed communal kitchens and professionalized housework. The break from "domestic politics" was both theoretical, as they embraced a more individualistic and scientific ethos questioning the importance of biological difference, and practical, as they moved farther from the female-dominated spaces of settlements and associations.

Paradoxes of Modernity

The power of scientific thought, bureaucratic organization, and professional expertise—all key signals of modernity—may have liberated individuals but it also corroded communal bonds and voluntary association. This paradox changed the meaning of many "achievements" and "advances" won by women during the years at the turn of the century, empowering individuals while undermining the sources of female solidarity.

The domestic science movement was an attempt to professionalize housework; to make it scientific, efficient, and rational; to bring the methods of scientific management from the factory into the home. Large corporations had discovered the importance of efficiency and sought to develop more scientific physical arrangements and job definitions to enhance productivity. Classes in settlement houses and college home economics departments similarly emphasized the values of efficiency, productivity, and scientific accuracy as they stressed the importance of nutrition, sanitation, and careful consumerism. In this way they helped to institutionalize a middle-class worldview. Home economists, for example, waxed eloquent over the making and uses of white sauce, describing "white meals," bland in both taste and texture. Within the popular culture, where women's magazines actively promoted the symbolism of this vision of domesticity, white sauce found an analog in the concept of the American melting pot which dissolved the pungent spiciness of diverse immigrant cultures. Women in settlement houses and clubs actively participated in "Americanizing" immigrants through classes in language, decorum, and cooking, marking their much needed educational outreach with an often unconscious cultural arrogance.[45]

The attempt by home economists to institutionalize some dimensions of a subculture rooted in communal female relationships, however, had the ironic consequence of isolating the individual woman in her "scientifically planned" kitchen and home while devaluing communal "common sense." It connected her to the values associated with a bureaucratic middle class without the institutional connections to political and economic power enjoyed by men in the "scientific management" movement. Men in these same strata invented scientific management to control their labor force and the flow of goods and services; women's use of scientific management, however, was a form of cultural control, and control of private space.

Similarly, social work evolved from the voluntarism of "friendly visitors" and settlement house workers to a profession with graduate training schools teaching the "scientific" case method. On the one hand, this meant the creation of a profession in which women predominated, and a base of expertise from which to influence policy. Civic housekeeping in which professionals exercised their expertise through the instrument of a "mother state," however, signaled the erosion of voluntary, private, and female-dominated efforts. Specifically, the professionalization of settlement-house work changed and restricted the female space of settlements through which thousands of women had experienced a new sense of their own possibilities. As settlement houses moved toward hiring professional staffs, they had less and less room for volunteers who had been the heartbeat of this community for so long. The new profession of social work also contributed to the gendered framework within which the modern welfare state would take shape. "Mothers' pensions" and family preservation strategies presumed an intrusive, parental (not to say maternal) state overseeing the lives of poor women and children.[46]

Modern science and professionalism even shaped the cultural revolt of "sex radicals," many of whom had begun to call themselves feminists. Female bohemians and radical intellectuals mounted an attack on Victorian norms and inhibitions using the scientific language of sexologists and Freudians. They asserted that an active and expressive female sexuality was "normal" according to the new science of psychology. That scientific language also included a new cataloging of sexual "perversion" which defined female/female loving relationships as pathological, a dangerous consequence of "mannish lesbians." Thus evolved new grounds for attacking female solidarity.[47]

New Life in the Suffrage Movement

Such paradoxes were barely visible, however, in the early 1900s. Women's collective voice and strength was growing as young college-educated women, some schooled in settlements, others in bohemian circles, fostered a dramatic shift in organizing methods within the suffrage movement and reached out to build alliances with working-class women. By 1900 there were five thousand female college graduates whose confidence about their right to occupy public spaces reflected the hard-won victories of pioneering generations that preceded them. Voting, to them, was a logical and natural extension of their public activity, and they grew impatient. Bypassing their elders and the internal quarrels of the NAWSA, younger women after 1900 initiated a new level of grassroots activity. Associations such as the College Equal Suffrage League and the Boston Equal Suffrage Association for Good Government invented fresh tactics and a new model of movement building. Door-to-door campaigns in neighborhoods reached poor and working-class areas as well as middle- and upper-class suburbs. Groups of women toured Massachusetts by trolley, making speeches at every stop and holding spontaneous outdoor meetings wherever crowds could be found. Finding crowds was easy. The scandalous spectacle of a woman speaking on a street corner drew curious listeners by the score.[48]

164

News of increasingly militant suffrage activity in England spurred American suffragists further. There, after 1903, Emmaline Pankhurst and her daughters Christabel and Sylvia seized the political initiative with marches, mass meetings, and a campaign to heckle British cabinet ministers whenever they appeared in public. After 1910 British suffragists escalated their tactics to include violence, riots, and arson.

American women watched events in England closely. Woman suffrage had become an international movement with the formation of the International Woman Suffrage Alliance in 1902; their own Carrie Chapman Catt was the international president. Speakers from the British movement became popular throughout the country. In Boomer, Iowa, two English suffragists attracted a large crowd and inspired a spontaneous parade in 1908. In the next two years Emmaline Pankhurst herself spoke to enormous crowds in Boston and New York. Even more important, the European travels customary among wealthier college graduates brought a number of American women into direct participation in the British movement where they gained a new education in organizing strategies and tactics.

The first political success of this renewed activism came in Washington State in 1910. A quiet but meticulous campaign there brought the message to unions, grange meetings, state and county fairs, and the popular Chautauqua lecture series—an informal adult-education movement that provided traveling speakers to small towns throughout the country. The WCTU agreed to keep a low profile to avoid arousing the liquor interests which had become major funders of the antisuffragists. Billboards, plays, a monthly newsletter, a cookbook, editorials, and sermons all conveyed the message, "Give the women a Square Deal." And on election day the *Woman's Journal* reported that "Many young women, middle-aged women and white-haired grandmothers stood for hours handing out the little reminders. It rained—the usual gentle but very insistent kind of rain . . . but the women would not leave their places . . . for fear of losing a vote."[49] The following year a six-month campaign in California set a new standard for massive organization and flamboyant tactics.

As the grass-roots revival indicated a heightened sense of possibility and self-assertion among a very broad base of American women, victories in smaller western states began to generate momentum. After Washington in 1910 and California in 1911 came

Kansas, Oregon, and Arizona in 1912. In Illinois entrenched political elites and patterns of corruption made a direct route through referenda an unlikely strategy. Suffragists perfected their lobbying techniques and found an alternative: by legislative vote they won the right for women to vote in presidential elections. The failure of state referenda in Michigan, Ohio, and Wisconsin, however, frustrated rising expectations and renewed interest in the possibility of a constitutional amendment that could at one blow admit women to full citizenship.

A federal amendment had been the subject of continuing strategic disagreements within NAWSA, a debate that went back nearly half a century to the original split between Stanton and Anthony, and Stone and Blackwell. Its revival required new leadership, a new constituency, and new organization all of which were sparked by an ambitious and charismatic young woman, Alice Paul, who joined the NAWSA Congressional committee in 1913 with her friend Lucy Burns.

Both Paul and Burns had lived in England and participated in the British suffrage movement. A Quaker social worker, Paul went to England in 1907 just in time to witness the meteoric rise of Emmaline Pankhurst and to join in mass demonstrations, also experiencing jail, hunger strikes, and force feeding. Paul and Burns joined the moribund NAWSA Congressional committee and convinced NAWSA leaders to let them organize a suffrage parade on the day before the inauguration of President-elect Woodrow Wilson. They set up headquarters in Washington, D.C., raised over $25,000, and began an aggressive lobbying and publicity campaign for a federal amendment. When Woodrow Wilson arrived for his inaugural on March 3, 1913, his greeters had already left to see the woman suffrage parade. Five thousand women stole the scene, as they pressed their way through a hostile crowd down Pennsylvania Avenue.[50]

Aware that the NAWSA was unwilling to build on this momentum, Paul and Burns established a separate organization, the Congressional Union, in April 1913 to provide a new base for national activity. Leaders of NAWSA, in turn, resented the use of their offices and letterhead in the creation of a rival organization. The two organizations went their separate ways after February 1914 when the Congressional Union entered the congressional elections, brandishing the political power of women enfranchised in nine states. They remained bitter competitors through the rest of the suffrage campaign and well beyond.

166

The differences between Paul and NAWSA were multilayered. The split with the Congressional Union had the important impact of reigniting NAWSA interest in a federal amendment, but the two organizations were never able to cooperate because their strategic disagreements ran deep. Alice Paul remained convinced that the British experience was an appropriate model for the American movement. In addition to adopting their flamboyant tactics, she advocated the practice of holding the party in power responsible for the failure to achieve woman suffrage. With a Democratic president and Democrats in control of both houses, this meant that the Congressional Union organized everywhere to defeat Democrats regardless of any specific candidate's stand on the issue.

As a political strategist, Paul failed to grasp the essential differences between the British and the American systems. In the United States, where the Congress and president were separately elected, where each party represented an undisciplined coalition of interests, the passage of a suffrage amendment required bipartisan support. On the other hand, by its willingness to attack many Democrats for their lukewarm support and failure to pressure their political colleagues, the Congressional Union and its successor, the National Woman's Party (NWP), provided a radical voice within the suffrage movement redefining the parameters of the debate. Their activities kept the issue in the limelight and made the increasingly disciplined and effective work of the NAWSA seem moderate and reasonable by comparison. Despite their enmity, the two organizations needed each other; together they succeeded more rapidly than either could have alone.

The Congressional Union and the National Woman's Party also galvanized the political energies of radical young women who in 1912 and 1913 had began to call themselves feminists. The sudden appearance of feminism crystallized the cultural revolt of female socialists, "sex radicals," intellectuals, and artists. Formed in 1912, a New York discussion group, Heterodoxy, typified the new ethos in its sole requirement that any member "not be orthodox in her opinions." Members included Industrial Workers of the World (IWW) organizer Elizabeth Gurley Flynn, theorist Charlotte Perkins Gilman, and journalists Mary Heaton Vorse and Rheta Childe Dorr. Feminists challenged previous generations' emphasis on female difference. As Dorr put it: "I wanted all the freedom, all the opportunity, all the equality there was in the world. I wanted to belong to the human race, not to a ladies' aid society, to the human race."[51] Another key figure in Heterodoxy, Crystal

Eastman, formulated "the problem of women's freedom" as a series of questions:

> How to arrange the world so that women can be human beings, with a chance to exercise their infinitely varied gifts in infinitely varied ways, instead of being destined by the accident of their sex to one field of activity—housework and child-raising. And second, if and when they choose housework and child-raising, to have that occupation recognized by the world as work, requiring a definite economic reward and not merely entitling the performer to be dependent on some man.[52]

Flouting convention in the name of sexual equality and self-expression, feminists were deeply attracted to militant action. Mary Heaton Vorse praised the violence of British suffragettes: "I cannot imagine anything that would affect better the moral health of any country than something which would blast the greatest number of that indecent, immoral institution—the perfect lady—out of doors and set them smashing and rioting."[53] The National Woman's Party provided a vehicle for such sentiments and the energy behind them.

Pressure for new direction and leadership in NAWSA grew with the challenge from Paul and the subsequent loss of state referenda in four key eastern states in 1915: New York, Pennsylvania, Massachusetts, and New Jersey. The logjam had been broken with western victories, and the endorsement of woman suffrage by the General Federation of Women's Clubs in 1914 signaled a new level of mainstream respectability, but newer and smaller organizations appeared to have the initiative. The election of Carrie Chapman Catt to the presidency of NAWSA, however, pointed in a new direction.

Catt had been an active suffragist since the mid-1880s and prominent in the national movement for more than two decades. When Susan B. Anthony retired in 1900, Catt was her chosen successor. She brought administrative order to the NAWSA, but her first presidency from 1900 to 1905 also coincided with the illness and death of her husband. Subsequently, widowed and financially independent, she worked for many years in the International Woman Suffrage Alliance and participated in the grass-roots revival in New York. The 1915 referendum campaign in New York showcased her achievements and provided a model that was followed closely in many other states. It also made Carrie Chapman Catt the logical leader for a revitalized NAWSA.

Under Catt's direction the Woman Suffrage Party of Greater New York, organized in 1909, developed the capacity to reach across the boundaries of class and ethnicity. In the ten-month campaign of 1915, women in the suffrage movement canvassed 60 percent of enrolled voters and collected 60,535 new memberships for their organization. They held thousands of outdoor meetings and hundreds of indoor meetings, and distributed nearly 3 million leaflets. "Suffrage days" for firemen or barbers or street cleaners featured parades and visiting delegations of women who left flyers and symbolic souvenirs. Street dances, outdoor concerts, religious services, and bonfires all made neighborhood women imbedded in communal daily life visible to themselves and to their communities and made their demand for rights something that all could celebrate. Catt's well-oiled political organization, furthermore, understood clearly that the campaign should be viewed as the prelude to a second effort in 1917. Two days after a narrow loss, they raised $100,000 for the next campaign fund and announced: "We know that we have gained over half a million voters in the State, that we have many new workers, have learned valuable lessons and with the knowledge obtained and undiminished courage we are again in the field of action."[54]

By 1916 woman suffrage had clearly entered the national political agenda. Both Republican and Democratic conventions were besieged by women. In Chicago Republicans marveled as ten thousand women marched in a driving rain to demand that they endorse the Susan B. Anthony amendment. Just days before, Alice Paul's Congressional Union reorganized as the National Woman's Party and prepared to demonstrate women's electoral power in the 1916 elections. Soon after, Democratic delegates to their party convention had to run a gauntlet of women with yellow sashes, banners, and signs demanding their endorsement. Both party platforms included planks calling on states to give women the right to vote.

President Wilson himself appeared before a NAWSA convention in September 1916 to announce his support, though hardly his leadership. "I have not come to ask you to be patient, because you have been, but I have come to congratulate you that there has been a force behind you that will beyond any peradventure be triumphant and for which you can afford a little while to wait."[55]

The National Woman's Party, however, had no intention of waiting. On January 10, 1917, they began picketing the White

House. Silently, they stood at the gate with banners asking "Mr. President, What Will You Do for Woman Suffrage?" and "How Long Must Women Wait for Liberty?" For six months they kept up the vigil, unharassed. But curious and sympathetic crowds turned hostile once the United States declared war on the Axis powers. In the fever of patriotism and sudden mobilization for World War I, protest against the president looked unpatriotic.[56]

In the meantime, Catt had won the support of the NAWSA leadership for a strategic approach to building an inexorable momentum for the federal amendment. The "Winning Plan" involved a carefully disciplined and centrally directed effort in which each state and local suffrage group had a role: Where state referenda could be won, campaigns were to be waged to maintain the momentum and increase the number of congressmen dependent on female as well as male votes. In states where women could vote, NAWSA would lobby and petition their delegations to introduce and fight for the passage of the federal amendment. Where referenda were unlikely, suffragists were charged with working for presidential suffrage or the right to vote in party primaries. Catt believed the remaining bastions of resistance would crumble if they could choose and win a southern state and an eastern state. The critical nature of these campaigns would not be self-evident to their opponents as long as they could "keep so much 'suffrage noise' going all over the country that neither the enemy nor friends will discover where the real battle is."[57]

The plan worked like clockwork, taking only four years instead of the six Catt had predicted. Arkansas broke the barrier in the south in 1917 and New York, where activists had continued to work without missing a beat after their 1915 defeat, contributed an east coast victory. The "suffrage noise" of the National Woman's Party pickets surely aided the cause as well.

The backdrop to these victories, however, was the brief but intense American participation in World War I from the spring of 1917 until Armistice Day on November 11, 1918. Many suffragists faced a difficult confrontation with the pacifist principles they had developed in the women's peace movement. Since 1900 most women's organizations had established peace departments following a line of argument that went well back into the pre–Civil War peace movement. The presumption that women were naturally moral and pure made war a powerful symbol of male evil. In 1869 Elizabeth Cady Stanton had remarked, "The male element

170

is a destructive force, stern, selfish, aggrandizing, loving war, conquest, acquisition, breeding . . . discord, disorder, disease, and death."[58]

The Woman's Peace Party was founded in 1915 after a number of American women attended the International Women's Congress at the Hague. Carrie Chapman Catt chaired the initial meeting to create a platform for the "mother half of humanity." Riding on the wave of antiwar sentiment that swept the country as war erupted in Europe, soon the Woman's Peace Party had twenty-five thousand members. Their voice was heard in the halls of Congress when Jeanette Rankin of Montana, the first woman elected to the House of Representatives, cast her vote against the declaration of war in 1917.

Nonetheless, the deeply held pacifism of leaders such as Jane Addams and Florence Kelley could not sustain such a membership once war had been declared. Socialists and radicals who viewed the war as an unnecessary battle among capitalist nations joined pacifists in opposition to the war and suffered with them an unprecedented loss of civil liberties and freedom of speech. Carrie Chapman Catt decided that the movement had too much to lose to risk opposition to the war despite her own prior activism in the Woman's Peace Party. Instead, she instructed her people to work unrelentingly for *both* the war effort *and* suffrage. The NAWSA supported a hospital in France and its leadership visibly shared the tasks of knitting socks, raising and canning food, selling Liberty Bonds, and preparing supplies for the Red Cross. They also drew contingents of Red Cross women, office workers, and "farmerettes" into their suffrage parades, symbolically claiming the citizenship rights they had earned in this "war to make the world safe for democracy."

The suffrage movement did benefit from the highly visible support of women for this extremely popular war. Women entered numerous occupations in war industries from which they had previously been excluded. Female clerical workers suddenly appeared everywhere in the swelling government bureaucracy, especially the War Department. Even though there was no remarkable change in the female labor force in absolute numbers, public perceptions of working women changed.[59] Women pitched in feverishly to help the war effort and they received considerable public praise. Anna Howard Shaw, former head of the NAWSA, headed the Women's committee of the Council of National De-

171

fense, an agency designed to coordinate women's voluntary activities, and Carrie Chapman Catt served on the committee as well. Though they had little power or influence, they succeeded in claiming the mantle of patriotic citizenship for women's efforts.

In 1918, in the midst of the war, the House of Representatives passed the federal suffrage amendment. Suffragists in the House balcony spontaneously broke into a traditional hymn, praising God for what seemed an imminent victory, while National Woman's Party pickets at the White House decided to lay down their signs. They felt part of an invincible wave of democratization as Great Britain, Canada, and postrevolutionary Russia also successfully enfranchised women. But the Senate voted the amendment down and while NWP pickets resumed their vigil, Catt mobilized her experienced, but tired, troops for one final effort. More than a year and several state campaigns later, on August 26, 1920, the Nineteenth Amendment became a part of the United States Constitution after ratification by thirty-six states.

For a moment at least American women could bask in the glow of their great victory. But their achievement was filled with ironies. With one stroke the Nineteenth Amendment enfolded women into a particular version of the American political heritage defining citizenship as a relationship between the individual and the state, whose key expression was the act of voting. To win this right women had to organize together, to act as a group. But the right itself undermined collectivity. Indeed, throughout the nineteenth century, as male politics came to be associated more and more with voting, female politics had developed its own separate track outside the electoral arena. Women learned to create institutions, to demand that governments accept some responsibility for community life whether in the form of pure drinking water or of libraries and schools.[60] Many of the leaders of the suffrage movement believed that once women had the right to vote they would, as individuals, express these female values through the electoral process and there would be no more need for collective organization.

But those "female values" really represented the politicized domesticity of middle-class women with its associated prejudices towards blacks, immigrants, and the working class. They rested on shared experience in the female spaces of associations and institutions from the WCTU to settlement houses. The pressures of individualism had already undermined these values and the female solidarity they presumed more than suffrage leaders could realize. Suffrage, as a symbol, condensed a wide spectrum of female discontents and allowed a broad coalition which could not hold together around any other issue. The female professional, the young working girl, the enticements of popular culture's emphasis on pleasure and leisure all undermined the solidarity of nineteenth century middle-class women's culture rooted in domesticity.

Women, especially those with college educations, were indeed becoming more "modern" in the sense of greater detachment from tradition and community. Between the 1890s and 1920 they had appropriated the language of "science" to assert their individual rights, but in the process they unknowingly undermined their own collective power. The irony of the vote is that what was won with a great collective effort permitted women to confront their newly attained citizenship in the solitude of the voting booth. That irony paralleled others in those same years as women—in the roles of housewives, professionals, and sexual beings—entered the scientific age. From suffragist to citizen, from housewife to home economist, from volunteer to social worker, from silence and euphemism to Freudian psychology, in each case modernity brought both gains and losses eroding the female community that had flourished in Victorian America.

The radical edge of the prewar years would be dulled in the subsequent decade. In September 1919 Emma Goldman, that quintessential female individualist and indefatigable fighter for sexual as well as political independence for women, emerged from two years in prison for opposing conscription during the war. Three days before Christmas, immigration officials seized her for deportation. She was later sent to Russia along with 248 other immigrants. Goldman lost her citizenship because the government had denaturalized her former husband and by law at that time a woman's citizenship followed her husband's. In the 1920s this legal bind became an important issue for female reformers. Hostility to "foreigners" and "reds" during the war had prompted many moderates such as Catt to distance themselves from socialists and other leftists. The postwar red scare showed the bitter fruit of such divisions between former allies. The forces that deprived Goldman of her citizenship and exiled her from her adopted homeland signaled a changed political climate for female reform and women's rights in the 1920s.

8

Flappers, Freudians, and All That Jazz

Suffragists celebrated their great victory in a nation out of war and emerging from a postwar depression to the first flush of newfound power and affluence. In this setting younger women seemed to turn their backs on the achievements of their mothers and grandmothers. Politics bored them. They wanted to have fun. Newspapers, magazines, movies, and novels all told Americans that womanhood had changed, again. Young, hedonistic, sexual, the flapper soon became a symbol of the age with her bobbed hair, powdered nose, rouged cheeks, and shorter skirts. Lively and energetic, she wanted experience for its own sake. She sought out popular amusements in cabarets, dance halls, and movie theaters that no respectable, middle-class woman would have frequented a generation before. She danced, smoked, and flaunted her sexuality to the horror of her elders.

"I like the jazz generation," said Zelda Fitzgerald in 1924, "and I hope my daughter's generation will be jazzier. I want my girl to do as she pleases, be what she pleases regardless of Mrs. Grundy." Zelda, wife of novelist F. Scott Fitzgerald, had become a popular symbol of the new female expressiveness; she consciously set herself against the image of generations of feminist reformers and career women. "Mrs. Grundy" represented prudery and sacrifice as opposed to the new standards of pleasure and consumption. As Zelda spelled out the contrast: "I think a woman gets more happiness out of being gay, light-hearted, unconventional, mistress of her own fate, than out of a career that calls for hard work, intellectual pessimism and loneliness. I don't want [my daughter] Pat to be a genius. I want her to be a flapper, because flappers are brave and gay and beautiful."[1]

Movie star Colleen Moore, heroine of the 1923 film *Flaming Youth*, echoed Zelda's rebellious tone. "Don't worry, girls," she reassured her fans. "Long skirts, corsets, and flowing tresses have gone. . . . The American girl will see to this. She is independent, a thinker [who] will not follow slavishly the ordinances of those who in the past have decreed this or that for her to wear."[2]

Yet for all their bravado, the triumph these flappers proclaimed was a complicated and contradictory one. The twenties formed an era when changes long under way emerged into an urban mass culture emphasizing pleasure, consumption, sexuality, and individualism. On virtually every specific, the changes proclaimed as "new" in the twenties can be traced back to the period before World War I. After all, "sex o'clock" had struck in 1913 with dance crazes, rising hemlines and slimmer silhouettes, public amusements, jazz, and bohemian culture. The difference was that activities once on the fringes of society or associated with specific subcultures became normative for white middle-class America in the 1920s. Jazz came out of the black ghetto and into the mainstream. Sexual experimentation and new Freudian ideas spread from Greenwich Village to college campuses. Public amusements frequented by the working class at the turn of the century now attracted middle-class women as well as men. Rouge, powder, and eyeshadow, once the mark of prostitutes, now adorned the most respectable young women.

The Companionate Marriage and the Reemergence of Female Sexuality

The sensuality of the flappers marked a powerful current of behavioral and ideological change in American culture. Youth were a force in American life as never before. Organized into educational institutions (a process enhanced by the passage of child labor laws in the 1910s) such as high schools and colleges, young people found environments in which they could experiment with new norms and challenge tradition with relative freedom. The dramatic growth of coeducational state universities created a setting in which young women and men created new rituals for courtship and new patterns for heterosexual relations. Heady with their newfound freedom, they flaunted new forms of plea-

176

sure-seeking such as petting, dancing, smoking, and drinking. "Are we as bad as we're painted?" asked a young woman at The Ohio State University. "We are. We do all the things that our mothers, fathers, aunts and uncles do not sanction, and we do them knowingly. We are not young innocents—we've got the dope at our finger ends and we use it wisely for our own protection."[3]

Yet the college generation of the twenties was not nearly as rebellious as they and their elders believed. The new norms they created reworked the older values with which they had been raised. And the power of peer culture created a degree of conformity in behavior previously unknown. How much individualism is there in a fad?[4] Indeed, the emergence of youth culture, where courtship commonly took place within the youthful institutions of college and high school, dramatically narrowed the age range within which most women and men married, creating far more uniformity than ever before.[5]

To Victorian mothers and fathers, however, the public acceptance of female sexuality was indeed revolutionary. Ideas expounded earlier only by radicals like Emma Goldman or Greenwich Village bohemians were now widely disseminated. An elite of psychologists, particularly the followers of Sigmund Freud, declared war on Victorian ideology, labeling it superstitious, unscientific, and unhealthful. They pronounced sexuality a positive, energy-producing (rather than depleting), and pervasive force in human life, and they redefined "normal" adulthood to include sexual expression. At the same time, they drew careful boundaries around the definition of "normal sex": it must be heterosexual and marital.[6] Indeed, birth control moved into the middle-class mainstream as part of a new ideal of marriage as an emotionally fulfilling companionship. Leaders like Margaret Sanger no longer advocated birth control as a source of female and working-class autonomy, but rather worked for its dissemination under the watchful control of doctors.[7]

If such ideas constituted a revolution for women, it was certainly a complex and restricted one. After a century of denial, middle-class culture acknowledged the existence of female sexuality, and indeed prescribed sexual pleasure separate from procreative intention. At the same time, it reinforced the traditional goal of marriage in the context of an increasingly competitive "marriage market." By emphasizing the emotional centrality of romance and marriage and the competition among women for male attention, the emphasis on female sexuality undermined and called into question some of the powerful bonds among women. Indeed, it stigmatized homosexuality, and by inference most intimate relationships between women, as "deviant."[8]

New courtship patterns presumed a new kind of marriage in which romantic love, sexual pleasure, and companionship were central. Responsibility for such relationships, however, rested primarily on the shoulders of women, who had the most to lose. Male identity and economic security still rested primarily on work, whereas women understood that their economic security, emotional fulfillment, and social status all depended on a successful marriage. If they failed to marry, they risked becoming "dried-up old maids." The very epithets used insinuated a new valuation of the single and presumably celibate life as unfulfilled, worthless, deviant.[9]

Anxieties about marital success curbed some of the flappers' new physical freedoms. If a young woman hoped to find a mate, she could not put all her energies into other pursuits such as sports and careers. Female athletics had grown dramatically in the twenties, providing new heroines such as tennis star Helen Wills and Gertrude Ederle, who swam the English Channel in 1928 breaking previous world records set by men. As the decade wore on, many expressed fears that competitive athletics could make young women too masculine to be acceptable wives and, perhaps, even uninterested in marriage. As a result many colleges abandoned intercollegiate competition for "play days" in which there would be no "stars" and no unwomanly behavior.[10]

Womanliness, in turn, had a growing commercial dimension. By the 1920s, Americans were aware of themselves as consumers and of consumption as a central facet of American life. Marketing experts used sexuality, especially female sexuality, to sell all manner of products. In this sexualized consumer economy young women learned to market themselves as products. Sales of cosmetics skyrocketed. Magazines tutored women on the ingredients of an attractive "personality." Social sororities flourished on campuses where they coached their select few in the social skills, proper appearance, and behavioral boundaries of the future wife-companion.[11] Beginning in 1921 the Miss America Beauty Pageant in Atlantic City emphasized the competitive display of female beauty, cloaked in rhetoric about wholesome femininity. Samuel Gompers of the American Federation of Labor described the first

Miss America for the *New York Times:* "She represents the type of womanhood America needs—strong, red-blooded, able to shoulder the responsibilities of home-making and motherhood. It is in her type that the hope of the country resides."[12]

As advice books urged married couples to "be friends," advertisements and movies warned women that the task of remaining an attractive and interesting wife required constant vigilance. According to Penrhyn Stanlaws, costume designer for the movie industry, "a woman who is properly gowned can rule nations, while a misplaced hairpin has caused more tragic mistakes than a misplaced commandment!"[13] And movie star Dorothy Phillips announced that "Women are matrimonial ostriches. They . . . refuse to admit that marriage is a competitive game in which *getting* a husband is merely the first trick."[14]

Advertisements played on anxieties, warning women of failure due to "housewife hands," "halitosis," or body odor and offering products to ward off the dangers. Movies, in turn, demonstrated the proper use of new products and clothes with models like the "it" girl, Clara Bow. Or Gloria Swanson, the dowdy housewife who lost her husband and then, transformed into a flapper, won him back again. Zelda Fitzgerald summarized the calculated marketing of self when she praised "flapperdom" for "teaching [young women] to capitalize their natural resources and get their money's worth. They are merely applying business methods to being young."[15] Gloria Swanson hinted at contempt for the objects of all this manipulation when she said, in *Why Change Your Wife?*, "The more I see of men, the more I like dogs."[16]

Companionate marriage was supposed to supply the emotional support and companionship which women and men had previously found most often with members of their own sex. As women broke out of the strictures of Victorian morality, their experience of female community diminished and they lost the conviction of a common female mission. At work, in the home, or in politics women were on their own, individuals yet still defined and limited by their gender.

The emphasis on heterosexual companionship and the stigmatizing of female community forced lesbians to recognize themselves as a distinct group. In a previous era, women who chose to spend their lives with other women and whose affections for each other found sexual expression did not consider themselves particularly "different." In a culture that denied female sexuality of all sorts,

179

they remained invisible and, therefore, unthreatening. Within the subculture built on women's domestic identities, powerful emotional and sensual relationships among women were the rule rather than the exception. That some of these were lifelong, committed, and passionate attachments went largely unremarked. Jane Addams and Mary Rozet Smith, for example, shared their lives for forty years during which time Addams became one of the most famous, idealized, and beloved women in the United States.

Freudian ideas labeled homosexuality "deviant" and emphasized intense and privatized heterosexual relations with men. In this context, a lesbian identity began to form among women who knew their sexuality did not fit the norms delineated by the "experts," and who needed new and discreet ways to find each other in a hostile world. Some of them found community in the worlds of single professional women and female athletes. Others began to articulate in literature the lonely search for self-affirmation. Novels such as Radclyffe Hall's *The Well of Loneliness* and the powerful writings of Gertrude Stein from her self-imposed exile in Paris initiated an expression of a new identity in formation.[17]

The isolation of lesbians from a broader community of women rooted in female reform and women's colleges mirrored the growing isolation of the housewife within the companionate marriage. The image of the ideal wife-companion presumed an intense focus on private life and specifically on the marital relationship. Emotionally centered as much on her husband as on her children, the "modern" housewife presided over a shrinking household in which modern technology replaced domestic servants and consumption itself had become a major task.[18]

Housework had always been labor-intensive, harsh work. From the colonial goodwife to the rural farm woman to the domestic servant in the middle-class home, women had produced food and clothing with calloused hands and sweated brows. As electricity and indoor plumbing reached the majority of homes (and over two-thirds of nonfarm homes) in the 1920s, however, the nature and organization of that work changed.

Perhaps it changed so rapidly because the expanding middle classes could no longer find servants to do the work except in the south where black women had few other job options.[19] Young white women flocked to new jobs in sales and clerical work and there were few new immigrants to replace them. Ads after World

War I no longer presumed the presence of servants at home. Instead, they urged housewives to let electricity be their servant.

> Electric servants can be depended on—to do the muscle part of the washing, ironing, cleaning and sewing. They will cool the house in summer and help heat the cold corners in winter. There are electrical servants to percolate your coffee, toast your bread and fry your eggs. There's a big, clean electrical servant that will do all your cooking— without matches, without soot, without coal, without argument—in a cool kitchen.[20]

The urban housewife no longer produced, or supervised production. Rather, purchasing and using the new technologies became a form of personal expression and an opportunity for guarding the health and welfare of her family. Vigilantly she attended to family nutrition with new canned and packaged products, cleaned the new bathroom to guard against germs, and decorated to enhance the cheer of her home. If she followed the advice of home economists she could become an expert at her main job, consumption, and ensure that her family had the best possible within her budget. In 1928 the *Ladies Home Journal* depicted the happy housewife who showed her commitment and creativity in her bright, gay kitchen decor: "It is a rainbow, in which the cook sings at her work and never thinks of household tasks as drudgery."[21] With science at her side she could remain interesting, slender, and elegant.

Motherhood itself became a job to be scientifically managed. It elicited a flood of advice from experts. Do it yourself, mother; don't allow anyone else (i.e., servants) to raise your children, they urged. At the same time they rushed in to teach her how to carry out responsibilities for which, they presumed, she was ill-equipped. For example, researchers Robert and Helen Lynd described mothers in Muncie, Indiana, who devoted their lives to their children, giving up church and club work and social activities.[22] The experts in scientific child rearing warned against too much emotional involvement and prescribed scheduled feedings and other methods of regulating what had previously been seen as a "natural" relationship. No longer could a "good mother" simply feed and clothe her little ones and send them off to school on time. Now she weighed her babies and visited doctors on a regular schedule, oversaw children's clubs and music lessons, studied nutrition, and participated in the PTA.[23]

The Secretary as Single Girl

While preparing herself for a companionate marriage, the young woman in the 1920s who was not in college was likely to be working. Between 1920 and 1930 the proportion of women in the labor force remained stationary at about one in four. The most dramatic gains had been in the two previous decades. Yet the twenties glamorized and enshrined the working girl, consolidating a new ideology about the proper public places for women. The growth in the female labor force before World War I had been viewed largely as an unfortunate and certainly unwomanly activity on the part of women outside the white middle-class mainstream. Women's participation in the war effort had broken a few barriers and certainly earned some public approval, but factory workers and domestics remained marginal and negative figures in popular culture. Nevertheless, with one in four women over sixteen in the labor force, some accommodation was in order. The changes in the working woman's locations offered an opportunity to reweave the working girl back into the fabric of socially approved womanhood. By 1920, 30 percent of women workers were in clerical and sales work. Clerical work—white collar, respectable, and available primarily to white, native-born women— provided the opportunity for a new ideology that recognized a period of work outside the home in many women's lives but separated that work from the idea of career so valued by nine-teenth- and early-twentieth-century new women seeking economic independence.[24]

The image of the secretary as the quintessential modern working girl joined the youthful independence and consumer orientation of the flapper to the wife-companion ideology. Magazines portrayed her as glamorous and offered her advice on how to get ahead. They also prescribed in both fiction and features her ultimate goal: marriage. Like the college girl, she needed "personality" to get ahead. And indeed, the office, like the university, represented a marriage market rife with opportunities. Floyd Dell, a prominent exponent of the new sexuality, argued that "The idea of work as a *goal* would be repudiated by working women; to them it is a *means to an end,* and the end is love, marriage, children, and homemaking."[25] Movies about working girls emphasized romance at the expense of sisterly bonds. Common scenes included the roommate left alone on Saturday night while her companions are out on dates or a group of working girls before a mirror, each absorbed in her own reflection.[26]

The glamor of the working girl lay in her proximity to men in the office context. Indeed, the secretary worked so closely with her boss that their relationship could be described in familiar, domestic terms. At the turn of the century when secretaries still were most commonly male, they were apprentices preparing for a long climb into managerial ranks. The boss was a mentor, a father figure. By 1930 the metaphor had changed from father/son to husband/wife, and, as the title of one popular film proclaimed, *The Office Wife* was at the top, not the bottom, of her professional possibilities.[27] *Fortune* magazine described the needs of the businessman in these terms:

> What he wanted in the office was something as much like the vanished wife of his father's generation as could be arranged—someone to balance his checkbook, buy his railroad tickets, check his baggage, get him seats in the fourth row, take his daughter to the dentist, listen to his side of the story, give him a courageous look when things were the blackest, and generally know all, understand all.[28]

Clerical work thus redefined offered an excellent vehicle for the new image of the young working women. It solved the growing needs of corporate bureaucracies while offering women jobs with limited possibilities for ambitions or careers. The office was no longer a male preserve but a public environment in which males and females were accorded separate and unequal roles analogous to their traditional roles in the home.[29]

At the same time the office was critically and fundamentally different precisely because the environment itself was public. Rife with potentially disruptive romantic opportunities, offices were redesigned to control this sexualization. Clerical workers operated in separate rooms, often adorning reception and information desks at the entrance. Many employers complained that young women dressed too frivolously for the serious business of the office. Indeed, given their low horizons of opportunity at work and popular culture's encouragement to find meaning in romance and leisure activities, they were expressing in their dress a very different sense of priorities. They were dressed for a party because that is where they wanted to go.[30]

Some writers at the time compared the beauty of women in the office to other aspects of the environment, to be controlled and used productively. An article in the *New York Times Magazine* in 1924 remarked that "consciously and at a cue beauty has entered into the world of business. . . . Not mere casual, sporadic beauty, blond or brunette, but the selected kind, chosen for type, stature, manner and personality and arranged in patterns about the establishment from the information desk to the offices at the back, as harmonious a whole as one might find on the stage." To the skeptical the author said "it pays dividends in morale and in salesmanship and in prestige." Somewhat tongue-in-cheek the author then discussed the process of matching employees to office decor and personalities to company image.[31]

The office worker, like the college girl, fit the image of the flapper. Flirtatious, fun-loving, the flapper had resources; she was middle- or even upper-class. Her working-class sister, however, also experienced some of these changes. Decades before it was respectable she danced in public halls. As working girls became acceptable, more and more of them lived separately from their families of origin and retained a growing proportion of their earnings to spend as they pleased.[32]

In Elizabethton, Tennessee, for example, the opening of two large rayon plants in 1925 and 1926 attracted a predominantly female labor force of nearly five thousand. Teenage girls and young women in their twenties represented the first generation in their Appalachian families to enter the cash economy. There is evidence, however, that even in this relatively isolated mountain community, working girls kept a portion of their earnings for personal expenditures on clothes and cosmetics. In 1929 five hundred young women led a walkout that became the first of a series of massive textile strikes in the south. The company brought in guards, machine guns, and ultimately the force of the state to quell the strike. They also recorded the strike on film. Pictures of the strikers clearly demonstrate the transmission of cultural artifacts through mass marketing: for all the world they look just like flappers with bobbed hair, close-fitting hats, and fur-trimmed coats. Newspaper stories described the celebratory mood after the first walkout as young women tootled around the town in automobiles, honking and yelling out the windows.[33]

The flamboyant and striking solidarity of Elizabethton women was the exception. Generally, the atmosphere of consumerism and optimism obscured continuing realities of economic hardship for rural women and working-class families. Income was rising, as were expectations, but hunger and hardship remained the lot of many. Salesgirls found it difficult to maintain the required ingratiating friendliness as they sold wealthy women goods that they themselves could never afford to buy. Racist hiring policies prevented black women who joined the great migration out of the rural south from experiencing the economic fruits of an expanding service sector. After a brief experience of enhanced opportunity during World War I, they found themselves forced into a very narrow range of job possibilities: the least desirable factory jobs and domestic service. Racist and anti-immigrant attitudes also underlay immigration restriction, the virtual exclusion of black women and men from political participation in southern states, and the revival of the Ku Klux Klan in northern cities. Although immigration from overseas virtually stopped, a new immigration from Mexico developed in the aftermath of the Mexican Revolution in 1910, fueled by the demand for labor in the United States during World War I.

Recruited by agricultural businesses like the Great Western Sugar Company, most Mexicans came in family groups, and like other immigrants, familial and ethnic patterns insulated them from the individualism so prevalent in popular culture. Women in such families labored not only in the fields but also to bring forth large numbers of children to join them and their husbands there. Their traditional subordination within the family was reinforced by the agribusinesses' practice of paying women's wages to their husbands. Economist Ruth Allen observed in 1924 that "She does not collect her own money; she does not know how much is paid for her services; she seldom knows how much cotton she picks a day or how many acres she chops. The wage paid is a family wage, and the family is distinctly patriarchal. . . ."[34]

Though the cash economy had been primarily the province of men, a community of women, in fact, had been the core of Mexican village life as they ministered to spiritual needs, produced a substantial portion of the diet in their gardens, plastered homes, and participated in an active barter economy. Migrant women in communities of farm laborers often found their traditional sources of autonomy, power, and authority undermined. But in the older Hispanic communities in southwestern cities, younger women experienced new possibilities.[35]

Like black women, Mexicans found severely limited options in the realm of wage work because they faced the dual obstacles of racial and sexual discrimination. Most of them worked in domestic and personal service (44.3 percent in 1930) or agriculture (21.2 percent). A growing proportion found low-skilled jobs in industries such as sewing garments or pecan-shelling (19.3 percent in 1930). On the whole, despite desperately poor living conditions, cultural preferences meant that Mexican-American women were far less likely to work outside the home than either black or white women. Yet the powerful currents of individualism in American culture affected them as well. Interviewers in the 1920s received frequent complaints from Mexican men about women who had lived and worked in the United States. They were too independent, "like American women," no longer content with subservient domesticity.[36] That new independence would encourage the transfer of the strength Mexican women traditionally exerted within the family and the church to more public and visible roles. One result was important female leadership in labor struggles such as the Texas pecan strike in 1927 and later in the massive farm strikes of the thirties.

The Decline of Female Reform

The cultural emphasis on surface appearances, on competition, and on consumption helped to undermine the prewar reform agenda developed by a broad range of women's organizations and premised on female sensibility and the collective strength of women. As urban life triumphed over rural, automobiles, movies, and radio brought urban mass culture even into the countryside. Urban culture eroded the traditional dependence on and authority of the family and facilitated youthful self-expression and individualism. Yet as the internal strictures of Victorian repression lifted, external forces of governmental repression and conservatism grew, and an era of Progressive reform came to a sudden end. Red scares jailed and deported thousands. Race riots in places like Chicago brought crowds of whites into black neighborhoods shooting and beating the new migrants in random violence. The Ku Klux Klan revived in northern cities to promote "100% Americanism" and hostility to immigrants, Jews, and Catholics. In 1924 the National Origins Act stemmed the flow of immigration from Eastern Europe and Asia. Republicans brought business leaders back to the center of government, proclaiming "the chief business of America is business."[37]

Suffragists seemed to recognize the changed context when they transformed the National American Woman Suffrage Association in 1920 into the League of Women Voters (LWV). They presumed that enfranchised women should be understood as individuals, citizens with a direct relationship to the state via the franchise. Their duty was to train women to be good citizens. The training they provided, rather like earlier work of groups such as the National Consumers' League, emphasized an issue-oriented politics based on thorough research and effective public education.

The National Woman's Party (NWP), by contrast, announced that its commitment to "the removal of all forms of the subjection of women" required a renewed commitment to end legal discriminations against women. The NWP claimed the banner of prewar feminists, to win "the final release of woman from the class of a dependent, subservient being to which early civilization committed her."[38] In practice, however, the single-minded focus on legal discrimination narrowed the meaning of feminism. In 1921 the NWP began a state-by-state campaign for Equal Rights Bills and in 1923 secured the first congressional hearings on the Equal Rights Amendment (ERA), which stated that "men and women shall have equal rights throughout the United States and every place subject to its jurisdiction."[39]

In an important sense the ERA represented another version of female individualism. Its premise was equal treatment of the individual before the law so that working women could have "an equal chance with men to compete in the labor market for their livelihood."[40] NWP supporters tended to be professional women for whom the barriers to individual success and advancement in the public arena were most onerous. Their campaign effectively narrowed the feminist vision, rejecting links to other reform issues. When black women, for example, demanded that the National Woman's Party protest the systematic denial of voting rights to black women in southern states, Alice Paul asserted that this was a "race issue" not a "woman's issue."[41] Although their former allies in the suffrage movement were almost as reluctant as the National Woman's Party to deal with the oppression of black women, NWP's restricted version of women's rights clashed sharply on other issues with the continuing drive for female progressive reform.

Former suffragists like Carrie Chapman Catt in the League of Women Voters believed there was no more need for an organization specifically concerned with women's rights, but they also assumed that women would bring a nurturing sensibility and reforming vision into the political arena. Most of them continued to work within a very wide range of reform organizations to better the conditions of working women, to curb child labor, to investigate and humanize prison systems, and to provide services to the urban poor.[42] Their reform vision remained rooted in politicized domesticity, and they focused on cross-class alliances in which middle-class women fought for the "protection" of their poor and working-class sisters by a nurturing feminized state. As a result, they could not imagine women as simply another selfish "interest group." The conflict between these two very different visions of female solidarity was deep and bitter. It permeated the continuing activities of feminists even as their base eroded among the broader female population.[43]

The female reform impulse, nourished especially in the intensely female environments of settlement houses and in the activities of religious women's organizations, the YWCA, women's clubs, the National Women's Trade Union League and the National Consumers' League, continued to spark social and political innovations in spite of the increasingly hostile environment. Communities of women proved strong enough to sustain such organizations though they could no longer provide a broad, unified vision like the nurturant cooperation of maternal commonwealth to counterpose to the rising power and diminished civic participation of the bureaucratic state. These organizations, in turn, trained a new generation of leaders who were ready to seize the new opportunities that emerged in the 1930s.

For the first time since abolition, black and white women began to make tentative steps toward interracial cooperation around a common agenda. Pressure from black women struggling against segregation within the YWCA and from white women in the Southern Methodist Women's Missionary Council forced the Council for Interracial Cooperation (CIC), founded in 1920, to set up a women's committee. These early contacts between southern white women and black activists remained tense and difficult. White women failed to acknowledge black women's broad claim for "all the privileges and rights granted to American womanhood." In a series of emotion-charged meetings black leaders such as Charlotte Hawkins Brown told southern whites that "the Negro women of the South lay everything that happens to the members of her race at the door of the Southern white woman." Calling on their shared religious heritage, she reminded them that at the final judgment white Christians would reach a hand out to God in the same way that she would, adding "I know that the dear Lord will not receive it if you are crushing me beneath your feet." Contact with middle-class blacks, singing hymns and praying with them, led white leaders such as Carrie Parks Johnson to recognize in "the hearts of those Negro women . . . all the aspirations for their homes and their children that I have for mine." The CIC Women's committee achieved little that was concrete in the 1920s, but it initiated a new alliance of middle-class black and white women in the south. Black women continued to work separately on the issues of education, working conditions of domestics, child welfare, public segregation, suffrage, and lynching. By the 1930s their agenda began to have a greater impact on the work of whites as well.[44]

A more visible political victory for women reformers was the Sheppard-Towner bill for maternal and infant health education passed by Congress in 1921. Proponents argued that high infant mortality rates could be lowered by educating mothers in prenatal and early childhood nutrition, sanitation, and child care practices. Careful to avoid encroaching on the growing professional power of physicians, they proposed that public health nurses under the supervision of the Children's Bureau provide education but no direct medical services.

Nevertheless, the program met sustained opposition from those opposed to state-supported health and welfare activity. The opposition to Sheppard-Towner marked yet another area within which female collective concerns and capacities gave way to a more individualized, scientific, and male-dominated profession. The most vociferous opposition came from physicians who were in the process of consolidating their newly won hegemony over medical practice. They did not want nurses to function in an autonomous way, outside their direction and direct supervision, nor did they want government-sponsored programs that might compete with their own practices. Sheppard-Towner, they implied, was a Bolshevik plot. By the end of the decade the funds for Sheppard-Towner had been cut entirely and doctors took over the preventive health care practices such as physical examinations and well-baby clinics pioneered by women.[45]

Similarly in the 1920s, the emerging specialty of obstetrics finally

189

eradicated the work of midwifery. Accused of being dirty, unedu-
cated, and responsible for maternal and child mortality, midwives—most of whom were blacks or immigrants—were driven
out of business except in remote, rural areas. As a result, the
experience of giving birth moved from the home to scientifically
controlled urban hospitals. In that transfer the woman giving
birth was further isolated from the support and proximity of other
women who traditionally attended the birthing mother at home.
Although the practices of experienced midwives, particularly those
who trained in Europe, resulted in far lower maternal and infant
mortality than most hospitals could report, the hospital birth became the acceptable form.[46]

In a context of growing political conservatism, most female
reformers ran into right-wing smear campaigns labeling their efforts alien and subversive. Peace, for example, had been a central
issue for many women's organizations. Though peace activists
disagreed in their degree of opposition to the world war, they
shared a view emphasizing the perspective of motherhood as an
essential point of view on world affairs. Women's consciousness
of the value of life, they believed, must be brought to bear in
the international arena where men too easily turn to militarism
and war when disputes arise. After the war the Woman's Peace
Party changed its name to the Women's International League
for Peace and Freedom (WILPF) and began to work in coalition
with the LWV, the Women's Joint Congressional Committee, and
even the Daughters of the American Revolution (DAR) to oppose
militarism and to abolish the National Defense Act of 1920.

This activity aroused the opposition of the War Department
which began a campaign against the WILPF in 1922. In 1923
the office of Brigadier General Amos A. Fries, head of the Chemical
Warfare Service, mailed out a "spider web" chart to patriotic
groups throughout the country. This chart purported to show
that "the activities of all women's societies and many church groups
may be regarded with suspicion." It named twenty-one women
and seventeen organizations, linking them to radical groups and
implying communist control. Interestingly, the DAR, which later
circulated the chart widely, was named in the original version.

The consequence of this red-baiting was that many organizations
and individuals drew back from coalitions and work with WILPF.
In 1925 Carrie Chapman Catt guided the formation of a broad
peace coalition excluding WILPF. Meeting as the first National

Conference on the Cause and Cure of War, the coalition included the LWV, the American Association of University Women, the General Federation of Women's Clubs, the YWCA, and the Woman's Christian Temperance Union. WILPF purged its own radical leadership, including women such as Crystal Eastman, and shifted its focus from militarism to the economic causes of war. In spite of these attacks, however, the women's peace movement retained a visible presence on the American political scene. It was a major force behind the 1928 Kellogg-Briand Pact, a multinational agreement renouncing the use of force in international relations, and it gained new strength in the 1930s.[47]

The work of middle-class reformers in alliance with working-class women came under similar suspicion by conservative antilabor forces. But it was also undergoing internal changes which transformed the relationships of middle- and working-class women. Settlement houses, which had been free spaces where women lived together, explored new ideas, and developed reform programs, were slowly becoming more structured, routinized, and professionalized. Directors and workers were more likely to be trained social workers pursuing professional agendas and less likely to live in and become part of the settlement house itself. Lines of responsibility became more formal and hierarchical as proliferating agencies expanded administrative responsibilities thereby diminishing the informal bonds of mutual dependence and cooperation. And, increasingly, men were likely to move into the upper echelons of social welfare bureaucracies, a trend which became far more pronounced in the 1930s.[48]

Women's alliances with unions, already badly eroded due to labor's disinterest in organizing women, virtually disappeared during the twenties. Union women and their allies continued to build communities on the edges of the union movement in women's locals, the Women's Trade Union League, the Women's Bureau, and summer schools for women workers. The most innovative of these were the Summer Schools for Women Workers initiated by trade union women together with M. Carey Thomas, the president of Bryn Mawr College, and Hilda Smith, an instructor there. The summer schools began at Bryn Mawr College in 1921 and continued in several places until the mid-1930s. This worker education movement brought hundreds of young women from their homes and factories to a two-month experience that changed many of their lives. They took courses in history and economics as well

191

as labor law and the skills of organizing and negotiating. Though the union movement remained inhospitable to women and was generally experiencing hard times in the 1920s, the summer schools trained many women who assumed leadership in later labor struggles.[49]

Worker education was one of several alternative strategies developed in response to the hostility of the union movement and the low level of unionization among working women. The most important of these, however, was protective legislation, which generated the most direct conflict between feminists.

Protective legislation had been achieved beginning early in the twentieth century largely as an alternative to unionization. If women could not protect themselves through organization, society could establish maximum hours, minimum wages, regulations against night work, and limitations on the weights they could lift. Furthermore, when the courts made it clear that they would not permit such legislation for all workers, reformers prevailed with the argument that women, like children, needed special protections because of their physical weakness as well as the social necessity of protecting future motherhood.

Though unions increasingly supported protective legislation for women and children, female unionists were reluctant to embrace this strategy because it diverted energy and resources away from organizing. Indeed, for many women in organizations like the WTUL, protective legislation was a last resort to which they turned in despair after other alternatives failed. Unions in the twenties protected their members' interests in part by excluding groups, like women, who might undermine their unity and discipline.[50] Union leaders used the rhetoric of the difference between women and men to keep women relegated to the sidelines, protected not by unions but by legislation. Thus unions turned against women workers using the very ideas underlying the militant and successful union drives of the 1910s, especially among garment workers. Such organizing had drawn on the sense of honor and dignity imbedded in female culture, its moral appeal reaching across class boundaries to a broader sisterhood. In the twenties, union women and men spoke different languages, but the men controlled the institution.[51] Women clung to protective legislation in part because they had so little else.

Unionists and women reformers supported the establishment of a Women's Bureau in the Department of Labor in 1920 to collect information and advocate government action in the interests of wage-earning women. This victory created an important institutional niche for advocates of working women and a constant source of data and new policy proposals addressing the needs of women in the labor force. Yet, on the heels of the creation of the Women's Bureau, the body of protective legislation so painstakingly won in the Progressive era and defended in the courts came under attack both from the political right and from feminists in the National Woman's Party.

When the NWP proposed an Equal Rights Amendment they pointed to the continued existence of discriminatory legislation in every state. For instance, remnants of the old common law tradition gave husbands in some states control over the earnings of their wives and minor children; denied women the right to serve on juries; allowed husbands to determine their wives' legal residence; placed the burden of responsibility for illegitimate children on the mother; limited women's inheritance from a husband without a will to one-third of his property while granting widowers complete control over a deceased wife's real estate. The NWP catalogued continuing discrimination against women professionals who were barred from many of the finest schools and relegated to subordinate roles within their professions. And they charged that protective legislation simply placed women in an inferior position and deprived them of their rights.[52] For their opponents who believed in protective legislation they had only scorn: "They are trying to make our legislators believe that we women in industry are a class of weaklings, a special class of creatures devoid of both moral strength and physical stamina, totally unfit, mentally, morally and physically, to decide for ourselves, to judge between right and wrong, good and bad."[53]

Progressive women reformers responded with horror and anger at this threat to decades of reform activity. They charged that the NWP consisted of professional women who wanted all doors open for their own advancement but who had neither sympathy nor understanding for working-class women trapped in sweatshops and factories. What, they argued, does equality mean when women are disadvantaged to begin with?

This battle over means and ends poisoned the international women's movement as well as the domestic one and it persisted until the 1960s.[54] Clearly protective legislation provided needed improvements for many women. Particularly in female-domi-

193

nated jobs, hours became more reasonable, wages rose, and working conditions improved. At the same time, protective legislation made women less able to compete for traditional male jobs requiring overtime, nightwork, or heavy lifting. Thus, it may have contributed to the continuing sex segregation of the labor force and encouraged women to seek work in newer areas of the economy such as clerical and service work where they would not face as much competition. Once feminized, those jobs reflected the same characteristics associated with other "female jobs," namely low pay, little job mobility, and low status.[55]

While the Progressive reformers won their battle to defeat the ERA in the twenties, their vision of a politicized domesticity allowing women to enact publically the values of the home brought responses as hostile as those experienced by their opponents in the National Woman's Party. They could defeat the ERA in part because the spectre of the independent woman evoked increasing hostility as the decade wore on. And yet, female reformers themselves frequently pursued public roles as unmarried social workers, nurses, or teachers whose status was more and more precarious. Opponents of the Sheppard-Towner bill like Senator James Reed of Missouri ridiculed as "unnatural" the unmarried, professional women employees of the Children's Bureau. "Female celibates," he sneered, "women too refined to have a husband. . . . It seems to be the established doctrine of the bureau that the only people capable of caring for babies and mothers of babies are ladies who have never had babies." Waxing eloquent about the natural delights of "mother love," he attacked the "bespectacled lady, nose sharpened by curiosity, official chin pointed and keen . . . [who] sails majestically and authoritatively to the home of the prospective mother and demands admission in the name of the law." While his colleagues chortled, he proposed that a better plan would be to set up a mothers' committee "to take charge of the old maids and teach them how to acquire a husband and have babies of their own."[56]

This reemergence of the domestic ideal in its more privatized form occurred, ironically, as younger women announced their intention of pursuing a new style of feminism including both a career and marriage. In many ways they shared Senator Reed's denigration of the suffragist generation. In 1927 Dorothy Dunbar Bromley wrote in *Harper's Magazine:*

"Feminism" has become a term of opprobrium to the modern young woman. For the word suggests either the old school of fighting feminists who wore flat heels and had very little feminine charm, or the current species who antagonize men with their constant clamor about maiden names, equal rights, woman's place in the world, and many another cause . . . *ad infinitum*.[57]

Yet she claimed for "modern young women" the right to economic independence, individual choice, and the combination of marriage and career. Popular magazines contained numerous feature stories about this new breed and their optimistic claim that they could "have it all." Their individualism left them painfully alone in a world that continued to discriminate against women. Naively they thought they could have it all without the social support of organized women. Yet the cultural gap between themselves and their more Victorian predecessors left a gulf of misunderstanding and a dearth of generosity on both sides. If they sniffed at "the old school of fighting feminists," women like Charlotte Perkins Gilman, in turn, criticized their "selfish and fruitless indulgence" in romantic sexuality displaying "an unmistakable tendency to imitate the vices of men."[58] Clearly the space for collective female action had eroded but not disappeared.

Perhaps the new freedoms and new attitudes of the twenties represented a necessary experimentation with individualism especially on the part of young women.[59] Yet they were shaped and bounded by economic and cultural forces to such a degree that in retrospect some of these freedoms seem illusory. Changes in public life in the twenties accompanied the disintegration of the Victorian female community and the incorporation of women into the individualistic ethos of a consumer economy. The "separate spheres" of public and private were no longer so separate as women visibly worked and played in public places and as they refashioned domesticity into the "public" roles of professionalized social work, nursing, teaching, and white collar clerical work. The separation of home and work, the structural basis for the traditional middle-class gender ideology, had changed almost beyond recognition. Indeed, consumerism, together with growing corporate and governmental bureaucracies, inverted the meanings of these categories. Consumer culture defined public spaces—department stores or popular entertainment centers—in terms of purchases meeting privatized, individualized needs. And politics increasingly moved away from the daily life of communities to become the arena of experts, specialists, and hidden interests. Indeed, instead of the emergence of a "mother state" as female reformers had hoped, the domestic realm itself became increasingly contingent on a technical, corporate, and professionalized state. Yet female reform had in many ways reshaped the political landscape—laying the groundwork for what would be called, in the 1930s, the "welfare state."

9

Surviving the Great Depression

*I*n 1930 movie star Joan Crawford underwent a dramatic transformation. As a star of the silent screen in the twenties she
had been a flapper, slender and doll-faced. Now in the new talkies
she exuded a more mature sexuality. With squared off shoulders
and nipped-in waist, smooth shoulder-length hair, and larger eyes
and mouth, she was a sophisticated lady. She joined a new breed
of Hollywood stars, the femmes fatales such as Greta Garbo, Marlene Dietrich, and Bette Davis whose self-confidence and mannish
ways filled the screens in the thirties. Americans had no more
time for adolescent play. The Great Depression had begun.

In the thirties women had to be grownups, partners in the
struggle for survival in a way the culture had not acknowledged
for well over a century. Since the demise of the colonial goodwife,
popular images had moved from the submissive domesticity of
Victorianism to the girlish exuberance of the flapper, effectively
subverting the autonomous potential of the turn-of-the-century
new woman. With no socially sanctioned model of independent
female adulthood, both the prospect and reality of strong and
resourceful women were profoundly frightening. In the movies
this ambivalence played itself out as Bette Davis or Katharine
Hepburn inevitably met her match in an even stronger man to
whom she capitulated in the end. The battle of the sexes they
enacted no doubt reflected serious tensions felt by many. Perhaps
women had to be strong, but in a topsy-turvy world where many
men were finding it impossible to be breadwinners, there was
an undercurrent of male anger which frequently broke through
the surface. In many movies marriage and domesticity provided

197

the resolution. In others women suffered physical and verbal abuse. In 1931 James Cagney smashed a grapefruit in Mae Clark's face in *Public Enemy,* in a scene praised by critic Gilbert Seldes for restoring masculinity damaged by feminism and the Depression.[1] The conflation of sexuality, violence, and putting women in their place reached a subtle apogee in *Gone with the Wind* when proud and selfish Scarlett O'Hara was overcome (raped) by Rhett Butler and emerged tamed and transformed.

Outside the movie theaters American women and their families faced an unambiguous disaster. The stock market crash in 1929 exposed the optimism of the twenties as an illusion. While profits and paper fortunes had skyrocketed, wages had risen only slightly, farmers were locked in an agricultural depression, and the gap between rich and poor had grown. In the next three years low wages gave way to unemployment as a hundred thousand workers lost their jobs each week.

Cities began to resemble war zones. Unemployment reached 50 percent in Cleveland; 80 percent in Toledo. With no safety net, people scavenged garbage cans for food or waited in soup lines extending for blocks. Evicted families moved in with relatives, or lived in cars or makeshift cardboard shacks. By the mid-thirties the Depression had become a way of life that would scar a generation. Few escaped hardship, but experiences differed dramatically according to circumstances. Ideas about proper roles of women and men crashed headlong into harsh realities, shaping responses, limiting options, but unable to govern behavior all of the time.

Women participated actively, powerfully, in labor and social movements and in the redefinition of American politics and public life that was the New Deal, bringing to fruition ideas they had nurtured for generations. Yet they did so following the demise of a widespread women's movement capable of articulating female interests and mission. As a result, their victories in many ways went unclaimed. Domestic concerns finally succeeded in reshaping the state, but they were disconnected from women's broader claims for independence and citizenship.

The Retreat into Privacy: Family, Work, and Personal Life

The psychic shock for many families whose status and social position depended on the occupation and income of the husband was exacerbated because the traditional sex roles of male breadwinner and dependent spouse no longer worked. Unemployed men were ashamed; they felt like failures. Women could not understand. They kept asking, "Why don't you go out and get a job?" Their husbands begged social workers to explain to their wives that there simply were not any jobs. Some men left home, disappeared; others turned to alcohol; a few committed suicide. One man, out of control with anger and humiliation, almost beat his wife to death after hearing she had accepted food from a neighbor.[2]

A black man interviewed by Studs Terkel maintained that black men, who had been economically depressed from long before the crash, "had one big advantage. Our wives, they could go to the store and get a bag of beans or a sack of flour and a piece of fat meat, and they could cook this. And we could eat it. . . . Why did these big wheels kill themselves? They weren't able to live up to the standards they were accustomed to, and they got ashamed in front of their women."[3]

The Depression forced even people accustomed to eating beans from survival to desperation. Black women, who had always worked in far greater numbers than white women, faced unemployment with few resources. As available manufacturing and clerical jobs were closed to them, black women crowded into the field of domestic labor, working for whatever they could get. Between 1930 and 1940 the numbers of private household workers increased 25 percent, and most of these were black. In 1930 55 percent of all household workers were nonwhite, by 1940 the proportion had risen to 64 percent or nearly two-thirds.[4]

To add to their difficulties, relief programs discriminated blatantly against blacks. Hundreds of black women wrote to the president to complain that whites controlling the New Deal relief programs in the south excluded blacks who had nowhere else to turn. "We are wondering what is going to become of this large number of widow women with and without children," wrote one woman in Greenwood, Mississippi. "I was in the [Public Works Administration] office a few days ago. A woman was there she had five children and a husband not able to work. They told her to go hunt washings [rather than seek government-sponsored relief work]. . . . The white people dont pay anything for their washing. She cant do enough washing to feed her family."[5]

The Depression stretched kinship relations to their limits. In the face of evictions, families doubled and tripled up, enduring

199

the emotional irritants of crowding and the loss of privacy. Women revived their foremothers' skills in home production to stretch family resources. They patched and remade clothes, split worn sheets down the middle and sewed the outside edges together, made-over children's clothes from adult garments, relined coats, planted gardens, canned vegetables, and saved the tiniest bits of leftover food for another meal. Home production and constant recycling allowed families to reduce their dependence on the cash economy while maintaining some semblance of respectability.

The harsh realities of the Depression had serious consequences for personal relationships. When the flapper disappeared from popular culture she took with her the rising expectations of sexual liberation. Contraception became commonplace in the middle classes and even legal in 1936, but its primary purpose was to prevent the birth of children families could not afford. Fertility rates declined precipitously, bottoming out in 1932 with a low that would not be reached again until the late 1960s. Young people debated whether to marry in the face of financial insecurity and many decided to wait. Meridel LeSueur, herself a young radical and single mother in the thirties, wrote stories about the despair of young women who knew there was no work for men and who could not imagine themselves as breadwinners:

> I don't want to marry. I don't want any children. So they all say. No children. No marriage. They arm themselves alone, keep up alone. The man is helpless now. He cannot provide. If he propagates he cannot take care of his young. The means are not in his hands. So they live alone. Get what fun they can. The life risk is too horrible now. Defeat is too clearly written on it.[6]

Others were not so much defeated as careful. If the 1929 marriage rate had continued through the decade of the thirties there would have been an additional 800,000 marriages. But marriages were delayed by economic insecurity. Even so, young people sought each other out more for emotional security than playful experimentation: "The Depression made love a defense against loneliness." Birthrates remained low through the decade; however, marriage rates began to inch up in 1934.[7] With the family as a refuge from the ravages of the Depression, the cultural perception of woman as wife and mother assumed renewed force and frequency.

The need for a labor-intensive family economy reinforced the previous decade's emphasis on the housewife who does it all herself. Ads encouraged consumption of household products by playing on women's anxiety about not doing enough for their families and their fears of losing status. The right soap powder could help avoid "tell-tale gray." Body soaps and mouth washes prevented offensive odors and consequent social rejection. A host of products promised to stretch housewives' income and to avoid public embarrassments like "Pocket Book Panic," "Housework Hands," "Dated Skin," or "Flour Face" while they juggled their resources and energies to make ends meet.[8]

As communities stretched their resources to meet the massive need in their midst, again women were on the front lines. Churches and synagogues collected food and clothing for members who had fallen on hard times. Local charities and religious women's groups set up soup kitchens and flophouses for the destitute. At the grass-roots level, the bulk of community relief efforts relied, as always, on the labor of women.

Because home production and community relief were rarely sufficient for urban families, many women and older children sought wage-earning work. In the depths of the Depression, however, the difficulties of finding work were compounded by growing public hostility toward women workers, especially married ones. Anger and frustration at the loss of jobs made women easy scapegoats. As one man wrote to his congressman in 1931:

> If less women were employed it would make room for the employment of many of the idle men in our country . . . in the last analysis woman's true place is her home where she can see to the proper raising of her children while the man earns the living. This . . . is nature's decree . . . and I do not believe we are again going to have normal and prosperous times until women do return to their homes.[9]

By that year several states, cities, and school boards had devised legislation to prohibit or limit the employment of married women. In 1932, Section 213 of the Economy Act provided that in any reduction of government personnel "married persons" whose spouses were also employed by the government should be fired first; it also discouraged any future hiring of spouses of government workers. Despite its neutral language, the provision both in intent and in actual enforcement discriminated against married women.[10]

Public opinion polls confirmed the widespread belief that mar-

201

ried women who worked outside the home were taking jobs away from men. Though a steadily growing proportion of married women had joined the labor force since the turn of the century, more than 80 percent of Americans expressed the belief that their only proper place was the home. The executive committee of the AFL passed a resolution that "married women whose husbands have permanent positions . . . should be discriminated against in the hiring of employees."[11]

Contrary to popular belief, however, separate labor markets ensured that only rarely did women and men compete for the same jobs. The consequence of firing women was not that men gained access to jobs but simply that more households faced destruction: withdrawal of support from unemployed children or elderly parents, mortgage defaults, and sometimes divorce. Hostility to women workers contributed to the continuing decline in the proportion of women in the professions as well. Even in the female-dominated areas of teaching, librarianship, and social work, women lost ground in the 1930s as growing numbers of men entered the fields and quickly dominated higher-level positions.

Even though the tendency to scapegoat women by blaming them for the loss of male jobs contributed to discrimination at the professional level, in other parts of the economy the segregation of the labor force into male and female jobs offered women some protection from unemployment. Jobs in clerical, trade, and service areas where women were concentrated disappeared more slowly and later than did those in heavy industry. Hostility to working women generally ignored the fact that women were not holding traditionally male jobs, but it probably strengthened the resistance to opening such opportunities to the growing numbers of women desperate for work. Unemployment statistics indicate a gradual deterioration in women's position in the labor force relative to men over the course of the Depression due to the increased competition among women struggling to enter a labor market that had only a few areas designated as female jobs.[12]

Throughout the Depression unemployed women remained relatively invisible. According to cultural norms, they represented a contradiction in terms: Women were not supposed to be employed in the first place. Their places were in their homes, where men would provide for them. It was not acknowledged that such women were most often concentrated in particularly marginal and vulnerable groups: older women and widows, minorities, single women, and the very young. In 1934 there were seventy-five thousand homeless single women in New York City. They sat in train stations, rode the subways, and visited employment agencies. Meridel LeSueur noticed their absence from the streets in Minnesota cities and wondered why such women remained so invisible, their desperation and starvation so quiet and private. "It's one of the great mysteries of the city where women go when they are out of work and hungry," she wrote. "There are not many women in the bread line. They are no flop houses for women as there are for men, where a bed can be had for a quarter or less."[13]

In a haunting description of women sitting in the employment bureau in Minneapolis, LeSueur spelled out their terror of the coming winter. Knowing that there was no work, the women in the room "look at the floor dreading to see that knowledge in each other's eyes. There is a kind of humiliation in it." The desperation of young girls whose farm families could not support them or older women whose children had no bread matched the nightmares of the lady behind the desk, haunted by suffering she saw and could not relieve. When a young girl, out of work for eight months, homeless, and living on crackers, became hysterical the woman in charge raged back at her.

> So they stood there the two women in a rage, the girl weeping and the woman shouting at her. In the eight months of unemployment she had gotten ragged, and the woman was shouting that she would not send her out like that. "Why don't you shine your shoes," she kept scolding the girl, and the girl kept sobbing and sobbing because she was starving.[14]

Rural women faced similar hardships. Thousands of farm families lost their land to mortgage foreclosures. While urban families starved, farmers could not sell their produce for what it cost them. In the rural south, tenancy had become a way of life. Margaret Hagood, who traveled through the south interviewing women on tenant farms, described their lives bounded by extremely high fertility, poverty, constant work in house and field, and patriarchal families. They exercised great ingenuity making clothes for children from flour sacks, raising "patches" of vegetables and putting them up. But the constant state of debt often shifted family priorities toward cash crops like tobacco, leaving the family short of food.

Tenant farm women's lives followed the older patterns of the preindustrial family economy: cooking "from scratch" on wood stoves, drawing water from wells, working long hours in the fields, letting the man "tote the pocketbook," bearing children almost constantly, and watching anxiously over their daughters' sexual purity. One such woman told Margaret Hagood she had so little energy at the end of the day that "I just *smear* up instead of cleaning up."[15]

Mexican migrant farm workers found themselves in fierce competition for work with rural families driven off the land by debt and drought. Deported in massive numbers from the United States, which wanted no more responsibility for them now that there was no work, the Mexican population in 1940 was only half of what it had been in 1930 and it was predominantly urban. In rural areas migrant Mexican families often earned less than $100 per year. Although women bore many children, in one California county nearly one in ten infants died. Chicanas remained far less likely to hold jobs outside the home than women in other ethnic groups, but during the Depression their entry into the labor force began to rise. Daughters especially escaped the authority of their unemployed fathers to find work in relief programs or factories.[16]

Despite the stresses of the Depression, the rise in the female labor force did not accelerate previous trends. The continued increase in married women's labor force participation in the face of overt hostility and renewed popular emphasis on domesticity indicates that at least in some families values had shifted. Women worked out of economic necessity. The definition of necessity in the emerging consumer economy was itself changing, particularly within middle-income families. Married women did not withdraw from the labor force once a male income provided enough for subsistence; rather they continued to raise their families' standards of living with a minimum level of household consumer goods such as refrigerators, automobiles, and washing machines, and with increased education for their children. The mold for postwar patterns was already being set.[17]

The Female Reform Tradition and the New Deal

The election of Franklin D. Roosevelt (FDR) in 1932 near the bottom of the Depression signaled a historic shift in women's political roles. The New Deal which his administration introduced transformed Americans' beliefs about the nature and responsibilities of the state. Suddenly the federal government assumed major responsibilities for regulating the economy and for supplying the basic needs of citizens unable to care for themselves—the poor, the unemployed, the elderly, and single mothers. The modern welfare state which had been gradually taking shape since the 1890s came into full bloom, to be subsequently expanded and modified but never dismantled. This not only meant a New Deal for women as recipients, but it was also in many way a *women's* New Deal.

For more than a hundred years, women had painstakingly built a reform tradition on the politicization of domestic concerns and goals. By the 1920s they had begun to institutionalize and professionalize their work in social welfare, education, and health, and to carve out niches in the larger political arena previously barred to them through their organizations—the League of Women Voters, the National Consumers' League, the Women's Trade Union League, and the Women's and Children's bureaus of the Labor Department. Through them, women reformers in the twenties evolved a political agenda based the values of female reform anticipating the welfare state. The training ground in political leadership skills that these organizations provided had prepared a generation of women to assume key roles when their agenda was suddenly also the nation's.

In the 1930s as the nation struggled out of economic depression Eleanor Roosevelt, Frances Perkins, Mary Anderson, Molly Dewson, and hundreds of others, principally social workers, found their concerns for social welfare were suddenly at the forefront of American politics. When Franklin Roosevelt assumed the presidency in 1933, they had an unprecedented access to the corridors of political power both because their skills and knowledge were needed and because Roosevelt's wife, Eleanor, was one of them. Female reformers had already laid the groundwork for a new concept of social responsibility for the poor and the unemployed; now a small but critical network of professionals and activists was in a position to bring their ideas to bear on the emerging shape of the welfare state. The scope of women's role in shaping and executing the New Deal has long been overlooked. There was no vocal women's movement in the 1930s to call attention to their achievements or to claim them as victories. Yet they represented the culmination of more than a century of organized activity on the part of ordinary women, something most Americans had already forgotten.

An exceptional group of women with a common perspective built on shared history and long-term friendships had attained highly influential positions. They were the last generation of women educated in the Victorian world of female social reform networks that had shaped the Progressive movement. Whether married or unmarried, they participated in a wide-flung network of female friends who shared common experiences in settlements and other reform organizations. The mutual support and understanding which these women could supply to one another, both politically and personally, helps to explain their remarkable achievements.[18]

Eleanor Roosevelt was the emotional center of the network. Born into an upper-class family, she had worked in a settlement house and in the National Consumers' League before her marriage in 1905. After bearing five children between 1906 and 1916 she turned in the twenties toward an active political life through the League of Women Voters, the Women's Trade Union League, the peace crusade, and the Democratic party. In politics she established her independence and at the same time became indispensable to Franklin Roosevelt, whose affair with Lucy Mercer had precipitated an emotional crisis and transformed their relationship from a traditional marriage to a political partnership. Politically sophisticated and deeply compassionate, Eleanor Roosevelt used her position as First Lady to gain publicity for groups on the margins of society such as women, the unemployed, and blacks. Her concern for women's rights and access to positions of power was evident. For example, to force many newspapers to treat women seriously, she held regular press conferences to which only female reporters were admitted. There and in her frequent radio shows, articles in women's magazines, and a syndicated column entitled "My Day," Roosevelt talked about the problems of women, children, and minorities. To call attention to the invisibility of unemployed women and the discrimination against them in most relief programs, she held a White House Conference on the subject. Her activity on the part of minorities and the unemployed led thousands of people to write her, telling her their stories, asking for help. And she answered them, sending personal replies to up to fifty in a day, and passing on others to people in agencies and organizations who might be able to help.

Eleanor Roosevelt did not try to speak exclusively on behalf of women, but she understood her audience as being primarily female. Her articles and radio shows reflect a political worldview rooted in domesticity. Take care of your families first, she told women, and included household hints, such as low-cost menus that would have made Catharine Beecher proud. Then, she advised, take the humane and nurturing values of the home into the world to make it a better place. Hers was a more complex, twentieth-century version of Jane Addams's "civic housekeeping." Across the country women hung on her words. Never before had a First Lady spoken out in her own right, nor had people on the margins had someone speak for them from the White House.

The second pillar of this extraordinary group of socially progressive women was Molly Dewson, veteran of the National Consumers' League and an old friend of Eleanor Roosevelt from her days in the Women's Division of the New York Democratic party. Appointed by FDR to head the Women's Division of the Democratic National Committee, she actively organized a grassroots base for the party and through Eleanor fed hundreds of women's names to the president for eventual appointment. Her organizing abilities made women a recognized force in the Democratic coalition. Her persistence had much to do with the placement of women in numerous key positions throughout the administration.

Secretary of Labor Frances Perkins, the first woman cabinet member, a social worker, and former Industrial Commissioner of New York, completed the key leadership in this closely linked network of women in the New Deal. As a young woman she had worked with the Consumers' League and witnessed the Triangle Shirtwaist Fire that in 1911 killed 146 workers, most of them women. Her subsequent career as a professional and as a volunteer, first in New York where she became a close personal and political friend of the Roosevelts and then in the federal government, was devoted to improving the health, safety, and working conditions of American workers. Initially, the labor movement was suspicious of someone whose connections lay primarily with social reformers rather than unions, but they quickly learned that Perkins was a strong and able ally. During her tenure at the Department of Labor, the Women's Bureau headed by Mary Anderson (formerly of the WTUL), and the Children's Bureau under Grace

Abbott (a social worker and protégé of Jane Addams) became hotbeds of female leadership and initiative.

Mary McLeod Bethune, Negro Affairs Director for the National Youth Administration from 1936 to 1944, led a different network of black appointees to administrative posts. Her position as the unofficial leader of the "Black Cabinet" (a group of black officials in federal agencies who advised Franklin Roosevelt on an informal basis) illustrates the narrowness of the women's network at the apex of its power and influence. Bethune, a prominent black educator, founded and served as president of Bethune-Cookman College. She was also a former president of the National Association of Colored Women's Clubs, founder of the National Council of Negro Women, and prominent in numerous other professional and civic associations. Even though she had worked on many of the same issues as white women, the bonds of friendship and shared work followed racially segregated lines. Her network rested on the local and national activities of black women's church groups, clubs, and settlement houses. Her priorities emphasized the issues of racial discrimination more than those of sex. Writing in 1941 this daughter of former slaves described her strenuous responsibilities as president of a college and supervisor of government training programs for sixty thousand black youth. She refused her doctor's advice to slow down, "For I am my mother's daughter, and the drums of Africa still beat in my heart. They will not let me rest while there is a single Negro boy or girl without a chance to prove his worth."[19]

Native-American women leaders remained outside the female political networks of the New Deal though they had gained considerable influence, and leadership training, through women's voluntary networks such as the YWCA and the General Federation of Women's Clubs. Indeed, few Indians of either sex were consulted regarding the dramatic shift in federal policy, called the "Indian New Deal." The Indian Reorganization Act (IRA) transformed government policy from one of overt suppression of traditional Indian cultures to a position advocating respect for tribal autonomy, encouragement of traditional religion and ceremonies, and greater protection for the integrity of Indian lands. Newly developed tribal constitutions, based on white concepts of political participation and civil rights, had mixed consequences for women. In tribes which traditionally excluded women from formal political participation, women gained new rights to vote and run for office

208

as well as encouragement to develop voluntary civic activities (such as clubs, parent-teacher associations, and guilds) like those of white women. From these emerged new female leadership in subsequent decades. At the same time, tribal constitutions overlooked the more traditional female political roles in tribes like the Iroquois where women as a group had deposed chiefs and exercised considerable, if indirect, influence over major tribal decisions. Instead they incorporated white patriarchal assumptions about male-headed families and female dependence which disadvantaged women economically. The Papago tribal constitution, for example, stated that "Every member . . . who is the *head* of a family that does not own any land . . . shall be entitled to receive an assignment of new land."[20]

Through the New Deal, Indian women for the first time had access to education acknowledging their traditional economic roles rather than insisting on training men to do tasks traditionally allocated to women. Director of Indian Education William Beatty claimed in 1942: "Today we are recognizing that in many Indian homes there will be no garden, no chickens, and no goats if the woman doesn't provide them—we are training girls to do these things well." They also received increased access to training for traditionally female jobs outside the reservation such as clerical work and nursing.[21] Thus, Indian women increasingly shared the discriminations as well as the opportunities of women in the majority culture.

With the prodding of Molly Dewson, FDR appointed numerous "first" women not only in the cabinet but also in the judiciary, where Florence Allen was the first woman on the United States Circuit Court of Appeals, and in the foreign service where Ruth Bryan Owen served as the first woman ambassador. More important, women filled numerous key positions in the new relief agencies and in the Department of Labor. Although women did not make many inroads in established agencies such as the Department of Commerce or the War Department, they were well positioned to take advantage of the creation of new agencies to respond to the economic emergency. Most social workers were already women; they simply moved from private agencies and settlements into public service. And, in the first few years of the New Deal when there were few ready-made answers to massive social welfare issues, female reformers had an agenda already prepared.[22]

For a century, women had led in constructing social and institutional responses to the human problems of modern society. By World War I they sought to redefine government as a maternal commonwealth providing protections for the weak and assistance to those in need. In the 1920s they translated their vision into specific proposals for the regulation of labor, health education, and social welfare. The Roosevelt administration, in effect, enacted most of these proposals into law in the creation of the welfare state. Wage and hour legislation, for example, in the National Recovery Administration and later the Fair Labor Standards Act, finally achieved protective legislation for male as well as female workers. Provisions for Aid to Dependent Children, developed in the Children's Bureau of the Labor Department, drew on decades of female experience in settlement houses and private charities. Indeed, the entire concept of social security, government-sponsored insurance for the unemployed, the elderly, and fatherless children, as well as expanded public health programs, could be traced not only to innovations in western Europe but also to the earlier activities of female-led private charities, settlement houses, and the provisions of the Sheppard-Towner Act in the 1920s.

The actual administration of relief programs at the federal and local levels drew intensively on the experience of women. At the same time, those same programs often discriminated against women by refusing jobs to married women, providing stereotypically female jobs such as sewing, and paying women especially low wages. Such programs continued to be premised on the idea that only men needed jobs and relief to support their families; this premise effectively rendered the needs of women invisible.

Social Movements: Activism without Feminism

The achievements of the New Deal must take their place against the broader backdrop of a society effervescent with social movements. Organizations and spontaneous protests sprang up at every level of society generating immense pressure for change. Throughout the decade, women played critical roles in religious, civic, and labor organizations. Their activities were bounded, however, by the changing parameters of public and private. As the Victorian world and values had disappeared, so had the female culture undergirding the women's rights movement earlier in the century. The absence of a movement which articulated women's specific

210

concerns and interests, even as women attained new positions of power, deprived many activists outside the New Deal of the supportive networks of other women as well as a feminist perspective with which to interpret the sexism pervading their lives. In one instance, however, women's organizations provided the base for a cultural challenge, albeit a limited one, to definitions of womanhood. The Association of Southern Women for the Prevention of Lynching, founded and directed by Jessie Daniel Ames, represented one of the last opportunities for women to generate organized power outside the corridors of public political life by drawing on traditional women's networks.

Jessie Daniel Ames, a Texas suffragist and social reformer, had worked with the League of Women Voters in the 1920s on a broad range of social reforms from the Sheppard-Towner Act to equal pay for women, the eight-hour day, mother's pensions, child welfare and child labor laws, peace, prison reform, and public education. She became highly skilled at the league's methods of intensive research coupled with effective publicity. At the same time, she increasingly understood that the political manipulation of racial prejudice continually undermined reform efforts in the south and she turned her activity toward the Council for Interracial Cooperation (CIC), the most important interracial reform organization in the south after World War I.[23]

The women's committee of the CIC was one of the few places where white and black women's networks met and influenced each other. There, black leaders like Mary McLeod Bethune pressed people like Ames to confront the issue of lynching. The illegal killing of blacks by mobs of whites had been an instrument of terror since the nineteenth century, with the approval of white elites who routinely failed to prosecute perpetrators. Southern newspapers publicized lynchings before they happened and continually reiterated the social mythology justifying such crimes in both racial and sexual terms by accusing black men of raping white "ladies." Black women, of course, were far more vulnerable to rape and sexual harassment, but the same mythology portrayed them as promiscuous and society offered them no protection whatever.

In 1930 CIC Director of Women's Work Jessie Daniel Ames led in the creation of a new organization, the Association of Southern Women for the Prevention of Lynching (ASWPL). Closed to blacks from the outset, the organization built its strategy around

211

a carefully orchestrated manipulation of the image of the white southern lady. Most important, they openly repudiated violence carried out in their name. Careful research revealed what black journalist Ida B. Wells-Barnett had shown more than thirty years before: Few lynching victims were even accused of sexual assault and most lynchings were terrorist acts against blacks who encroached on the economic power of white men. They came to understand that lynching not only functioned as an instrument of terror against black men but it also reinforced the dependency of white women and kept them "in their places" as well.

Though Ames had become an activist within the networks of female reform, her principal constituency for the ASWPL lay in the religious networks of organized women, such as the Methodist Women's Missionary Council and the National Council of Jewish Women. Reminiscent of nineteenth-century women's organizing, their method had been to build and use a range of self-consciously female institutions, outside the centers of male political power, through which to implement their values and beliefs. In essence, Ames set out to organize the wives and mothers of the lynchers themselves and to mobilize them to exercise their authority as the moral guardians of the home.

The ASWPL conducted extensive educational campaigns to expose the myths surrounding lynching, and it investigated lynchings, exposed the perpetrators, and forced prosecution. At the state and local levels, the ASWPL extracted pledges from police and elected officials to uphold the law. In the event a lynching was threatened, women would call the newspapers and urge them to avoid sensational and provocative coverage and call or visit the sheriff or mayor to remind him of his pledge. In contrast to the decentralized creativity of nineteenth-century organizations such as the Woman's Christian Temperance Union which allowed local chapters great autonomy in choosing issues and tactics, however, the ASWPL operated in a highly disciplined and centralized manner. Only a few women in each state provided most of the direction and actual work. Others simply signed pledges and responded to a specific call for action when a lynching was threatened.

There is some evidence that their efforts reduced the incidence of lynching. At the same time, their appeals to law and order and their racially segregated membership expressed a social conservatism still bounded by class and race. The ASWPL was a force

212

for racial peace and social order rather than for fundamental social reform. They were unable to accept the political agenda of black leaders in the 1930s who urged federal antilynching legislation. But they offered one of the few grass-roots challenges to cultural stereotypes about women in the 1930s—reminiscent of the WCTU in the 1880s—and they demonstrated the continuing political possibilities of grass-roots women's organizations. That did not happen again until female networks were repoliticized in the late 1960s in a very different manner. The demise of the ASWPL in 1942 signaled the limits of the traditional female subculture as a base for organizing in the twentieth century. Though organizations remained extensive and vibrant, fewer women accepted a uniquely female mission to transform society. As a result, women's networks remained key training grounds in civic and leadership skills, but their focus was narrower, less visionary, and less political.

By contrast, women's participation in the great union drives of the 1930s opened new possibilities for collective activity and changes in the conditions of women's lives. Even though an elite group of social reformers shaped the welfare state, the passion and lifetime commitment that had once characterized the women's rights movement had flowed into radical organizations where "the woman question" remained a secondary issue. The Communist party in the 1930s was at the center of a radical ferment encompassing a wide range of socialist and anarchist groups. Horrified by the human desperation around them and the rise of fascism in Europe, and moved by visions of a world without want, many young people debated the possibilities and mechanisms of change. Within such radical circles there was discussion of "the woman question," but feminism was considered a bourgeois reform in the context of the socialist revolution.[24]

Radical women continued the tradition of the twenties' "feminists—new style" in their determination to combine activism with the roles of wives and mothers. According to Peggy Dennis, a Communist party organizer married to a prominent leader:

> The Communist Party organizational milieu provided little possibility for both, especially in the upper levels of leadership. . . . A woman had to be willing or able to relegate the children to an around-the-clock surrogate parent [and] one had to gamble with the destructive effect that long separations, due to independent assignments in different places, had on wife-husband relationships.

The most prominent women leaders, such as "Mother" Bloor and Elizabeth Gurley Flynn, had "neither children nor a permanent personal relationship" during their tenure. Dennis could have said the same of radical Catholic Dorothy Day, who initiated a religious, pacifist movement for social justice around her newspaper, *The Catholic Worker*. Others, such as Dennis herself or Vera Buch Weisbord, consciously subordinated their own activism to that of their husbands.[25]

Nevertheless, leftists on occasion actively encouraged female leadership when it served their larger goals. And they tried to mobilize working-class women both through union drives and in organizations aimed at housewives. Consumer groups, unemployed councils, and auxiliaries provided new arenas of activism and leadership training despite their limitations.

For example, when Minneapolis Teamsters initiated a trucker's strike in 1934 under Trotskyist leadership, women organized an auxiliary to support the strike. Quickly they found themselves preparing between five and fifteen thousand meals each day using donated foods. Meridel LeSueur walked in off the street and was immediately swept up in the intensity of the struggle and the organizational power of the women. She marveled at the "foreman . . . an efficient stout woman," bawling out "like any mother" a striker who had thrown his coffee dregs out an open window. On Bloody Friday, when police opened fire on strikers, women administered first aid to a stream of wounded men.[26] Yet the organizational efficiency of the women, their willingness to endure harassment, insult, and physical abuse, did not translate into feminist activism. Women mobilized in defense of their families with little or no attention to their own grievances as women.[27] Union leaders wanted that and no more. Trotskyists appointed men to take charge of the commissary and watchdogs to follow the activities of women's committees. At the end of the strike, when an opposition faction appeared to have gained strength among the women, Trotskyists dissolved the auxiliary and the women for the most part accepted the decision without a murmur.[28]

Equally ephemeral but even more exciting was the activity of the Women's Emergency Brigade during the Flint, Michigan, sit-down strike at General Motors Corporation in 1937. While men sat at their machines (the few women workers having been sent out at the outset of the strike), women organized the continual delivery of food and necessities making the forty-four day occupation possible. The Emergency Brigade, under communist leadership, went a step further by breaking windows when police threw tear gas into the building and appearing in their red berets whenever violence threatened.[29]

Even though women played critical roles in the mobilization of communities at the heart of the great union struggles in the 1930s, unions persisted in viewing the organization of female workers as a secondary priority. Women had actually pioneered the industry-wide organizations known as the "new unionism" in the great garment industry strikes that created the ILGWU. When the Congress of Industrial Organizations (CIO) broke away from the AFL in the thirties and set out to organize workers by industry rather than by craft, the new unions welcomed unskilled workers, many of whom were women. Because some of the organizers—especially radicals—were also committed to the equal inclusion of women in organizations and as organizers, the CIO presented the first real opportunity since the Knights of Labor for the mass organization of female workers.[30]

The result was a partial success. By 1940 eight hundred thousand women belonged to unions, an increase of 300 percent over 1930.[31] Yet, for the most part, unions continued to share the view that women belonged in the home, not in the factory. One vice-president of a United Auto Workers (UAW) local, for example, wrote in the local newsletter that "the working wife, whose husband is employed should be barred from industry," but explained that his pledge to enforce the contract seniority clause forced him to defend women workers despite his beliefs. Union priorities emphasized the organization of heavy industry—steel, rubber, and auto—where the labor force was heavily male. Organizers rarely operated with a sensitivity to the specific problems of women workers.[32]

Unions that succeeded in organizing women had to address the complexities of gender, ethnic, and work identities and to mobilize considerable communal and collective resources. As workers women were also mothers, wives, daughters, Irish, Polish, black, Catholic, Jewish, and Mexican. Black domestics organized associations to combat the low wages of urban "slave markets" where women waited on street corners for employers to drive by and make an offer. They succeeded in raising wages but soon disappeared as organizations.[33] Luisa Moreno, an international vice-president of the United Cannery, Agricultural, Packing and

215

Allied Workers of America, was a key organizer of the National Congress of the Spanish-Speaking People in Los Angeles in 1938.[34] For second- and third-generation ethnics, immigrant communities were no longer as closely knit, and the role of the union came to include the revitalization of community in ways providing critical roles for women more often as auxiliaries, however, than as autonomous organizations in their own right.

In southern textiles, women often provided spontaneous and militant leadership in the waves of strikes in 1929–1930 and 1934. The unions, however, rarely sent women organizers or encouraged female leadership. In the tobacco industry the unions were weakened by their inability to overcome the cleavages of race and sex. The fact that meetings were held in male-dominated public spaces and that women workers were doubly burdened with household duties limited women's ability to attend meetings and assume leadership within the union. In addition, unions remained separate from and alien to the community institutions of church and family so central to women's lives and worldviews. As a result, the union failed to include in its demands issues of particular interest to women.[35]

Similarly, the organization of transit workers in New York City remained outside the ethnic, social, and religious institutions primary to women's identities. Because organizers depended on the mobilization of Irish workers through the networks and the rhetoric of the Irish Republican Army (IRA), female workers were not recruited. Rather than using the language of church and family, the union drive relied on military metaphors, reinterpreting Irish political tradition of the paramilitary IRA through the male networks of pub and bar in the Irish community.[36] As a result, the only unit that voted against the Transit Workers was a section of female BMT ticket agents.

Even the progressive and democratic United Auto Workers cooperated in institutionalizing a separate labor market for women with separate, lower pay scales. Preexisting practices such as separate seniority lists for women and men, job segregation, and wage differentials were written into local contracts.[37] Meanwhile, industrial unions that had not organized office and clerical workers, raided office worker unions when women organized themselves.[38]

The consequences of the unions' failures to address working women's particular concerns and needs shaped women's subsequent place in the labor force and the labor movement. Many radical women, having been fired from professional or manufacturing work for their union activism, were locked into clerical jobs. In line with their commitments to labor organizing, they led in the formation of three office workers' unions within the CIO. Yet, their work continually received secondary priority, and successful locals in major industries were readily handed over to industrial unions instead of remaining affiliated with a clerical workers' union. When all three clerical unions were purged from the CIO in 1950 during the anticommunist scare, the key sector of the female labor force was left firmly outside the ranks of organized labor.[39]

In all of these cases female leadership lacked a base in an organized community of women committed to women's priorities and concerns. As a result they suffered individual defeats without resort to broader networks, and they could not build their minor victories into more concrete changes in the position and power of women as a group. Unions remained male dominated, and cultural assumptions about women and work remained limited and mired in stereotypes.

In 1941 women entered the war, still on the margins of the labor force, not allowed to compete for most jobs, often paid less even for exactly the same work, and rarely unionized. Thus, the ironies and paradoxes of women's political roles in the thirties multiplied. Within the Democratic party, women became a grassroots force for the first time. The openness and experimentalism of the New Deal and the presence of Eleanor Roosevelt in the White House allowed a key group of women reformers powerful ways to reshape the state along the lines of politicized domesticity. The expanded state, however, also redefined the meaning of "public," separating it from roots in citizen activism in local communities and infusing it with the values of efficiency, rational planning, and control by experts.

A female community and sense of mission based on middle-class domesticity could no longer flourish, and the mass movement for which it had provided a base no longer existed. In the absence of a movement specifically devoted to women's rights and a feminist critique of gender roles, radical women and labor organizers

217

found it difficult to manage multiple roles and assert the importance of women's needs; thus, the striking achievements of women within the New Deal were rapidly erased from memory. And so, although some women were powerful in the thirties, women as a group were not empowered.

10

10

Women at War
The 1940s

Terrible conflicts had raged in Europe and Asia since 1936. While diplomatic maneuvers kept the United States out of combat, the immense industrial power of the country began to move slowly back into gear and out of a decade of depression. As the specter of economic instability receded a bit, marriage and birthrates spurted ahead, and life became easier for many women and their families. Then the Japanese attacked Pearl Harbor on December 7, 1941. In a single stroke the wars abroad entered the lives of American women and men alike and transformed them irrevocably.

The massive mobilization for World War II politicized daily life on a scale never before seen. Women's most mundane activities were suffused with nationalistic fervor. They saved and recycled metal toothpaste tubes and tin cans; rationed short supplies of meat, sugar, and gasoline; stretched food supplies with "victory gardens"; volunteered at the Red Cross or the Civil Defense agency; bought war bonds; deferred consumer purchases; joined the armed services; and entered the labor force in unprecedented numbers. As in previous wars, activities once viewed as inappropriate for women suddenly became patriotic duties for which women were perfectly suited.[1]

The War Years: 1941–1945

The most powerful, immediate effects of the attack on Pearl Harbor and President Roosevelt's call for a Declaration of War were the surge of patriotism and the creation of new jobs. At the end of the 1930s, 25 percent of American workers remained unemployed, but now suddenly jobs were everywhere. Employers scrambled to find enough workers at the same time the government drafted young men into the armed services. Manpower was at a premium.

As jobs appeared in industrial centers, people flocked to them, creating overnight housing shortages and insurmountable domestic difficulties. Half the southern agricultural labor force migrated to cities. In these overcrowded and alien environments, most often women had to figure out how to set up homes in novel circumstances. Harriet Arnow in her novel *The Dollmaker* portrayed an Appalachian woman who, in her native countryside, could handle ánything. Tall, strong, and creative, she planted and plowed, cooked on a wood stove, carved wooden pieces, and shared a rich fantasy life with her youngest daughter. When her husband took a job in the auto industry in Detroit, Michigan, though, she found herself uprooted, in a new landscape with different cultural and physical realities. Suddenly she had to cope with economic dependence, the cramped spaces of prefabricated housing, the purchase rather than the production of food, unfamiliar appliances that rendered her skills obsolete, school bureaucracies, and the gradual loss of her children to a new culture she did not share. Her experiences matched those of thousands of migrants moving across the United States, uprooted by national mobilization and unable to use their traditional skills.[2]

A revived economy and wartime realities generated new patterns of marriage and childbearing. Nine months after the Selective Service Act passed in 1940 with a provision to exempt fathers from the draft, there was a sudden spurt in the birthrate. Even when the exemption was withdrawn, rates stayed high as young people married in great numbers, casting their lot with an uncertain future.[3] The "good-bye" babies resulting from these marriages represented the first wave of a baby boom that reached new heights after the war's end.

Well-schooled in voluntary activities, women responded in massive numbers to the social needs of wartime society. Three million of them volunteered with the Red Cross. Others drove ambulances and spotted airplanes for the Civil Defense, served food and entertained soldiers at USO canteens, sold war bonds, and organized their domestic tasks around the needs of the economy for scarce materials. As men began to leave civilian life, women took up the slack, assuming responsibility for families as well as for mobilizing the community for victory.[4]

Soon, however, the country needed women to do more than volunteer with the Red Cross or buy war bonds. By 1942 the economy had absorbed available supplies of male workers and there was widespread recognition that only the employment of women could meet industrial demand. U.S. Employment Service surveys reported marked shifts that year in employers' willingness to hire women. Between January and July, employers raised their estimates of the proportion of new jobs for which women would be acceptable from 29 to 55 percent.[5] One of the primary reasons given for refusal to hire women was the opposition of male workers who periodically walked out rather than work with, or for, a woman.[6] However, with fewer men in the factories and increased demands for industrial output, employers saw fit to tap the pool of female workers.

By 1943 *Fortune* magazine noted, "There are practically no unmarried women left to draw upon. . . . This leaves, as the next potential source of industrial workers, the housewives." That was even more disturbing than hiring single women. As *Fortune* put it: "We are a kindly, somewhat sentimental people with strong, ingrained ideas about what women should or should not do. Many thoughtful citizens are seriously disturbed over the wisdom of bringing married women into the factories."[7] If employers and co-workers were reluctant, so were many women. Although large numbers of women were clearly eager for well-paying jobs, many—especially those with children—faced practical obstacles. Some were unsure about the social ostracism they might encounter for crossing the boundary from acceptable female to decidedly male domains.

To entice women into the factories while allaying anxieties about the consequences of change, the government mounted a major propaganda campaign aided and abetted by the active cooperation of the media and industrial advertisers. Indeed, the mobilization of women for industrial work illustrates an extraordinary degree of governmental intervention in the economy and in molding values and attitudes achieved during the war. Through the War Production Board, the administration determined what would be produced and how scarce resources would be used. The War Manpower Commission allocated the labor supply. The War Labor Board intervened in labor disputes to prevent strikes or other disruptions. And the Office of War Information coordinated publicity and propaganda campaigns. Once the War Manpower Commission decided to recruit female workers, including married women, the War Labor Board indicated its intention to rule that women working in previously male jobs should be paid at the male rate, and the Office of War Information generated recruitment posters and pamphlets and established guidelines for fiction, features, and advertising in the mass media. The response was immediate.

"Rosie the Riveter" became a national heroine, gracing magazine covers and ads that emphasized women's civic and patriotic duty to work in the defense industry in no way undermined their traditional femininity. In Seattle, Washington, Boeing Aircraft placed large ads urging women to come to work. They displayed "pretty girls in smart slack outfits showing how easy it is to work on a wiring board."[8] Propaganda films such as *Glamour Girls of '43* assured women that industrial tasks and machines mimicked household work:

> Instead of cutting the lines of a dress, this woman cuts the pattern of aircraft parts. Instead of baking cake, this woman is cooking gears to reduce the tension in the gears after use. . . . After a short apprenticeship, this woman can operate a drill press just as easily as a juice extractor in her own kitchen.[9]

Similarly, a group of 114 electric companies extolled the "modern magic" of electricity: "She's 5 feet 1 from her 4A slippers to her spun-gold hair. She loves flower-hats, veils, smooth orchestras— and being kissed by a boy who's now in North Africa. *But, man, oh man, how she can handle her huge and heavy press!*"[10]

Labor shortages affected the military as well, and from the outset of the war women's organizations demanded that women be allowed to serve their country. The result was the creation in 1942 and 1943 of women's branches in the army (WACs), the navy (WAVES), the Coast Guard (SPARS), and the marines (MCWR) in addition to the army and navy nursing corps. Close to three hundred fifty thousand women served in these various branches and an additional thousand flew commercial and air force transport planes for the Women's Airforce Service Pilots (WASP). As in the case of women in industry, glamorized servicewomen appeared everywhere in the media, looking for all the world like Joan Crawford or Katharine Hepburn with their squared shoulders and sophisticated smiles. In another version these "girls" or "gals" peeked prettily out from under their sailor hats, looking too cute to be threatening. A Sanforized ad in 1942 epitomized the latter with a headline "Maidens in Uniform" and the following verse:

> Oh, aren't we cute and snappy
> in our cover-alls and slacks?
> And since the tags say "Sanforized"
> we'll stay as cute as tacks![11]

In retrospect, such reassurance seems excessive. The breakdown in the sexual division of labor was clearly limited to the war effort from the start. In the armed services women's work sustained the traditional values and labor force segregation of the civilian world. Most women worked in clerical and supply areas or as nurses. Each of the services avoided placing women in positions where they might give orders to men and prohibited overseas duty as long as they could (1943 for WACs and 1944 for WAVES). They also prohibited the enlistment of women with children, actively persecuted lesbians, and segregated black women.

Similarly, though women entered manufacturing industries in large numbers, many new jobs such as riveting and wiring aircraft were simply redefined from male to female work. Women were hired in far greater numbers in light industry than in heavy, and they often found themselves confined to entry-level and lower-skilled positions. In addition, many areas of growth were in jobs like clerical work and teaching previously defined as female. As the numbers of female clerical workers grew by 85 percent they dominated the field more than ever, raising their proportion of all clerical workers from 50 to 70 percent. A nationwide teacher shortage induced many localities to withdraw prohibitions on the employment of married women thus increasing the numbers of female teachers as well.[12]

Discrimination against women in traditionally male blue-collar jobs continued in spite of the crisis. Employers were reluctant to invest in training women for skilled work, as they presumed women workers were only temporary. And for the most part, they flatly refused to hire black women. When they tried to lower the wages of women workers holding formerly male jobs, however, unions protested vigorously. Even if unions were less than enthusiastic about their new female members, unions were unambiguous about protecting the wages they had fought for and they worried that lower wages for women might create an incentive for industries to retain female workers after the war. As a result they waged the first effective battles for equal pay for equal work.

Practical obstacles lay in the paths of most working women as well. Critical shortages of housing and transportation limited their options. Government agencies in Washington, D.C., for example, suddenly expanded their clerical labor force to meet wartime demands. In 1942 the Pentagon opened with office space for 35,000 workers, the largest office building in the world. Yet as thousands of young women flooded into Washington, D.C., to fill clerical jobs in the swelling federal bureaucracy, they doubled and tripled up in shabby boardinghouses and tiny rooms, unable to find decent places to live. Their conditions, however, were probably easier to bear than those of industrial workers' families crushed into prefab housing and tiny apartments in places like Detroit and Mobile. Single young women on government wages quickly learned the value of cooperative housekeeping. "The result was a whole collection of strangely-bonded female groups."[13]

Mothers of small children found virtually no help. When the Federal Works Agency finally decided in 1943 to fund day-care centers for defense workers, their efforts met only a tiny proportion of the demand. Newspapers ran stories of infants locked in cars parked in employee lots, young children shut up in apartments most of the day, and juvenile delinquents. Local communities tried to address the problems. More than 4,400 communities had established child care and welfare committees by the summer of 1943, but their efforts paled in comparison to the need. Most women relied on family members, but a Women's Bureau survey in 1944 found that 16 percent of mothers in war industries had no child-care arrangements at all.[14] The federal government never considered measures like those in Britain which relieved the double burdens of working mothers with time off for shopping; extended shopping hours; and restaurants offering inexpensive, take-home prepared food. As a result of these stresses, women workers' absenteeism was 50 percent higher than that of men and their turnover was twice as high.[15]

Nevertheless, the government campaign to fill defense needs with women workers was hugely successful. Six million women who had never worked outside the home joined the labor force during the war years while millions more shifted from agricultural, domestic, or service work to industrial work. Their profile represented a marked shift toward older and married women from the traditional young and single worker, and most of them did not want their new status to be temporary. When questioned about their future intentions, women in defense industries indicated an overwhelming preference for retaining their jobs after the war.[16] If the stresses of managing home and workplace were acute, the gains were also real. For the first time, women had access to high-paying industrial jobs requiring specialized skills and affording status. Black women, though blocked from higher-level industrial jobs, began to enter the female jobs which had previously been virtually all white, such as clerical work and nursing, and significantly reduced their reliance on domestic service. In Detroit in 1942 and 1943 black women demonstrated for jobs and housing with the support of the UAW. Two busloads of women finally stormed a Ford plant to call attention to discriminatory hiring. Perhaps most important, half the rural black female labor force left the countryside and found employment in cities.[17]

From the beginning, business owners and government planners worried that women might not willingly give up higher paying industrial jobs once they had access to them. Some managers consciously tried to hire the wives of the servicemen they were replacing, "reasoning that the women will not be reluctant to yield their jobs to their own husbands."[18] Surveys of women workers confirmed planners' fears.

Shipyard worker Katherine Archibald described the constant resentment of men in the shipyard where she worked. From overt harassment in the beginning, men retreated to "a vague and emotion-charged atmosphere" in which women were always suspect of sexual improprieties. And they regaled one another with anecdotes proving that women were unsuited for the work: " 'Take a look around at the women and what they're doing,' one disgruntled workman urged. 'From one end of the hull to the other they're jawing or prettying up their faces or bothering some man and keeping him from his work.' "[19] The Minneapolis *Tribune* editorialized in August 1942, "WACS AND WAVES and women welders. . . . Where is it all going to end? . . . Is it hard to foresee, after the boys come marching home and they marry these emancipated young women, who is going to tend the babies in the next generation?"[20]

Government and media propaganda consistently reassured

Americans that while women would do their civic duty for the duration, they would certainly return to their traditional roles once the emergency was over. Ads that praised working women also emphasized the temporary nature of their positions. The Eureka Company, for example, noted women's many contributions to the war effort including filling over 70 percent of the positions on their own assembly lines "for the duration. But," the ad continued, "a day is coming when this war will be won. And on that day, like you, Mrs. America, Eureka will put aside its uniform and return to the ways of peace . . . building household appliances."[21]

Unions reflected the prejudices of their constituents, especially fears that women would displace male workers at lower rates of pay. In the beginning, unions objected strenuously when women were hired, frequently to the point of going on strike.[22] "Women don't know how to be loyal to a union," said a skilled craftsman. "They're born, and they grow up, dirty dealers. There isn't a straight one among 'em."[23] Once the War Labor Board announced its intention to rule that women must be paid at male rates for the same work, unions expressed their willingness to support women workers and accept them as members. Because unions began to see organizing women as the key to protecting jobs and wage rates in previously all male work settings, and because the War Labor Board protected labor's right to organize, the unionization of women as well as men made enormous strides during the war. The number of organized women grew between 1940 and 1944 from eight hundred thousand to three million, and the female proportion of organized labor from 11 to 23 percent.[24]

Even though popular culture extolled the adventures of strong female heroines, its messages were always mixed. Middle-class journals were most likely to present women as assertive, proving that they were as good as any men. In the pages of the *Saturday Evening Post*, for example, women appeared as welders, engineers, executives, and taxi drivers, heroically claiming their own capacities against the doubts and denigration of men around them. In actuality, female adventure and achievement represented little threat for middle-class men because women were being recruited either into female-dominated white-collar positions or into blue-collar industrial work.[25] For working-class women, however, the complexities were more serious. They faced hostility from men in their own communities who were threatened by the loss of prerogatives at work as well as authority in their homes.[26]

In pulp magazines like *True Story*, fictional female war workers' happiness rested not on their achievements but on stoic willingness to continue unrewarding work for the larger goal of victory. Boring assembly-line work, for example, took on new meaning when imbued with patriotism: "The noise of the factory [became] an articulate voice, saying: more planes, more planes, more planes— we're making them, we're building them, we're sending them out." Status in *True Story* fiction still depended on a romantic relationship with the right man.[27] Advertisements in such magazines sustained women's consumer roles, imbuing everything with a gendered, domestic patriotism. In 1942 a columnist in *True Romance* quoted Ruth Merson, a "well-known corset designer and stylist," on the necessity of corsets in wartime: "Right now with the country embarking on its gigantic task of self-preservation it is essential that the women of America do not let down their men. Women must keep up the morale of their men and still continue to be their guiding star. To this end they must be their trim and shapely selves."[28]

If wartime patriotism had gendered meanings and class dimensions, it also aroused racial prejudice especially toward Japanese-Americans. In 1942 Franklin Roosevelt, responding to fears of a Japanese fifth column on American shores, signed an order removing Americans of Japanese descent from west coast states to inland relocation camps. They were allowed to bring only what they could carry, and many sold their houses and businesses at a great loss. They experienced the terror of the refugee—uprooted, deprived of control over their destiny—and the humiliation of implied disloyalty. Many were Nisei, American-born citizens. Their Japanese-born parents, the Isei, had been prohibited by law from becoming naturalized citizens. Women generally fared better than men because they were able to pursue their traditional roles in the camps and were, therefore, more resilient. Domestic tasks remained to be done while productive work outside the home did not exist. At the war's end, however, these women and their families had to begin anew to build their lives despite bitter hardship and hurt.[29]

The war, a time of vastly expanded centralized planning and control of individual lives, witnessed the final transformation of the birth-control movement from an insurgent, feminist movement to an established and accepted organization. In 1942 the Birth Control Federation of America under the leadership of Margaret Sanger changed its name to the Planned Parenthood Federation of America. Its new reformist orientation emphasized family stability rather than individual freedom, utilizing the bureaucratic language of scientific, rational social planning and familial welfare.[30] At a time of unprecedented governmental mobilization and control of both economic and social life, this shift seemed so logical that it went virtually unremarked.

The theme of sexual liberation, relatively submerged during the Depression years, reemerged among young people whose economic autonomy and separation from their home communities offered unprecedented opportunities for experimentation. Men in the military, urban teenagers, and women war workers discovered a new freedom that many found irresistible. "When I was sixteen I let a sailor pick me up and go all the way with me . . . mainly because I had a feeling of high adventure and because I wanted to please a member of the armed forces." For young men, such attitudes were a kind of heaven. "Where I was, a male war worker became the center of loose morality. It was a sex paradise." The intensity of wartime emotion contributed to short-term affairs, "The times were conducive for this sort of thing," as well as to sudden marriages.[31]

Less visible to most Americans, World War II represented a turning point in the birth of a self-conscious homosexual identity among lesbians and gay men. The slow development of an urban gay subculture in the twenties and thirties had touched the lives of only a few. On the eve of the war most homosexuals remained isolated in a hostile culture. But just as heterosexual women and men found that the war diminished the authority of traditional norms and expectations, so also homosexuals discovered that World War II had "created a substantially new 'erotic situation' conducive both to the articulation of a homosexual identity and to the more rapid evolution of a gay subculture."[32]

For lesbians the war created a dramatically different situation in two ways: First, the women's armed services recruited primarily young, unmarried women providing an all-female environment in which intimate, erotic relationships could grow despite official prohibitions. Indeed, at the height of the war the army was distinctly uninterested in losing personnel or generating unpleasant publicity. As a result, "for a time, many [homosexual] women in the military enjoyed a measure of safety that permitted their sexuality to survive relatively unharassed."[33] Second, the fact that women visibly dominated so many public places, whether for work or recreation, provided a new safety for lesbians. They could meet each other without fearing that their presence in an all-female environment labeled them deviant. One result was that lesbian bars began to appear in cities all over the country, no longer confined only to the largest and most anonymous urban centers.[34] In effect, specifically lesbian spaces were created that, though always threatened and vulnerable, provided the necessary conditions for group identity.

The Postwar Years: 1945–1949

At the end of the war women knew that they, as well as men, had made victory possible. The outpouring of energy and patriotic emotion had given a new dimension to citizenship and to their sense of self. Yet there was no way to institutionalize such emotions when public life itself was so thoroughly dominated by the state. The political focus of wartime activity had only one purpose— victory. There was little to debate either about means or ends. Only military and technocratic experts could know what was needed to mobilize and direct the massive resources of America. Women's duty was simply to respond, to do what was necessary "for the duration," and to maintain the family as the essential foundation for democracy.[35] As a result, the exhilaration of wartime communal effort had neither structural nor ideological support for continuation after the war. At the same time, the changes, even if temporary, were shocking and deeply unsettling, and their consequences must be read far into the postwar era.

As men were mustered out of the army, women were mustered out of the factories; both were sent home to resume increasingly privatized lives. What the war had accomplished, with a reinvigo-rated economy and pent-up consumer demand, was a new expectation that most Americans could enjoy the material standard of living promised by the consumer economy in peace. The purpose of work outside the home was to procure the resources to sustain this standard of living (which now included a private house; appli-ances such as a refrigerator, stove, and vacuum cleaner; and a car). The female task was to oversee the quality of this private life, to purchase wisely, and to serve as an emotional center of the family and home.

The principal obstacle to this vision, however, was the possibility that women might not choose to play their publicly condoned role. Anthropologist Margaret Mead wrote at the end of the war that the media's "continuous harping on the theme: 'Will the women be willing to return to the home?'" reflected widespread anxieties. A returning serviceman was likely to wonder, "Will she have learned to be so independent that she won't want to give up her job to make a home for me?"[36]

Articles addressed to women warned them about the care they must exercise to support the egos of returning men. One marriage counselor suggested women should "let him know you are tired of living alone, that you want him now to take charge." Others emphasized the "feminine" qualities returning vets valued including "tenderness, admiration, or at least submissiveness."[37] Even before the war ended the pressure to quit began. "In the great factories, the ominous sound of the old saw, 'A woman's place is in the home,' is heard above the music now piped into the workrooms to make conditions more attractive for the still badly needed women workers," wrote A. G. Mezerik in the *Atlantic*.[38]

The UAW Women's Bureau held a conference for women union leaders in April 1945 to discuss the postwar situation. Union women expressed great concern that seniority must operate in a nondiscriminatory way so that women would have equal opportunity when postwar layoffs came. Two delegates reported that their unions had surveyed women workers regarding their work needs. "In one shipyard, 98 percent of the women want to continue working in shipyards or at least continue working in those skills which they have been able to pick up there. Many of them worked in service industries before the war." Another survey in a New York manufacturing industry indicated that 82 percent of the women intended to continue working. The report of the conference noted that "several delegates proposed for labor in general a program to show that women are not just a temporary wartime group." They shared stories of struggles within unions, many successful, to win and enforce equal pay for equal work. But they earmarked for future work ongoing concerns about the wage gap between women and men due to the fact that "women work on jobs historically women's or in separate women's departments where rates are traditionally lower."

Some suggested that a job evaluation system analyze skills and experience in such a way that different job categories could be compared.[39] Both the ideas and the techniques for "comparable worth," an issue which would not emerge full grown until the

1980s, were present in this discussion.[40] But the principal concern expressed in this meeting and by writers, such as Lucy Greenbaum in the *New York Times Magazine,* was for women who would still need to work after the war. Greenbaum wrote in April 1945, "All organizations working with and for women in industry expect that pressure will be brought to bear on the married women to stay at home and mind the children. In war she heard promises; peacetime will be full of prohibitions."[41]

Greenbaum was right. Even if four out of five industrial women workers preferred to keep their jobs, few had much choice. When military orders ceased, industries shut down to prepare for reconversion, laying off women workers. For a moment unemployment was high again and everyone feared the return of the depression. Plants reopened rapidly, however, and for the most part they refused to rehire women regardless of their skills or seniority rights. In the Detroit auto industry after the war, the proportion of women in the work force fell from 25 to 7.5 percent and women's share of work in durable goods industries throughout the nation dropped 50 percent.[42]

Women who went to the U.S. Employment Service were incredulous to discover that the only jobs available to them paid only half what they had made in war industries. Skilled industrial jobs were no longer open to them. One union organizer reported that the U.S.E.S. in her area told women, "No, these jobs are for men; women can't do them."[43] As one woman complained: "They say a woman doesn't belong behind a factory machine or in any business organization. But who will support me, I ask? And who will give my family the help they have been getting from me? No one has thought to ask me whether or not I need my job."[44]

Women fought back, staging picket lines protesting their exclusion. But they met with little sympathy or support even from their unions, and often they found themselves blamed for their situation. Margaret Pickel, dean of women at Columbia University, said women's own shortcomings accounted for their loss of jobs. She charged that as workers they had proved to be emotionally unstable, to "lack the gift for teamwork," to "have no gift for finality," and to "lack the corporate loyalty that makes for effective unionization." While advocating the view that "marriage and sensible motherhood are probably the most useful and satisfying of all the jobs that women can do," she nevertheless characterized "marriage mortality" (i.e., women quitting work when they marry) as "women's greatest handicap." Flaying women with the cultural stereotypes their employers and male co-workers held, Pickel accused them of being "unprofessional" and displaying "a weakness for the personal." As a result, "they do not age well. By middle age, when men are at their best, a devoted woman worker is apt to degenerate into a strained fussiness or worse."[45] The nastiness of Pickel's charges was not typical, but it was not uncommon either as women once again provided easy scapegoats in a time of anxiety and change.

So, many women returned to the home only to be confronted by the economic challenge of postwar prices. The dramatic inflation that doubled many prices in the months after wage and price controls were lifted brought strong protests from women. In New York, when hamburger rose from thirty-five to seventy cents per pound, Women's Trade Union League leaders organized a coalition to stage a meat boycott advising women not to buy meat for more than sixty cents a pound. For a time they succeeded as store after store advertised "specials" for fifty-nine cents.[46]

Women's protests were sporadic and unconnected, however. The leadership came primarily from trade union women who had only minimal support within their labor unions. Though Congress almost passed the ERA in 1941, women's social reform networks in the federal government had been relatively forgotten during wartime priorities and had atrophied further as the Truman administration focused on America's new role as a global power in the postwar world. Remnants of the early-twentieth-century feminist movement such as the National Woman's Party remained small and relatively isolated. The ERA had gained further support during the war from groups like Business and Professional Women and the National Federation of Women's Clubs; even Eleanor Roosevelt had been converted. Many of the old-line women's groups such as the League of Women Voters consciously shunned "women's issues" to avoid the appearance of being a self-interested special interest group as well as ideas considered distinctly marginal and out-of-fashion. Even though the league remained an important training ground for women leaders, it operated within an understanding of citizenship that was issue-oriented, consciously isolated from political parties, and focused on the informed individual. The national agenda emphasized peace, prosperity, and domestic security. This was not the environment in which a feminist movement could grow though it prepared leaders who would play key roles when a movement re-emerged. Only a few spaces remained where the ideals of women's rights and female equality could be kept alive. Among the most important of these were the Women's Bureau of the United Auto Workers and the continued activities of the YWCA and other religious women's organizations.

Several unions, most notably the United Electrical Workers and the United Auto Workers, had actively organized women during the war, holding special women's conferences and employing greater numbers of female organizers. Within the UAW a network of women convinced the executive board in 1944 to create a Women's Bureau within its war policy division. Under the interracial leadership of Mildred Jeffrey and Lillian Hatcher, the Women's Bureau spearheaded efforts to ensure equal pay and seniority rights, supported measures such as child care, and protested the expulsion of women from the auto industry during reconversion (despite the acquiesence of most male union leaders).

After the war, UAW women leaders decided that "to be classified forever as a female worker was hurting the working woman . . . because there were many jobs that were tagged male occupations that women could perform as well as any other person."[47] At the 1946 UAW Convention, the Council of Women Delegates asked for "increased attention and aid . . . to the status of women workers." Specifically they condemned the classification of jobs as male or female and the existence of separate seniority lists. In response to their demands, the executive board made the Women's Bureau a permanent part of their Fair Practices and Anti-Discrimination Department. In effect they created an institution that could build networks among working women, offer leadership training, and develop strategies for change. No other group of working women "owned" an institution in the same way from which they could launch a campaign for working women's rights.[48]

With few exceptions, middle-class women's organizations remained firmly within boundaries defined by class and race. The UAW Women's Bureau is notable not only for its advocacy of working-class women but also for its interracial leadership from the beginning. When the National Council of Negro Women under the leadership of Mary McLeod Bethune initiated an interracial coalition of women's organizations called the Co-ordinating Committee for Building Better Race Relations, the principal participants were women's religious organizations, the YWCA, and the National Women's Trade Union League. The League of Women Voters, Business and Professional Women, and the American Association of University Women, despite their deep roots in female reform, remained unwilling to challenge racial discrimination or to participate actively in interracial coalitions. In limited and halting ways the YWCA and religious organizations provided ongoing spaces where white and black middle-class women could rethink the meaning of womanhood across cultural, racial, and class boundaries.[49]

Women at the Crossroads

In the postwar era American women were at a crossroads. The entry of married women into the labor force since the 1920s had been a constant source of controversy. Now it was approaching the norm. During the same time, a new definition of the housewife's role—child-centered, consumer conscious, and fully responsible for all housework—had begun to take shape. The undertow of anxiety about the consequences of this dual change erupted in the immediate postwar period in an acrimonious debate in which traditional views of female domesticity were strongly reasserted.

In part the dominance of traditional attitudes about women's roles reflected the pessimism that permeated the atmosphere in the late 40s. People had lived through fifteen years of war and depression. Celebrations at the end of the war were haunted by images of the Nazi death camps and the shadow of the atomic bomb. The magnitude of human evil and the potential for global destruction were hard to comprehend even after a war in which millions died. VE and VJ days had barely been celebrated when a new threat loomed, the onset of the cold war. Soon the Truman foreign policy was governed by hostility to Russia, defense of Western Europe from Russian expansion, and an aggressive assault on "subversives" within the United States.

If women were praised during the war years for taking up men's jobs and carrying on the war at home, they were criticized for failing to raise their sons properly. Republican motherhood, in the view of some critics, no longer defined women's mission. Early in the war, Americans were shocked to learn that many young men were physically or mentally unfit for service in the

234

military. In the ensuing discussions "Mom" took most of the blame for the physical and emotional weaknesses of the young men who failed to pass the entrance tests for the armed forces as critics expressed growing unease about changes in women's roles. In the middle-class world of consumerism and abundance, they charged, women had lost a sense of duty and turned instead to emotionally devouring their children, especially their sons. "Momism" was the term coined to describe this failure. Writer Philip Wylie argued in 1942 that since women attained the vote the world had witnessed rising corruption, degeneration, depression, chaos, and war. "I give you Mom," he said, "I give you the destroying mother."[50] A military psychiatrist, Dr. Edward A. Strecker, echoed Wylie's sentiments in 1946, charging that "Mom" had too often failed to cut "the emotional apron string," leaving sons immature and mentally ill.[51]

More sympathetic social scientists debated what they saw as the "dilemma" of the modern woman. Sociologist Mirra Komarovsky proposed that college women were caught between the "feminine" role which presumed that women were "not as dominant, or aggressive as men" and the "modern" role which demanded similar behaviors and virtues of both women and men. Margaret Mead noted that both women and men were "confused, uncertain, and discontented with the present definition of women's place in America." This disturbance, most pronounced among the best educated women, took two forms: discontent with the social role of housewives and confusion about whether to define themselves principally as persons or as women.[52]

Della Cyrus, a social worker, proposed that modern society had failed to make "motherhood satisfying or even bearable to mothers themselves." She criticized the practice of educating women "to be interested in and responsible for the needs and problems of their world" and then isolating "them in houses as soon as they become mothers." She proposed that communities needed to develop plans "to end the isolation of individual mothers and children." Interestingly, Cyrus was one of the few to discuss women's relationship to the broader community. Although the debate centered on women's proper roles at home and in the labor force, the question of women's civic responsibilities (or conversely the responsibilities of communities for family life and domestic burdens) were rarely discussed except to the degree that women's failures in traditional domesticity were perceived to have harmful social consequences. Despite criticisms such as Cyrus's, the presumptions of a radically privatized domesticity that sharply separated women, the home, and family life from the public arena appeared triumphantly persuasive at least to the *Atlantic*'s readers.

When the *Atlantic* held a symposium of responses four hundred readers replied, "most of them furious with Mrs. Cyrus." Rhona Ryan Wilber charged that Mrs. Cyrus's ideas were

> dated. . . . She smacks too much of feminism and the selfish twenties to find any echo in the hearts of most of the young wives of my acquaintance. I suspect that the war brought a change of feeling to most of us who got married during those sad years. . . . We like this business of running a home after a few years of contemplating what life would be like without our husbands.[53]

Life magazine entered the debate on women's place in 1947 with a series of articles offering a variety of viewpoints. A pictorial essay about young housewife Marjorie McWeeney expressed some of the ambiguity of domesticity in the postwar world. She appeared with a broom in her hand, surrounded by images of her week's work: "35 beds to make; 750 pieces of glass and china, 400 of silverware to wash; 175 pounds of food to prepare; 250 pieces of laundry to handle." Though she proclaimed herself happy with her lot, *Life* noted that many consider it a "life of drudgery."[54] A *Fortune* poll in the fall of 1945 demonstrated strong majorities of both women (57 percent) and men (63 percent) believed that married women whose husbands earned enough to support them should not be allowed to hold jobs even if they wanted to work. When the phrase "with no children under 16" was added some months later, the proportions dropped to 38 and 46 percent.[55]

In view of such attitudes, it is not surprising that following the war the women who left the labor force altogether were predominantly young women, the same cohort that participated in the demographic phenomena of rising marriage rates and baby booms. Older married women found themselves forced into lower-paying, female-dominated jobs, but they refused to withdraw altogether. A new pattern of intermittent labor force participation, once characteristic of working-class women, was becoming normative for the middle class despite cultural admonitions to the contrary.

In the chilled atmosphere of the cold war, unions and a wide variety of progressive organizations were suddenly suspect, forced to prove their "patriotism" by expelling anyone suspected of communist sympathies. The CIO drove from its leadership many of those who had built the organization, even purging entire unions including three unions of clerical workers. In such an atmosphere, women demanding significant changes in their traditional roles were suspect as well. The WTUL disbanded in 1950 declaring that its goals had been accomplished. Civil-rights activists and radical unionists joined other reformers upset with these new directions to prompt a split from the Democratic party and support the candidacy of Henry Wallace under the banner of the Progressive party. Harry Truman, however, deftly manipulated widespread anticommunist sentiments to win an unexpected victory, and the politics of red-baiting was in full swing, with the family as a bulwark against the threat of communism. Republican motherhood took on a new twist.[56]

The public political arena, now defined as the province of government and increasingly run by large-scale bureaucracies, had lost the gloss of civic virtue it had during the war. Voluntary support activities which had flourished during the war quickly evaporated. Voluntary associations such as suburban churches took on the sentimentality associated with domesticity and private life, far removed from civic and political overtones. Anticommunism and the sudden awareness of the dangers of the nuclear bomb reinforced the notion that only experts really knew how to manage an international scene that failed to deliver the peace for which everyone thought they had fought and sacrificed. And conservative pressure on progressive organizations made activism and visionary protest subject to immediate charges of subversion.

The sense of danger, within and without, accompanied deep yearnings for security and stability at the end of the war. As author Betty Friedan put it, "We were all vulnerable, homesick, lonely, frightened. A pent-up hunger for marriage, home, and children was felt simultaneously by several different generations; a hunger which, in the prosperity of postwar America, everyone could suddenly satisfy."[57] The consequence was the ferocious pursuit of private domesticity. Marriage rates and birthrates skyrocketed. The marriage rate peaked in 1946 at 118 per 1,000 women fifteen years and older compared to 79 per 1,000 women in 1926.[58] The median age at first marriage fell over the course of the decade from 21.5 to 20.3 for women and from 24.3 to 22.7 for men. With the support of the GI bill, college campuses were suddenly

237

flooded with veterans and their families, many living in "Victory Villages" of tiny prefabricated housing. These new families continued to have babies at an astonishing rate (see Table 1).

TABLE 1

Birthrate per 1000 Women
15–44 Years Old

	White	Nonwhite
1930	87	106
1940	77	102
1945	83	106
1950	102	137
1955	113	155

SOURCE: U.S. Bureau of the Census, *Statistical Abstract of the United States: 1960,* 81st Edition (Washington, D.C.: U.S. Government Printing Office, 1960), Table 57, p. 56.

Middle-class young mothers discovered that, where their parents had been advised to adopt a strict regimen of "scientific" child rearing, by the mid-1940s the content of child-centered family life had changed. With the advent of permissive child rearing advocated by psychologist Arnold Gesell and popularized by Dr. Benjamin Spock, mothers operated with fewer rules and greater responsibilities. The mother was urged to watch and follow her child's inclinations, moods, and needs; to avoid setting strict rules and boundaries for fear of stifling its development. The problem, of course, was that such attention and care often made it impossible to accomplish other domestic tasks. And they reinforced reliance on psychologists and pediatricians who were taking to the air waves and media to preach their creed.

This highly emotion-charged domesticity, less focused on the couple than on the family unit, was powerfully reinforced by leading ideologues who linked the privatization of women within the family with social tranquility. Just as the cold war began to dominate American policy, Marynia Farnham and Ferdinand Lundberg argued in *The Modern Woman: The Lost Sex* that only a return to the traditional home, "a social extension of the mother's womb," could reclaim "women's inner balance" and reduce the level of hostility in the world.[59] According to their popularized

238

"Freudian" analysis, virtually all social problems were products of neuroses. Because women were primarily responsible for the home and for child rearing, where most neuroses originated, women were the basic cause of most social problems. They attacked feminism as "a deep illness" rooted in penis envy, and set out to locate the essence of female nature and female sexuality in motherhood. "The rule is: the less a woman's desire to have children and the greater her desire to emulate the male in seeking a sense of personal value by objective exploit, the less will be her enjoyment of the sex act and the greater her general neuroticism."[60]

Between the attacks of social critics and the advice of experts, women experienced extreme pressures to take their patriotic and public activities of the war years back into the enclosed safety of motherhood and the home. The home, in turn, as bulwark against communist subversion and aggression gained new political meanings as the cold war progressed.[61] Yet simple withdrawal was not possible, as evidenced by the continued growth of the female labor force soon after the war.

The impact of World War II on women cannot easily be measured in the immediate postwar era. Other wars such as the Civil War and World War I had clearly broadened the boundaries of acceptable behavior for men and women and had hastened changes already in process such as suffrage, but their impact on women's status—their culturally defined roles—remained similarly ambiguous and ephemeral. The American Revolution had the most powerful symbolic and culturally formative impact on women prior to the twentieth century. That war, concerned with the definition of public life and the citizen, created new republican political consciousness and practice. Women, like men, found themselves engaged in political struggles and acts despite the solidly masculine military. And male politicians wrestled with the problem of whether women who acted thus were citizens and, if so, in what sense. The result was the powerful new ideology of republican motherhood that acknowledged women's political engagement but contained it within the ideal of motherhood. Women's political work was the rearing of good citizens.

The context for women in World War II was vastly different from that of their revolutionary foremothers, though each war was understood to have been fought to preserve liberty and overthrow tyranny. By the mid-twentieth century public life had come to be defined by the growing activities of the state. Where women during the Revolution had spontaneously organized boycotts and petitions, governmental control of both media and economy during World War II ensured efficient use of voluntary energies. There was little discussion of the political meaning of women's changed participation in public life, only assurance that it would be temporary. Women lacked collective, public spaces within which to redefine themselves as a group in relation to society or to critique a social order that simultaneously called on them and restricted their possibilities. Many traditional women's organizations remained bounded by class and race, unable to achieve a broader vision of women's needs.

Millions of women left the labor force, voluntarily and involuntarily; the women who stayed represented an increase in labor force participation consistent with previous trends. In other words, one could argue that the war itself made little difference. Ideologically, wartime propaganda justified the erosion of gender boundaries "for the duration" and no more. The intense pressure on women to return to domesticity coincided with the wishes of a younger cohort of women and men to focus on their private lives. This privatization promised a dramatically new level of isolation within the family as bulldozers began to reshape the landscape in preparation for growing suburbs.

At the same time, there were some long-term consequences of the changes in women's behavior during the war. Even though the trends the war exaggerated, toward the employment of older, married women, were clearly in place before the war, only the expanding economy created during and after the war could have allowed those trends to continue. As a result, the war removed some of the legal and cultural barriers to the employment of married women. Laws, for example, against married women teachers were removed in several states, and the equal pay for equal work standard was adopted by many unions and by eleven states.[62]

However, World War II also witnessed the end of an ascendant women's network that had operated within the New Deal and the beginning of an era as hostile to reform as the twenties had been. Mobilization for war marginalized women in the administration along with their reform agenda; the Truman administration, which began in 1945, lacked both links and sympathy with female reformers. Individuals, however, continued to make their marks.

240

Appointed to the U.S. delegation to the newly created United Nations, Eleanor Roosevelt turned her attention to the global problem of human rights. When the General Assembly passed the United Nations Declaration on Human Rights in 1948, it gave her a standing ovation in recognition of her central role in its creation.

As older networks faded, newer ones began to take root. New generations in the YWCA and women's religious organizations indicated greater willingness to challenge racial barriers. The creation of a permanent women's department within the United Auto Workers meant that despite the death of the WTUL there would be an institution keeping alive the concerns of working women and preparing a reform agenda until the 1960s. In this sense, as in the case of female labor force participation, the war was a turning point, the intersection of long-term trends.

The longer-term consequence of a generation of women shaped by their wartime experiences, like that of their predecessors seared by the Great Depression, can only be inferred, but its importance should not be underestimated. The mothers of the baby boom generation experienced a moment of independence and cultural validation (whether personally or vicariously) during the war years; this may well have shaped the mixed messages they gave their daughters who loudly proclaimed the rebirth of feminism two decades later and politicized daily life once again with the slogan "the personal is political." In between, however, lay the contradictory and illusion-filled decade of the 1950s.

241

11

The Cold War and
the "Feminine Mystique"

*I*n 1947 when Christian Dior introduced the New Look, American women were horrified. Instead of simple, loose-fitting, square-shouldered attire reminiscent of the war era, he proposed a dramatically new silhouette. Skirts dropped to within inches of the floor; waists were sharply defined and tightly belted beneath well-defined bosoms. Resistance to the new fashion was rather short-lived. Femininity was back—along with foundation garments that could add or subtract where necessary to achieve the prescribed shape.

With the New Look, American women provided a visual symbol of their exit from the male industrial labor market and of the renewed emphasis on polarized images of femininity and masculinity. Lowered skirts hinted at maturity and meshed with the somber mood of the country. The postwar world would not emphasize girlish experimentation as much as the security of family life to which mothers were central. If women continued to work, as many did though no longer in traditionally male jobs, they struggled alone to balance the demands of jobs with family and community life and to conform to cultural images of femininity at the same time. As a postwar recession kept economic fears alive, cold war insecurities grew with every news report. In 1949 the Soviet Union exploded an atomic bomb, making atomic war a possibility. And China "fell" to a communist revolution. The House Committee on Un-American Activities warned Americans that communists and subversives lurked in the very heartbeats of their communities, their schools, setting off hysterical witch-hunts among teaching faculty. In 1950 North Korea invaded South Korea and very soon the United States was at war again.

Cold War and Warm Hearths

The red scare accompanying the onset of the cold war powerfully shaped the political mood of the postwar era. The radical effervescence of the thirties gave way to scapegoating and pressures to conform. Unlike the briefer red scare following World War I, however, cold war rhetoric and attacks on "subversives" led by figures like Senator Joe McCarthy had marked sexual overtones. Mixed in with deep cultural anxieties about global politics were fears about the changing place of women and changing sexual norms. The association was not, on the surface, evident, but it can be detected in the rhetoric that conflated these very different anxieties.[1]

The House Un-American Activities Committee published a pamphlet to warn people about the dangers of the communist conspiracy to conquer and rule the world and particularly about the "deadly danger" of communists in the schools. Explaining why school teachers (presumably mostly female) constituted such a dangerous population, the pamphlet quoted John Hanna, a Columbia University professor: "The girls' schools and women's colleges contain some of the most loyal disciples of Russia. Teachers there are often frustrated females. They have gone through bitter struggles to attain their positions. A political dogma based on hatred expresses their personal attitudes." The committee asserted that based on its files, "the Communists have always found the teaching group the easiest touch of all the professional classes."[2]

This scapegoating of women existed in the context of a right-wing resurgence characterized by a politics of victimization and powerlessness. Right-wing organizations such as the newly formed John Birch Society and in the south the Ku Klux Klan and White Citizens' Councils preyed on and dramatized widespread anxieties about cultural change. Defensive and parochial, they practiced a politics of division and exclusiveness, attacking anyone outside the norms of white middle-class culture. Nostalgically appealing to an imagined past in which men were men, women were women, and community leaders freely enforced rigid standards of morality,

244

right-wing demagogues urged a retreat from social or communal problem solving into privatized conformity. It should not be surprising, then, that they linked fears of communists, subversive of the traditional family and, therefore, of the social order.

Cold war rhetoric added a dimension of sexual fear. Anticommunism meshed with homophobia in a campaign to purge public employment and the military of "sexual perverts." Lesbians and rumored lesbians were summarily dismissed from the armed services as "undesirable." Police harassment of gay and lesbian bars became commonplace. And Senator McCarthy demanded that the government seek out and fire all homosexuals. Guy Gabrielson, national chairman of the Republican party, sent an alert to party workers warning that "sexual perverts" who were "perhaps as dangerous as the actual Communists" had "infiltrated our Government in recent years." A subsequent Senate investigation report in December 1950 concluded that "one homosexual can pollute a Government office." Yet "even the most elaborate and costly system of investigating applicants for Government positions will not prevent some sex perverts from finding their way into Government office."[3]

More covert was the generalized fear of sexuality. One Harvard physician's analysis of the consequences of atomic war, published in the *Journal of Social Hygiene*, emphasized social and sexual disorder as a primary concern of public health professionals in the event of an attack. Without "drastic preventive measures" he suggested that venereal disease would increase 1,000 percent and that prostitution, promiscuity, and drunkenness would be rampant.[4] More often than not, the sexuality that was threatening was female, as in the cold war metaphor for sexy women: "bombshells."

At the same time, in their proper place, women symbolized safety and security not only for families but also for the globe. In an article for *Atlantic Monthly* entitled "Women Aren't Men," Agnes E. Meyer put it this way: "Women have many careers but only one vocation—motherhood. . . . It is for woman as mother, actual or vicarious, to restore security in our insecure world."[5] Prescriptions for teenagers betrayed anxieties imbedded in admonition. In "How to Be a Woman," *Seventeen* magazine told the young woman that she was "a partner of man . . . not his rival, his enemy, or his plaything. Your partnership in most cases will produce children, and together you and the man will create a

haven, a home, a way of life for yourselves and the children."
The contrast, then, lay between rivalry or enmity, and a family-
centered haven. After extolling the "exciting career" of wife and
mother, the article concentrated on advice designed to prevent
what apparently was the principle obstacle to such a future: premarital sex.[6]

Through the fifties, however, anxiety gave way to optimism.
The enormous strength of the American economy following the
war, boosted by the Korean War and sustained military spending
afterward, generated an expanding economy further stimulated
by pent-up consumer demand. Visions of material progress born
in the late nineteenth century and reshaped in the twenties to
emphasize consumption and pleasure reigned triumphant. Burgeoning suburbs absorbed not only middle- and upper-middle-
class but also working-class families as rising incomes placed home
ownership within reach of nearly 70 percent of Americans.[7] Family
formation hit new highs, evidenced statistically in a rising propensity to marry, falling marriage ages, and soaring birthrates.

The dominant optimistic mood (later reflected in nostalgic views
of the fifties such as the TV series "Happy Days") turned anxieties
on their head, purging complexity and denying change. Capitalism, pundits declared, works for the benefit of all. Political com-
mentator Walter Lippmann noted "We talk about ourselves these
days as if we were a completed society." And sociologist Seymour
Martin Lipset echoed, "The fundamental problems of the industrial revolution have been solved."[8] Faith in technological progress
coupled with economic growth led many to predict an end to
social divisions such as class and to ideologies based on such divisions. Some even predicted that soon there would be no need
for welfare. The dominant domestic ideology, known to a later
generation as the "feminine mystique," which defined women
almost exclusively in terms of wife and mother, functioned
smoothly both to shape changes in women's roles and to deny
their disruptive power.[9]

The feminine mystique defined women's place in the postwar
family-centered, prosperous, middle-class life-style. It wedded prewar ideas about the centrality of homemaking and motherhood
to more popularized versions of Freudian sexuality to produce a
sexualized and modernized version of republican motherhood.
This version, however, was not very politicized, for politics had
retreated either to the simple act of voting or to the activities of

246

distant governmental experts. Citizens had become "private citizens." The duty of the modern mother was to create a warm haven, a happy family life, a goal *McCall's* defined in 1954 as "togetherness." As such, the fifties mother maintained the home as a bulwark of social stability rather than a training ground for future citizens. She also joined in a wide range of community activities as an extension of this domestic vision. Indeed, women's participation in organized activities hardly diminished in the 1950s despite their depoliticization. Church groups, PTAs, the YWCA, branches of the League of Women Voters, and women's clubs of all sorts flourished in cities, towns, and suburbs. In the new suburbs, women assumed the role of community builder as they had done in numerous frontier towns, providing the organizational energy behind new churches, schools, park systems, and libraries that, when institutionalized, rarely placed women in positions of institutional control.

It would require a redefinition of politics and of citizenship to draw women's activities away from the sidelines of political life even though they continued to sustain the grass-roots organizations on which politicians relied. Women occupied less than 5 percent of public offices, even locally. Social scientists advocated a division of labor that reserved for women the "expressive functions" of emotion and nurture. Political life was associated with the "instrumental functions" of wage earning and public activity allocated to men. Indeed, in 1952 when the Democratic party abolished its Women's Division, it provided a powerful manifestation of the disassociation of women and private life from politics. The Women's Division had been source of strength and autonomy for Democratic women. Party leaders called their action a "reorganization" that would integrate women's activities into the party structure. India Edwards, Director of the Women's Division, was made a vice-chairman of the Democratic National Party and Director of Women's Activities, but she no longer had a staff. The same year, the Republican party announced a similar restructuring.[10] Behind the scenes women continued to work within the political parties through the 1950s, pressing for increased representation, but their efforts remained invisible and only marginally effective.[11]

Lessening anxiety about whether women would stay (and be happy) within their prescribed roles affected material and popular culture as well as expert pronouncements. By 1950 women's fashions retained the longer skirts of the New Look but had shifted to the "baby doll" image with full skirts over layers of crinoline petticoats. Movie stars no longer offered independent and assertive alternatives. Girl-women, they varied from the silly, fluffy characters played by Doris Day and Debbie Reynolds to the sexy but innocent Marilyn Monroe. Coquettish, pleasers of men, they were a far cry from the assertive presence of earlier stars like Katharine Hepburn or Joan Crawford.

The feminine mystique limited male anxieties about changing female sexuality by prescribing the boundaries of change. In the 1950s women could—even should—be sexual (a return to Victorian denial of female sexuality was not possible), but they could not be in control. Freudian popularizers no longer encouraged the independence of the single girl as they had in the twenties. Rather, they redefined sexuality in terms of motherhood. Marynia Farnham and Ferdinand Lundberg asserted in 1947 that "The woman needs to have in her unconscious mind the knowledge that for her the sex act, to yield maximum satisfaction, terminates only with childbirth or the end of the nursing period."[12]

Thus at the same time that birth control had become standard practice for the majority of the population, experts took great pains to reassert the essential link between female sexuality and reproduction. Similarly, advertisers linked sexual attractiveness with marital prospects: "She's engaged! She's lovely! She uses Pond's!"; "Camay, for skin that says, 'I do!' "[13] The unspoken fear, of course, was that by detaching sexuality from procreation, birth control was likely to facilitate nonmarital sexual encounters, as indeed it did. But popular wisdom calmed such anxieties with ditties and aphorisms that portrayed marriage as the inevitable consequence of love.

Within marriage the experts encouraged a new sexual norm, the simultaneous orgasm. Even though Marie Robinson's best seller, *The Power of Sexual Surrender,* described female orgasm as "a sensation of such beauty and intensity that I can hardly think of it without weeping," she and others used Freudian categories to describe women's sexual experience as essentially passive. Anais Nin wrote in her diary about the two kinds of orgasm—the "immature" clitoral versus the "mature" vaginal orgasm—according to psychoanalysts and novelist D. H. Lawrence: "One [vaginal] in which women lay passive, acquiescent and serene. The one orgasm came out of the darkness miraculously dissolving and invading.

248

In the other [clitoral] a driving force, an anxiety, a tension . . . confused and unharmonious, cross currents of forces, short circuits which brought an orgasm that did not bring calm satisfaction but depression."[14] By 1959 Marie Robinson could dismiss all women who reached orgasm via the clitoris as frigid. It did not matter that Alfred Kinsey had pointed out in his 1953 study that the vagina had few nerve endings or that the most sexually satisfied group he interviewed were lesbians. The result was that many women struggled with definitions that denied their own physiology.[15]

The Kinsey Report in 1953 demonstrated, however, that behavior was changing quite apart from prescriptions. Approximately one in four college women engaged in premarital intercourse and a strong majority of them expressed no regrets. By quantifying both acceptable and forbidden behaviors as forms of "sexual outlet" Kinsey began a process of demystification. His attack on the idea that homosexuality was pathological provided affirmation for many lesbians and contributed to a long process of attitudinal change.[16]

Architecture gave spatial expression to the intensification of domesticity. Suburbs emphasized the privatization of family life. Pastoral, separated from the conflicted public realms of work and politics, suburban houses no longer segregated formal and informal or male and female spaces as older Victorian homes had done. Rather, in the popular California ranch house the walls of the kitchen became counters and open spaces. Integrating women's primary workspace into other active areas of the household, particularly the increasingly popular family room, home design personified the togetherness of the family unit.

By the later fifties, the tone of celebration in the mass culture presumed that the argument over women's place had been won. In a special issue about American women in 1956, *Look* magazine editors waxed ecstatic about "this wondrous creature" who "marries younger than ever, bears more babies and looks and acts far more feminine than the emancipated girl of the 1920s or even '30's. Steelworker's wife and Junior Leaguer alike do their own housework." Older arguments seemed beside the point as she began to find "a new true center, neither Victorian nor rampantly feminist. Today, if she makes an old-fashioned choice and lovingly tends a garden and a bumper crop of children, she rates louder hosannas than ever before. . . . If, by contrast, she chooses

249

to take six to ten years out for family, then return to the work for which she was educated, no one fusses much about that either."[17]

Cultural Contradictions

The very economic expansion facilitating this sense of material well-being and self-satisfaction also generated conditions that would undermine it. The revised American dream of a high-consumption-, pleasure- and leisure-oriented society appeared to be possible for most Americans. In their zeal to consume, however, few recognized at first the new problems that would soon overtake them. In a thousand ways, middle-class Americans denied the reality of social changes rapidly eroding old ways. Ideas about domesticity and womanhood were part of this broader pattern.

While the *Saturday Evening Post* portrayed on its covers the dense social relations of small-town America, the most rapid population growth was taking place in a new environment, the suburbs. Women in suburban families, especially housewives with young children, found themselves in a female ghetto as public and private spaces resegregated along geographic lines. Some enjoyed the company and support of other young mothers. Twenty-nine-year-old Eileen Moore described for *Look* the easy visiting patterns and trading of equipment and advice in her Chicago suburb. In addition, she and her husband enjoyed having a neighborhood where everyone was new on the block and close to the same age. That way they avoided the snobbishness and the "get ahead of the Joneses" competition of older suburbs.[18]

Middle-class women often found themselves caught up in a frantic round of volunteer activities and carpooling. Indeed, the station wagon became symbolic of a suburban life-style organized around children's expanding social and cultural opportunities and activities. If her husband were an upwardly mobile corporate executive, she shared his "two-person career" by providing useful social contacts and proper entertaining. *Life* described the "achievements" of one such wife whose husband earned $25,000 a year (nearly four times the median). Marjorie Sutton cooked and sewed clothes for her four children, worked with the Campfire Girls and the PTA, did charity fund-raising, sang in the choir, entertained fifteen hundred guests a year, and exercised on a trampoline "to preserve her size 12 figure."[19]

Most suburban housewives' husbands earned far less than Marjorie Sutton's, however. And these housewives found such demands more difficult to meet. Untold numbers were cut off from extended networks of kin and friends who traditionally had offered support and solace. They were burdened with housework whose standards rose with every new appliance and product and whose performance bore little relation to material rewards. In such circumstances, many experienced isolation and loss of self-esteem. Now that most houses had electric washing machines, standards of cleanliness and quantities of clothing escalated. Advertisers offered a variety of products guaranteed to get laundry "whiter than white" and showed women eyeing one another's clotheslines competitively over back fences. Ad agencies quickly realized that guilt and feelings of inadequacy were easily manipulable. Cake mix manufacturers found that their product gained popularity after they removed the eggs from the mix. Women felt too guilty to serve cakes that required only the addition of water. Once they could add their own fresh eggs and associated warm cakes with family love rather than time off, women began to use cake mixes in great quantities.

The problem remained that no one was sure that housework was really "work" in a culture and an economy which consistently measured value with dollar bills. By the late fifties the pressures of consumption-oriented domesticity allowed advertisers to shift their appeals back to time saving, especially when the drudgery of housework could be replaced with emotion-centered family activities: "Clean and shine pots and pans faster, have more time for *family fun,* spend less time in the kitchen." In another ad, a mother in her scout leader's uniform closed the door of her Kitchenaid dishwasher as father and Cub Scout son waited at the door. "More time for living" read the text.[20]

Such domestic scenes were uniformly white and middle class, for suburbs had also effected a new racial and economic segregation of American society. The rural poor, many of them black, moved to the cities as more affluent whites moved to the suburbs. There blacks joined communities of ethnic blue-collar workers who could not afford or did not want the novelty and the uniformity of suburbia. Growing numbers of female-headed households among the urban poor—at a time when social scientists such as Seymour Martin Lipset glibly declared that "the fundamental problems of the industrial revolution have been solved"—evoked moral condemnation rather than social concern.[21] Female single parents, especially the never-married, had no place in a world that saw itself through the television lens of "I Love Lucy," "Father Knows Best," and "Leave It to Beaver," nor did the poor, racial minorities, or working-class ethnics, whose relative invisibility allowed them to be dismissed and ignored by the popular culture.

As the geography of urban spaces divided along class, race, and gender lines, the mass media provoked further cultural fragmentation. Television entered 5 million new homes per year with a powerful capacity to generate cultural norms and present a homogenized image of middle America that blurred differences of ethnicity and class. Differences along the lines of gender were perhaps the most powerful social division recognized and enforced in this portrayal of American life as relentlessly white and middle class. Daytime television replaced the old radio soap opera programming aimed at women, providing ongoing socialization into the mysteries of domesticity. At the same time, popular music and the medium of radio shifted toward more specialized audiences along lines of race, class, and age as well. Urban black culture offered an audience for commercial music rooted in jazz, gospel, and rhythm and blues. Simultaneously white youth forsook their parents' musical tastes with the birth of rock and roll that borrowed heavily from rhythm and blues. The shocking and sensuous pulsations of rock and roll (represented most powerfully by Elvis Presley) marked a new stage in the evolution of youth culture and the emergence of sexuality into commercial mass culture.

Popular culture based in a consumer economy depended ironically on the massive growth of the female labor force that allowed millions of families to enter the amorphous "middle class." Women provided the most important source of new workers throughout the fifties, providing half the total growth in the labor force. In contradiction to privatized images of family life and the glorification of motherhood, white married women with children entered the labor force at an accelerating rate. From 1950 to 1960 their labor force participation rate grew from 17 to 30 percent.[22]

Economists explain such shifts with reference to supply and demand. In fact, there were powerful forces at work creating jobs for women (demand) and women who wanted jobs (supply). On the demand side, the reestablishment of labor force segregation following World War II ironically reserved for women a large proportion of the new jobs created in the fifties due to the fact that the fastest growing sector of the economy was no longer

252

industry but services. The service sector, in turn, generated jobs already established as appropriate for women. Clerical work; lower-level jobs in education, health care, and social services; waitress and housekeeper jobs in hotels; airline stewardesses; and sales clerks all had become associated with women's traditional serving and nurturing responsibilities in the home.[23]

Clerical workers increased their predominance among working women with the growth of huge corporate and government bureaucracies. Education expanded so rapidly in response to the baby boom and urban growth that retaining prejudices against married women teachers proved impractical. Nurses found new opportunities as well as new problems in an expanding health industry. Hospitals replaced private duty as the locus of most nurses' employment. Placed under the direct supervision of physicians and hospital administrators, many nurses felt robbed of autonomy and artisanal pride, but hospital employment was more secure and jobs were plentiful. New divisions of labor resulted in paraprofessions for nurses aides and Licensed Practical Nurses (LPNs). Within hospitals nurses began to develop specialized expertise associated with cardiac, obstetric, and intensive care wards. Female nurses also discovered new bonds of solidarity with other nurses while working together as a team on hospital wards, and they initiated informal methods of resisting doctors' authority.[24]

As jobs opened for women workers, there was no apparent hesitation as the women, most of them married, seized these opportunities. Long-term factors had shaped the increasing availability of married women through the twentieth century. Women lived longer and had fewer children—despite the baby boom, the long-term trends remained clear. They also married younger and concentrated their childbearing in the early years of marriage. Together, these changes resulted in a new post–child-rearing life stage, relatively free of child care responsibilities. Most women lived in urban areas, the location of most new jobs. Increased educational opportunities and a rising propensity to marry had sharply reduced the supply of single working girls. Young women were likely to move straight from school to marriage expecting to work until they had children and possibly again when the children were older.[25]

Such expectations reflected a shift in values under way since the 1930s and accelerating in the 1940s. Educated, middle-class married women were taking the path pioneered by their black and working-class counterparts, combining work inside and outside the family home. Highly educated married women began to demonstrate a greater tendency to work outside the home in the 1940s, in part because many of the new jobs required significant literacy skills and special training. Then in the 1950s the link between husbands' income and female labor force participation began to change. In 1950 the less a man earned, the more likely his wife would be employed. Through the 1950s and 1960s, however, this pattern gradually changed until by 1968 the wives most likely to work were married to middle-income men.[26] Indeed, married women in middle-income families entered the labor force faster than any other group in the population through the 1950s and 1960s. Although women in very low-income families continued to work outside the home in disproportionate numbers, it appears that many working-class families, capable of living on a single wage for the first time, chose to live out the values of domesticity glamorized by the popular media.[27]

The powerful forces of supply and demand meshed with the values of booming consumer capitalism to generate an ideological shift that justified women's new roles. The definition of what was essential had expanded to include home ownership, automobiles, refrigerators and other appliances, televisions, and college educations for children. Thus many families felt the urgent need for a second income for only with that could they enter the "middle class." As long as this second income was defined as secondary and dispensable (regardless of the actuality) it could be acceptably earned by a woman (wife). If women worked to "help out" the family, they were no longer violating social convention. As *Look* put it in 1956: "No longer a psychological immigrant to man's world, she works rather casually, as a third of the U.S. labor force, and less toward a big career than as a way of filling a hope chest or buying a new home freezer. She gracefully concedes the top job rungs to men."[28] Similarly, after reveling in the "achievements" of a housewife, the beauty of young women, and the delights of motherhood, *Life*'s 1956 special issue on women offered a picture essay on working women which visually emphasized numbers, sameness, and passivity. Nurses and teachers, for example, could easily have been depicted on the job, exercising authority and creativity. Instead, they appeared as large audiences, listening impassively to lectures from male experts. Similarly, in a typing pool 450 women were shown pounding away on identical machines. A line of chorus girls presented the only active image of working women.[29]

If popular culture accepted women's work outside the home, then, it did so in a way that validated a segmented labor force. It also denied the economic or psychological importance of jobs for the women who held them and masked the continuing realities of discrimination and denial of opportunity. Professional, clerical, and blue-collar women chafed at this reality, but there were few environments in which they could move beyond individual grievance or find a shared language with which to challenge cultural assumptions.

Female Organizations: Fragmented Publics

Indeed, as the public economy assumed many serving and nurturing tasks in health, education, and personal services traditionally associated with women, and as large numbers of women worked outside their homes, traditional boundaries between public and private spaces no longer made much sense. This erosion of the boundaries, however, did not allow the feminine mystique to become an ideological base for female self-assertion in the way that its nineteenth-century predecessor, the cult of true womanhood, had done. There was no strong sense of public or civic life where women could put into practice the values of domesticity, nor were those values easily expressed in communal terms. Thus Adlai Stevenson's exhortations to women to take up the banner of republican motherhood in a commencement address at Smith College in 1955, only reemphasized the isolation of the housewife. He began with a recognition that women "feel frustrated and far apart from the great issues and stirring debate for which their education has given them understanding and relish. Once they wrote poetry. Now it's the laundry list." Nevertheless, Stevenson urged that a woman could perform her political duty by inspiring "in her home a vision of the meaning of life and freedom . . . help[ing] her husband find values that will give purpose to his specialized daily chores . . . [and] teach[ing] her children the uniqueness of each individual human being."[30]

The fact was that even middle-class women no longer shared a sense of female "mission." The aging remnant of the National Woman's Party illustrated the irrelevance of its tradition. Sharing a powerful sense of sisterhood rooted in early-twentieth century images, they sustained a tight network providing ongoing support for members. Their daily lives and their work wove together in a seamless web of community that allowed them to buck the tide of the mid-twentieth century and to lobby relentlessly for the Equal Rights Amendment guaranteeing women legal equality under the Constitution. Their perspectives, however, were shared by few others and their community was not a free space within which younger women, raised in a different time, could build from their own inheritance to a new sense of possibility. A close-knit and self-enclosed group, they had neither the language nor the method to reach out.[31]

Yet the blandness of the fifties' domestic ideology and cold war conformity masked new signs of discontent and change. Although most women experienced problems as individuals, collective activity within a wide variety of groups in the population signaled possibilities which would surface in subsequent decades. Working-class women, for example, experienced continuing discrimination based on traditional stereotypes. Union leaders, uniformly male, generally shared traditional attitudes toward women and were only gradually pushed to work against gender discrimination. Their hostility to the ERA and defense of legislation protecting women workers led to a public posture that emphasized female weakness and difference. The demise of a broad female reform coalition which had undergirded Progressivism and laid the groundwork for the New Deal had severed the links between working- and middle-class reform-minded women. Working-class women had few environments in which they could define their own problems or work for change. Two exceptions to these patterns are notable because they illustrate the conditions necessary both for women to develop a shared agenda and to push effectively for change. In the very different circumstances of New Mexico's salt mines and the United Auto Workers' Women's Bureau, women did just that.

In 1950 Chicano miners in New Mexico went out on strike protesting unsafe conditions and wage cuts at the Empire Zinc Company. In their isolated mining village, the employers owned everything including the workers' houses. Women, who were the backbone of the village community, had long complained about the poor conditions of company shacks lacking such basics as hot running water. They knew very well the importance of the strike for the safety of their husbands and brothers and for their own livelihoods because there were no opportunities for women to earn money. They also understood the terrible consequences of a prolonged or lost strike. Their own dependence led many to respond reluctantly at first to the strike announcement.

As the community mobilized, however, the women began to ask why family needs for decent housing were not included in the strike demands. The men laughed. How ridiculous. Didn't they understand what was really important here? The tables turned, however, when an injunction forbade miners from picketing and the company trucked in strikebreakers to take their places. Women, whose leadership skills had been honed invisibly in churches and on front porches, stepped forward and took over the picket line. Suddenly, men found themselves home, feeding children, changing diapers, and washing clothes (without hot water) while their women faced the police. Men were not on strike any more. The community was. Women, empowered by their experiences, found a unique free space on the picket lines and in the packed jail cells. The jailer hardly knew what to do with cells full of singing women and crying babies. When a young woman complained that her baby needed formula, not milk, the women chanted "We want the formula" until the walls rang. Cowed, the jailer agreed to go and get it. With a new sense of their own rights, women returned home to face men who also understood in a new way the legitimacy of their demands. Their story was immortalized just a few years later in the film *Salt of the Earth,* in which many villagers played themselves. The film was suppressed, however, as part of a Hollywood purge of suspected "subversives."[32]

In a very different way the female staff of the United Auto Workers' Women's Bureau developed an agenda for change through the fifties. Because of their institutional position, they received complaints and appeals from women throughout the international union, and they began to see broad patterns which challenged union orthodoxy. In particular, they became aware of the ways in which protective laws were used to discriminate against women. Unrealistic restrictions on hours or weight-lifting kept women out of higher paying jobs and limited their promotions. For example, simply by adding a single instance of lifting over the prescribed weight limit a company could change a job from "female" to "male."

The record of the UAW in the 1950s was a limited one, however.

With some success the Women's Bureau opposed discrimination against married women, but attempts to eliminate separate seniority lists and job classifications based on sex won little favor. Because the Women's Bureau worked to increase women's participation in ways encouraging loyalty to the union local without facilitating women's own solidarity, the national office's growing awareness of pervasive discrimination and unequal pay was not widely shared. Nevertheless, the UAW Women's Bureau provided a key environment in which the realities of work for women in industry could become visible, the need for change articulated, and future leadership trained. No other union provided such a space.[33]

Tiny seeds of self-organization sprouted among lesbians in the 1950s as well. The heterosexual and family preoccupations of postwar culture had reemphasized the deviance of lesbians leaving them simultaneously more self-conscious and more vulnerable. On September 21, 1955, Del Martin and Phyllis Lyon, a lesbian couple living in San Francisco, held the founding meeting of the Daughters of Bilitis (DOB), named for a poet who was supposed to have lived on the Greek island of Lesbos in the time of the lesbian poet Sappho. Dissatisfied with bar culture and with relationships they believed mimicked male/female roles, DOB founders sought to create "a home for the Lesbian. She can come here to find help, friendship, acceptance and support. She can help others understand themselves, and can go out into the world to help the public understand her better."[34]

The DOB participated with other homosexual organizations in a movement to change public attitudes and advocate homosexual rights. Always aware of the specific needs of lesbians, many of whom were mothers or trapped in heterosexual marriages, they refused to become subordinated to male-dominated organizations. The constituency of DOB remained small, primarily professional women who could afford the risks and who disliked the working-class ambience of bars. Most lesbians remained isolated and socially marginal, but their invisibility to the culture and to themselves was beginning to fade.[35]

Black women also began to take on more visible roles working for change. Those who had tasted equality during the war were reluctant to return to the wages and demeaning personal relations of domestic work. With their families they moved in massive numbers into cities, sharing the rising expectations generated by the expanding economy and increasingly looking for their rights as citizens and Americans. More than any other wives, married black women worked outside the home. They had built a collective tradition of activism within the black church, and as school teachers they instilled a new generation of black children in the urban south with racial pride that could withstand the daily humiliations of segregation. Again and again in the stories of rising racial protest through the fifties, women appear in key roles.[36]

The moment many see as the birth of the civil rights movement came in the fall of 1955 in Montgomery, Alabama. Rosa Parks, a seamstress, churchgoer, secretary of the local NAACP, and beloved community member, boarded the city bus feeling bone-weary. The "colored" section at the back was full, so she sat at the rear of the "white" section. When the rest of the bus filled, the driver angrily demanded that she give up her seat. Rosa Parks refused. Soon the black community buzzed with news of her arrest. Joanne Robinson of the Local Women's Political Council, a black counterpart to the white League of Women Voters, immediately put into action the bus boycott she and her organization had discussed for more than a year. In the middle of the night she and two students duplicated thousands of boycott notices at Alabama State College, where she was an English professor. Soon, everyone in the black community knew. With the support of other black leaders such as E. D. Nixon, head of the state NAACP and the Brotherhood of Sleeping Car Porters, and black churches under the leadership of Martin Luther King, Jr., the boycott lasted for more than a year. Blacks in Montgomery walked, carpooled, and built an unshakable sense of community solidarity and pride. As one elderly black woman put it, when offered a ride by a white reporter: "No, my feets is tired but my soul is rested."[37]

Long before the bus boycott Ella Baker had worked with Parks organizing NAACP chapters in Alabama. When the Southern Christian Leadership Conference (SCLC), headed by Martin Luther King, Jr., emerged out of the boycott Baker went to Atlanta to set up an office and coordinate the first southwide project. She understood the voter registration project called "Crusade for Citizenship" as a process of movement building. "The word Crusade connotes for me a vigorous movement with high purpose and involving masses of people. . . . It must provide for a sense of achievement and recognition for many people, particularly local leadership." Baker stayed on to run the SCLC office for two and a half years when there were virtually no resources, though she knew that the leadership was looking for "a man and a minister" to serve as director.[38]

The context for this new movement in the south was rising expectations and rising repression following the Supreme Court ruling in *Brown* v. *Board of Education* that outlawed school segregation. White southerners in the mid-1950s had mounted a massive campaign of rioting, violence such as the Emmett Till case, and school closings to resist integration. In community after community, black women were among the key figures who refused to give in to violent threats and intimidation. In 1956 Authurine Lucy faced Governor George Wallace as he sought to bar her entrance as the first black student at the University of Alabama. She knew that federal officials would force him to step aside but she was also aware that a riotous mob had gathered and violence was imminent.

In 1957 Daisy Bates, president of the Little Rock, Arkansas, NAACP, won a suit to require the integration of Little Rock High School. When Governor Orville Faubus called out the National Guard to prevent the entry of nine black students, President Dwight Eisenhower responded by sending federal troops to protect them. In her autobiography Bates described the courage of children such as fifteen-year-old Elizabeth Eckford and sixteen-year-old Minnijean Brown who faced down mobs, returning to school day after day despite constant harassment and violence from white students and their parents.[39]

Growing racial violence signaled the fact that behind the ideological blinders of the feminine mystique, togetherness, and social harmony, the 1950s were rife with conflict over the meaning and structure of American society. The educated middle class worked to fulfill a vision of domestic bliss in the expanding suburbs while urban blacks began to make their own claims on an American dream they had been denied. The popular fifties female image glorified domesticity at the same time that women entered the labor force more rapidly than ever before. Pundits declared the end of class divisions and of ideologies based on them as the poor concentrated in urban ghettos and popular entertainment fragmented along lines of race and class. Upper-middle-class men in gray flannel suits yearned for proof of their manliness in faceless bureaucracies as they were revered as breadwinners at home. Domesticated wives could soothe men's bruised egos. As a 1955 "Harvard man" put it: "She can be independent on little things, but the big decisions will have to go my way. The marriage must be the most important thing that ever happened to her."[40] Yet in spite of these hopes and domestic expectations (shared by many women as well), women with college educations were more likely to work outside the home than those without. As the consumerist ethos and high mobility seriously eroded traditional communal bonds, not only were housewives increasingly isolated, but also some of their middle-class men began to resist domesticity that made too many claims on them as providers. They preferred consumerism not tied to families, an ethic of pleasure without responsibility articulated by editor Hugh Hefner as the "*Playboy* philosophy."[41]

Traditional women's service organizations with their roots in nineteenth-century female culture could not provide a base from which to challenge the complexities of women's place in mid-twentieth-century America. Nevertheless, they continued to provide a training ground for leadership and to lay the groundwork for future change. The 1950s marked a resurgence of religious observance, often derided for its status orientation and theological emptiness. Yet student groups sponsored by the YWCA and other mainline religious organizations held intense discussions of the relationship between Judeo-Christian values and the social order. They challenged racial segregation and noticed the ferment of anticolonial independence movements in Asia and Africa. While youthful beatniks in Greenwich Village proclaimed their hostility to a hypocritical, consumerist society, other young people began to organize a movement to stop the testing of nuclear weapons.

The signs of ferment on campuses reflected in part the dramatic expansion of higher education in the postwar era that had an additional consequence of enlarging the number of professional women by 41 percent between 1940 and 1960. Professional women were, perhaps, the most natural audience for the feminist message of the National Woman's Party. Their position was an extremely precarious one because despite their growing numbers, the proportion of women in most professions continued to decline and they remained limited primarily to female-dominated fields such as teaching and nursing. Extensive training and commitment to their work made them the dreaded career women described in the tradition of Farnham and Lundberg as the "fatal error" of feminism. A few pioneers, like a woman physicist, could be portrayed as exceptions, proof that the unusual woman could do anything she wished. But suspicions that such women might abandon their "natural" roles brought ritualistic affirmations of the primacy of marriage and family in professional women's lives. A study of female executives in 1956 indicated that all the women interviewed valued home and family above their jobs but believed they could satisfy the demands of each "if they want to badly enough."[42] Such articles rarely explored the ways discrimination limited women's horizons. Discontent was rising, but voices of protest remained fragmented, isolated, and defensive.

The weakness of women's protests in the fifties illustrates the power of domesticity to define the parameters of change. Domestic ideology redefined a new reality—female labor force participation—to remove the potential threat of female power and autonomy by making women's work legitimate only as an extension of traditional family responsibilities. Locked into jobs defined as female, they could be paid less, denied opportunities for training and promotion, and laid off easily. Yet, the problems women faced were deep, structural, and increasingly urgent. Fewer and fewer lived the prescribed domestic and highly privatized life. Professional and blue-collar women alike increasingly chafed at the discrimination and lack of respect they experienced in the world of work. Younger women grew up with mixed, contradictory messages. The cultural ideal informed them that their only true vocation lay in marriage and motherhood. But they observed their mothers' realities, which were substantially different. And, black women had begun a process of protest that would soon shatter illusions of stability and challenge American society to live up to some of its most deeply held values. All of these groups were about to move into action far more dramatic than they knew at the time.

12

Decade of Discovery
"The Personal Is Political"

The chair of the House Un-American Activities Committee (HUAC) subcommittee was beside himself. For three days in mid-December 1962 his hearing room had been packed with hundreds of women who hissed, booed, applauded, and shushed their wailing babies. He was trying to prove that Women Strike for Peace (WSP) was infiltrated by communists, and he was accustomed in such cases to interviewing terrified witnesses. But these witnesses baffled him. They claimed their organization had no members, that they were all leaders. Retired schoolteacher Blanche Posner took the Fifth Amendment time after time, even when the committee counsel asked whether she wore a paper daisy to identify herself as a member of WSP. The audience cheered. Over the sputtering objections of the chair, Posner lectured the committee: "You don't quite understand the nature of this movement. This movement was inspired and motivated by mothers' love for children. . . . When they were putting their breakfasts on the table, they saw not only the Wheaties and milk, but they also saw Strontium 90 and Iodine 131."[1]

By the time Women Strike for Peace founder Dagmar Wilson appeared, Chairman Clyde Doyle was near the end of his rope. He had outlawed standing when the audience stood in silent solidarity with the first witness. Next they applauded and he outlawed that. Then they ran to the front of the room to kiss the witnesses. Journalists described Doyle's defeat with delight: "By the third day the crowd was giving standing ovations to the heroines with impunity."

As Dagmar Wilson headed for the stand, a woman with a baby

on her hip pushed through the crowd to hand her a large bouquet of flowers. Trim, serene, and impeccably dressed in red wool, Wilson calmly answered questions that in the fifties had made other witnesses cower. Was it her idea to send a delegation to a peace conference in Moscow? "No, I wish I had thought of that." Well then, whose was it? "This is something I find very difficult to explain to the masculine mind." Finally, the committee counsel asked if she "would knowingly permit or encourage a Communist Party member to occupy a leadership position in Women Strike for Peace" "Well, my dear sir," she said, "I have absolutely no way of controlling, do not desire to control, who wishes to join the demonstrations and the efforts that women strikers have made for peace. In fact, I would also like to go even further. I would like to say that unless everybody in the whole world joins us in the fight, then God help us."[2]

HUAC's defeat came at the hands of an organization of middle-class housewives who proclaimed their concern for peace in the name of mother love. Their actions were harbingers of women's reentry into political action in the name of womanhood and the initiation of a decade of activism that would shatter cold war assumptions. By the end of the decade, growing numbers of women possessed a new sense of rights, sisterhood, and language with which to describe personal experiences in group and political terms. This reemerging feminism issued a broad challenge to American culture—a challenge that would reverberate for the rest of the century. The politicized femininity of Women Strike for Peace was not the source of the new feminism, but it helped create an environment in which the passivity and apolitical nature of the feminine mystique could be challenged.

Signs of Change

Movements for women's rights generally emerge in the ferment of widespread social change when women discover and create spaces in which they can develop a collective identity and a shared sense of rights and possibilities. In 1960 there were signs of change on many levels, though no one at the time could have put the pieces together to find a pattern. In February four black college students in Greensboro, North Carolina, sat at the lunch counter of Woolworth's and refused to leave despite violent threats and finally arrest. Their action inspired young blacks across the south who began to sit-in, kneel-in, stand-in, wade-in, and otherwise challenge racial segregation wherever they could. The civil rights movement that grew from these activities provided a new model for social change and a language about equality, rights, and community that transformed public discourse in a decade. "Freedom now," the movement proclaimed. Movement-sponsored citizenship schools taught the basic skills of public participation and reinvigorated the ideals of civic duties and rights. All such ferment changed the idiom of politics, reemphasizing themes of community and civic participation that had long been eclipsed. The election of youthful and energetic John Fitzgerald Kennedy in 1960 further encouraged the new civic idealism as he challenged Americans to "ask not what your country can do for you. Ask what you can do for your country." A renewed public life for middle-class women in the 1960s was a far cry from the politics of domesticity a hundred years before; this public life carried with it the burdens, as well as the freedoms, of the modern age.

The changes of the fifties had left women in a new and unsettled position, experiencing new dimensions of work, education, and community action but trapped in a language of domesticity that suppressed the broader implications of these new realities. The mass media in 1960, including the *New York Times, Newsweek, Redbook, Time, Harper's Bazaar,* and CBS Television, suddenly discovered the "trapped housewife." Twice as many women attended college as a decade before, leading *Newsweek* to worry about "Young Wives with Brains: Babies, Yes—But What Else?"[3] Obviously the "what else" in most cases included labor force participation, but the concentration of women in low-paid clerical and service jobs had reduced women's wages from 63.9 percent of men's in 1955 to only 60 percent in 1960. A few universities began experiments to help women cope with their "dual role" as housewives who would also work outside the home at some stage in their lives. The continuing education movement opened higher education to older women who wanted to complete degrees or plan for returning to the labor force in meaningful jobs.[4]

The reemergence of the single young woman represented another alternative obscured by the popular obsession with domesticity. After 1957 marriage ages had begun to creep up and birthrates to fall. Slowly, invisibly, the headlong rush into domesticity had begun to reverse, revealing itself as an aberration in the long-term trends. At the same time, in 1960 the Food and Drug Administration approved a new form of contraception, the birth control pill. For the first time contraception was thoroughly separated from the act of sexual intercourse. And the effectiveness of the pill broadened the possibilities of recreational sex, enjoyed for its own sake in contexts not linked to procreation or even domesticity.

The convergence of these ongoing changes and vaguely sensed possibilities took place in a context in which cold war verities were rapidly dissolving. From the late 1950s, world events signaled the end of self-congratulation and a reemergence of social criticism. New countries in Asia, Latin America, and Africa met in 1955 to declare themselves uncommitted either to the Russian-led communist world or the United States–led capitalist world. The cold war bifurcation into "free" and "communist" countries no longer sufficed. In 1957 Ghana won independence from British colonialism, to be followed by a flood of newly liberated nations in the late fifties and early sixties; each new nation joined the nonaligned movement. Also in 1957 Russia launched the first artificial satellite and sent shock waves through a complacent American educational establishment. Then in 1959, Cuban guerrillas led by Fidel Castro overthrew an American-supported dictatorship and proclaimed a socialist state only ninety miles from the Florida coast.

Americans were suddenly on the defensive and they began a new self-examination. Intellectuals and "experts" of all kinds began to ask new questions and challenge bland orthodoxies. The passivity of the child-mother image no longer fit the times. Several studies of working women and a National Manpower Council report indicated both that working women with children required substantially increased social support for the double burdens they carried and that educated women remained significantly underemployed.[5] At a time when leaders worried that the United States was losing the cold war, underemployed women suddenly looked like a wasted resource.

On the fringes of college campuses, young people gathered to listen to folk music, to talk about the terrors of nuclear war, and to criticize the materialism and hypocrisy of American culture.[6] Beatniks like Jack Kerouac challenged American mass culture but hardly its sex roles. Their praise of sex, drugs, and Zen tended to portray women as simply the mechanism for achieving the cosmic orgasm. There were few liberating possibilities

266

for women in this subculture, though it prepared the way for more egalitarian sexual experimentation. By contrast, when pacifists in the Committee for Non-Violent Action and the Fellowship of Reconciliation discovered a new audience concerned about the morality of warfare and the dangers of the nuclear arms race, groups like Women Strike for Peace found their voice. And when Michael Harrington, former associate of Dorothy Day, shocked optimistic liberals with descriptions in *The Other America* of millions of Americans who remained hungry and impoverished in the midst of affluence, he shocked young women and men alike into idealistic activism.[7]

For all kinds of women changes in the 1960s paradoxically generated greater stresses, new possibilities, and new consciousness. Housewives, still the majority of adult women, perhaps faced the most difficult dilemmas. Sociologist Helena Lopata spent most of the 1960s interviewing women in the Chicago area to produce a profile of urban and suburban, black and white, and middle- and working-class women. She found tremendous variation, but most of all a continuing conflict between the very restrictive cultural definition of women's proper domestic roles, reflected in the self-denigrating response, "I'm just a housewife," and women's own descriptions of varied, creative, and active lives.[8]

Suburban housewives, in particular, had arrived in their new suburban environment during the fifties leaving behind the old neighborhoods and the extended family networks that defined much of their mothers' daily lives. Relying largely on one another and on "experts," they began to construct a life-style with few concepts to describe or validate what they did. The more educated women had evolved an activist life-style in which they extended mothering roles into the community and through voluntary associations brought community into the home. Such organized domesticity began to change the texture of public life in local communities. Suburbs vibrated with the activities of PTAs, girl scouts, churches, charitable fund-raisers, and volunteer-supported neighborhood recreation programs. Yet, most women understood their activities simply as "an attempt to fill empty time." American culture offered them no way to explain and justify their increasing competence and experimentation.[9] At the same time, few recognized the social and economic vulnerability of their position as housewives as divorce rates, which had dropped during the 1950s, began to rise again in the 1960s.[10] The multifaceted life of a

267

middle-class suburban housewife could become, overnight, a single mother's struggle for economic survival.

The growing community activities of middle-class women briefly generated a new form of politicized domesticity, a political claim on society in the name of family loyalty. Five women who had been active in the Committee for a SANE Nuclear Policy started Women Strike for Peace. They were disgruntled with the way cold war witch-hunts had turned peace activists against each other and wanted a way to act quickly in response to international events such as the atmospheric testing of nuclear weapons. Updating a tradition that began with the WCTU, they wanted an organization that could raise "mother's issues," such as radioactive contamination of milk, to their rightful place on the public agenda.

They issued a call for women to go on a one-day "strike" for peace on November 1, 1961, as a radioactive cloud from a Russian nuclear test floated across the United States. Word of the strike spread through female networks in PTAs, the League of Women Voters, peace organizations, and personal contacts. By November 1 an estimated fifty thousand women left their jobs and kitchens to lobby government officials to "End the Arms Race—Not the Human Race." Within the next year they organized local groups in sixty communities. Most activists in WSP were educated, middle-class mothers. Sixty-one percent did not work outside the home. Intellectual and civic minded, these middle-aged women had been liberal or radical in the 1940s and then had withdrawn into domesticity in the 1950s. They found themselves impelled, by growing fears for their children's futures as well as by the courageous examples of civil rights activists in the south, back into politics, this time in positions of leadership. Women's rights were on their agenda only so far as they emphasized the right of housewives to be heard as citizens. Conscious that "the housewife was a down-graded person," Dagmar Wilson set out to show "that this was an important role and that it was time we were heard."[11]

Although WSP enjoyed a momentary triumph, domesticity could not provide the political base it had for Victorian women. For too many the home was conceptualized as a "closed off cloister unconcerned with what goes on outside," and while the actual boundaries between public and private were fuzzy, political life that involves citizens, as opposed to politicians, had lost a distinctive, vibrant dynamic of its own.[12] Working-class and lower-class housewives had a far more restrictive definition of domesticity

268

than their middle-class counterparts, along with far less self-confidence about their own achievements. Less neighboring and less involvement in the community reinforced women's isolation inside a constantly precarious family economy and gave them little sense of control over their lives or their children. When such women did not work outside the home, they frequently explained that their husbands would not let them. Researcher Lillian Rubin described a painful discussion with a mother of four who, like her house, appeared "unkempt and uncared for." The woman explained, "No, I don't work." "My husband doesn't like me to work. He thinks a wife ought to be home taking care of the children and her husband." In a wistful voice she remembered how much she had enjoyed her work at a bank, where "I was the best girl in the office, too. You know, it's funny, but I'm very organized when I work. . . . I even used to be more organized around the house when I was working."[13]

Economic dependence on men whose own opportunities were severely restricted led many such women, both white and black, to express considerable anger at men for failing to fulfill their roles as breadwinners. One woman complained that she never got enough money from her husband "to feed and clothe my family," not recognizing that with a total income of less than $5,000 he did not have "enough" to give. Others complained about unemployed men: "They don't care to work" and "Men just think women are work horses."[14]

Among poor black women, especially in northern urban ghettos, decades of severe unemployment among black men left growing numbers with sole responsibility for the support of their children. As the numbers of female-headed households rose, so did illegitimacy rates, from 17 to 29 percent of all black births between 1940 and 1967. The proportion of black women in the labor force reached 58 percent in 1960.[15] A government report by Daniel Patrick Moynihan issued in 1965, *The Negro Family: The Case for National Action*, appeared to place the blame for black poverty on the "pathology" of this "matriarchal" black family.[16]

Yet the survival strategies of poor black women drew on the traditional elasticity of the black family that had never conformed to middle-class images. Kin and fictive kin (that is, friends referred to with the labels of kinship: "sister," "aunt") formed networks within which resources could be shared and children cared for. Women were central to such networks while men floated in and out of them depending largely on their level of employment. When one member of the network had a job or a welfare check, resources flowed out to the network as a whole. When members were jobless, homeless, or ill, resources in the form of gifts and services flowed to them. Such gift-giving and swapping exchanges contrasted sharply with middle-class competitive and individualistic values. As one woman said, "You ain't really giving nothing away because everything that goes round comes round in my book."[17]

Struggles for Minority Rights: Black Women and Chicanas

For middle-class black women domesticity as organized through church and community groups had always been politicized. From the earliest black women's clubs, through settlements like the Atlanta Neighborhood Union, or work in the colored YWCA, black women had worked for the welfare of the black community. By the 1960s, however, the black community was becoming increasingly diverse—ranging from north to south, from city to countryside, and from extreme poverty to educated middle class.

In contrast to the white middle class, black community activists for the most part worked outside the home as well. Indeed, working black women's intensely active life-style involved them in religious and community groups more than any other group of women.[18] The activist tradition of black women, primarily through their churches, placed them in central leadership positions in the civil rights movement that spread across the southern states after 1960. As young blacks throughout the south confronted segregation, they drew on the courage and experience of earlier actions such as the Montgomery bus boycott. When the movement shifted its focus to voter registration, it became essential to mobilize entire communities; organizers quickly learned that, as in Montgomery, churches were the key institutions within the black community. On one level this emphasized the public leadership of black male ministers. On another, it required the active support of community women. Young volunteers in southern communities quickly learned to know the "mamas," powerful women whose courage and strength provided the backbone of the local movement as they had within their churches.

Born in 1917, Fannie Lou Hamer was the twelfth of twenty children; her parents were Mississippi sharecroppers. Until she went to her first mass meeting in 1962, she didn't know that a Negro could register and vote. . . . When they asked for those to raise their hands who'd go down to the courthouse the next day, I raised mine. Had it up as high as I could get it. I guess I'd had any sense I'd a-been a little scared, but what was the point of being scared. The only thing they could do to me was kill me and it seemed like they'd been trying to do that a little bit at a time ever since I could remember.[19]

When her employer in Sunflower County, Mississippi, instructed her not to register to vote, she replied, "But you don't understand, I'm not registerin' for *you,* I'm registerin' for *me!*"[20] As a result, she and her husband lost their jobs and were evicted from their home. But for Hamer the movement had become a way of life. She organized citizenship schools and voter registration projects, endured brutal beatings in jail, and founded the Mississippi Freedom Democratic party to challenge the all-white political structure in that state. Young black and white volunteers recalled the transforming power of women like Fannie Lou Hamer singing gospel hymns, organizing their communities, risking and suffering for freedom with indomitable pride and dignity.[21]

The opportunities for female leadership in the civil rights movement were most open at the grass roots. Within Martin Luther King, Jr.'s Southern Christian Leadership Conference women such as Ella Baker, Septima Clark, and Dorothy Cotton conceived and led the Citizenship Education program that laid the groundwork for many local civil rights demonstrations. Women were also key leaders in the youthful radical wing of the civil rights movement, the Student Nonviolent Coordinating Committee (SNCC). SNCC was founded because Ella Baker had persuaded SCLC to sponsor a meeting in April 1960 for participants in the sit-in movement. SNCC set out to embody the goals of the movement, "the beloved community" people called it. Blacks would claim their dignity and citizenship rights regardless of intimidation or violence. Blacks and whites would live and work together equally, showing to the world the meaning of the equality for which they were fighting.

The intensely personal nature of participation in SNCC and the openness to youthful initiative made it possible for many women to join and lead demonstrations against segregation and to organize communities for voter registration. Refusing bail, they experienced jail again and again, gaining the respect and admiration of their colleagues. Rubye Doris Smith Robinson, a central staff member of SNCC, according to one of her co-workers was

271

"The nearest thing I ever met to a free person. I mean really free, free in the sense that be you Black or white, you could not commit a great indignity or injustice about Rubye and have it go undealt with. . . . Rubye just stood up to *anybody*. . . . That's just not the way Blacks acted in the south. As a result, she made you stand taller."[22]

The civil rights movement transformed many parts of the south between 1960 and 1967 by eliminating the humiliations of public segregation, integrating school systems, and empowering black voters. On other levels its achievements seemed excruciatingly minimal. Black Americans remained disproportionately poor while discrimination assumed increasingly subtle forms. For black women, however, there were some dramatic consequences. Public opinion shifted decisively toward a belief that racial discrimination was wrong, and the Civil Rights Act in 1964 made it illegal. In 1960 black women remained confined to domestic and other segregated, menial jobs or professional jobs within the black community. After 1964, however, their economic opportunities broadened to include jobs previously open only to white women. The proportion of black women in clerical and sales jobs increased between 1960 and 1970 from 17 to 33 percent in northern states and from 3 to 11 percent in the south. The proportion of black women in domestic service dropped from 36 percent in 1960 to 15 percent in 1970. And in the north, black women earned 95 percent of the wages of white women compared to less than 80 percent in 1960.[23] Of course, white women's wages remained about 60 percent of white men's.

Black women were left with a dilemma. The poorest faced deteriorating conditions as single parents in inner-city ghettos. Swirling around them in the late 1960s was not only the rage expressed in ghetto riots but also the arguments, sometimes echoed by black men, that their very strength and survival undermined the black community. On the other hand, working- and middle-class black women found new opportunities in the late 1960s in spite of continuing racial prejudice. By the 1970s they also found a new voice.

The infectious nature of the black struggle, with its stirring stories of courage and reclaimed dignity, spurred numerous other groups to action as well. Chicana farm workers like Jesse Lopez de la Cruz had labored for decades in the grape, apricot, beet, and cotton fields of the southwest, moving from farm to farm, setting up house in shacks and fields. When Cesar Chavez visited the home of 43-year-old de la Cruz in 1962 and talked about building a union of farm workers she immediately joined as a volunteer organizer.

Chavez's background in community organization led him to emphasize community issues and communal solidarity, matters of deep concern to women. The farm workers' union combined the spirit of labor organizing with that of a civil rights movement rooted in the culture of Mexican Americans. In the beginning it focused not on workplace issues, where a series of union efforts had failed in recent decades, but rather on strengthening the Mexican-American community. Union members built a credit union and a consumer coop. They offered counseling for welfare recipients and immigrants seeking citizenship and waged battles against racism in the schools and rent-gouging landlords. When workers in the Delano, California, grape fields struck in 1966, the United Farm Workers drew on the deep cultural symbolism of the religious pilgrimage as workers marched 230 miles to Sacramento, staying in farm workers' homes each night, drawing new marchers every day, and becoming a presence on the national nightly news for twenty-five consecutive days.[24]

Though Chicanas experienced continuing resistance to activism even within their own communities, many joined and a few emerged as leaders in *la causa*. De la Cruz, who joined the staff of the United Farm Workers in 1967, saw her principal task as bringing women into the union. "Women can no longer be taken for granted—that we're just going to stay home and do the cooking and cleaning," she would tell them. "It's way past the time when our husbands could say, 'You stay home! You have to take care of the children! You have to do as I say!' "[25] A new generation of Chicana leaders emerged from this struggle. The farm workers' movement, in turn, inspired student activists who joined a massive grape boycott in the late 1960s. And in the 1970s it served as a model for new forms of organizing among urban working women.

Reemergence of Feminism

The civil rights movement in the black community also inspired a renewed struggle for women's rights. From the beginning a number of black women were involved: Dorothy Height, president of the National Council of Negro Women, lawyer Pauli Murray, union leaders Aileen Hernandez and Addie Wyatt, Representative Shirley Chisholm, and Fannie Lou Hamer herself. The dual oppression of women in racial minorities and the difficulties of fighting sexism while maintaining racial solidarity, however, took black and other minority women, for the most part, on a different trajectory toward feminism in the 1970s.

The initiation of a new feminist sensibility came from two groups of middle-class women, both inspired by the civil rights movement. The first group consisted primarily of professional women. The second, in many ways parallel to feminists in the 1910s, drew on younger radical activists and posed a broader cultural challenge to accepted definitions of femininity and sexuality but without the seasoned political expertise of the older, more moderate group.

Through the fifties a small network around the Women's Bureau of the Department of Labor and the tiny remnant of the National Woman's Party had sustained mutually antagonistic voices in behalf of women's rights. But when President Kennedy appointed Esther Peterson to head the Women's Bureau, he brought back into the center of the federal government a female reform sensibility shaped by the labor movement. Peterson had served as recreation director of the Bryn Mawr Summer School for Women Workers in the early thirties and had worked as a labor lobbyist in Washington for several years.

Peterson persuaded Kennedy to appoint a Presidential Commission on the Status of Women. Chaired by Eleanor Roosevelt and strongly directed by Peterson, the commission set about reassessing women's place in the economy, the family, and the legal system. Membership on the commission, its staff, and seven technical committees was drawn from labor unions, women's organizations, and government agencies.

Not surprisingly, a strong majority of the commission opposed the Equal Rights Amendment that had been kept alive by the National Woman's Party, gaining some new support from business and professional women in the postwar years. Striving for a position less divisive than in the past, their report declared that "equality of rights under the law for all persons, male or female is so basic to democracy . . . that it must be reflected in the fundamental law of the land." They argued that this was already achieved under the Fifth and Fourteenth amendments to the Constitution. Therefore, they could conclude that a constitutional amendment was not needed "now." The only member of the commission who

274

supported the ERA, feminist lawyer Marguerite Rawalt, insisted on the insertion of the word "now" to leave the door open for change if the Supreme Court failed to accept their interpretation.[26]

The commission's final report, issued in 1963, together with numerous subcommittee reports documented in great detail problems of discrimination in employment, unequal pay, lack of social services such as child care, and continuing legal inequality. Though the committee paid careful obeisance to the centrality of women's traditional roles, it also spelled out the realities of inequality. One immediate consequence was a presidential order requiring the civil service to hire for career positions "solely on the basis of ability to meet the requirements of the position, and without regard to sex."[27] A second was passage of the Equal Pay Act in 1963 that made it illegal to have different rates of pay for women and men who did equal (i.e., the same) work.[28] For the first time the federal government restricted discrimination against women by private employers.

The commission itself activated a network of professional women whose growing concerns during the past decade had found no outlet. Its various subcommittees drew on a large number of women who had been active both in their professions and in their communities. Within a year of their report, most states had also formed commissions. These environments fostered concern about women's status and creative thinking about solutions. No longer bifurcated by their positions on the ERA, union women, lawyers, academics, and organizational leaders were stunned by what they learned. The depth and pervasiveness of discrimination and the hardships accompanying women's "double burden" in the home and the labor force gave quantified validation to problems they themselves had experienced or observed in more individual ways.[29]

The same year the commission issued its report, Betty Friedan published her book *The Feminine Mystique*. Blaming educators, advertisers, Freudian psychologists, and functionalist sociologists for forcing women out of public life and into a passive and infantilizing domesticity, Friedan advocated meaningful work outside the home as the solution to "the problem that has no name." She was unprepared for the deluge of mail that her book inspired. From all over the country, women by the thousands wrote to thank her for naming their unhappiness and to tell her their own painful stories. "My undiluted wrath," wrote one, "is expanded

275

on those of us who were educated and therefore privileged, who put on our black organza nightgowns and went willingly, joyfully, without so much as a backward look at the hard-won freedoms handed down to us by the feminists (men and women)." Another upper-middle-class housewife and mother of five explained, "In seeking that something 'more' out of life, I have tried large doses of everything from alcohol to religion, from a frenzy of sports activities to PTA . . . to every phase of church work. . . . Each served its purpose at the time, but I suddenly realized that none had any real future." While she saw herself as about to make some different choices, other writers conveyed notes of despair. A suburban housewife claimed that she and her female neighbors were depressed and self-destructive. Describing herself as brilliant with "an I.Q. in the 145–150 range," a compulsive eater, and occasionally suicidal, she summarized her life: "I 'caught' a husband at 19, married him on my twentieth birthday, quit school pregnant, and now have six children! I am the typical stay-at-home, domineering mother and wife. I love my children yet I hate them, have actually wished them dead."[30]

All of this set the stage for debate on the 1964 Civil Rights Act. Howard Smith, an elderly congressman from Virginia, encouraged by constituents in the National Woman's Party, suggested that the prohibition in Title VII against discrimination in employment on the basis of race, creed, and national origin should also include "sex." As a long-time supporter of the ERA he offered the amendment seriously, but as an ardent segregationist he probably also hoped it would help to kill the bill.[31] While their colleagues chuckled at the very idea of including sex in a civil rights bill, Congresswoman Martha Griffiths and Senator Margaret Chase Smith set to work to pass the amendment which made Title VII the strongest legal tool yet available to women.

Once the Civil Rights Act passed, the newly created Equal Employment Opportunity Commission (EEOC) found itself flooded with women's grievances. Most people, including the EEOC, still considered the inclusion of sex a bit of a joke. The *New York Times* referred to it as the "bunny law." What, the editors worried, would happen if a man applied to a Playboy Club for a position as a bunny? Could he charge discrimination if the owners refused to hire him?[32]

Friedan and others within the networks surrounding the presidential and state commissions became increasingly alarmed.

276

Sharing Space

In 1920 the National American Woman Suffrage Association assumed a new name, the League of Women Voters. It took on the task of voter education, as in this 1935 Minnesota State Fair booth, and became indispensible to grass-roots American politics. The league's vision of an informed citizenry has enriched the concept of democracy in the twentieth century. *(Minnesota Historical Society)*

A more autonomous and individualistic ethos opened new opportunities for leisure and for work after 1920. These three "girls" (above) pose with their small roadster in 1925 as they embark on a trip to California. *(Minnesota Historical Society)* For black women, who rarely had the resources to enjoy the consumerism of the flapper, religion continued to provide a cornerstone for community and an arena for new public roles. The revival preacher below proclaimed her message in 1942 with energetic authority. *(Library of Congress)*

Women also found themselves increasingly in public, and politically potent, settings as a consequence of their continuing commitment to their families. Women's auxiliaries, for example, were largely responsible for the domestic and communal activities of numerous male religious, civic, and political organizations. The women above are running a strike commissary during the bloody 1934 Minneapolis Teamsters' strike. *(Minnesota Historical Society)* The Mexican women shown below waiting at the U.S. Immigration Station in El Paso, Texas, in 1938 had to fend for themselves and their families in seeking entrance to the United States. Twentieth-century immigrant women have had to skillfully negotiate ever-changing governmental regulations and bureaucracies to realize their dream of a better life. *(Library of Congress)*

Women created some of their most powerful public roles by building institutions and professions in response to the issues of poverty, public health, and child welfare. Settlement houses (left) and health clinics (below), shown here in the 1920s, made domestic issues into matters of community concern and laid the groundwork for the emergence of the modern welfare state. *(Minnesota Historical Society)*

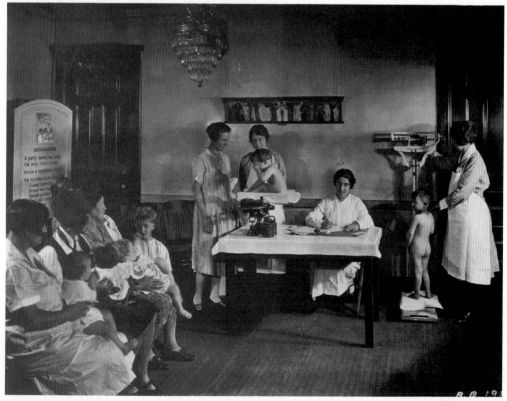

Above, the New Deal policies of the Roosevelt administration in the 1930s drew on the leadership and experience of female reformers. Mary McCloud Bethune, director of Negro relations for the National Youth Administration, had founded Bethune-Cookman College and served as president of numerous organizations including the National Council of Negro Women. Right, Eleanor Roosevelt received her training in the settlement house movement, the National Women's Trade Union League, and grass-roots Democratic party politics in New York State. *(Library of Congress)*

Women entered the labor force in massive numbers during World War II. While most continued to work in gender-segregated and sex-stereotyped jobs (above) *(The Archives of Labor and Urban Affairs, Wayne State University)*, the requirements of war industries opened many previously male blue-collar jobs to women such as the young welder below left. *(Library of Congress)* Images of female strength and self-confidence, as well as unabashed female sexuality, were also promoted by Hollywood, as in Joan Crawford's sultry stare (below right). *(Collection, The Museum of Modern Art, New York)*

The civil rights and feminist movements called American society back to its democratic heritage and a broadened, more participatory definition of citizenship. Black women, such as the protester above, under arrest in Birmingham, Alabama, were key leaders in the civil rights struggle. *(Photo by Bruce Davidson. ©1970 Magnum Photos)* The civil rights movement was also a training ground for future leaders of a reborn feminist movement (right). The revival of feminism, together with movements for racial justice, proposed an active, equitable, and inclusive vision of democratic citizenship. *(Photo by Arthur Tress. Magnum Photos)*

EQUAL PAY FOR EQUAL WORK

Though sexual inequality remains a hallmark of American society, even as the twentieth century draws to a close, the gendered meanings of public and private spaces are clearly undergoing redefinition. In the photograph above, in 1983 Dorothy Pink reads from the Torah at her Bat Mitzvah, a ritual first celebrated in 1922 and popular since 1960. In classical Judaism, women were not allowed to touch or to read the Torah, nor were they instructed in Hebrew. The Bar Mitzvah marked ritual adulthood for males exclusively. *(Minnesota Historical Society. With permission of the* Minneapolis Star and Tribune*)*

Women, they realized, had no organized advocates in Washington or the states. The EEOC had even approved the continued use of separate want ads for male and female employment. Organizations such as the League of Women Voters and the American Association of University Women were decidedly uninterested in working specifically for women's rights or being labeled "feminist." Clearly women lacked the political clout to demand that laws similar to Title VII be enforced.

Several delegates to the third National Conference of State Commissions on the Status of Women, including women from the United Auto Workers and leaders of several state commissions, arrived with this concern. They held an informal meeting in Betty Friedan's hotel room and decided first to submit a resolution to the conference. When they learned that the conference would not allow resolutions or action of any kind, even the reluctant members of the group decided a new organization was required. Friedan recalled that they "cornered a large table at the luncheon, so that we could start organizing before we had to rush for planes. We all chipped in $5.00, began to discuss names. I dreamed up N.O.W. on the spur of the moment."[33] Thus the National Organization for Women, NOW, was born with a clear statement of purpose: "To take action to bring women into full participation in the mainstream of American society now, assuming all the privileges and responsibilities thereof in truly equal partnership with men."[34]

NOW articulated the clear dilemmas of professional women for whom continuing discrimination violated deeply held convictions about their rights to equal treatment and for whom traditional attitudes about family roles were obsolete. "It is no longer either necessary or possible," they argued in their founding statement, "for women to devote the greater part of their lives to child-rearing."[35] NOW represented in some ways a modernized version of the Seneca Falls Declaration by reclaiming for women the republican ideals of equal participation and individual rights. But its organizers were skilled at lobbying, not movement building.[36] For the first year, organizational mailings went out from the offices of the United Auto Workers' Women's Bureau, and local chapters were slow to develop. Activities targeted the enforcement of federal antidiscrimination laws. This included pickets and demonstrations against the continued existence of sex segregated want ads; pressure for the inclusion of "sex" on the list of discriminations prohib-

277

ited for federal contractors and for enforcement of Executive Order 11375 once it was amended on October 13, 1967; and continuous pressure on the EEOC to enforce Title VII. As the cases piled up, it became clear that Title VII could eliminate the use of protective legislation to discriminate against women as well as such blatant discrimination as the airlines' policy of firing stewardesses who married or turned thirty-two.

With some successes, several law suits pending, no organized local base, and an increasingly diverse membership, the NOW national conference in 1968 encountered serious disagreements. Endorsement of the Equal Rights Amendment forced United Auto Workers women to withdraw. Within their union they were working for change, but until their union changed its position—which it did two years later—they could not remain within NOW. The issue of abortion precipitated another split as lawyers who wanted to focus on legal and economic issues left to found the Women's Equity Action League (WEAL).

NOW did not immediately grow into a national movement in part because its founders did not have the required organizing skills. In addition, its focus on rights and individuals, abstracted from communal relations, did not speak to large numbers of women. The founders of NOW understood that women were seriously disadvantaged in the American political and legal system, but they presumed a model of political activity which was essentially individualist, recalling the late suffragist focus on the direct relationship between citizen and state. In the beginning, the bonds of sisterhood remained unarticulated and depoliticized. Indeed, NOW was very careful to insist that it was an organization "for" women but not necessarily "of" women, a sharp contrast to the centrality of female solidarity (without the feminism) in Women Strike for Peace.

The fact is that most women still could not identify with the clear-cut dilemmas of the professional woman. Trapped in the mystifying complexities of a popular culture that simultaneously endorsed individual opportunity and the feminine mystique, a gender-segregated economy that drew women into low-paid, low-status jobs, and a child-centered family premised on the full-time services of a wife/mother, they could not abstract issues of rights from the underlying questions of identity.

Even younger women preparing for professional vocations found themselves caught in a web that was both internal and external. Sara Ruddick finished four years of graduate work at Harvard and followed her husband to his first academic job planning to write her dissertation. She found herself paralyzed, unable to work because she had no models, no image of herself as a worker. "In my generation, women's work histories were so buried in our life histories as to be barely visible."[37] Similarly, Marilyn Young with a Ph.D. in Chinese history found herself caring for young children and playing the role of the faculty wife in the mid-1960s. She wrote in her journal in 1967 at the age of thirty: "How ineffective. I shall live out the rest of my life as if it weren't really happening and then die surprised. . . . I have no proper work, and for me that is hard. And I grow lazier, mentally, by the hour."[38] Both Ruddick and Young found new direction in the intense relationships and personal support of another, younger branch of the emerging women's movement. They were not so much interested in changing the EEOC's enforcement policies as in transforming their own sense of self. Ruddick recalled that the women's movement "enabled me to achieve a new self-respect at home, made me confident and clear about my need for the friendship of women." It also transformed her sense of women's aspirations. "I had carried an invisible, almost amorphous weight, the weight of guilt and apology for interests and ambitions that should have been a source of pride. When that weight was lifted, I felt almost literally lighter, certainly more energetic, more concentrated."[39]

The groups in which Young could speak of "the bitterness of those years" and Ruddick could find a new definition of selfhood were part of another, younger branch of feminism that emerged about a year after the formation of NOW.[40] What was called the "women's liberation movement" grew from the angry critique of a small group of radical young women who challenged the very definitions of public and private, of politics and personal life, and who asserted women's needs for personal support and group solidarity as well as for political action.

The young women who proclaimed, in the late 1960s, that "sisterhood is powerful" were children of the postwar middle class. Their parents had achieved unprecedented material success in a culture characterized increasingly by rootlessness. The student movements of the sixties represented a backlash on the part of such youth against the materialism of American society, the absence of authentic community, and the failure of America to live up to its moral claims. In the process young people not only demanded changes but also began to experiment with new and visionary forms of democratic relationships.

These movements provided young women with a social space within which they could question received definitions of domesticity and female nature. They shared their generation's intense search for community and discovered there the power of sisterhood. As a result, they challenged the definitions of politics more fundamentally than women had done since the days of the WCTU, and definitions of gender more radically than anyone had since the Greenwich Village radicals in Heterodoxy. With their declaration that "the personal is political" they repoliticized the bonds among women and rediscovered the ground for collective action.

Within the black civil rights movement, middle-class white women experienced a politicizing transformation analogous to that of their abolitionist and settlement house foremothers. In the beginning there were very few whites, but in the summers of 1964 and 1965 hundreds of college students flooded the south at the invitation of civil rights organizations, particularly SNCC. Many women found that they had to stand up to the opposition of parents frightened by the continuing violence in the south. "It is very hard to answer to your attitude that if I loved you I wouldn't do this," wrote one woman to her parents. "I can only hope you have the sensitivity to understand that I can both love you very much and desire to go to Mississippi. . . . There comes a time when you have to do things which your parents do not agree with."[41]

Bolstered by a radical commitment to equal rights, often with religious roots, they broke the mold of passive domesticity by organizing voter registration drives and freedom schools, risking arrest, enduring jail, and witnessing firsthand the dignity and self-respect of impoverished rural black communities. They also learned from black women on whose strength much of the movement rested. These "mamas" offered a vision of womanhood that further reinforced an emerging sense of self-assertion.

When Students for a Democratic Society (SDS) initiated a series of community organizing projects in imitation of SNCC's southern projects, it unwittingly created an environment in which women could develop new skills and self-confidence. Even more than in the civil rights movement, women's experiences in SDS were filled with irony and mystification. Men were the public leaders of every project, but women were frequently the most skilled organizers. While men tried to organize street gangs and winos, young women effectively organized a large, stable, female constituency, many of them welfare recipients, around community issues. Yet everyone worried about the "problem" of having so many women leaders, and community issues never received the respect and attention of strategies focused on male employment.

Nevertheless, community organizing projects offered women opportunities to develop leadership skills and political analysis talents, as well as supplying role models—all of which they later used to begin a new women's movement. Within SDS projects, women developed communal bonds among themselves and a deep identification with the female leadership of poor communities both in the north and in the south.

The new left student political movement as a whole became a less hospitable environment for women after the mid-sixties. In the south, racial anger and the need of the black community for self-definition made it impossible for whites to participate in an increasingly nationalist black movement. "Black power," often defined as a movement to reclaim black "manhood," also rendered black women increasingly invisible. President Lyndon Johnson began, in the spring of 1965, an escalation of the war in Vietnam that quickly provided the central focus for student activists in the north. In the traditions of the Women's International League for Peace and Freedom and the Women Strike for Peace, many women devoted themselves to the cause of peace. Nonetheless, the anti–Vietnam War movement, with its emphasis on draft resistance, was far more male dominated than community organizing had been.

The emergence in the late 1960s of a youthful counterculture celebrating love and community—feminine values—might have reversed this trend, but its focus on drugs and sex was often extremely exploitative of women. The counterculture represented a complex continuation of the sexual revolution that had been working its way through American culture since the beginning of the twentieth century. By the 1960s the association between pleasure, consumption, and heterosexuality thoroughly permeated popular culture. With the availability of the birth control pill in 1960, for the first time contraception could be separated from any specific sexual interaction and could be almost 100 percent effective. Heralded as "the perfect contraceptive," the pill made it possible for women to separate sexuality and procreation with a confidence never before known. Yet, as young people experimented with new frontiers of sexual freedom, they did so with no critique or reevaluation of female sexuality. Instead, the promiscuity, emotional detachment, and consumption orientation associated with cultural definitions of male sexuality became defined as sexual "freedom." Women raised with needs for security and affection found themselves accused of being "uptight" and "out of it." In the midst of these new pressures some did indeed explore new dimensions of themselves, others withdrew in distrust, and still others experienced what they would later name as abuse.

As early as 1964, women in the student movement had begun to explore the possible consequences of applying democratic principles to their relationships with men. Just at the moment when women had begun to apply the egalitarian ideology of the new left to themselves and their condition in American society, they discovered the realities of sexual inequality. The very settings that had taught them the value of egalitarian community also harbored the prejudices of the broader society.

When women raised the question of their equality within the student movement, they met a combination of indifference, ridicule, and anger. In 1964 SNCC leader Stokeley Carmichael joked that "the only position for women in SNCC is prone." At a conference in 1967 Shulamith Firestone stood at the microphone demanding to present a set of women's rights resolutions. After effectively preventing the resolutions from reaching the floor, the chair patted Firestone on the head and said, "Move on little girl; we have more important issues to talk about here than women's liberation." Like the founders of NOW in a similar situation, sponsors of the resolutions met immediately to begin organizing a separate movement for women. Using their organizing skills and the networks of activist women across the country, they began to set up small discussion groups and to create a process they called "consciousness-raising."

The early meetings were intense and exhilarating. In a style they had learned in the civil rights movement and the new left, women explored the political meaning of their personal experiences. Again and again, individuals were shocked to discover that their lives were not unique but part of a larger pattern. The warm support and understanding of other women empowered them as they reclaimed the lost legacy of sisterhood.

282

Convinced that they would and could change history, radical young women initiated a variety of forms of outreach. While theoretical papers circulated—What is the root cause of women's oppression? Who is the enemy?—guerrilla theater attracted the mass media. At the 1968 Miss America pageant they crowned a live sheep, tossed objects of female torture—girdles, bras, curlers, issues of the *Ladies Home Journal*—into a "freedom trashcan," and auctioned off an effigy: "Gentlemen, I offer you the 1969 model. She's better every year. She walks. She talks. She smiles on cue. *And* she does housework." Other groups leafleted bridal fairs and "hexed" Wall Street.

The lack of structure in this new movement contributed to its growth because it had such a large, ready-made base of activist women in every city. The small consciousness-raising groups proved a brilliant organizing tool. Anyone could start one, in an office, a school, a neighborhood. Soon it had spread well beyond the boundaries of the new left.

In Washington, D.C., Arvonne Fraser, a longtime activist in the Democratic party who worked in her husband's congressional office and managed his campaigns, invited about twenty women to her home in 1969 to talk about the new women's movement. She had tried to join NOW but her letter had been returned—probably a casualty of NOW's disorganization after the UAW withdrew support. Like many of her friends she found women's liberation groups too young and too radical, but she easily adopted their organizing strategy by organizing her own group. At the first meeting women decided not to introduce themselves through relationships with men (though many were related to or on the staff of prominent men). They said they would be a discussion group, not a consciousness-raising group. "Many of us realized later," according to Fraser, "that the main difference between the two was in name only."[42] Out of that group came key insider networks that in the 1970s carried out major legislative advances for women.[43] Fraser herself went on to become not only a national officer in the Women's Equity Action League (WEAL) but also increasingly active in international women's networks.

Del Martin, one of the founders of the Daughters of Bilitis, became an early activist in NOW. DOB had made some slight and controversial shifts in the mid-1960s toward a more militant stance, but remained a tiny organization, still distant from the the growing lesbian culture that flourished in urban bars. Femin-

283

ism added a dynamic and stressful dimension. Activists debated whether their primary loyalties lay with the homophile movement, where many experienced sexist treatment from gay male activists, or the new feminist movement where they painfully discovered the homophobic prejudices of other feminists. With feminism, however, they had a powerful analytic tool for examining their own social realities as well as an experience of solidarity and community—sisterhood—which provided a "psychic space" that allowed many women to claim their identity as lesbians.[44] The explosive emergence of gay liberation in 1969 further fueled this process and set the stage for more dramatic changes in the 1970s.

By the late sixties, feminist challenges were in the headlines and opposition to the war in Vietnam had toppled a president. Inflation aroused anxiety that the boom might be ending. Race riots and a divisive war abroad destroyed the optimism of the early sixties. Both cold war verities and their cousin, domestic ideology, were under serious stress. Indeed, Women Strike for Peace, so effective in the beginning of the decade, found itself accused of being reactionary. Younger radical women pointed out that WSP still played on traditional roles of wife and mother, roles in which women's identities remained derivative and dependent.

In January 1968 women in the peace movement mobilized thousands to march in Washington in opposition to the war in Vietnam. They called their march the Jeanette Rankin Brigade to honor the first woman in Congress and the only congressperson to vote against American entry into both world wars. A small contingent at the march called a separate meeting of women interested in struggling for their own liberation. Among themselves there was immediate division over ideological issues: Were men the enemy or was it "the system"? Should women continue participation in the male-dominated left or should they break away and work only with other women?

For the moment these angry young women seemed a rude and irritating interruption of the mass movement of women in the mold of Women Strike for Peace. In fact, they were the core of the burgeoning new women's liberation movement that by 1970 had eclipsed and apparently rendered obsolete agitation based on women's traditional roles. Declaring that "the personal is political," they introduced a radical challenge to the cultural definitions of male and female. Yet with youthful ingratitude, they failed to recognize the debt they owed previous generations as well as the complex power of women's traditional identities and associations. That failure also prevented them from understanding the long-run import of the movement they had begun.

13

The Politicization of Personal Life
Women Versus Women

*B*y 1970 "women's lib" was on everyone's lips. Between January and March substantial stories on the women's liberation movement appeared in virtually every major journal and broadcast network.[1] People were fascinated, intrigued, and often angered by the flamboyant tactics of feminist radicals. The combined effects of the women's liberation movement's agitation and the legal and legislative strategies of organizations such as the National Organization for Women and the Women's Equity Action League appeared to be changing the landscape. In January a front-page article in the *New York Times* noted, "The walls of economic and psychological discrimination against women in the American job market are beginning to crack under the pressures of the Federal Government, the women's liberation movement, and the efforts of thousands of individual women themselves."[2] The same day the article appeared, WEAL filed a complaint with the U.S. Department of Labor demanding a review of all colleges and universities holding federal contracts to determine whether they complied with antidiscrimination regulations. Two hundred and fifty institutions were targets for more specific charges of sex discrimination. By the end of the year, suits brought by women now willing to make public charges against discriminatory employers both for themselves individually and for women as a class had more than three hundred and sixty institutions of higher education in court.[3]

While lawyers took to the courts, radical feminists grabbed headlines with more direct tactics: They had already "hexed" Wall

Street and bridal fairs, disrupted congressional hearings to demand legalized abortion, conducted a rape speak-out where victims for the first time publicly shared their experiences, and announced self-defense karate classes for women. On March 18, 1970, two hundred women occupied the offices of the *Ladies Home Journal* and stayed for eleven hours of sharp debate and negotiation. A journal for women, they argued, should provide day care for its own employees, pay a minimum of $125 a week, hire more minorities, and replace its male editor with an entirely female senior staff. As a result the *Journal* agreed to give them an eight-page supplement to the August 1970 issue. The editor, John Mack Carter, introduced the supplement with his own account of the encounter. "Beneath the shrill accusations and the radical dialectic, our editors heard some convincing truths about the persistence of sexual discrimination in many areas of American life." More important, perhaps, "we seemed to catch a rising note of angry self-expression among today's American women, a desire for representation, for recognition, for a broadening range of alternatives." The accompanying articles, written collectively, explored sex discrimination in the labor force and education, childbirth, divorce, appearance and beauty, love, sex, and how to start a consciousness-raising group.[4]

With perfect timing the *Journal* special issue coincided with the fiftieth anniversary of the passage of the Nineteenth Amendment to the Constitution granting women the right to vote. When the National Organization for Women called for a Women's Strike for Equality on August 26, 1970, the new movement suddenly gained visibility, setting off another round of explosive growth. Thousands of women marched and demonstrated in cities across the country, some of them taking a stand for the first time in their lives; others, former suffragists, had waited a long time to march again for women's rights.[5] Following the strike, new members flooded into NOW chapters bringing into the organization members of the younger generation who had shaped the radical branch of women's liberation.

Women's liberation was contagious. When a *Newsweek* writer began to work on a story on the movement she discovered that many of her colleagues were preparing an EEOC complaint against *Newsweek*. With careful planning they held a press conference to announce their complaint just as *Newsweek* hit the stands with a major story on women's liberation.[6] Sophy Burnham laughed

288

when she received an assignment from *Redbook* to do a story on the women's movement. "A lunatic fringe," she thought. But "within a week I was so upset, I could hardly focus my ideas." In four months of listening to women's anger, pain, and quest for identity "chords were struck that I had thought long dead. . . . I thought I had come to terms with my life; but every relationship—husband, child, father, mother—was brought into question." By the end she was a convert: "I am now offended by things that would never have bothered me before. I am now a feminist. I am infused with pride—in my sisters, in myself, in my womanhood."[7]

The power of the women's movement lay in its capacity to stimulate such deep rethinking, to pose, *as a problem*, concepts such as femininity and motherhood and relationships previously taken for granted. Most Americans, both male and female, unlike Sophy Burnham, were not converted. They were angry, defensive, confused, but they were thinking about gender nonetheless.[8] Millions tuned in on September 20, 1973, to watch tennis star Billie Jean King battle Bobby Riggs, a 1939 Wimbledon winner and defender of manhood. Riggs had brilliantly hustled the media with his taunts against King's campaign for more opportunities and more money for women tennis professionals. "You insist that top women players provide a brand of tennis comparable to men's. I challenge you to prove it. I contend that you not only cannot beat a top male player, but that you can't beat me, a tired old man." Though the odds in Las Vegas were 5 to 2 for Riggs; King won three sets with ease, 6–4, 6–3, 6–3.[9] Riggs' rout in this "battle of the sexes" sparked debates, and female pride, in households and workplaces across the country.

The central organizing tool of the women's liberation movement, the small consciousness-raising group, proved an effective mechanism for movement building. Within such groups, women discovered that their experiences were not unique but part of a larger pattern, and they rediscovered female community. The intensity and power of the new bonds among women prompted them to name themselves a sisterhood, a familial metaphor for an emerging social and political identity that captured the key qualities of egalitarianism, love, and mutual responsibility. Because the groups had little or no structure, they could be formed anywhere—from offices to churches to neighborhoods. In effect, consciousness-raising defined the personal issues of daily life—

housework, child rearing, sexuality, etiquette, even language—as political issues susceptible to collective action and solution. Nothing was beyond discussion.

This spreading debate in thousands of formal and informal small groups soon affected informal female networks such as office friendships, religious groups, neighborhood kaffeeklatsches, and other voluntary associations. The new feminism necessitated extensive redefinition of roles, attitudes, and values because the traditional definitions of women and men were so at odds with women's actual experience. Women, in effect, reintroduced the personal experience of being female into the political discourse of the day, challenging the obsolete language that bifurcated public and private life along lines of gender. Their debates brought new analyses to the questions raised by earlier feminisms. Among themselves, feminists argued vehemently about whether the division between public and private was universal or particular to American society in recent times, and whether women were essentially different from or the same as men. The heat of their debate opened new windows on women's lives as individuals and as citizens and marked the difficulty of devising new categories for their changing reality.

Political Momentum and Cultural Critique

The new feminist movement continued to gain momentum in the early part of the 1970s. There were more rallies and demonstrations in behalf of women's rights every year until they peaked in 1975 with more than three hundred nationally reported feminist events.[10] Legislative victories, however, probably reached an apex in 1972. After decades of inattention, Congress suddenly recognized the political power of women and the importance of women's claims for equity. The feminist political awakening frightened lawmakers who rushed to appease a constituency that potentially represented more than half of the voting public, making it possible to gain hearings, votes, and legislative victories with breathtaking speed. While the media explained and explored the meaning of consciousness-raising and arguments over the use of "Ms." instead of "Miss" and "Mrs.," Congress passed more legislation in behalf of women's rights than it had considered seriously for decades. The ranks of ERA supporters now included the League of Women Voters, Business and Professional Women, the YWCA, the American Association of University Women, Common Cause, and the United Auto Workers, a coalition capable of mounting a massive two-year campaign that generated more mail on Capitol Hill than the Vietnam war. On March 22, 1972, Congress finally approved the ERA. By the end of the year, twenty-two of the needed thirty-five states had ratified it.

Other women's rights legislation passed by Congress in 1972 included Title IX of the Higher Education Act, providing "No person in the United States shall, on the basis of sex, be excluded from participation in, be denied the benefits of, or be subjected to discrimination under any education program or activity receiving federal financial assistance," setting the stage for the growth of women's athletics later in the decade. An Equal Opportunity Act broadened the jurisdiction of the EEOC and strengthened its enforcement capacity. And working parents received a tax break for their child-care expenses. Representative Bella Abzug recalled 1972 as "a watershed year. We put sex discrimination provisions into everything. There was no opposition. Who'd be against equal rights for women? So we just kept passing women's rights legislation."[11]

Abzug, a flamboyant activist who had belonged to Women Strike for Peace in the 1960s, joined with Betty Friedan and Representative Shirley Chisholm in 1971 to found the National Women's Political Caucus (NWPC). A bipartisan organization intended to increase female visibility and participation in the political arena, the NWPC further demonstrated women's political strength in 1972: The proportions of women attending the national party conventions that summer jumped to 40 percent in the Democratic party (up from 13 percent in 1968) and 30 percent in the Republican party (up from 17 percent in 1968).[12] That year Representative Shirley Chisholm mounted the first serious presidential campaign by a black woman. Texas state legislator Sissy Farenthold, a surprise nomination for vice president from the floor of the Democratic Convention, received 420 delegate votes. And both political parties, which had virtually ignored women four years before, adopted most of the NWPC platform including planks for ratification of the ERA, antidiscrimination legislation, elimination of tax inequities, educational equity for women, and extension of the Equal Pay Act. They balked only on the issue of abortion.[13]

When the Supreme Court handed down its decision on abortion in *Roe* v. *Wade* in 1973, it seemed that feminists had a golden

291

touch. Jane Roe, a pseudonym for a pregnant, single woman in Dallas County, Texas, had brought a federal suit claiming that the Texas criminal abortion laws unconstitutionally abridged her personal privacy by denying her the right to a medically safe abortion. She sued "on behalf of herself and all other women" in the same situation. The *New York Times* editorialized that "the Court's seven-to-two ruling [invalidating state laws that prohibit abortion in the first three months of pregnancy] could bring to an end the emotional and divisive public argument over what always should have been an intensely private and personal matter."[14] Though the Court's ruling followed a rather dramatic shift in public opinion, however, it propelled into action a deeply convinced minority opposed to abortion. The boundary separating issues that should be subjects of public policy and state control from those that properly remained private concerns continued to be a contested one.

Division over women's changing roles, in fact, was just beginning, not about to end. Its terms, however, were new. Joseph Adelson, writing a hostile article in the *New York Times Magazine* entitled "Is Women's Lib a Passing Fad?", dismissed some feminist goals as "banal simply because everyone seems to agree with them, men and women and alike. . . . Everyone believes in equal pay for equal work; most everyone believes that women should not be sharply limited in the economic roles available to them; and so on." Such words delighted and frustrated feminists who knew that these issues were hardly "banal" and that they did not represent the reality for most women. Adelson went on to argue against feminist advocates of "radical changes in sexual socialization and identity [and] radical changes in the family."[15]

These more disruptive ideas were being discussed and experimented with primarily among feminists who chose to work outside the legislative halls and political parties. Like feminists in the 1910s, these younger women were bent on challenging the system of gender in its broadest dimensions, and they saw specific legislative reforms as too limited and short-term. Theirs was a cultural radicalism. They wanted to transform the very definition of "female" and to shatter every barrier to women's autonomy—not just laws, but attitudes and values, methods of child rearing, marriage, and sexual norms. They operated in an atmosphere of radical experimentalism critical of virtually all existing institutions and determined to reclaim female power and liberate women's erotic potential. The meaning of female autonomy and authentic femininity varied dramatically according to whether they assumed that women were fundamentally the same or fundamentally different from men. Debates raged, groups split and reformed around different ideological constellations. Some, especially those most committed to continued alliance with other groups in the anti–Vietnam War movement and the student new left, joined more moderate feminist reformers in a deep suspicion of any assertion of female difference, knowing how it had historically been used in the service of biological determinism to assert female inferiority. Yet others chose to use the process of consciousness-raising to comprehend and give political meaning to their own experiences. All of these efforts, however, by emphasizing "women" as a group, and implicitly assuming a white and middle-class norm, obscured differences *among* women along lines of race, class, and ethnicity.

The power of female solidarity and community in consciousness-raising groups, and such groups' insistence on examining the world from women's point of view, led to an emphasis on issues uniquely female. Rape, wrote Susan Griffin in 1970, "is a kind of terrorism which severely limits the freedom of women and makes women dependent on men."[16] Such issues required female-controlled environments such as rape crisis centers and shelters for battered women within which women could be empowered to resist oppression and work for change. Like women reformers in the nineteenth century, feminists created institutions in response to women's unmet needs and their desire to be free from dependence on male-dominated institutions and ideas.

Thus outside the framework of traditional electoral politics, feminists began to construct a new public terrain giving priority to issues affecting women's lives and issues previously kept outside public surveillance. Rape crisis centers, battered women's shelters, women's health clinics, and feminist publications, coffee houses, and bookstores suddenly appeared in cities across the country. In Boston a women's health collective wrote a book to help women make knowledgeable decisions about their own bodies and health care alternatives. After selling two hundred thousand copies in a newsprint edition from a nonprofit press, *Our Bodies, Ourselves* came out in a commercial, revised edition in 1973. Its fourth edition was published in 1984. Another health collective formed in Chicago to advise women seeking abortions—before *Roe* v. *Wade* made them legal—soon began to provide the abortions themselves.[17] Acting on their own behalf and in their own space, women discovered that their space was very wide indeed.

The emphasis on the personal nature of political action, reminiscent of the civil rights movement, empowered lesbians to pursue the sexual revolution begun in the sixties and proclaim the political importance of sexual preference. Although lesbians battled continually in the more formally structured, moderate wing of feminism for visibility and recognition of their oppression, in the radical branch of the movement, their struggle led to separatism. Those, like Charlotte Bunch, who "came out" and proclaimed their lesbianism after joining the women's liberation movement, "did not realize how savagely we would be disinherited by our 'sisters'."[18] Lesbian feminists argued that lesbianism represented the most complete form of female autonomy. They called attention to the exploitation of homophobia as a means of undermining feminism. Like red-baiting, the charge that women who challenge traditional gender boundaries were lesbians (and that lesbians were somehow "unnatural") had been used to contain feminist insurgency throughout the twentieth century. "As long as the label 'dyke' can be used to frighten women into a less militant stand, keep her separate from her sisters, keep her from giving primacy to anything other than men and family—then to that extent she is controlled by the male culture."[19]

Lesbian collectives such as the Furies in Washington, D.C., recognized that lesbians themselves had to struggle for a new identity against the grain of cultural prejudice and began an exploration of the meaning of lesbian community, identity, and sexuality. "As separatists, we stopped trying to justify our lives to straight society and instead concentrated on ourselves."[20] Together they could move beyond the haunting fears of discovery and rejection, the self-hatred and invisibility inflicted by a culture that labeled them abnormal. Together they could claim, celebrate, and explore the meaning of their sexuality that the rest of society seemed to find so frightening. As they announced and defended their love for other women, they also explored barriers to female autonomy and female community restricting heterosexual women as well. Soon lesbian feminism informed the central theoretical debates within the movement.[21]

Finally, the *personalized* quality of women's newly created public spaces, with their emphasis on personal openness and transformation, tended strongly to create assumptions of or demands for commonality—a normative foundation of "sisterhood"—that made differences, when they emerged, all the more painful and difficult to address. Having discredited the gender hierarchy of patriarchal society, women's liberation activists challenged all forms of distinction and expressed a fear that any *differentiation* would be hierarchical, divisive, and regressive. Groups experimented with rotating leadership, using a lot system to determine who could speak in meetings, and consensus decision making. The lack of structure in groups facilitated their rapid spread—anyone, anywhere could start one—but gave them an ephemeral quality as well. There was no way to sustain regional or national structures. Yet, though the use of formal leaders was suspect, informal leadership inevitably emerged based on personal friendships and charismatic appeal. This conflation of personal relations and semipublic roles proved to be a severe weakness. It placed a premium on homogeneity and trust, all too easily undermined when differences arose. Jo Freeman in a famous critique of the "tyranny of structurelessness" recalled that between 1969 and 1971 feminists who gained public attention were attacked as "elitists." Some withdrew from the limelight; others persisted in the public arena but experienced alienation from their sisters. "Removed from the reaches of group pressure, they were no longer responsible for what they publicly said to anyone but themselves."[22] In proclaiming that "the personal is political" the women's liberation movement had attempted to personalize public life. In so doing, however, it had neglected the realities of political discourse and processes. Feminist ideas and practices demanded a rethinking of political power, as a fact of life subject to challenge and change but never obliteration, and of public life as an arena where difference and contention are constantly in play.

The Politicization of Female Networks

What few feminists in the women's liberation movement understood, particularly given their suspicion of all traditional institutions, was their impact on preexisting women's networks. Women's organizations, which for decades had avoided the "feminist" label associated with the National Woman's Party and shunned "women's issues," now reinterpreted their mission in feminist terms. The Girl Scouts devised a new curriculum to acquaint young women with a broad range of life choices. The American Associa-

295

tion of University Women, the YWCA, and the League of Women Voters took up feminist issues regarding female identity, rights, and autonomy, with vigor. From these organizations, with their long histories of organizational experience and community concern, came the women who moved most quickly into the electoral arena once the feminist movement had opened up that possibility. As the number of women holding elected offices began to rise, participation in women's organizations was one of the strongest characteristics of these new politicians, and they were more likely to have been active in the League of Women Voters than in NOW or even in the National Women's Political Caucus.[23]

Religious women mounted both an institutional and an ideological challenge. The illegal ordination by several male bishops of fourteen female Episcopal priests in Philadelphia in 1974 threw that staid old denomination into a crisis that was finally resolved in 1976 in women's favor.[24] Theologians like Mary Daly and Rosemary Radford Reuther explored female spirituality as distinct from male and the implications of female as well as male images of God. While one (Daly) broke with the church altogether and the other (Reuther) elected to remain, their paths represented journeys shared by thousands.[25]

Middle-class housewives also took up the challenge in 1972. The steep inflation of an overheated Vietnam War economy confronted them every day in a battle to stretch family resources at food markets. Like Jan Schakowsky in a Chicago suburb, many found in the new feminism an affirmation not only of their right to speak out but also of community support. "I started reading, you know, even women's magazines and watching the talk shows." With two children in diapers, she felt trapped; yet, she felt supported by "all those unseen people" about whom she had read. "I knew that if I ever met Gloria Steinem we would be best friends. . . . *Ms.* magazine, I read it totally uncritically . . . it was my magazine." Unaware of any local women's groups, Schakowsky joined with friends to initiate a consumer protest. "We felt the consumer group was part of the women's movement. We talked about how the problems we faced related directly to the fact that we were women and the kinds of changes as women that we had to go through in order to face those things."[26] Her group helped to spark a nationwide meat boycott in 1972 slowing the rise in prices.

Less visible were the responses of black and working-class

women. Black women had remained deeply suspicious of the new women's movement, perceiving it as "basically a family quarrel between White women and White men." Intensely focused on the black struggle, they resented white women's comparisons of their own plight to that of black people. As Dorothy Height, president of the National Council of Negro Women, put it: "Fifty years ago women got suffrage . . . but it took lynching, bombing, the civil rights movement and the Voting Rights Act . . . to get it for Black women and Black people."[27] They found themselves and their issues shunted to the side within the predominantly white movement whose universalist claims about the nature of women's oppression denied the realities of racism. The antirape movement, for example, with its animus against all male perpetrators, had no sympathy for the black community's historic suspicion of rape charges against black men, charges used again and again to justify lynching and other forms of terrorism.[28]

In the late 1960s and early 1970s the black activist movement was in decline in the face of government repression, internal dissension, and continuing frustration. Particularly among black nationalists in the north, black women became scapegoats, accused of robbing their men of their "manhood." Black feminist Paula Giddings argued, "In the North, the exhibitionism of manhood was not mitigated by the strength of Black institutions whose most vital resource was women."[29] As Sonia Pressman complained in an article on job discrimination and black women in 1970, "When most people talk about civil rights, they mean the rights of Black people. And when they talk about the rights of Black people, they generally mean the rights of Black males."[30] Though black women were not visibly part of the women's movement, their double oppression and their historic strength and assertiveness meant that in the early 1970s black women significantly outdistanced whites in their support for the ERA and approval of feminist activism.[31]

The Shirley Chisholm presidential campaign in 1972 exemplified the dilemma of black women. She received only lukewarm support from feminists in the National Women's Political Caucus, but she encountered active hostility from black male political leaders. "There she is—that little Black matriarch who goes around messing things up," said one politician when she was in earshot, calling up all the hostile, misogynist imagery validated by the Moynihan report.[32]

297

By the late 1970s and early 1980s, however, black feminist voices began to emerge. Writers such as Alice Walker, Audre Lorde, Toni Morrison, and Angela Davis began to explore the complexities of the dual oppression of gender and race, the meanings of blackness for women, the realities of male chauvinism and homophobia in the black community, and the strengths in black women's heritage. In St. Louis's public housing projects Bertha Gilkey, a young welfare mother and former Black Panther party member, cajoled her neighbors into painting their hallways. Cochran Gardens was one of the most violent, despair-filled projects in the country. Halls reeked of refuse and urine. People cowered in their apartments, afraid of the daily shootings and knifings. So Gilkey convinced gang members to serve as guards for elderly residents afraid to walk to the bus stops. Then she fast-talked a local company into supplying a coin-laundry machine to buildings with a reputation for violence so severe that even police hesitated to come in. She invited the mayor to the ribbon cutting for the laundry machine! Bertha Gilkey had found ways to empower and build self-respect in the face of a brutalized and chaotic social environment. As Cochran Gardens changed, its residents began to demand more of, and for, themselves. The city authorities had contemplated razing the housing project, as they had done to a nearby high-rise. Instead, they turned its management entirely over to tenants. Today Cochran Gardens is clean and safe. The grass and flowers growing by the sidewalks thrill Gilkey's soul every time she looks at them. Hallways stay clean— no graffiti, no trash, no odors of urine and garbage. Only gradually did Gilkey recognize that the people who transformed Cochran Gardens were, for the most part, black *women,* and that their victory represented an achievement to be shared with poor women of all races across the country.[33]

Similar to blacks, women in other minority groups remained distant from the new feminist ferment. Hispanic women, most of whom were Catholic, found it difficult to become involved in a movement that made abortion a central issue. Although they responded defensively to attacks on the patriarchal family, growing numbers of Chicanas joined movements like the Farm Workers' Union and began to raise questions about the effects of machismo.[34] Similarly, native-American women resisted feminist perspectives that emphasized individual choice over communal relations and obligations as contrary to their deepest cultural val-

298

ues. In each minority group, as among white and black feminists, the voices of lesbian women often spoke with great clarity as they struggled to explain their dual allegiance to feminism and to the communities in which they were raised. To white women, minority lesbians proclaimed the centrality of racial oppression and the importance of sustaining ethnic solidarity and cultural integrity. However powerful, sisterhood could not mean forsaking these roots. To their own people they insisted on the empowerment of women and an end to prejudice against homosexuals. Experiencing sexism and homophobia in their own communities was especially painful and alienating.[35]

Activism among working-class women frequently proved more racially diverse than among the mostly white middle-class feminists. In 1974 clerical workers in Boston and Chicago initiated a new kind of organization, modeled on community organizations rather than on unions and inspired in part by the Farm Workers.[36] The goal of Nine-to-Five in Boston and Women Employed in Chicago was to activate the female networks within offices. In Chicago on February 3, 1977, fifty secretaries from the downtown Loop took their lunch hour to protest the firing of Iris Rivera, a legal secretary. Rivera had lost her job because she refused to make coffee arguing that "(1) I don't drink coffee, (2) it's not listed as one of my job duties, and (3) ordering the secretaries to fix the coffee is carrying the role of homemaker too far." Women Employed demonstrators conducted a facetious lesson in how to make coffee (including Step 5, "Turn switch to on. This is the most difficult step, but with practice, even an attorney can master it.") and presented Rivera's boss with a bag of used coffee grounds as a "coffee demerit badge."[37]

The brilliance of Women Employed's tactics paid off. Their demonstration captured the network nightly news, generating hundreds, possibly thousands, of minor office revolutions across the country. It posed the problem of clerical workers in terms that moved beyond union-style claims for better wages and working conditions to expose the daily, gender-specific humiliations of being treated like a domestic servant in the office. It also got Rivera her job back.

Women Employed and Nine-to-Five adroitly used Title VII and affirmative action guidelines to build campaigns against discriminatory employers and to win legal victories. They developed colorful public celebrations of Secretaries' Day with slogans like

"Raises Not Roses" and awards to the stingiest boss of the year. Nine-to-Five grew into a national network of organizations and in the 1980s joined with the Service Employees International Union to take their organizing methods into a union setting.[38]

The same year that Women Employed and Nine-to-Five started, 1974, women in the labor movement created their own organization, the Coalition of Labor Union Women (CLUW). The founders of CLUW included Olga Madar, Edith Van Horne, and Dorothy Haener of the United Auto Workers and Addie Wyatt of the Meatcutters—all of whom had been among the earliest activists in NOW.[39] Structurally, CLUW was conservative, remaining within the labor movement, restrained from independent action, particularly in the area of organizing. Yet CLUW broke down the isolation of women within specific unions and forced the labor movement to recognize women as an important constituency for the first time. The appearance of three thousand women at CLUW's founding meeting in Chicago when only eight hundred had been expected signaled the intensity of women's interest and their need for solidarity.[40]

The new feminism made a lasting impact on higher education across the United States. By the late sixties the numbers and proportion of women seeking postgraduate degrees had begun to rise, providing plaintiffs for the Women's Equity Action League's class-action suits and then women to seize the opportunities that resulted from their success. By 1979, 23 percent of medical school graduates and 28.5 percent of law graduates were women compared to 8.4 percent and 5.4 percent respectively in 1970.[41] Within the basic disciplines of the humanities and the social sciences, changes were intellectual and curricular as well as numerical. Undergraduate students, touched by the feminist ferment, began to demand courses about women. Graduate students and a few faculty turned their research interests toward the study of women as well, and those who were already working in this area found themselves suddenly recognized. Women's studies courses began in 1970 and quickly grew into programs and departments offering major and minor concentrations. By 1975 there were 150 women's studies programs and by 1980 thirty thousand courses about women were listed by colleges and universities.[42]

Feminist scholars formed caucuses in many disciplines and initiated conferences and journals where they could present and debate new findings. From the outset the new scholarship on women

300

was interdisciplinary as were journals such as *Women's Studies* (1972), *Feminist Studies* (1972), and *Signs* (1975). The underlying paradigms of most disciplines, when scrutinized critically for their gender-based assumptions, proved unequal to the task of studying women. They presumed a male norm—as in the many sociological and psychological studies using only male samples—assuming either that male experience could validly stand for the whole or that female experience, if different, was insignificant. Theorizing that had begun in underground feminist journals moved onto the more respectable terrain of academic debate, and conferences like the Berkshire Conference on the History of Women (beginning in 1972) or the National Women's Studies Association Annual Meeting (beginning in 1977) exhibited a hybrid atmosphere in which the passion of a social movement was contained, but not suppressed, within a more rigorous and disciplined scholarly discourse.

The arguments were not easily won, however; women continued to be a small proportion of tenured professors. And their new scholarship, for all its revolutionary potential, remained isolated from much of the ongoing mainstream.[43]

Emergence of the Female-Headed Household

As had been true before, feminism arose in a time of dramatic change and deep social conflict. An analysis of the changing economic and demographic position of women in American society in the 1970s helps to explain both the explosive appeal of modern feminism and the fierce opposition it aroused. At the same time the measurable "place" of women indicated some fundamental changes and apparently intractable dilemmas.

Labor force participation became normative for women in the 1970s. By 1980, 51.5 percent of all adult women held jobs outside the home including more than 60 percent of women with children between the ages of six and seventeen and 45 percent of women with children under six. By 1985, 53.4 percent of women with preschool children were in the labor force.[44] Despite its ideological power, then, the notion that women "belong" in the home had lost much of its material basis. Throughout the twentieth century the rate of change in female labor force participation has been such that each generational group created a new pattern, so that they could not look to their mothers and grandmothers for guidance about what to expect.[45] Yet women retained primary responsibility for housework. Husbands of employed women in the 1970s apparently assumed a higher proportion of child rearing duties than similarly situated men in the 1960s, but feminist discussions of the "politics of housework," in which household tasks remained primarily female responsibilities even when men were willing to "help out," struck a nerve precisely because women continued to bear a double burden.[46]

The reemergence of the single woman in the 1960s after the intensely familial 1950s has turned out to be a long-term trend with ironic twists. As average marriage ages continued to rise, from 20.3 in 1960 to 20.8 in 1970 to 22 in 1980 and 23 in 1984, a growing proportion of women (about one in six) opted not to marry.[47] The numbers of unmarried women have also grown as a result of a burgeoning divorce rate which doubled between the early 1960s and mid-1970s.[48] At its height, the number of divorces was nearly half the number of marriages per year, leading some statisticians to predict that marriages had only a fifty-fifty chance of survival.

Higher divorce rates may reflect in part women's increased ability to support themselves and a consequent decreased willingness to remain in unsatisfactory marriages. At the same time, divorce had devastating economic consequences for many women. Changes in divorce laws toward a more egalitarian "no-fault" divorce drastically reduced awards for alimony despite comparatively limited mobility and opportunity in the workplace for women. As a result, in the first year following a divorce the standard of living for men increased 42 percent and for women it decreased 73 percent.[49] Of white, female-headed households below the poverty line in the mid-1980s, half had become poor because of change in family composition, primarily divorce.[50] This was less the case for black women, who were more likely to have been poor even before a divorce.

Single women included growing numbers of never-married mothers of young children. Although adolescent pregnancy rates declined after 1960, the likelihood that pregnant adolescents would marry also declined sharply. Furthermore, as birthrates among married women continued to fall, the proportion of births to unmarried teenagers grew. Four percent of unmarried eighteen-year-old white women in the mid-1980s were mothers as were 27 percent of unmarried black women.[51]

Finally, single women were increasingly old. The greater longevity of women compared to men meant a growth in the number of widows, who have always been disproportionately poor. In contrast to single mothers and racial minorities, however, older women on the whole saw a dramatic improvement in their economic status since 1960 due primarily to government programs such as Medicare, food stamps, and housing subsidies.[52]

Women appeared to be caught in a series of tragic ironies. They had more options regarding work, marriage, and childbearing and greater legal support for fighting discrimination. Yet, growing numbers of female-headed households filled the ranks of the poor, a phenomenon named in 1978 "the feminization of poverty."[53]

Women assumed their new roles in the labor force and as heads of households within the constraints of the late-twentieth-century U.S. economy. The dramatic entry of millions of women into the labor force, and the passage of new antidiscrimination laws, did not significantly change the gender segregation of most jobs. Those who worked had few choices outside traditionally female-dominated, low-paid work. In 1973 more than half of all female professionals were still teachers and nurses. Nearly half of all working women could be found in clerical and service work, 40 percent in only ten occupations including secretary, nurse, waitress, elementary school teacher, domestic service worker, and typist.[54] And the wages of full-time women workers remained less than two-thirds those of men.

Pressures to increase women's wages, however, were undercut by recessions in 1973–75 and 1982–83 signaling the end of the economic boom. In the face of surging inflation, real wages for all workers began a serious decline in the mid-1970s and income inequality rose.[55] In some ways, labor force segregation advantaged women in a contracting labor market. The service sector continued to expand, generating jobs in traditionally female-dominated fields. Meanwhile, the manufacturing sector, where males dominated, was shrinking dramatically. Only one million new jobs were available in manufacturing between 1968 and 1978 compared to four times that many in the previous decade. Between 1978 and 1983 three million manufacturing jobs were lost.[56]

The consequent downward pressure on all wages meant that women's jobs alone, without the addition of a male income, were rarely sufficient for family support. The political atmosphere,

303

shaped by the newly emerging economic vulnerability and insecurity of the middle class, fed an angry backlash against a whole range of justice and equity issues raised in the 1960s and 1970s. In this setting antifeminism and the new right arose. By the end of the decade, women were embattled *with each other* over the meaning of gender and the proper place of women in society.

Female Conservatism: Antifeminism and the New Right

Media attention to women's liberation in the early 1970s had stimulated a number of organizations among women who proclaimed their continuing satisfaction with the status quo. "Women Who Want to Be Women," "Happiness of Womanhood," and "Females Opposed to Equality" announced their antifeminist intentions. They gained a powerful leader with keen organizing skills in 1972 when right-wing activist Phyllis Schlafly founded STOP ERA and began an incessant barrage of criticism in public speeches and in her newsletter, the *Phyllis Schlafly Report*. Characterizing feminists as "a bunch of bitter women seeking a constitutional cure for their personal problems," Schlafly brilliantly orchestrated an attack designed to arouse deeply held fears.[57]

She labeled feminists as both marginal and dangerous, "See for yourself the unkempt, the lesbians, the radicals, the socialists." They were, she and others agreed, women who had rejected womanhood—the God-given roles of wife- and motherhood. The presumption that feminists were women-who-wanted-to-be-men fueled interpretations of the ERA that supporters found impossible to answer on a plane of rational political discourse. "Please don't send my mommy to war!" read signs held by small children. Supporters differed among themselves in their feelings about the likelihood and consequences of women being drafted under the ERA, but when the carnage in Vietnam appeared on TV news every night, images of women with rifles evoked a topsy-turvy world gone mad.[58] Similarly, right-wing opponents charged that the ERA would decriminalize rape, legitimize homosexuality, integrate public restrooms, and guarantee abortion rights.[59]

The defensiveness of not only traditional women, especially housewives whose role was rapidly losing status, but also many working-class women who would have chosen that role if given a chance, revealed a deep sense of vulnerability rooted in precisely the same cultural and economic changes that motivated feminist

304

activism. Where one side sought political equality with which to defend their own interests better, the other feared an almost total loss of self and female identity. The ERA became a symbolic focus for each side. Schlafly's first attack on the ERA linked it with *Ms.* magazine and "women's lib." *Ms.*, she charged, was

> anti-family, anti-children, and pro-abortion. It is a series of sharptongued, high-pitched, whining complaints by unmarried women. They view the home as a prison, and the wife and mother as a slave. . . . Women's lib is a total assault on the role of the American woman as wife and mother, and on the family as the basic unit of society. . . . They are promoting Federal "day-care centers" for babies instead of homes. They are promoting abortions instead of families.[60]

Parallel to the growth of the anti-ERA movement, a national pro-life (i.e., antiabortion) movement developed in the wake of *Roe* v. *Wade*. By 1980 the National Right to Life committee, created by the family life division of the National Conference of Catholic Bishops, claimed 11 million members. Though public opinion remained decidedly tolerant of abortion, most Americans believed that abortion was acceptable under certain conditions and not others. For right-to-life activists, however, abortion offended basic values about the meaning of womanhood, of sexuality, and of human life. They quickly became a significant political force because of their single-issue intensity, and by 1976 Congress prohibited the use of federal funds for the abortions sought by poor women.[61]

As issues at the heart of personal life—family, sexuality, and reproduction—entered political agendas across the political spectrum, it was hardly surprising that a revived political right wing in the mid-1970s should adopt these same issues as key themes for their agenda. The "new right," as it was called, drew on older themes of anticommunism and laissez-faire economics, but its potency in reclaiming control of the Republican party lay in its claim to represent a "moral majority" on issues of family and sexuality, namely the ERA and abortion.[62]

Political Feminism in Decline

As the new right gained strength, feminists in NOW warred with each other for control of the organization. An insurgent group ousted the leadership in 1974–75 with the slogan "out of

305

the mainstream and into the revolution," implying an intention to radicalize NOW and move away from traditional politics focused on lobbying, legislation, and legal initiatives. In fact, the change-over made little substantive difference. By 1977 when membership had declined significantly, the election of Eleanor Smeal refocused NOW on the ERA as its central issue.[63] The renewed emphasis on the ERA represented, however, a response to the growing power of the right-wing anti-ERA movement headed by Schlafly. In fact, the momentum for the ERA had been lost after 1972 when 22 states ratified it. There were eight more ratifications in 1973, three in 1974, one in 1975, and one in January 1977. In 1975, popular referenda on the ERA lost in both New York and New Jersey (states that had already ratified). And yet, public opinion polls continued to show majority support for the ERA.[64] Feminists, despite widespread support, were unable to overcome a tightly organized and politically sophisticated opposition.

In 1977 feminists and antifeminists clashed publically in celebrations organized around the United Nations International Women's Year. A national conference in Houston, Texas, had been funded by the federal government and planned by a presidential commission. Newly elected President Jimmy Carter appointed Bella Abzug to chair the commission, replacing more cautious Republican appointees. The Houston conference itself, and the fifty state conferences that preceded it, displayed both the breadth and the internal conflicts of the new feminism. State conferences, called to elect delegates for the Houston conference, became arenas for battle between feminists and the right wing. Even though liberal feminists prevailed for the most part, they were unprepared for the strength of antiabortion and anti-ERA forces in several states.

The Houston conference, consisting of about two thousand delegates and eighteen thousand observers, made visible a women's movement that had spread well beyond its original white middle-class base. Thirty-five percent of the delegates were nonwhite; nearly one in five was low income, and Protestants were in the minority (42 percent) with 26 percent Catholics and 8 percent Jews.[65] By significant majorities, the conference with considerable emotion enacted a plan for action that not only had the ERA as its centerpiece, but also included major planks on reproductive freedom and minority and lesbian rights.

The contacts, and conflicts, among differing groups of women generated moving stories of change and reconciliation. A small delegation of twelve including three native-American women "developed a deep level of intimacy . . . as the hours went on." One of the whites recalled that "we grew to respect each other's opinions and ended up influencing the delegation on issues, such as reproductive freedom and lesbianism, which the native-Americans had previously been against. When the Minorities resolution passed, we all danced in the aisle and cried tears of joy." Other delegates reported stereotype-shattering conversations on coffee breaks. One alternate from Tennessee spoke to an Indiana conservative and found "(to her and my amazement) that we agreed on a lot of things." A New Yorker found out third hand, from a cousin in the California delegation, about the working conditions of Asian-American women in west coast sweatshops. "I thought they passed with my parents' generation—those awful sweatshops we knew as children in New York."[66] The planks on abortion and lesbianism, in particular, provoked intense divisions. And in a counterconference on the other side of Houston, Phyllis Schlafly's "Pro-Family Rally," the possibility of dialogue did not exist.

In the end, the 1970s were a frustrating decade for feminists. Even with a two-year extension, the ERA could not be passed. New laws against discrimination worked with glacial slowness, if at all, in a stagnating economy. And the politicization of personal life, which had raised the consciousness of millions of women of all ages, helped breathe new life into right-wing politics that came to power with the presidency of Ronald Reagan in 1980. Even so, feminist concerns were firmly on the national political agenda and clearly there to stay.

Ironies of the 1980s

Within the conservative ethos of the Reagan administration, political feminism found hard times, but organizational strengths and cultural transformations gave it advantages it had never had before. Despite the effective use of cultural themes—family, sexuality, and reproduction (issues initially politicized by feminists)—the Reagan revolution was unable to significantly alter the gender shifts that had already taken place: new roles for women in the labor force, the changing demographics of marriage and family size, the reemergence of single women, and greater sexual freedom. The real battle was over the *meaning* of those changes both for individuals and for society.

307

New realities deeply affected the daily life experiences and expectations of all women. As a stream of young female graduates entered business and professions after the mid-1970s, they met more subtle forms of discrimination than their predecessors had experienced. They found themselves in a world that proclaimed equality of opportunity but defined career paths in the rhythms of a male life cycle. In response, many women put off marriage and childbearing, accelerating earlier trends. A spate of new magazines, such as *Savvy* and *Working Woman*, coached them in "dressing for success" and "how to have it all." By the mid-1980s this cohort produced a baby boomlet and introduced the world to "yuppie [young, upwardly mobile professional] moms." Many found the life of superwoman extremely stressful as they strove to meet the standards of success for *both* professionals and housewives.

The high-consumption life-style associated with two-income professional families meshed with the new admiration for wealth and business of the Reagan administration. Gourmet foods, aerobic exercise, and soaring house prices stamped the coming of age of the baby-boom generation with a high-energy search whose goals, beyond money, remained unclear. Some of the internal contradictions of this life-style for women could be seen in new household technologies and consumption patterns. Kitchens, for example, increasingly facilitated labor-intensive gourmet cooking with Cuisinarts and specialized cookware. At the same time, growing numbers of households also included microwave ovens, useful for heating frozen entrees and for eating-on-the-run, a style characterized as "grazing." For the first time, hours spent on housework began to decline.[67]

If greed was in, one male version was the driving aggression of business and international intrigue. Movie star Sylvester Stallone's "Rambo" epitomized that untamed, macho image as screen violence hit new highs. The female version was not the businesswoman or female lawyer—they were there, still anomalous, women-acting-like-men—but the consumer. Television evangelist Tammy Faye Bakker with her six houses, air-conditioned dog house, garish makeup, and love of shopping provided a contrasting female caricature.

While two-income professional families generated a new, high-consumption standard of living, the numbers of low-income female heads of households grew as the Reagan administration cut back traditional social programs. The poor, disproportionately female, did not share in the Reagan boom. Yet poor and working-class women brought new issues and new definitions of public life into the political arena against the grain of the conservative, look-out-for-number-one, ethos of the 1980s.

In San Antonio, Texas, Communities Organized for Public Service (COPS) brought its battle for dignity and rights in the Mexican community to the whole city. In 1978 they gained majority support on the city council for an alternative development plan, and in 1983 they elected the first Hispanic mayor of a major city, Henry Cisneros. Instigated by organizer Ernesto Cortez and organized primarily through Catholic parishes, COPS rapidly developed a strong core of female leadership. As staff director Sister Christine Stephens put it, COPS "didn't begin with people who were the politicos or who were in public life, the people who wheeled and dealed. It grew from the people who run the festivals, who lead the PTAs, whose lives have been wrapped up in their parishes and their jobs and with their children. What COPS has been able to do is give them a public life, the tools whereby they can participate."[68] Five of the six presidents of COPS who served between 1973 and 1988 were women. Only the first was a man.

COPS began with a campaign to force the city to enclose the open drainage ditches flowing through the Mexican section of town. With every major rain floods forced people from their homes and one or more children drowned. Drawn up in 1945, the official plan for improving the system had never been implemented. As it moved from success to success, COPS built a new political organization that consciously furnished its participants with the basic tools of participation. According to Ernesto Cortes, "COPS is like a university where people come to learn about public policy, public discourse, and public life." In doing so it necessarily drew on the talents of women. As former president Beatrice Cortez put it, "Women have community ties. We knew that to make things happen in the community, you have to talk to people. It was a matter of tapping our networks." Activating female-dominated communal networks in San Antonio offered a definition of public life with communal roots, a self-conscious discourse about values and family, and a refreshing attitude toward politicians. Sonia Hernandez, another former president of COPS, explained. "Politicians' work is to do your work. When you've got somebody working for you, you don't bow and scrape. It's not meant to show disrespect. When politicians deliver, we applaud them. Not until then."[69] The success of COPS provided a model for dozens of new community organizations across the country in Hispanic, black, and white ethnic communities.

The growing strength of women in unions such as the American Federation of State, County, and Municipal Employees (AFSCME) along with the formation of CLUW, Nine-to-Five, and Women Employed had given working women a new voice and new leverage. Together with political feminists in state and federal agencies, they generated a continuing debate through the 1970s over the persistence of the gap between women's and men's wages despite the legal tools of affirmative action and equal pay for equal work. Numerous research projects revealed an underlying cause: the labor market, though less racially segregated after the 1960s, continued to be sharply sex segregated. In general, women had access only to the least skilled, lowest-paying jobs, few of which paid well enough to support a family.

The concept of equal pay for work of comparable worth, dating from the World War II era, reappeared in policy debates and union negotiations in the mid-1970s. At the same time that feminist theorists were searching for the origins of patriarchy as a system, some union organizers and members of the EEOC were recognizing that women's economic disadvantages were complex and systemic. The division of the labor market into male and female jobs had allowed assumptions rooted in the older division of work/home, public/private, male/female to shape the emerging postindustrial economy. Only in the late 1970s and the 1980s, however, did this discrepancy become the object of social protest. In 1980 Eleanor Holmes Norton, chairwoman of EEOC, proclaimed comparable worth the "issue of the eighties." Despite active opposition by the Reagan administration, by 1987 more than forty states and seventeen hundred local governments had taken major steps toward implementing a comparable worth policy to raise the wages of female-dominated job classes.[70]

As the 1980s drew to a close, American women continued century-old debates in new ways. Women's actions, within the limitations of a declining patriarchy, had powerfully reshaped the structure and meaning of family and private life as well as a variety of public arenas from voluntary associations to electoral politics. Some challenged given definitions head-on; others advocated a return to an imagined past. New contexts reframed issues in ways their grandmothers could never have fathomed.

Peace activists continued, in the tradition of Jane Addams's Women's Peace Party, Women's International League for Peace and Freedom, and Women Strike for Peace. Women provided the backbone of a campaign in 1984 urging a freeze on nuclear weapons. Women Against Military Madness (WAMM) joined feminist/pacifist actions across the world in confronting the horror of global holocaust with what they viewed as a female vision of a humane world.

The spirit of Frances Willard's WCTU found new focus in a powerful lobby as Mothers Against Drunk Driving (MADD) made alcohol consumption a political issue again. Using their moral force as mothers whose children had been killed or maimed by inebriated drivers, they lobbied for stiffer penalties and surer sentences. In the name of protecting innocent loved ones, laws against drunk driving were strengthened across the country.[71]

Advocates of traditional gender roles emerged in new guises. Like nineteenth-century women's advocates favoring moral reform and an end to prostitution, twentieth-century women divided over the question of pornography in ways that confounded a left-wing/right-wing political spectrum. Similarly, nineteenth-century opponents of birth control resembled in some ways the opponents of abortion and homosexual rights in the late twentieth century, but the former could not have imagined either of those latter issues even being discussed in a public setting. Women who organized to oppose the vote for women on the grounds that it would disrupt family life and force women into manly ways would have recognized many of their arguments in the presentations of Phyllis Schlafly, though Schlafly herself matched precisely the image of the independent professional woman who was her target.

Certainly suffragist foremothers of late-twentieth-century American women would have cheered at the increased female presence in political parties. Women had been only 3.5 percent of state office holders in 1969, but by 1983 they were 13 percent. In local governments their proportion grew from 4 percent in 1975 to 10 percent in 1981.[72] Geraldine Ferraro's nomination for the vice-presidency by the Democratic party made the previously unthinkable, thinkable. A woman at the top? Maybe. When Congresswoman Patricia Schroeder seriously considered running for the presidency in 1987, however, political women knew both how far they had come and how far they had to go. A member of the House Armed Services Committee, Schroeder was a credibly knowledgeable and experienced candidate. Even so, reporters dogged her with questions about what Mr. Schroeder would eat for supper if she were president and why she was running "as a woman." Her favorite answer was "Do I have any choice?" Although a very significant proportion of the electorate was clearly prepared to accept her feminism as part and parcel of her thoughtful, liberal politics, there were not enough for her to be a viable candidate.

In the eighties feminists themselves, however, increasingly divided over what their agenda should include. Should all laws be written in a gender neutral way, or were there occasions when women needed to be treated separately to make genuine equity possible? Feminists split, for example, over the issue of maternity leave (linked to the biological fact of bearing a child) versus parental leave; over the problem of sex neutral divorce laws that had the consequence of plunging thousands of women into poverty; and over whether restrictions on the growing pornography industry amounted to dangerous (and antisex) repression or an essential prerequisite to female liberty.

More fundamental, women of all persuasions grappled with the dilemmas of reproductive technology. Abortion followed a deep fault line that did not quite match other political divisions, but even that seemed to pale a bit in the raging controversy over contract motherhood. For the first time, women could carry and bear children genetically unrelated to them. With artificial insemination, they could bear children for infertile couples and agree to surrender the child for adoption upon birth. With increasing infertility among middle-class couples that had postponed childbearing and very few infants available for adoption, the conditions existed for a new industry. Lawyers established themselves quickly as the go-betweens, making enormous sums of money in the process.

Such arrangements posed knotty problems. If the biological mother changed her mind, as Mary Beth Whitehead and numerous others did, could she keep the child? In such a situation, who was the "real mother"? The legal battle of Mary Beth Whitehead and William Stern over custody of "Baby M" exposed the class and gender dimensions of surrogate motherhood. Whitehead was a working-class housewife; Stern, a lawyer, and his wife, a pediatrician. Whitehead's behavior, kidnapping Baby M, and her obsessive insistence that biology was the only relevant definition of motherhood convinced many that she was unbalanced. The prosecution's derisive characterization of her as a bad mother because she played "pattycake" the wrong way brought many to her defense. The debate over the problem of parental equity in claims to children posed once again the cultural problematics of defining femaleness and its relationship to female biology.[73]

The debates over Baby M took place in a society wracked with political scandal (the Iran-contra hearings were the same year) and about to experience a jolt to the macho economics of speculation and corporate takeovers. In October 1987 a record stock market plunge of more than 500 points led *Newsweek* to proclaim the "end of the eighties" era of greed, as the year ended.[74] Though the proclamation was premature there were other, smaller signs of a shift toward communal interests and a diminished focus on individual consumption and self-interest. Applications to schools of social work began to rise again in 1985. The percentage of high-achieving college students interested in public school teaching rapidly increased. The terrible AIDS epidemic devastated the gay male community, bringing out the generous best and the homophobic worst in the surrounding society. As AIDS spread into the heterosexual population, it prompted a general reassessment of sexual experimentation and a terrifying realization of interdependence. From within their smaller households, American people hungered for community.[75]

In such a context, perhaps women once again will take leadership roles in the redefinition of our common life. They have a long history on which to build. From the beginning of Indian and then European settlement, women have refashioned the meanings and challenged the conventional dichotomies of public and private, female and male, black and white. In the process, women created a new public terrain through voluntary associations that became areas where citizenship could take on continuing and vital meanings, personal problems could be translated into social concerns, and democratic experiments could flourish.

Not only did new forms of public life force an ongoing reconceptualization of the responsibilities of the state (reflected once again in the 1970s as governments began to fund shelters for battered women and rape crisis centers), but they also provided varied and widespread foundations for a reactivated civic life, even in the face of massive corporate and government bureaucracies. Such possibilities coexist with obstacles as diverse as women's own conditions. Black, white, Asian, native-American, Hispanic, native-born and immigrant, urban and rural, wealthy and poor, educated and illiterate, working in the economy's female ghettos, raising the next generation against great odds, American women still struggle to make the issues of personal life matters of public concern. And they seek to claim for themselves the status of full participants in the construction of the American dream.

Notes

Introduction

1. The historians who have paid the most attention to this intersection have been Linda Kerber in her study of women in the American Revolution, *Women of the Republic: Intellect and Ideology in Revolutionary America* (Chapel Hill: University of North Carolina Press, 1980) and Paula Baker in a brilliant overview of both male and female politics in the nineteenth century, "The Domestication of American Politics," *American Historical Review* 89 (June 1984): 620–49.

2. Hannah Arendt, *The Human Condition*, pt. 2 (Chicago: University of Chicago Press, 1958).

3. Jean Bethke Elstain, *Public Man, Private Woman: Women in Social and Political Thought* (Princeton, N.J.: Princeton University Press, 1981), 162, 165.

4. See Barbara Nelson, "Women's Poverty and Women's Citizenship: Some Political Consequences of Economic Marginality," *Signs* 10 (Winter 1984): 209–31, and "The Gender, Race, and Class Origins of Early Welfare Policy and the U.S. Welfare State: A Comparison of Workman's Compensation and Mothers' Aid" in *Women, Change and Politics*, ed. Louise Tilly and Patricia Gurin (New York: Russell Sage Foundation/Basic Books, forthcoming, 1989).

5. For a fuller discussion of the lacuna among feminist political theorists, see Mary Dietz, "Context Is All: Feminism and Theories of Citizenship," *Dedalus* 116 (Fall 1987): 1–24.

6. The key exceptions to this are Linda Kerber, *Women of the Republic*, and Paula Baker, "The Domestication of American Politics"; Joan Scott, "Gender: A Useful Category of Historical Analysis," *American Historical Review* 91 (1986): 1053–75. In addition, the literature on women's organizations tends to prioritize the search for the roots of feminism and feminist consciousness. See, for example, Barbara

Epstein, *The Politics of Domesticity: Women, Evangelism, and Temperance in Nineteenth Century America* (Middletown, Conn.: Wesleyan University Press, 1981); Carroll Smith-Rosenberg, "Beauty, the Beast and the Militant Woman: A Case Study in Sex Roles and Social Stress in Victorian America," *American Quarterly* 23 (October 1971): 562–84; Keith E. Melder, *Beginnings of Sisterhood: The American Woman's Rights Movement, 1800–1850* (New York: Schocken Books, 1977); Ruth Bordin, *Woman and Temperance: The Quest for Power and Liberty, 1873–1900* (Philadelphia: Temple University Press, 1980); Nancy Cott, *The Bonds of Womanhood* (New Haven, Conn.: Yale University Press, 1977), and *The Grounding of Modern Feminism* (New Haven, Conn.: Yale University Press, 1987).

1 / The First American Women

1. Louis Hennepin, *A Description of Louisiana,* trans. John Gilmary Shea (New York: John G. Shea, 1880), 278–80, in *The Colonial and Revolutionary Periods,* vol. 2 of *Women and Religion in America,* ed. Rosemary Radford Reuther and Rosemary Skinner Keller (San Francisco: Harper & Row, 1983), 20–21.

2. See Carolyn Niethammer, *Daughters of the Earth: The Lives and Legends of American Indian Women* (New York: Collier Books, 1977); Ferdinand Anton, *Women in Pre-Columbian America* (New York: Abner Scham, 1973); and Gary B. Nash, *Red, White, and Black: The Peoples of Early America* (Englewood Cliffs, N.J.: Prentice-Hall, 1974). The Indians did not have any written languages. Even though archaeologists can tell us a great deal about aspects of Indian subsistence such as diet, settlement patterns, and population size and density, to date they have not developed adequate methods for studying gender. Pot shards, for example, are not labeled "made by a woman" or "made by a man" nor do tools indicate who used them. Unfortunately, we do not really know what division of labor or other gender relations looked like archaeologically. Inferences about men and women based on archaeological findings too often tend to be little more than speculations based on our own stereotypes about gender. See Janet D. Spector and Meg Conkey, "Archeology and the Study of Gender," *Advances in Archaeological Method and Theory* 7 (1984): 1–38.

3. Janet D. Spector, "Male/Female Task Differentiation among the Hidatsa: Toward the Development of an Archeological Approach to the Study of Gender," in *The Hidden Half: Studies of Plains Indian Women,* ed. Patricia Albers and Beatrice Medicine (Washington, D. C.: University Press of America, 1983), 77–99.

4. James Seaver, *Life of Mary Jemison: Deh-he-wa-mis* (1880), 69–71,

quoted in Judith Brown, "Economic Organization and the Position of Women among the Iroquois," *Ethnohistory* 17 (1970): 151–67, quote on 158. Similar to the Iroquois, Pueblo women in the Southwest owned their fields, though their concepts of ownership bore little resemblance to Western notions of private property. Their lands were not as rich as those of the Iroquois, however, and men were charged with tending the fields so that women could gather additional foods. After the harvest, women completed the processing of crops, including the constant and grueling task of grinding dried corn. See Niethammer, *Daughters,* 120–21.

5. Quoted in Robert Grumet, "Sunksquaws, Shamans, and Tradeswomen: Middle Atlantic Coastal Algonkian Women during the 17th and 18th Centuries," in *Women and Colonization: Anthropological Perspectives,* ed. Mona Etienne and Eleanor Leacock (New York: Praeger, 1980), 57.

6. Laura F. Klein, "Contending with Colonization: Tlingit Men and Women in Change," in Etienne and Leacock, *Women and Colonization,* 88–108.

7. This section draws heavily on Jacqueline Peterson and Mary Druke, "American Indian Women and Religion," in Reuther and Keller, *Women and Religion,* 1–41; see also Niethammer, *Daughters,* chap. 10.

8. Grumet, "Sunksquaws, Shamans, and Tradeswomen," 43–62; see also Niethammer, *Daughters,* chap. 6.

9. Brown, "Economic Organization"; Diane Rothenberg, "The Mothers of the Nation: Seneca Resistance to a Quaker Intervention," in Etienne and Leacock, *Women and Colonization,* 66–72.

10. Quoted in Brown, "Economic Organization," 154.

11. Elizabeth Tooker argues that women's power derived from their domestic roles within matrilineal households. She questions those who portray Iroquois women as a matriarchy because the economic relationship between women and men is more correctly portrayed as one of exchange rather than dominance. See Elizabeth Tooker, "Women in Iroquois Society," in *Extending the Rafters: Interdisciplinary Approaches to Iroquois Studies,* ed. Michael K. Foster, Jack Campisi, and Marianne Mithun (Albany: State University of New York Press, 1984), 109–123. Daniel Richter further clarifies the links between domestic life and warfare by showing that in the seventeenth and eighteenth centuries war was a means by which families replaced members who had died. See Daniel K. Richter, "War and Culture: the Iroquois Experience," *William and Mary Quarterly* 40 (1983): 528–59.

12. The demography of precontact and postcontact native-American

populations is a subject of controversy due to the difficulty of developing accurate population estimates. See Henry Dobyns, "Estimating Aboriginal American Population: An Appraisal of Techniques with a New Hemispheric Estimate," *Current Anthropology* 7 (1966): 395–412; William M. Denevan, ed., *The Native Population of the Americas in 1492* (Madison: University of Wisconsin Press, 1976); Russell Thornton, *American Indian Holocaust and Survival: A Population History since 1492* (Norman: University of Oklahoma Press, 1987); Henry Dobyns, "Native American Population Collapse and Recovery," in *Scholars and the Indian Experience: Critical Reviews of Recent Writings in the Social Sciences,* ed. William R. Swagerty (Bloomington: Indiana University Press, 1984).

13. See June Nash, "Aztec Women: The Transition from Status to Class in Empire and Colony," in Etienne and Leacock, *Women and Colonization,* 134–48.

14. Niethammer, *Daughters,* chaps. 5–6.

15. Anthony F. C. Wallace, *The Death and Rebirth of the Seneca* (New York: Alfred A. Knopf, 1970), 28.

16. Leacock, "Montagnais Women and the Jesuit Program for Colonization" in Etienne and Leacock, *Women and Colonization,* 27. Similarly, Cherokee women gradually lost their traditional agricultural roles and economic power in the face of a "civilization" campaign. See Theda Purdue, *Slavery and the Evolution of Cherokee Society, 1540–1866* (Knoxville: University of Tennessee Press, 1979), 52–53.

17. One scholar argues that as a result, women in these areas were particularly resistant to the efforts of French priests to convert them to Christianity. Finding their own economic autonomy threatened, they rejected a set of beliefs and structures emphasizing male authority. See Carol Devens, "Separate Confrontations: Gender as a Factor in Indian Adaptation to European Colonization in New France," *American Quarterly* 38 (1986): 461–80.

18. See Sylvia Van Kirk, *"Many Tender Ties": Women in Fur Trade Society in Western Canada, 1700–1850* (Winnipeg: Watson & Dwyer, 1980); Jennifer S. Brown, *Strangers in the Blood: Fur Trade Company Families in Indian Country* (Vancouver: University of British Columbia Press, 1980); and Jacqueline Peterson, "The People in Between: Indian-White Marriage and the Genesis of a Metis Society and Culture in the Great Lakes Region, 1680–1830" (Ph.D. diss., University of Illinois at Chicago Circle, 1981).

19. Quoted in Van Kirk, *"Many Tender Ties,"* 63.

20. Ibid., 33.

21. Ibid., 88.

22. Ibid., chap. 4.

23. Sylvia Van Kirk concluded that "in reality, the more acculturated a mixed-blood woman became the more she lost that sphere of autonomy and purpose which native women had been able to maintain." *"Many Tender Ties,"* 145. See also chaps. 5–10.

24. Niethammer, *Daughters,* 127–29.

25. Alan Klein, "The Political-Economy of Gender: A 19th Century Plains Indian Case Study," in Albers and Medicine, *The Hidden Half,* 143–73; Niethammer, *Daughters,* 111–18.

26. See Klein, "The Political-Economy of Gender."

27. See, for example, quote from Geo. Sword, *Manuscript Writings of Geo Sword* vol. 1 (ca. 1909), quoted in Raymond J. DeMallie, "Male and Female in Traditional Lakota Culture," in Albers and Medicine, *The Hidden Half,* 238.

28. Ibid., 241–47, quote from 245; also Niethammer, *Daughters,* 132–37.

29. In Beatrice Medicine, "Warrior Women—Sex Role Alternatives for Plains Indian Women," in Albers and Medicine, *The Hidden Half,* 273, see also 267–80.

30. Thomas Jefferson quoted in Bruce Johansen, *Forgotten Founders: Benjamin Franklin, the Iroquois and the Rationale for the American Revolution* (Ipswich, Mass.: Gambit, 1982), 112, 114.

31. Quoted in Leacock, "Montagnais Women," in Etienne and Leacock, *Women and Colonization,* 27.

32. Quoted in Van Kirk, *"Many Tender Ties,"* 17.

33. Grumet, "Sunksquaws, Shamans, and Tradeswomen."

34. "Journal of William Allinson of Burlington" (1809) quoted in Rothenberg, "Mothers of the Nation," in Etienne and Leacock, *Women and Colonization,* 77.

2 / The Women Who Came to North America, 1607–1770

1. *New England Historical and Genealogical Record* 28: 36–39. Quoted in Laurel Thatcher Ulrich, *Good Wives: Image and Reality in the Lives of Women in Northern New England, 1650–1750* (New York: Alfred A. Knopf, 1982), 161.

2. Quoted in Natalie Zemon Davis, "City Women and Religious Change," *Society and Culture in Early Modern France* (Palo Alto, Calif.: Stanford University Press, 1975), 91.

3. John Milton, *Paradise Lost,* ed. John T. Shawcross (New York: New York University Press, 1963), 295, quoted in Darrett B. Rutman, *Winthrop's Boston: A Portrait of a Puritan Town, 1630–1649* (New York: W. W. Norton, 1972), 7–8.

4. A separate system of equity courts could modify some of the harsher consequences of common law though it rarely did so in practice. Norma Basch, *In the Eyes of the Law: Women, Marriage, and Property in Nineteenth-Century New York* (Ithaca, N.Y.: Cornell University Press, 1982), 19–26, Marylynn Salmon, *Women and the Law of Property in Early America* (Chapel Hill: University of North Carolina Press, 1986), chaps. 3, 5–7. Joan R. Gunderson and Gwen V. Gampel, "Married Women's Legal Status in Eighteenth-Century New York and Virginia," *William and Mary Quarterly*, 3d series, 39 (1982): 114–34.

5. Natalie Zemon Davis, "Women on Top," *Society and Culture*, 124–51.

6. See, for example, Mary Beth Norton, "Gender and Defamation in Seventeenth-Century Maryland," *William and Mary Quarterly*, 3d series, 44 (January 1987): 3–39.

7. Bernard Bailyn, *The Peopling of British North America: An Introduction* (New York: Alfred A. Knopf, 1986).

8. Quoted in *Notable American Women: A Biographical Dictionary*, ed. Edward T. James, Janet Wilson James, and Paul S. Boyer (Cambridge, Mass: Belknap Press, 1971): 222. *The Works of Anne Bradstreet in Prose and Verse*, ed. John Narvard Ellis (New York: Peter Smith, 1932), 5.

9. Anne Bradstreet, "Here Follows Some Verses upon the Burning of My House, July 10, 1666," ed. Adelaide P. Amore (Washington, D.C.: University Press of America, 1982), 83.

10. See Robert V. Wells, *The Population of the British Colonies in America before 1776* (Princeton, N.J.: Princeton University Press, 1975); James T. Lemon, *The Best Poor Man's Country: A Geographical Study of Early Southeastern Pennsylvania* (Baltimore: Johns Hopkins University Press, 1972); Susan Klepp, "Five Early Pennsylvania Censuses," *The Pennsylvania Magazine of History and Biography* 106 (October 1982): 483–514; and Bailyn, *The Peopling of North America*.

11. Quoted in Joan Jensen, *Loosening the Bonds: Mid-Atlantic Farm Women, 1750–1850* (New Haven, Conn.: Yale University Press, 1986), 4.

12. Elizabeth Springs to John Springs, Maryland, 22 September 1756, in *Root of Bitterness: Documents of the Social History of American Women*, ed. Nancy Cott (New York: E. P. Dutton, 1972), 89.

13. Two recent historians have argued that "women were less protected but also more powerful than those who remained at home [in England]." Lois Green Carr and Lorena S. Walsh, "The Planter's Wife: The Experience of White Women in Seventeenth-Century Maryland," *William and Mary Quarterly*, 3d series, 34 (1977): 542–71.

14. Ibid.

15. See Allan Kulikoff, "The Origins of Afro-American Society in Tide-water Maryland and Virginia, 1700 to 1790," *William and Mary Quarterly*, 3d series, 35 (1978): 226–59; Allan Kulikoff, "The Beginnings of the Afro-American Family in Maryland" in *American Family in Social-Historical Perspective*, ed. Michael Gordon, 2d ed. (New York: St. Martin's Press, 1978), 444–66; Peter Wood, *Black Majority* (New York: W. W. Norton, 1974); Russell Menard, "The Maryland Slave Population, 1658–1730," *William and Mary Quarterly*, 3d series, 32 (1975): 29–54; and Deborah White, *Ar'n't I A Woman: Female Slaves in the Plantation South* (New York: W. W. Norton, 1985), chap. 2.

16. Ulrich, *Good Wives*, chaps. 1–2; John Demos, *A Little Commonwealth: Family Life in Plymouth Colony* (New York: Oxford University Press, 1970), pt. I.

17. Ulrich, *Good Wives*, 43–46.

18. Ulrich, *Good Wives*, 30. Previous section based on Ulrich, 13–33.

19. Carr and Walsh, "The Planter's Wife," quote from 561.

20. Peter Wood, *Black Majority*, 59–62.

21. See also Kulikoff, "Origins of Afro-American Society" and "*Beginnings of the Afro-American Family*," and Jacqueline Jones, *Labor of Love, Labor of Sorrow: Black Women, Work, and the Family from Slavery to the Present* (New York: Basic Books, 1985), 11–43. Chapter 1 deals with women's labor in slavery, not much specifically in Chesapeake.

22. Mary P. Ryan, *Womanhood in America: From Colonial Times to the Present*, 2d ed. (New York: New Viewpoints, 1979), 25; Russell Menard, "Immigrants and Their Increase: The Process of Population Growth in Early Colonial Maryland," in *Law, Society, and Politics in Early Maryland*, ed. Aubrey C. Land, Lois Green Carr, and Edward C. Papenfuse (Baltimore: Johns Hopkins University Press, 1977), 88–110. This pattern contrasts sharply with the much lower fertility of native-American women.

23. Ulrich, *Good Wives*, 126–45.

24. Carr and Walsh, "The Planter's Wife," 552.

25. Ulrich describes motherhood as "extensive rather than intensive," *Good Wives*, 153. On instrumental attitudes see Nancy Cott, "Eighteenth-Century Family and Social Life Revealed in Massachusetts Divorce Records," *Journal of Social History* 10 (Fall 1976): 20–43.

26. See Peter C. Hoffer and N. E. H. Hull, *Murdering Mothers: Infanticide in England and New England, 1558–1803* (New York: New York University Press, 1984), quotes on 57–58.

27. Her "disorderliness" consisted of the fact that she held mixed meetings of women and men and that she spoke "in a prophetical way" thereby rendering the entire meeting "disorderly." James Kendall

Hosmer, ed., *Winthrop's Journal,* vol. 1, p. 234, in *Original Narratives of Early American History,* vol. 7 (New York: Barnes and Noble, 1953).

28. Quoted in Lyle Koehler, "The Case of the American Jezebels: Anne Hutchinson and Female Agitation during the Years of Antinomian Turmoil, 1636–1640," *William and Mary Quarterly,* 3d series, 31 (January 1974): 55–78, quote on 64.

29. See Carol F. Karlsen, *The Devil in the Shape of a Woman: Witchcraft in Colonial New England* (New York: W. W. Norton, 1987).

30. Ibid.

31. John Demos, "Underlying Themes in the Witchcraft of Seventeenth-Century New England," *American Historical Review* 75 (1970): 1311–26.

32. Ulrich, *Good Wives,* 224; see also Karlsen, *The Devil,* chap. 7.

33. Daniel Scott Smith and Michael Hindus, "Premarital Pregnancy in America, 1640–1971: An Overview and Interpretation," *Journal of Interdisciplinary History* 5 (1975): 537–70; Daniel Scott Smith, "Parental Power and Marriage Patterns: An Analysis of Historical Trends in Hingham, Massachusetts," *Journal of Marriage and the Family* 35 (1973): 419–28.

34. See Ulrich, *Good Wives,* 69; Rhys Isaac, *The Transformation of Virginia, 1740–1790* (Chapel Hill: University of North Carolina Press, 1982), 302–5.

35. Mary Beth Norton, *Liberty's Daughters: The Revolutionary Experience of American Women, 1750–1800* (Boston: Little, Brown, 1980), 5–9, 20–25; and Ulrich, *Good Wives,* 113–24 on "genteel and domestic" urban women.

36. Julia Cherry Spruill, *Women's Life and Work in the Southern Colonies* (1938; reprint, New York: W. W. Norton, 1972), chaps. 13–14. Mary Beth Norton, "A Cherished Spirit of Independence: The Life of an Eighteenth-Century Boston Businesswoman," in *Women of America,* ed. Carol Berkin and Mary Beth Norton (Boston: Houghton Mifflin, 1979): 48–67 on Elizabeth Murray. Elisabeth Anthony Dexter, *Colonial Women of Affairs,* 2d ed., rev. (Clifton, N.J.: Augustus M. Kelley, 1972, chaps. 1–3.

37. New York *Journal,* 1733, quoted in Dexter, *Colonial Women of Affairs,* 18.

38. Joan Jensen, *Loosening the Bonds: Mid-Atlantic Farm Women, 1750–1850* (New Haven, Conn.: Yale University Press, 1986), 79–91. Jensen argues that women's activity as producers and consumers was essential to the new commercial infrastructure of the mid-Atlantic region that developed in the late eighteenth and early nineteenth centuries.

39. Quoted in Isaac, *Transformation*, 61, from Farish, ed., *Journal of Fithian*, 29.

40. Quoted in Anne Firor Scott, "Self-Portraits: Three Women," *Making the Invisible Woman Visible* (Urbana: University of Illinois Press, 1984), 3–36, quote on 21. On Eliza Lucas Pinckney see also Spruill, *Women's Life and Work*, 308–311, and James, *Notable American Women*, 69–71.

41. Kulikoff, "Origins of Afro-American Society"; and Isaac, *Transformation*, 30–32.

42. Kulikoff, "Beginnings of the Afro-American Family in Maryland."

43. Sara M. Evans and Harry C. Boyte, *Free Spaces: Sources of Democratic Change in America* (New York: Harper & Row, 1986), chap. 2.

44. This discussion draws on Winthrop Jordan, *White over Black: American Attitudes toward the Negro, 1550–1812* (Chapel Hill: University of North Carolina Press, 1968).

45. Quoted in Jordan, *White over Black*, 146.

46. Mary Maples Dunn, "Saints and Sisters: Congregational and Quaker Women in the Early Colonial Period," *American Quarterly* 30, no. 5 (Winter 1978): 582–601.

47. Ulrich, *Good Wives*, quote from 114, see 113–17.

48. Dunn, "Saints and Sisters"; Ulrich, *Good Wives*, chap. 12; Barbara Epstein, *The Politics of Domesticity: Women, Evangelism, and Temperance in Nineteenth-Century America* (Middletown, Conn.: Wesleyan University Press, 1981), 11–44; see also Susan O'Brien, "A Transatlantic Community of Saints: The Great Awakening and the First Evangelical Network, 1735–1755," *American Historical Review* 91, no. 4 (October 1986): 811–32.

49. Quoted in Paul Lucas, *American Odyssey, 1607–1789* (Englewood Cliffs, N.J.: Prentice-Hall, 1984), 197.

50. Hoffer and Hull, *Murdering Mothers*, chap. 3.

51. Cott, "Eighteenth-Century Family and Social Life," 32.

52. Hoffer and Hull, *Murdering Mothers*.

53. Mary Beth Norton, "Eighteenth-Century American Women in Peace and War: The Case of the Loyalists," *William and Mary Quarterly*, 3d series, 33 (July 1976), 386–409. Lorena S. Walsh, "The Experiences and Status of Women in the Chesapeake, 1750–1775," in *The Web of Southern Social Relations: Women, Family, and Education*, ed. Walter J. Fraser, Jr.; R. Frank Saunders, Jr.; and Jon L. Wakelyn (Athens: University of Georgia Press, 1985), 1–18.

54. Quoted in Cott, "Eighteenth-Century Family and Social Life," 22.

55. Ibid.

3 / "But What Have I to Do with Politicks?"

1. Edmund Burke, *Parliamentary History* 18, 14th Parliament, 3d session, November 6, 1776. Debate in Commons on a Motion for the Revisal of All the Laws by Which the Americans Think Themselves Aggrieved, p. 1443. I thank Linda Kerber for this citation.

2. George Rude, *The Crowd in History: 1730–1848* (New York: John Wiley & Sons, 1964), especially chap. 1; Edward P. Thompson, *Making of the English Working Class* (New York: Pantheon Books, 1964); Linda Kerber, *Women of the Republic: Intellect and Ideology in Revolutionary America* (Chapel Hill: University of North Carolina Press, 1980), 154, on the courthouse as "the physical locale in which public political education took place"; Edward Countryman, *A People in Revolution* (Baltimore: Johns Hopkins University Press, 1981), 182–83; Gary B. Nash, "The Transformation of Urban Politics, 1700–1765," *Journal of American History* 60(2) (Dec. 1973): 605–32.

3. Quoted in Gordon Wood, *The Creation of the American Republic, 1776–1787* (Chapel Hill: University of North Carolina Press, 1969), 6. On Whig philosophy see Ibid., chap. 1, and Bernard Bailyn, *Ideological Origins of the American Revolution* (Cambridge: Belknap Press, 1967).

4. See Edwin G. Burrows and Michael Wallace, "The American Revolution: The Ideology and Psychology of National Liberation," *Perspectives in American History* 6 (1972): 167–306, quote on 197.

5. Quoted in Wood, *Creation*, 110.

6. Quotes from Wood, *Creation*, 110, 105, 53.

7. See Ruth H. Bloch, "The Gendered Meanings of Virtue in Revolutionary America," *Signs* 13 (Autumn 1987): 37–58.

8. See Kerber, *Women of the Republic*, chap. 1.

9. See Barbara Leslie Epstein, *The Politics of Domesticity: Women, Evangelism, and Temperance in Nineteenth-Century America* (Middletown, Conn.: Wesleyan University Press, 1981), 42–43. Cotton Mather, *Ornaments for the Daughters of Zion* (1692; reprint, Delmar, N.Y.: Scholars' Facsimiles and Reprints, 1987) was widely read during the Great Awakening.

10. Rhys Isaac, *The Transformation of Virginia: 1740–1790* (Chapel Hill: University of North Carolina Press, 1982), 183; Bloch, "The Gendered Meanings of Virtue." For similar imagery in the French Revolution see also Lynn Hunt, *Politics, Culture, and Class in the French Revolution* (Berkeley: University of California Press, 1984), 61–65, 87–119.

11. Quoted in Wood, *Creation*, 6.

12. Quoted in Kerber, *Women of the Republic,* 78.

13. Quoted in Mary Beth Norton, *Liberty's Daughters: The Revolutionary Experience of American Women, 1750–1800* (Boston: Little, Brown, 1980), 170, 171.

14. Quoted in Kerber, *Women of the Republic,* 37.

15. "The Female Patroits, Address'd to the Daughters of Liberty in America, 1768" reprinted in *William and Mary Quarterly,* 3d series, 34 (1977): 307–8.

16. Quoted in Kerber, *Women of the Republic,* 41; see also Norton, *Liberty's Daughters,* 161–62; Inez Parker Cumming, "The Edenton Ladies' Tea-Party," *Georgia Review* 8 (1954): 289–94. The treatment of this extremely decorus meeting makes an interesting contrast to the Boston Tea Party whose participants in fact dressed in Indian costume and acted the buffoon.

17. Quote from Kerber, *Women of the Republic,* 104–5; see also Norton, *Liberty's Daughters,* 187.

18. Quoted in Norton, *Liberty's Daughters,* 157.

19. Ibid., 202–204; see also Kerber, *Women of the Republic,* 46. Susan Brownmiller in *Against Our Will: Men, Women, and Rape* (New York: Simon & Schuster, 1975) has documented the persistent pattern of sexual exploitation by armies. It is no accident that the word "conquest" is used in both military and sexual settings.

20. Quoted in Norton, *Liberty's Daughters,* 204–5.

21. Kerber, *Women of the Republic,* 54–61; Norton, *Liberty's Daughters,* 174, 212–13.

22. See Julia Ward Stickley, "The Records of Deborah Sampson Gannett, Woman Soldier of the Revolution," *Prologue* 4 (1972), 233–41. For other stories of female activity and heroism see Linda Grant De Pauw, *Founding Mothers: Women in America in the Revolutionary Era* (Boston: Houghton Mifflin, 1975); Sally Smith Booth, *The Women of '76* (New York: Hastings House, 1973).

23. Norton, *Liberty's Daughters,* 209–12; Ira Berlin, "The Revolution in Black Life," in *The American Revolution: Explorations in the History of American Radicalism,* ed. Alfred F. Young (Dekalb: Northern Illinois University Press, 1976), 353–55.

24. Berlin, "The Revolution," 367.

25. Saunders Redding, "Phyllis Wheatley," in *Notable American Women; 1607–1950: A Biographical Dictionary,* ed. Edward T. James (Cambridge, Mass.: Harvard University Press, 1971), 573–74. See also Paula Giddings, *When and Where I Enter: The Impact of Black Women on Race and Sex in America* (New York: Bantam Books, 1984), 41.

26. See Gary Nash, "The Forgotten Experience: Indians, Blacks, and the American Revolution," in *The American Revolution: Changing Perspectives,* ed. William M. Fowler, Jr., and Wallace Coyle (Boston: Northeastern University Press, 1979): 27–46; and Francis Jennings. "The Indians' Revolution," in Young, *The American Revolution,* 319–48.

27. Norton, *Liberty's Daughters,* 212–24, quotes from 218, 219, 223–24.

28. Kerber, *Women of the Republic,* 34–44; Abigail Adams to John Adams, 31 July, 1777, in *The Book of Abigail and John: Selected Letters of the Adams Family, 1762–1784,* ed. L. H. Butterfield, M. Friedlander, and M. J. Kline (Cambridge, Mass.: Harvard University Press, 1975), 184–85.

29. See Eric J. Hobsbawm, *The Age of Revolution: 1789–1848* (New York: New American Library, 1962).

30. Charles Brockden Brown quoted in Kerber, *Women of the Republic,* 121. See also Gordon Wood, *Creation,* chap. II. Note that the emphasis on "actual representation" meant a strong attachment to the right to vote, a concept with deeply radical implications. See Wood, chap. V, esp. 181–88.

31. John Adams to James Sullivan, 26 May, 1776, *Works of John Adams,* vol. 9, 375, quoted in Wood, *Creation,* 182.

32. Quotes from Jean Bethke Elstain, *Public Man, Private Woman: Women in Social and Political Thought* (Princeton, N.J.: Princeton University Press, 1981), 165; and Jean-Jacques Rousseau in Kerber, *Women of the Republic,* 26.

33. Quoted in *The Feminist Papers from Adams to de Beauvior,* ed. Alice Rossi (New York: Columbia University Press, 1973), 10–11, 13.

34. See Mary Beth Norton, "The Evolution of White Women's Experience in Early America," *American Historical Review* 89 (June 1984), 615–16.

35. See Rhys Isaac, "Preachers and Patriots: Popular Culture and the Revolution in Virginia," in Young, *The American Revolution,* 125–56; also Jan Lewis, *The Pursuit of Happiness: Family and Values in Jefferson's Virginia* (New York: Cambridge University Press, 1983), chap. 2.

36. See Norton, *Liberty's Daughters,* 128–32; also Rhys Isaac, "Evangelical Revolt: The Nature of the Baptists' Challenge to the Traditional Order in Virginia, 1765 to 1775," *William and Mary Quarterly,* 3d series, 31 (1974): 345–68.

37. See Margaret W. Masson, "The Typology of the Female as a Model for the Regenerate: Puritan Preaching, 1690–1730"; Martha Tomhave Blauvelt and Rosemary Skinner Keller, "Women and Revival-

ism: The Puritan and Wesleyan Traditions," *Women and Religion in America*, vol. 2, 327; Epstein, *Politics of Domesticity*, 49–51.

38. See Kerber, *Women of the Republic*, chap. 9; Norton, *Liberty's Daughters*, 245–50, 298–99.

39. See Wood, *Creation*, 69.

40. Judith Sargent Murray, "On the Equality of the Sexes," reprinted in Rossi, *The Feminist Papers*, 18–24, quotes from 19, 23, 24. See also Kerber, "Daughters of Columbia: Educating Women for the Republic, 1787–1805," in *Our American Sisters*, 3d ed., ed. Jean E. Friedman and William G. Shade (Lexington, Mass.: D. C. Heath, 1982), 137–53; *Women of the Republic*, chap. 5; and Cott, *Bonds*, 104–109.

41. Quote from Kerber, "Daughters of Columbia," in Friedman and Shade, *Our American Sisters*, 149.

42. See Kerber, *Women of the Republic*, chap. 9 for a discussion of women's part in the creation of republican motherhood.

43. Helen Hornbeck Tanner, "Coocoochee: Mohawk Medicine Woman," *American Indian Culture and Research Journal* 3, no. 3 (1979): 23–41.

44. David Hackett Fischer has argued that the period 1780–1820 witnessed an important acceleration in the rate of change on many levels—economic, demographic, and cultural. See *Growing Old in America* (New York: Oxford University Press, 1977), 77–78, 100–101.

45. Mary P. Ryan, *Womanhood in America: From Colonial Times to the Present*, 2d ed. (New York: New Viewpoints, 1979), 46; Alan Dawley, *Class and Community: The Industrial Revolution in Lynn* (Cambridge, Mass.: Harvard University Press, 1976), chap. 1.

46. Ryan, *Womanhood in America*, 46–48, 53–54.

47. Kerber, *Women of the Republic*, 201; see also Cott, *Bonds*, 103.

48. Kerber, *Women of the Republic*, 200.

49. Ryan, *Womanhood in America*, 52–53.

50. Ryan, *Womanhood in America*, 49.

51. Carol Shammas, "The Domestic Environment in Early Modern England and America," *Journal of Social History* 14 (1980–81): 3–24, quote from 15.

52. Norton, *Liberty's Daughters*, 229–35, quotes from 230 and 234–235.

53. See Burrows and Wallace, "The American Revolution," for an analysis of patriarchal versus Lockean images of family.

54. Quoted in Norton, *Liberty's Daughters*, 235.

55. Quoted in Cott, *Bonds*, 77.

56. Kerber, *Women of the Republic*, chap. 6; Nancy F. Cott, "Divorce

and the Changing Status of Women in Eighteenth-Century Massachusetts," *William and Mary Quarterly*, 3d series, 33 (1976): 586–614.

57. Robert V. Wells, "Family Size and Fertility Control in Eighteenth-Century America: A Study of Quaker Families," *Population Studies* (1971): 173–82; Norton, *Liberty's Daughters*, 232–34, finds literary evidence of the conscious use of prolonged lactation. See also Daniel S. Smith, "The Demographic History of Colonial New England," in *American Family in Social Historical Perspective*, 1st ed., ed. Michael Gordon (New York: St. Martin's Press, 1973), 397–415; Philip J. Greven, *Four Generations: Population, Land, and Family in Colonial Andover, Massachusetts*, pt. 3 (Ithaca, N.Y.: 1970).

58. Marylynn Salmon, "Women and Property in South Carolina: The Evidence from Marriage Settlements, 1730 to 1830," *William and Mary Quarterly*, 3d series, 39 (1982): 655–85; and "Equality or Submersion: *Feme Covert* Status in Early Pennsylvania" in Berkin and Norton, *Women of America*, 92–111.

59. Kerber, *Women of the Republic*, 137–55, quotes from 146 and 153; Salmon, "Equality or Submersion."

60. Norton, *Daughters of Liberty*, 236.

61. See Cott, *Bonds*, 125.

62. Epstein, *Politics of Domesticity*, 45; Nancy F. Cott, "Young Women in the Second Great Awakening in New England," *Feminist Studies* 3 (Fall 1975): 15.

63. Quoted in Cott, *Bonds*, 129.

64. Suzanne Lebsock, *The Free Women of Petersburg: Status and Culture in a Southern Town, 1784–1860* (New York: W. W. Norton, 1984), 196; also Cott, *Bonds*, 132.

65. Cott, *Bonds*, 138.

4 / The Age of Association

1. Hannah Mather Crocker, *Observations on the Real Rights of Women, with Their Appropriate Duties Agreeable to Scripture, Reason and Common Sense* (Boston, 1818), 17, 20, cited in Keith Melder, *Beginnings of Sisterhood: The American Woman's Rights Movement, 1800–1850* (New York: Schocken Books, 1977), 9.

2. Alexis de Tocqueville, *Democracy in America*, abridged, edited, and with an introduction by Andrew Hacker (New York: Washington Square Press, Inc., 1964), 181.

3. Mrs. John Sandford, *Woman, in Her Social and Domestic Character* (Boston, 1842), 173, quoted in Barbara Welter, "The Cult of True Womanhood" in *Dimity Convictions: The American Woman in the Nineteenth Century* (Athens: Ohio University Press, 1976), 31.

4. Welter, "Cult of True Womanhood," pp. 21–41, quote on 31.

5. Quoted in Welter, "Cult of True Womanhood," 37.

6. Catharine Maria Sedgwick, *Clarence* (New York: George Putnam, 1849), 242.

7. Nancy Cott, *The Bonds of Womanhood: "Woman's Sphere" in New England, 1780–1835* (New Haven: Yale University Press, 1977), 80–83, quotes on 81 and 82. Some historians have argued that the companionate marriage resulted in substantially increased power for women, see especially Carl Degler, *At Odds: Women and the Family in America from the Revolution to the Present* (New York: Oxford University Press, 1980), chap. 2. Suzanne Lebsock, however, offers a convincing critique based on the fact that "marriage was fundamentally asymmetrical" in *The Free Women of Petersburg: Status and Culture in a Southern Town, 1784–1860* (New York: W. W. Norton, 1984), chap. 2.

8. Lebsock, *Free Women*, chap. 5.

9. Kathryn Kish Sklar, "The Founding of Mount Holyoke College," in Carol Berkin and Mary Beth Norton, eds., *Women of America: A History* (Boston: Houghton Mifflin, 1979), 181.

10. Anne Firor Scott, "The Ever-Widening Circle: The Diffusion of Feminist Values from the Troy Female Seminary, 1822–72," in *Making the Invisible Woman Visible* (Urbana: University of Illinois Press, 1984), 64–88.

11. Kathryn Kish Sklar, *Catharine Beecher: A Study in American Domesticity* (New Haven: Yale University Press, 1973), quote from 36.

12. Quotes from Sklar, "The Founding of Mount Holyoke College," in Berkin and Norton, *Women of America*, 200, 198, 196.

13. Quoted in Alice Rossi, ed., *The Feminist Papers from Adams to de Beauvoir* (New York: Columbia University Press, 1973), 258.

14. Welter, "The Feminization of American Religion," in *Dimity Convictions*, 88.

15. See Louis J. Kern, *An Ordered Love: Sex Roles and Sexuality in Victorian Utopias—the Shakers, the Mormons, and the Oneida Community* (Chapel Hill: University of North Carolina Press, 1981), chap. 4.

16. Barbara Epstein describes in some detail the differences between women's and men's conversion experiences in *The Politics of Domesticity: Women, Evangelism and Temperance in Nineteenth-Century America* (Middletown, Conn.: Wesleyan University Press, 1981), see especially 53–58.

17. Mary Ryan, *Cradle of the Middle Class: The Family in Oneida County, New York, 1790–1865* (Cambridge, Mass.: Cambridge University Press, 1981), 89–102.

Notes

18. See Ryan, *Cradle of the Middle Class,* chap. 2; Cott, *Bonds,* chap. 4.

19. Carroll Smith-Rosenberg, "Beauty, the Beast and the Militant Woman: A Case Study in Sex Roles and Social Stress in Victorian America," *American Quarterly* 23 (October 1971): 562–84.

20. Ibid., 570–71.

21. Ryan, *Cradle,* chap. 3, quote from 119.

22. This assertion rests on the assumption that illegitimacy rates paralleled the more measureable rate of premarital pregnancy (i.e., births within nine months of marriage). See Daniel Scott Smith, "The Dating of the American Sexual Revolution: Evidence and Interpretation," in Michael Gordon, ed., *The American Family in Social-Historical Perspective,* 2d ed. (New York: St. Martin's Press, 1978), 427, table 1.

23. See Ryan, *Cradle,* 140–42.

24. Amy Swerdlow, "Abolition's Conservative Sisters: The Ladies' New York City Antislavery Societies, 1834–1840," unpublished paper, 3rd Berkshire Conference on the History of Women, Bryn Mawr College, June 1976; also Rossi, *The Feminist Papers,* 262–64.

25. Paula Baker, "The Domestication of Politics: Women and American Political Society, 1780–1920," *American Historical Review* 89 (June 1984): 620–49. The custom of "treating" the voters had begun in the eighteenth century.

26. Elizabeth Cady Stanton, *Eighty Years and More: Reminiscences, 1815–1897* (New York: T. Fisher Unwin, 1898; New York: Schocken Books, 1971), 31–32; Norma Basch, *In the Eyes of the Law: Women, Marriage, and Property in Nineteenth-Century New York* (Ithaca, N.Y.: Cornell University Press, 1982), chap. 4; Lebsock, *Free Women,* chap. 3.

27. See D'Ann Campbell, "Women's Life in Utopia: The Shaker Experiment in Sexual Equality Reappraised: 1810 to 1860," *New England Quarterly* 51 (March 1978): 23–38; and Mark Holloway, *Heaven on Earth: Utopian Communities in America: 1680–1880,* 2d ed. (New York: Dover, 1966); quote from Edward Deming Andrews, "Ann Lee," in Edward T. James, Janet Wilson James, and Paul S. Boyer, eds., *Notable American Women: A Biographical Dictionary,* vol. 2 (Cambridge: Belknap Press of Harvard University Press, 1971), 386.

28. Celia Eckhardt, "Fanny Wright: The Woman Who Made the Myth" (undated manuscript), 20, 22–23; see also Celia Eckhardt, *Fanny Wright: Rebel in America* (Cambridge, Mass.: Harvard University Press, 1984).

29. See Nancy A. Hewitt, *Women's Activism and Social Change: Rochester, New York, 1822–1872* (Ithaca, N.Y.: Cornell University Press, 1984), quote from 93; Mary Maples Dunn, "Women of Light," in Berkin

and Norton, *Women of America,* 114–33; and Gerda Lerner, *The Grimke Sisters from South Carolina: Pioneers for Woman's Rights and Abolition* (New York: Schocken, 1966), esp. 60–61.

30. "The General Association of Massachusetts (Orthodox) to the Churches under their Care," in Rossi, *The Feminist Papers,* 305.

31. Angelina Grimke, *An Appeal to the Women of the Nominally Free States,* 1st ed. (New York: W. S. Dorr, 1837), quoted in Lerner, *The Grimke Sisters,* 161; Sarah Grimke, *Letters on the Equality of the Sexes and the Condition of Women* (Boston, 1838), in Rossi, *The Feminist Papers,* 307–8.

32. See Eleanor Flexner, *Century of Struggle: The Woman's Rights Movement in the United States,* rev. ed. (Cambridge, Mass.: Belknap Press, 1975), chap. 5.

33. Thomas Dublin, *Women at Work: The Transformation of Work and Community in Lowell, Massachusetts, 1826–1860* (New York: Columbia University Press, 1979), 37.

34. Thomas Dublin, "Women, Work and the Family: Female Operatives in the Lowell Mills, 1830–1860," *Feminist Studies* 3 (Fall 1975), 32, quoted from Henry A. Miles, *Lowell as It Was and as It Is* (Lowell, 1845), 144–45.

35. Dublin, "Women, Work and the Family," 33.

36. See Christine Stansell, *City of Women: Sex and Class in New York, 1789–1860,* pt. 2, "The Politics of Sociability, 1820–1850" (New York: Alfred A. Knopf, 1986).

37. Paul A. Gilje, "Infant Abandonment in Early 19th-Century New York City: Three Cases," *Signs* 9 (Spring 1983): 587.

38. *The National Laborer* (14 January 1837).

39. See Catherine Clinton, *The Plantation Mistress: Woman's World in the Old South* (New York: Pantheon Books, 1982), and Anne Firor Scott, *The Southern Lady: From Pedestal to Politics: 1830–1930* (Chicago: University of Chicago Press, 1970), chaps. 1–3.

40. See Lebsock, *Free Women,* chap. 7.

41. Quoted in Clinton, *Plantation Mistress,* 94.

42. Quoted in Clinton, *Plantation Mistress,* 93.

43. See Catherine Clinton, "Caught in the Web of the Big House: Women and Slavery," in *The Web of Southern Social Relations: Women, Family, and Education,* ed. Walter J. Fraser, Jr.; R. Frank Saunders, Jr.; and Jon L. Wakelyn (Athens: University of Georgia Press, 1985), 19–34.

44. Herbert Gutman, *The Black Family in Slavery and Freedom* (New York: Pantheon Books, 1976), chap. 5; see also Jones, *Labor of Love, Labor of Sorrow,* chap. 1.

45. Lebsock, *Free Women*, chap. 4, quote from 111.
46. Quoted in Theda Purdue, "Southern Indians and the Cult of True Womanhood," in Fraser, *The Web of Southern Social Relations*, 35–51, quote on 41.
47. Ibid., 46.
48. Ibid., 35–51.

5 / A Time of Division

1. See Elizabeth Cady Stanton, *Eighty Years and More: Reminiscences, 1815–1897*, introduction by Gail Parker (New York: Fisher Unwin, 1898; reprint, New York: Schocken Books, 1971); Lois W. Banner, *Elizabeth Cady Stanton: A Radical for Woman's Rights* (Boston: Little, Brown, 1980), chap. 2; Elizabeth Griffith, *In Her Own Right: The Life of Elizabeth Cady Stanton* (New York: Oxford University Press, 1984), chaps. 3–4.
2. Nancy A. Hewitt, "Feminist Friends: Agrarian Quakers and the Emergence of Woman's Rights in America," *Feminist Studies* 12 (Spring 1986): 27–50; Nancy A. Hewitt, *Women's Activism and Social Change: Rochester, New York, 1822–1872* (Ithaca, N.Y.: Cornell University Press, 1984).
3. Quoted in Norma Basch, *In the Eyes of the Law* (Ithaca, N.Y.: Cornell University Press, 1982), 156.
4. See Eleanor Flexner, *Century of Struggle,* rev. ed. (Cambridge, Mass.: Belknap Press, 1975); Ellen Carol Dubois, *Feminism and Suffrage: The Emergence of an Independent Women's Movement in America, 1848–1860* (Ithaca, N.Y.: Cornell University Press, 1978); Alice Rossi, ed., *The Feminist Papers* (New York: Columbia University Press, 1973), 239–426; Mari Jo Buhle and Paul Buhle, eds., *The Concise History of Woman Suffrage, Selections from the Classic Work of Stanton, Anthony, Gage, and Harper* (Urbana: University of Illinois Press, 1978), 89–98.
5. Kathryn Kish Sklar, *Catharine Beecher: A Study in American Domesticity* (New Haven: Yale University Press, 1973), chap. 11, quote from 159.
6. See Ann Douglas, *The Feminization of American Culture* (New York: Alfred A. Knopf, 1977).
7. Quoted in Douglas, *Feminization of American Culture*, 129–30.
8. Quoted in Johnny Faragher and Christine Stansell, "Women and Their Families on the Overland Trail to California and Oregon, 1842–1867," *Feminist Studies* 2 (1975): 150–66. For more detail see Johnny Mack Faragher, *Women and Men on the Overland Trail* (New Haven, Conn.: Yale University Press, 1979).

9. Mary Ann Longley Riggs to Mother, 16 October 1845, and 10 December 1846; Mary Ann Longley Riggs to Lucretia Longley Cooley, 1 July 1850, Riggs Collection, Minnesota Historical Society, St. Paul, Minnesota.

10. Stephen Riggs, *Mary and I: Forty Years with the Sioux* (Minneapolis: Ross and Haines, 1969), 96.

11. See Roy Meyers, *History of the Santee Sioux: United States Indian Policy on Trial* (Lincoln: University of Nebraska Press, 1967); Gary C. Anderson, *Kinsmen of Another Kind: Dakota-White Relations in the Upper Mississippi Valley, 1650–1862* (Lincoln: University of Nebraska Press, 1984). See also Robert Berkhofer, *Salvation and the Savage: An Analysis of Protestant Missions and American Indian Response, 1787–1862* (Lexington: University of Kentucky Press, 1965).

12. Mary H. Blewett, " 'I am Doom to Disappointment, . . .': The Diaries of a Beverly, Massachusetts, Shoebinder, Sarah E. Trask, 1849–1851," *Essex Institute Historical Collections* 117 (1981): 192–212.

13. Alan Dawley, *Class and Community: The Industrial Revolution in Lynn* (Cambridge, Mass.: Harvard University Press, 1976), quote from 82.

14. William H. Mulligan, Jr., "From Artisan to Proletarian: The Family and the Vocational Education of Shoemakers in the Handicraft Era," in *Life & Labor: Dimensions of American Working-Class History*, ed. Charles A. Stephenson and Robert Asher (Albany: State University of New York Press, 1986), 22–36.

15. Alice Kessler-Harris, *Out to Work: A History of Wage-Earning Women in the United States* (New York: Oxford University Press, 1982), chap. 3.

16. Maxine Seller, *To Seek America: A History of Ethnic Life in the United States* (Englewood, N.J.: J. S. Ozer, 1977), 77.

17. William Sanger, *History of Prostitution: Its Extent, Causes, and Effects Throughout the World* (New York: Harper and Brothers, 1859; reprint, New York: AMS Press, 1974), chaps. 32–34; esp. 473, 488, 524.

18. Quoted in Christine Stansell, "Women, Children, and the Uses of the Streets: Class and Gender Conflict in New York City, 1850–1860," *Feminist Studies* 8 (Summer 1982): 323.

19. Ibid., 309–35.

20. Suzanne Lebsock, *The Free Women of Petersburg: Status and Culture in a Southern Town, 1784–1860* (New York: W. W. Norton, 1984), chap. 7.

21. Christine Stansell, *City of Women: Sex and Class in New York, 1789–1860* (New York: Alfred A. Knopf, 1986), 212–14.

22. New York *Herald*, 12 September 1852, reprinted in Elizabeth Cady

Stanton, Susan B. Anthony, and Matilda Joslyn Gage, eds., *History of Woman Suffrage,* vol. 1 (New York: 1881), 853–54.

23. Orestes A. Brownson, "The Woman Question, Article I" [from the *Catholic World,* May 1869], in *Up from the Pedestal: Selected Writings in the History of American Feminism,* ed. Aileen S. Kraditor (Chicago: Quadrangle Books, 1968), 193.

24. Basch, *In the Eyes of the Law,* 190–91.

25. Anthony to Stanton, (1856) in *Elizabeth Cady Stanton/Susan B. Anthony: Correspondence, Writings, Speeches,* ed. Ellen Carol DuBois (New York: Schocken Books, 1981), 61; Stanton to Anthony (1857) quoted in Flexner, *Century of Struggle,* 90.

26. Stanton, Anthony, and Gage, *History of Woman Suffrage,* vol. 1, 427–28, also in Buhle and Buhle, *Concise History of Woman Suffrage,* 103–105. This source renders Truth's words as a white person's version of a southern black accent. She is said, however, to have had a Dutch accent. I have therefore chosen to modernize the spellings.

27. Quoted in Sklar, *Catharine Beecher,* 223.

28. Regina Morantz-Sanchez, *Sympathy and Science: Women Physicians in American Medicine* (New York: Oxford University Press, 1985), chap. 2; Carroll Smith-Rosenberg, "The Hysterical Woman: Sex Roles and Role Conflict in Nineteenth-Century America," *Social Research* 39 (Winter 1972): 652–78.

29. Morantz-Sanchez, *Sympathy and Science,* chap. 2, quote from 46.

30. Morantz-Sanchez, *Sympathy and Science,* chap. 3, quote from 48.

31. Quoted in Johnny Mack Faragher, "The Midwestern Farming Family, 1850," in *Women and Men on the Overland Trail,* 59–60.

32. Lucie Cheng Hirata, "Chinese Immigrant Women in Nineteenth Century California" in Carol Berkin and Mary Beth Norton, eds., *Women of America: A History* (Boston: Houghton Mifflin, 1979), 223–41.

33. See Joan Iversen, "Feminist Implications of Mormon Polygyny," *Feminist Studies* 10 (Fall 1984): 505–22, quote on 517; and Julie Dunfey, " 'Living the Principle' of Plural Marriage: Mormon Women, Utopia, and Female Sexuality in the Nineteenth Century," *Feminist Studies* 10 (Fall 1984): 523–36, quote on 534.

34. Charles L. Perdue, Jr., Thomas E. Borden, and Robert K. Phillips, *Weevils in the Wheat: Interviews with Virginia Ex-Slaves* (Charlottesville: University Press of Virginia, 1976), 88–89, quoted in Jacqueline Jones, *Labor of Love, Labor of Sorrow: Black Women, Work, and the Family from Slavery to the Present* (New York: Basic Books, 1985), 31.

35. Deborah White, *Ar'n't I A Woman: Female Slaves in the Plantation*

South (New York: W. W. Norton, 1985), chaps. 4 and 5; Jones, *Labor of Love, Labor of Sorrow*, 29–43; Jacqueline Jones, " 'My Mother Was Much of a Woman': Black Women, Work and the Family Under Slavery," *Feminist Studies* 8 (Summer 1982): 235–70; Angela Davis, "Reflections on the Black Woman's Role in the Community of Slaves," *The Black Scholar* 3 (December 1971): 2–15. White and Jones offer sharply contrasting interpretations of women's work inside and outside the slave family. I find White's discussion of the "female slave network" convincing which undermines Jones's assertion that differentiated gender roles within the family constituted a form of resistance. Yet the evidence remains partial and elusive and further studies are necessary to move toward greater clarity. A good example of this is John Campbell, "Work, Reproduction, and Family on Upcountry Cotton Plantations, 1790–1860" (Ph.D. diss., University of Minnesota, Minneapolis, 1988).

36. Herbert Gutman, *The Black Family in Slavery and Freedom* (New York: Pantheon Books, 1976), chap. 2; quotes from Lawrence W. Levine, *Black Culture and Black Consciousness: Afro-American Folk Thought from Slavery to Freedom* (New York: Oxford University Press, 1977), 280, and Jones, *Labor of Love, Labor of Sorrow*, 38. See also White, *Ar'n't I A Woman*.

37. Jones, " 'My Mother Was Much of a Woman,' " 235–70, quote on 237.

38. See White, *Ar'n't I A Woman;* Jones, *Labor of Love;* and John Campbell, "Work, Pregnancy, and Infant Mortality among Southern Slaves," *Journal of Interdisciplinary History* 14, no. 4 (Spring 1984): 793–812.

39. Quoted in Leon Litwack, *Been in the Storm So Long: The Aftermath of Slavery* (New York: Alfred A. Knopf, 1979), 8.

40. Margaret Walker, *Jubilee* (New York: Bantam Books, 1976), 60.

41. Jean M. Humez, " 'My Spirit Eye': Some Functions of Spiritual and Visionary Experience in the Lives of Five Black Women Preachers, 1810–1880," in *Women and the Structure of Society*, ed. Barbara J. Harris and JoAnn K. McNamara (Durham, N.C.: Duke University Press, 1984), 129–43, quote on 138.

42. See Sarah H. Bradford, *Harriet Tubman: The Moses of Her People* (Auburn, N.Y.: W. J. Moses, 1869), and John Hope Franklin, "Harriet Tubman," in James, *Notable American Women*, vol. 3, 81–83.

43. Quoted in Willie Lee Rose, *Rehearsal for Reconstruction: The Port Royal Experiment* (New York: Oxford University Press, 1964), 12.

44. Bradford, *Harriet Tubman*, 39–40.

45. Mary Elizabeth Massey, *Bonnet Brigades* (New York: Alfred A. Knopf, 1966), 32–34, quote on 34. See also Anne Firor Scott, *The Southern*

Lady: From Pedestal to Politics, 1830–1930 (Chicago: University of Chicago Press, 1970), chap. 4.

46. Massey, *Bonnet Brigades*, 44.

47. Ibid., 132–34, quote on 133 from Washington *Chronicle,* 8 November 1865.

48. See Barbara Wertheimer, *We Were There: The Story of Working Women in America* (New York: Pantheon Books, 1977), 151–58; Massey, *Bonnet Brigades,* 143–46; Philip S. Foner, *History of the Labor Movement in the United States,* vol. 1 (New York: International Publishers, 1947), 341–44.

49. *Fincher's Trades' Review,* 18 March 1865, reproduced in John R. Commons, et al., *A Documentary History of American Industrial Society,* vol. 9 (Cleveland: Arthur H. Clark Company, 1910), 72.

50. Richmond *Examiner,* April 4, 6, 24, 1863; Louis Manarin, ed., *Richmond at War: The Minutes of the City Council, 1861–1865* (Chapel Hill: University of North Carolina Press, 1966), 313, 321.

51. Sara Evans, "Woman at War: The Richmond Bread Riot, April 2, 1863" (unpublished paper, n.d.), 15.

52. Quotes from Bell Irvin Wiley, *Confederate Women* (Westport, Conn.: Greenwood Press, 1975), 177, 176.

53. See Adrian Cook, *The Armies of the Streets: The New York City Draft Riots of 1863* (Lexington: University of Kentucky Press, 1974), and James McCague, *The Second Rebellion: The Story of New York City Draft Riots of 1863* (New York: Dial Press 1968). Neither of these studies, however, uses gender as an analytical category in examining the riots.

54. See Lawrence W. Levine, *Black Culture and Black Consciousness: Afro-American Folk Thought from Slavery to Freedom* (New York: Oxford University Press, 1977), 138–58, quote on 141.

6 / "Maternal Commonwealth" in the Gilded Age

1. Leon Litwack, *Been in the Storm So Long: The Aftermath of Slavery* (New York: Alfred A. Knopf, 1979), 229–47, quote on 237. I have modified the spelling to avoid an overemphasis on black dialect as recorded by whites (e.g., "cryin' " appears here as "crying"). Not only might the dialect be rendered incorrectly, but also one rarely finds quotations of other ethnic or immigrant groups spelled in dialect. The grammar and idioms of black English as recorded in these sources, however, has been retained.

2. Litwack, *Been in the Storm So Long,* 236.

3. Peter Rachleff, *Black Labor in the South: Richmond, Virginia, 1865–1890* (Philadelphia: Temple University Press, 1984), 22–33.

4. See James Oliver Horton, "Freedom's Yoke: Gender Conventions among Antebellum Free Blacks," *Feminist Studies* 12 (Spring 1986): 51–76; quotes from Litwack, *Been in the Storm So Long,* 245. Jacqueline Jones sees such sentiments as part of a pattern of black resistance in which slaves chose and defended a strict gender division of labor within the family against the grain of white's more undifferentiated treatment of black labor. See *Labor of Love, Labor of Sorrow* (New York: Basic Books, 1985), chaps. 1–2.

5. Margaret Walker, *Jubilee* (New York: Bantam Books, 1976), 392. See also Nell Irwin Painter, *The Exodusters: Black Migration to Kansas after Reconstruction* (New York: Alfred A. Knopf, 1976) for a description of black migration to escape economic and political persecution.

6. Quoted in Frances Ellen Watkins Harper, "Coloured Women of America," *Englishwoman's Review,* January 15, 1878, in *Black Women in White America: A Documentary History,* ed. Gerda Lerner (New York: Vintage Books, 1973), 247.

7. Eric Foner, *Reconstruction: America's Unfinished Revolution, 1863–1877* (New York: Harper & Row, 1988), 290–91.

8. Quoted in Litwack, *Been in the Storm So Long,* 532.

9. Quoted in Ellen Carol DuBois, *Feminism and Suffrage: The Emergence of an Independent Women's Movement in America, 1848–1869* (Ithaca, N.Y.: Cornell University Press, 1978), 59, 60.

10. Dubois, *Feminism and Suffrage,* chap. 3, quote on 89.

11. See Dubois, *Feminism and Suffrage,* chaps. 4–6; Eleanor Flexner, *Century of Struggle,* rev. ed. (Cambridge, Mass.: Belknap Press, 1975), chaps. 10–12, 16. Though the AWSA remained more decorous than the NWSA, its broader concerns can be traced in the pages of its publication, *The Woman's Journal.*

12. Tamara Hareven, "Family Time and Industrial Time: Family and Work in a Planned Corporation Town, 1900–1924," *Journal of Urban History* 1 (May 1975): 365–89.

13. Key sources on the women's crusade and the WCTU include Ruth Bordin, *Woman and Temperance: The Quest for Power and Liberty, 1873–1900* (Philadelphia: Temple University Press, 1980); Mary Earhart, *Frances Willard: From Prayers to Politics* (Chicago: University of Chicago Press, 1944); Barbara Epstein, *The Politics of Domesticity* (Middletown, Conn.: Wesleyan University Press, 1981); Frances Willard, *Woman and Temperance: Or the Work and Workers of the Women's Christian Temperance Union,* 6th ed. (Evanston, Ill., 1897). On pre–Civil War activism see Jed Dannenbaum, "The Origins of Temperance Activism and Militancy among American Women," *Journal of Social History* 15 (December 1981): 235–54.

14. Quoted in Epstein, *The Politics of Domesticity,* 96.

15. Ibid., quoted on 100.

16. Quotes in Ruth Bordin, *Frances Willard: A Biography* (Chapel Hill: University of North Carolina Press, 1986), 9, 10.

17. Bordin, *Woman and Temperance*, 98.

18. Mari Jo Buhle, *Women and American Socialism, 1870–1920* (Urbana: University of Illinois Press, 1981), 57; quotes from Estelle B. Freedman, *Their Sisters' Keepers: Women's Prison Reform in America, 1830–1930* (Ann Arbor: University of Michigan Press, 1981), 98.

19. Epstein, *Politics of Domesticity,* 113–16.

20. Willard, *Woman and Temperance*, 471.

21. Open letter from a group of Boston women in the *Bridgeport Evening Farmer,* November 29, 1895, quoted in Bordin, *Frances Willard,* 170.

22. See Bordin, *Woman and Temperance*, Appendix, 163–75, for a summary of studies of WCTU leadership and her own figures on their demographic composition. Unfortunately, she does not do a regional analysis.

23. See Lawrence Goodwyn, *Democratic Promise: The Populist Moment in America* (New York: Oxford University Press, 1976), chaps. 2–5.

24. Buhle, *Women and American Socialism,* 84–89, quote on 89.

25. See Susan Levine, "Labor's True Woman: Domesticity and Equal Rights in the Knights of Labor," *Journal of American History* 70 (September 1983), 324.

26. Maxine Seller, *To Seek America: A History of Ethnic Life in the United States* (Englewood, N.J.: J. S. Ozer, 1977), 125.

27. Deborah Swork, "Immigrant Jews on the Lower East Side of New York: 1880–1914," in Jonathan D. Sarna, *The American Jewish Experience* (New York: Holmes and Meier, 1986), 102–3; Paula Hyman, "Culture and Gender: Women in the Immigrant Jewish Community," in *The Legacy of Jewish Migration,* ed. David Berger (New York: Brooklyn College Press, 1983), 157–68. See also Charlotte Baum, Paula Hyman, and Sonya Michel, *The Jewish Woman in America* (New York: Dial Press, 1976).

28. On European women, industrialization and the family economy see Louise A. Tilly and Joan W. Scott, *Women, Work, and Family* (New York: Holt, Rinehart, & Winston, 1978), chap. 6.

29. See Laurence A. Glasco, "The Life Cycles and Household Structures of American Ethnic Groups," *Journal of Urban History* 1 (May 1975): 339–64; John Modell and Tamara K. Hareven, "Urbanization and the Malleable Household: An Examination of Boarding and Lodging in American Families," *Journal of Marriage and the Family* 35 (August 1973): 467–79; Susan Strasser, *Never Done: A History of American Housework* (New York: Pantheon Books, 1982), chap. 8.

30. Quoted in Strasser, *Never Done*, 155.

31. Susan Kleinberg, "Technology and Women's Work: The Lives of Working Class Women in Pittsburgh, 1870–1900," *Labor History* 17 (Winter 1976): 58–72.

32. Elizabeth H. Pleck, "A Mother's Wages: Income Earning among Married Italian and Black Women, 1896–1911," in *The American Family in Social-Historical Perspective*, 2d ed., ed. Michael Gordon (New York: St. Martin's Press, 1978), 490–510; Virginia Yans McLaughlin, "Italian Women and Work: Experience and Perception" in *Class, Sex, and the Woman Worker*, ed. Milton Cantor and Bruce Laurie (Westport, Conn.: Greenwood Press, 1977), 101–119.

33. See Jacquelyn Dowd Hall, Robert Korstad, and James Leloudis, "Cotton Mill People: Work, Community, and Protest in the Textile South, 1880–1940," *American Historical Review* 91 (April 1986): 245–86.

34. Lynn Weiner, *From Working Girl to Working Mother: The Female Labor Force in the United States, 1820–1980* (Chapel Hill: University of North Carolina Press, 1985), 18–27.

35. See David M. Katzman, *Seven Days a Week: Women and Domestic Service in Industrializing America* (Urbana: University of Illinois Press, 1981).

36. Quotes from Katzman, *Seven Days a Week*, 10–11.

37. Quoted in Katzman, *Seven Days a Week*, 198–99.

38. Aurora Phelps, "The Working Women. White Slavery in New England," *Workingman's Advocate* 5 (May 8, 1869), in *America's Working Women: A Documentary History—1600 to the Present*, ed. Rosalyn Baxandall, Linda Gordon, and Susan Reverby (New York: Vintage Books, 1976), 107.

39. *Penman's Art Journal* quoted in Margery W. Davies, *Woman's Place Is At the Typewriter: Office Work and Office Workers, 1870–1930* (Philadelphia: Temple University Press, 1982), 37.

40. Ibid., 54–55, quote on 54.

41. Cited in Weiner, *From Working Girl to Working Mother*, 25.

42. See Flexner, *Century of Struggle*, 140–42.

43. *Workingman's Advocate*, 29 April 1871, quoted in Kessler-Harris, *Out to Work*, 85.

44. "Two Heads or One," *Workingman's Advocate*, 7 May 1870, quoted in Alice Kessler-Harris, *Out to Work* (New York: Oxford University Press, 1982), 84.

45. Susan Levine, "Labor's True Woman: Domesticity and Equal Rights in the Knights of Labor," *Journal of American History* 70 (September 1983): 323–39; see also Leon Fink, *Workingmen's Democracy: The Knights of Labor and American Politics* (Urbana: University of Illinois

Press, 1982) and Peter Jay Rachleff, *Black Labor in the South: Richmond, Virginia, 1865–1890* (Philadelphia: Temple University Press, 1984).

46. Quoted in Levine, "Labor's True Woman," 329.

47. Ibid., 323–39.

48. See Fink, *Workingmen's Democracy.*

49. Levine, "Labor's True Woman," describes the ideology of women in the Knights. She does not use the term "maternal commonwealth," however.

50. See Strasser, *Never Done,* chaps. 1–7; Robert V. Wells, "Family History and the Demographic Transition," *Journal of Social History* 9 (Fall 1975): 1–20.

51. Quoted in Flexner, *Century of Struggle,* 129.

52. Anne Firor Scott, "Education and the Contemporary Woman," in *Making the Invisible Woman Visible* (Urbana: University of Illinois Press, 1984), 356–57; Barbara Solomon, *In the Company of Educated Women: A History of Women and Higher Education in America* (New Haven, Conn.: Yale University Press, 1985), chaps. 4–7.

53. Anne Firor Scott, "Jane Addams," in *Making the Invisible Woman Visible,* 111–14, quote on 112.

54. Quoted in Sheila Rothman, *Woman's Proper Place* (New York: Basic Books, 1978), 65.

55. Karen Blair, *The Clubwoman as Feminist: True Womanhood Redefined* (New York: Holmes and Meier, 1980).

56. William L. O'Neill, *Everyone Was Brave: The Rise and Fall of Feminism in America* (Chicago: Quadrangle Books, 1969), 77–84.

57. Quotes from Weiner, *From Working Girl to Working Mother,* 50, 61.

58. Ibid., 49–63, quote from 55; see also Joanne J. Meyerowitz, *Women Adrift: Independent Wage Earners in Chicago, 1880–1930* (Chicago: University of Chicago Press, 1988).

59. Estelle B. Freedman, "Separatism as Strategy: Female Institution Building and American Feminism, 1870–1930," *Feminist Studies* 5 (Fall 1979): 512–29, and *Their Sisters' Keepers,* chap. 3.

60. Jones, *Labor of Love, Labor of Sorrow,* 142–46.

61. Barbara Melosh, *"The Physician's Hand": Work, Culture and Conflict in American Nursing* (Philadelphia: Temple University Press, 1982), 30–34.

62. *New York Tribune,* 5 March 1860, quoted in Nelson Blake, *The Road to Reno: A History of Divorce in the United States* (New York: Macmillan, 1962), 91.

63. James C. Mohr, *Abortion in America* (New York: Oxford University Press, 1978), 196–99. See also R. Sauer, "Attitudes to Abortion in America, 1800–1973," *Population Studies* 28 (March 1974): 54–60.

7 / **Women and Modernity**

1. Frances E. W. Harper, "Woman's Political Future," in *World's Congress of Representative Women*, vol. 1, ed. May Wright Sewell (Chicago, 1894), 433–34.

2. Peter Filene, *Him/Her Self*, 2d ed. (Baltimore: Johns Hopkins University Press, 1986), statistical table, "Higher Education, 1870–1980," 238.

3. Quoted in Barbara Solomon, *In the Company of Educated Women* (New Haven: Yale University Press, 1985), 118.

4. See Mary Church Terrell, *A Colored Woman in a White World* (c. 1940; New York: Arno Press, 1980).

5. Solomon, *In the Company of Educated Women*, 119–21, see esp. 120, table 4.

6. Carroll Smith-Rosenberg, "The New Woman as Androgyne: Social Disorder and Gender Crisis, 1870–1936," in *Disorderly Conduct: Visions of Gender in Victorian America* (New York: Oxford University Press, 1985), 245–96.

7. See Kathryn Kish Sklar, "Hull House in the 1890s: A Community of Women Reformers," *Signs* 10, no. 41 (1985): 658–77.

8. Jane Addams, *Twenty Years at Hull House* (New York: Macmillan, 1911), 85.

9. Quoted in Sheila Rothman, *Woman's Proper Place* (New York: Basic Books, 1978), 112.

10. Quoted in Allan Davis, *Spearheads for Reform: The Social Settlements and the Progressive Movement, 1890–1914* (New York: Oxford University Press, 1967), 13.

11. Dolores Hayden, *The Grand Domestic Revolution: A History of Feminist Designs for American Homes, Neighborhoods, and Cities* (Cambridge, Mass.: MIT Press, 1981), 153.

12. For the best account of the Illinois Women's Alliance see Meredith Tax, *The Rising of the Women* (New York: Monthly Review Press, 1980), chap. 4.

13. Quoted in Vida Scudder, *On Journey* (New York: E. P. Dutton, 1937), 139.

14. Karen Blair, *The Clubwoman as Feminist: True Womanhood Redefined, 1868–1914* (New York: Holmes and Meier, 1980), 84–85; see also Mildred White Wells, *Unity in Diversity: The History of the General Federation of Women's Clubs* (Washington, D.C.: General Federation of Women's Clubs, 1953) and Jane C. Croly, *History of the Women's Club Movement in the U.S.* (New York: H. G. Allen, 1898).

15. Blair, *Clubwoman as Feminist*, 85–86; Catherine Clinton, *The Other*

Civil War: American Women in the Nineteenth Century (New York: Hill and Wang, 1984), 168–69.

16. See Steven Buechler, *The Transformation of the Woman Suffrage Movement: The Case of Illinois, 1850–1920* (New Brunswick, N.J.: Rutgers University Press, 1986).

17. Ella D. Clymer speaking to the National Council of Women, 1891, quoted in Rothman *Woman's Proper Place*, 65.

18. See Alice Kessler-Harris, *Out to Work* (New York: Oxford University Press, 1982), 167, 171; and Lynn Y. Weiner, *From Working Girl to Working Mother* (Chapel Hill: University of North Carolina Press, 1985), 68.

19. Susan Porter Benson, *Counter Cultures: Saleswomen, Managers, and Customers in American Department Stores: 1890–1940* (Urbana: University of Illinois Press, 1986), chaps. 1 and 4, quotes on 17 and 130.

20. Mary Church Terrell, "What Role Is the Educated Negro Woman to Play in the Uplifting of Her Race?" in *Twentieth Century Negro Literature,* ed. D. W. Culp (Naperville, Ill.: J. L. Nichols, 1902), 175, quoted in Paula Giddings, *When and Where I Enter: The Impact of Black Women on Race and Sex in America* (New York: William Morrow, 1984), 97.

21. Eleanor Flexner, "Ida Bell Wells-Barnett," in Edward T. James, Janet Wilson James, and Paul S. Boyer, eds., *Notable American Women: A Biographical Dictionary,* vol. 3 (Cambridge, Mass.: Belknap Press, 1971, 565–67; Gerda Lerner, "Community Work of Black Club Women," in *The Majority Finds Its Past: Placing Women in History* (New York: Oxford University Press, 1979), 83–93; Cynthia Neverdon-Morton, "The Black Woman's Struggle for Equality in the South, 1895–1925," in *The Afro-American Woman,* ed. Rosalyn Terborg-Penn and Sharon Harley (Port Washington, N.Y.: Kennikat Press, 1978), 43–57; Giddings, *When and Where I Enter,* chaps. 5–6; Hazel V. Carby, " 'On the Threshold of Woman's Era': Lynching, Empire, and Sexuality in Black Feminist Theory," in *"Race" Writing and Difference,* ed. Henry Louis Gates (Chicago: University of Chicago Press, 1986), 301–16.

22. Eleanor Flexner, *Century of Struggle,* rev. ed. (Cambridge, Mass.: Belknap Press, 1975), 222–31.

23. *History of Woman Suffrage* 4: 308–309, in *The Concise History of Woman Suffrage,* ed. Mari Jo Buhle and Paul Buhle (Urbana: University of Illinois Press, 1978), 364–65.

24. *History of Woman Suffrage* 5: 178–79 in Buhle and Buhle, *Concise History,* 371.

25. Grover Cleveland, "Would Woman Suffrage Be Unwise?" *Ladies Home Journal,* 22 (October 1905): 7–8.

26. Charlotte Perkins Gilman, *Women and Economics* (New York: Source Book Press, 1970, ca. 1898), see also introduction by Carl N. Degler; *The Home: Its Work and Influence* (1903; New York: Charlton, 1910); *Human Work* (New York: McClure, Phillips, 1904); *Man-Made World* (New York: Charlton, 1911).

27. Aileen Kraditor, *Ideas of the Woman Suffrage Movement, 1890–1920* (1965; reprint, Garden City, N.Y.: Anchor Books, 1971), chaps. 6–7.

28. NAWSA *Proceedings,* 1893, 84, quoted in Kraditor, *Ideas of the Woman Suffrage Movement,* 110.

29. *History of Woman Suffrage* 5, 82.

30. See Rosalyn Terborg-Penn, "Afro-Americans in the Struggle for Woman Suffrage" (Ph.D. diss., Howard University, Washington, D. C., 1977) and "Discrimination Against Afro-American Women in the Woman's Movement: 1830–1920," in Terborg-Penn and Harley, *The Afro-American Woman,* 17–27; Giddings, *When and Where I Enter,* chap. 7, quote on 123.

31. Carby, "On the Threshold of Woman's Era."

32. Weiner, *From Working Girl to Working Mother,* 4, table 1, and 6, table 2.

33. See Kessler-Harris, *Out to Work,* 97–105.

34. David M. Katzman, *Seven Days a Week* (Urbana: University of Illinois Press, 1981), 53, table 2–2.

35. Hayden, *The Grand Domestic Revolution,* 13, 72–77.

36. Weiner, *From Working Girl to Working Mother,* 89, table 6.

37. The best account of the IWA is Tax, *The Rising of the Women,* chap. 4.

38. For a sensitive analysis of class and ethnic differences between women in the socialist movement see Mari Jo Buhle, *Women and American Socialism* (Urbana: University of Illinois Press, 1981).

39. See Nancy Schrom Dye, "Creating a Feminist Alliance: Sisterhood and Class Conflict in the New York Women's Trade Union League, 1903–1914," *Feminist Studies* 2, no. 2/3 (1975): 24–38; Robin Miller Jacoby, "The Women's Trade Union League and American Feminism," *Feminist Studies* 3, no. 1/2 (1975): 126–40.

40. Tax, *The Rising of the Women,* chap. 8, quote from the ILGWU, *Souvenir History of the Strike,* 207.

41. Ibid., 217.

42. See Kathy Peiss, "Dance Madness: New York City Dance Halls and Working-Class Sexuality, 1900–1920," in *Life and Labor: Dimensions of American Working-Class History,* ed. Charles Stephenson (Albany:

State University of New York Press, 1986), 150–76; John D'Emilio and Estelle B. Freedman, *Intimate Matters: A History of Sexuality in America* (New York: Harper & Row, 1988), chap. 8; Lois Banner, *American Beauty* (New York: Alfred A. Knopf, 1983), chap. 9; Filene, *Him/Her Self*, 61–68, 88–89.

43. Banner, *American Beauty*, 190.

44. See Smith-Rosenberg, "The New Woman as Androgyne"; Linda Gordon, *Woman's Body, Woman's Right: A Social History of Birth Control in America* (Middlesex, England: Penguin Books, 1977), 186–245; Ellen Kay Trimberger, "Feminism, Men, and Modern Love: Greenwich Village, 1900–1925," in *The Powers of Desire*, ed. Anne Snitow, Christine Stansell, and Sharon Thompson (New York: Monthly Review Press, 1983), 131–152; D'Emilio and Freedman, *Intimate Matters*, chap. 9; Joanne J. Meyerowitz, *Women Adrift: Independent Wage Earners in Chicago, 1880–1930* (Chicago: University of Chicago Press, 1988); June Sochen, *The New Woman in Greenwich Village: 1910–1920* (New York: Quadrangle Books, 1972); David Kennedy, *Birth Control in America: The Career of Margaret Sanger* (New Haven, Conn.: Yale University Press, 1970).

45. See Laura Shapiro, *Perfection Salad: Women and Cooking at the Turn of the Century* (New York: Farrar, Straus & Giroux, 1987), 91–95.

46. See Barbara J. Nelson, "Women's Poverty and Women's Citizenship: Some Political Consequences of Economic Marginality," *Signs* 10 (Winter 1984): 209–31; Michael B. Katz, *In the Shadow of the Poorhouse: A Social History of Welfare in America* (New York: Basic Books, 1986), chap. 5; Clarke Chambers, "Toward a Redefinition of Welfare History," *Journal of American History* 73 (September 1986): 407–33.

47. See Smith-Rosenberg, "The New Woman as Androgyne."

48. Sharon Hartman Strom, "Leadership and Tactics in the American Woman Suffrage Movement: A New Perspective from Massachusetts," *Journal of American History* 62 (September 1975): 296–315.

49. Buhle and Buhle, *Concise History*, 389–90; *History of Woman Suffrage* 6: 675–82, quote on 681.

50. *History of Woman Suffrage* 5: 377–81; Flexner, *Century of Struggle*, 256–74.

51. Rheta Childe Dorr, *A Woman of Fifty*, 2d ed. (New York: Funk & Wagnalls, 1924), 101.

52. *The Liberator* 3 (December 1920): 23–34, in *The New Feminism in 20th Century America*, ed. June Sochen (Lexington, Mass.: D. C. Heath, 1971), 65. See also Judith Schwarz, *Radical Feminists of Heterodoxy: Greenwich Village, 1912–1940* (Lebanon, N.H.: New Victoria Publishers, 1982).

53. This discussion of the birth of feminism draws on Nancy Cott, *The Grounding of Modern Feminism* (New Haven, Conn.: Yale University Press, 1987), chap. 1, quote from 36.

54. Buhle and Buhle, *Concise History,* 405; from "New York City Campaign, 1915," *History of Woman Suffrage,* vol. 6, 459–64, quote from 464.

55. Buhle and Buhle, *Concise History,* 434; *History of Woman Suffrage,* vol. 5, 496–508, quote from 498.

56. See Flexner, *Century of Struggle,* 292–94.

57. Quoted in Flexner, *Century of Struggle,* 291.

58. Buhle and Buhle, *Concise History,* 249–56, quote from 252.

59. See Maurine Weiner Greenwald, *Women, War, and Work: The Impact of World War I on Women Workers in the United States* (Westport, Conn.: Greenwood Press, 1980).

60. This interpretation draws on Paula Baker, "The Domestication of American Politics," *American Historical Review* 89 (June 1984): 620–49.

8 / Flappers, Freudians, and All That Jazz

1. Quoted in Nancy Milford, *Zelda* (New York: Avon Books, 1971), 160.

2. Quoted in Marjorie Rosen, *Popcorn Venus: Women, Movies and the American Dream* (New York: Avon, 1974), 77.

3. Quoted in Paula Fass, *The Damned and the Beautiful: American Youth in the 1920s* (New York: Oxford University Press, 1977), 307.

4. Ibid., 228–42; see also Peter Filene, *Him/Her Self,* 2d ed. (Baltimore: Johns Hopkins University Press, 1986), chap. 5.

5. John Modell, Frank Furstenberg, Douglas Strong, "The Timing of Marriage in the Transition to Adulthood: Continuity and Change, 1860–1975," in *Turning Points,* ed. John Demos and Sarane Boocock (Chicago: University of Chicago Press, 1978), 120–50.

6. Christina Simmons, "Companionate Marriage and the Lesbian Threat," *Frontiers* 4, 3 (1979): 54–59.

7. Sheila Rothman, *Woman's Proper Place* (New York: Basic Books, 1978), 198; Linda Gordon, *Woman's Body, Woman's Right* (New York: Grossman, 1976), 259–74; David Kennedy, *Birth Control in America: The Career of Margaret Sanger* (New Haven, Conn.: Yale University Press, 1970), chap. 7.

8. See Carroll Smith-Rosenberg, "The New Woman as Androgyne," in *Disorderly Conduct* (New York: Alfred A. Knopf, 1985), 245–96; Filene, *Him/Her Self,* 129–35.

9. Rosalind Moss, "Spinsters and Old Maids in Folklore and Oral History" (Paper presented to the 15th Annual Northern Great Plains History Conference, Duluth, Minn., October 1980).

10. Ellen Gerber, "The Controlled Development of Collegiate Sport for Women, 1923–1936," in *Her Story in Sport,* ed. Reet Howell (West Point, N.Y.: Leisure Press, 1983), 432–59; Henel Lenskyj, *Out of Bounds: Women, Sport and Sexuality* (Toronto: The Women's Press, 1986), 67–71.

11. Rothman, *Woman's Proper Place,* 162.

12. Lois Banner, *American Beauty* (New York: Alfred A. Knopf, 1983), 265–70, quote on 269.

13. "The Art of Dress," *Photoplay,* April 1921, 48.

14. "How to Hold Him," *Photoplay,* November 1920, 46.

15. Quoted in Milford, *Zelda,* 122.

16. Quoted in Mary Ryan, "The Projection of a New Womanhood: The Movie Moderns in the 1920s," in *Our American Sisters: Women in American Life and Thought,* 3d ed., ed. Jean Friedman and William Shade (Lexington, Mass.: D. C. Heath, 1982), 513.

17. See Estelle B. Freedman, "Sexuality in Nineteenth-Century America: Behavior, Ideology, and Politics," *Reviews in American History* 10 (December 1982): 196–215; Carroll Smith-Rosenberg, "The Female World of Love and Ritual: Relations Between Women in Nineteenth-Century America," *Signs* 1 (Autumn 1975): 1–29; Blanche Wiesen Cook, "Female Support Networks and Political Activism: Lillian Wald, Crystal Eastman, Emma Goldman," in *A Heritage of Her Own,* ed. Nancy F. Cott and Elizabeth H. Pleck (New York: Touchstone, 1979), 412–44; Vern Bullough and Bonnie Bullough, "Lesbianism in the 1920s and 1930s: A Newfound Study," *Signs* 2 (Summer 1977): 895–904; Lillian Faderman, *Surpassing the Love of Men: Romantic Friendship and Love between Women from the Renaissance to the Present* (New York: William Morrow, 1981); Leila J. Rupp, " 'Imagine My Surprise': Women's Relationships in Historical Perspective," *Frontiers* 5 (Fall 1980): 61–70. On the emergence of homosexual subcultures in the twentieth century see John D'Emilio, *Sexual Politics, Sexual Communities: The Making of a Homosexual Minority in the U.S., 1940– 1970* (Chicago: University of Chicago Press, 1983).

18. See Rothman, *Woman's Proper Place,* 187; Filene, *Him/Her Self,* 124– 28.

19. Ruth Schwartz Cowan, *More Work for Mother: The Ironies of Household Technology from the Open Hearth to the Microwave* (New York: Basic Books, 1983), 121–22; David M. Katzman, *Seven Days a Week* (Urbana: University of Illinois Press, 1981), 61, table 2–6.

20. *McClure's*, 1917 General Electric ad, in Susan Strasser, *Never Done* (New York: Pantheon, 1982), 77.

21. Quote from "Editorial," *Ladies Home Journal* (April 1928): 36. See also Ruth Schwartz Cowan, "Two Washes in the Morning and a Bridge Party at Night: The American Housewife between the Wars," *Women's Studies* 3, no. 2 (1976): 147–71, and "The 'Industrial Revolution' in the Home: Household Technology and Social Change in the Twentieth Century," in *Material Culture Studies in America,* ed. Thomas Schlereth (Nashville: American Association for State and Local History, 1982), 222–36; Strasser, *Never Done,* chap. 14; Bettina Berch, "Scientific Management in the Home: The Empress's New Clothes," *Journal of American Culture* 3 (Fall 1980): 440–45; Kimberley W. Carrell, "The Industrial Revolution Comes to the Home: Kitchen Design Reform and Middle-Class Women," *Journal of American Culture* 212 (Fall 1979): 488–99.

22. Robert Lynd and Helen Lynd, *Middletown* (New York: Harcourt, Brace, 1929), 146–47.

23. Cowan, *More Work for Mother,* 178–80; Strasser, *Never Done,* 237–40; Filene, *Him/Her Self,* 125–27.

24. See Alice Kessler-Harris, *Out to Work* (New York: Oxford University Press, 1982), chap. 8.

25. Floyd Dell, *Love in the Machine Age* (New York, 1930), 139, quoted in Judith Smith, "The New Woman Knows How to Type: Some Connections Between Sexual Ideology and Clerical Work, 1900–1930" (Paper presented at the Berkshire Conference on the History of Women, Cambridge, Massachusetts, November 1974).

26. Ryan, "Projection of a New Womanhood," 514.

27. Rosalind Urbach Moss, " 'With You/Without You': The Shifting Locus of Spinsterhood Presented in American Popular Films, 1900–1960" (Paper presented at the American Studies Association, San Diego, California, November 3, 1985).

28. "Women in Business," *Fortune* 12 (August 1935): 55.

29. Margery W. Davies, *Woman's Place Is At the Typewriter: Office Work and Office Workers, 1870–1930* (Philadelphia: Temple University Press, 1982), chap. 8.

30. Angel Kwolek-Folland, "The Business of Gender: The Redefinition of Male and Female in the Modern Business Office in the United States, 1870–1960" (Ph.D. diss., University of Minnesota, 1987), chaps. 3 and 5.

31. M. B. Levick, "Reign of Beauty in Business," *New York Times Magazine,* 15 June 1924, 5.

32. See Joanne J. Meyerowitz, *Women Adrift: Independent Wage Earners*

in Chicago, 1880–1930 (Chicago: University of Chicago Press, 1988).

33. Jacquelyn Dowd Hall, "Gender and Labor Militancy in the Appalachian South," *Journal of American History* 73 (September 1986): 354–82.

34. Quoted in Rosalinda M. Gonzalez, "Chicanas and Mexican Immigrant Families, 1920–1940," in *Decades of Discontent: The Women's Movement, 1920–1940,* ed. Lois Scharf and Joan M. Jensen (Westport, Conn.: Greenwood Press, 1983), 63–64.

35. Sarah Deutsch, *No Separate Refuge: Culture, Class, and Gender on an Anglo-Hispanic Frontier in the American Southwest, 1880–1940* (New York: Oxford University Press, 1987), see especially chaps. 2 and 6; Vicki L. Ruiz, *Cannery Women, Cannery Lives: Mexican Women, Unionization, and the California Food Processing Industry, 1930–1950* (Albuquerque: University of New Mexico Press, 1987), chap. 1.

36. Gonzalez, "Chicanas and Mexican Immigrant Families," 59–84, quote 74. Sarah Deutsch and Vicki Ruiz emphasize the lack of wage-earning opportunities rather than cultural preferences to account for women's labor force participation. The history of Chicanas and Hispanic women in general is clearly an area in which there is desperate need for more research.

37. Calvin Collidge. This famous quote may be found in William A. DeGregorio, *The Complete Book of U.S. Presidents* (New York: Dembner Books, 1984), 460.

38. Elsie Hill, "Shall Woman Be Equal Before the Law? Yes!" *The Nation,* 12 April 1922, 419.

39. Nancy F. Cott, *The Grounding of Modern Feminism* (New Haven, Conn.: Yale University Press, 1987), chap. 4.

40. Mrs. Mary Murray, testimony before the Judiciary Committee, quoted in Ruby A. Black, "The Congressional Hearings," *Equal Rights,* 14 February 1925, 6.

41. Giddings, *When and Where I Enter,* 166–69.

42. See Cott, *Grounding of Modern Feminism,* chap. 3; Clarke A. Chambers, *Seedtime of Reform: American Social Service and Social Action, 1918–1933* (Minneapolis: University of Minnesota Press, 1963).

43. For a powerful and persuasive discussion of these differences see Cott, *Grounding of Modern Feminism.* See also Felice Gordon, *After Winning: The Legacy of the New Jersey Suffragists, 1920–1946* (New Brunswick, N.J.: Rutgers University Press, 1986).

44. Jacquelyn Dowd Hall, *Revolt Against Chivalry: Jessie Daniel Ames and the Women's Campaign Against Lynching* (New York: Columbia University Press, 1979), chap. 3, quotes on 86–89. See also Gerda Lerner, ed., *Black Women in White America* (New York: Vintage, 1973), 211–15.

45. Rothman, *Woman's Proper Place*, 136–53. For a detailed political history of the Sheppard-Towner Act see Stanley Lemons, *The Woman Citizen* (Urbana: University of Illinois Press, 1973).

46. Gretchen G. Mettler, "The Midwife Controversy: A Lesson for Nurse Midwives" (M.A. thesis, University of Minnesota, 1984).

47. See Joan M. Jensen, "All Pink Sisters: The War Department and the Feminist Movement in the 1920s," in *Decades of Discontent: The Women's Movement, 1920–1940,* ed. Lois Scharf and Joan M. Jensen (Westport, Conn.: Greenwood Press, 1983), 199–222, and Cott, *Grounding of Modern Feminism,* chap. 8.

48. Chambers, *Seedtime for Reform,* chaps. 4–5; Roy Lubove, *The Professional Altruist: The Emergence of Social Work as a Career* (Cambridge: Harvard University Press, 1965).

49. Mary Fredrickson, "The Southern Summer School for Women Workers," *Southern Exposure* 4 (Winter 1977): 72–78; Joyce L. Kornbluh and Lyn Goldfarb, "Labor Education and Women Workers: A Historical Perspective," in *Labor Education for Women Workers,* ed. Barbara Mayer Wertheimer (Philadelphia: Temple University Press, 1981), 15–31; see also Kessler-Harris, *Out to Work,* 243–45.

50. Kessler-Harris, *Out to Work,* 120–21.

51. Alice Kessler-Harris, "Problems of Coalition Building: Women and Trade Unions in the 1920s," in *Women Work and Protest,* ed. Ruth Milkman (Boston: Routledge & Kegan Paul, 1985), 127.

52. "Cite 50 Ways Laws Hold Women to Be Inferior," *New York Times,* 2 March 1924, 9.

53. Mrs. Mary Murray, quoted by Ruby A. Black, "The Congressional Hearings," *Equal Rights,* vol. 11, 14 February 1925, 6.

54. In retrospect, historians have tended to take one side or the other in this debate. Some affirm the view of the NWP as elitist professionals, out for their own self-interest regardless of the consequences for working-class women. Others argue that reformers had mistakenly adopted a view of female difference that reinforced the cultural roots of discrimination by emphasizing the primacy of biology, of motherhood, and of women's weakness and vulnerability. The most subtle explication of this debate and the paradoxical implications of arguments over sameness and difference is in Cott, *Grounding of Modern Feminism.*

55. See Kessler-Harris, *Out to Work,* 205–14; Rothman, *Woman's Proper Place,* 157–65.

56. Quoted in Lela B. Costin, *Two Sisters for Social Justice: A Biography of Grace and Edith Abbott* (Urbana: University of Illinois Press, 1983), 141–42.

57. Dorothy Dunbar Bromley, "Feminist—New Style," *Harper's* 155 (October 1927): 552.

58. Charlotte Perkins Gilman, "The New Generation of Women," *Current History* 18 (August 1923), 733–36.

59. Alice Rossi speculates in *The Feminist Papers: From Adams to Beauvoir* (New York: Columbia University Press, 1973), 615–21, on a generational hypothesis that what one generation of women wins with collective struggle another internalizes on a more private and individual level.

9 / Surviving the Great Depression

1. Lois Banner, *American Beauty* (New York: Alfred A. Knopf, 1983), 214.

2. Peter Filene, *Him/Her Self*, 2d ed. (Baltimore: Johns Hopkins University Press, 1986), 153–57. See also Caroline Bird, *The Invisible Scar* (New York: David McKay Co., 1966), chap. 3.

3. Studs Terkel, *Hard Times: An Oral History of the Great Depression* (New York: Pantheon Books, 1970), 104–5.

4. Janet M. Hooks, "Women's Occupations through Seven Decades," Women's Bureau Bulletin, No. 218 (Washington, D.C.: U.S. Government Printing Office, 1947), 142–44.

5. Gerda Lerner, ed., *Black Women in White America* (New York: Vintage Books, 1973), 401.

6. Meridel LeSueur, "Women on the Breadlines," in *The American Writer and the Great Depression*, ed. Harvey Swados (Indianapolis: Bobbs-Merrill, 1966), 190.

7. Bird, *The Invisible Scar*, 283–88, quote on 283; Filene, *Him/Her Self*, 158–59.

8. See Ruth Schwartz Cowan, "Two Washes in the Morning and a Bridge Party at Night," *Women's Studies* 3, 2 (1976): 147–71; Bird, *Invisible Scar*, 277–78.

9. Quoted in Joy A. Scime, "Section 213 of the 1932 Economy Act: Government Policy, Working Women, and Feminism" (Paper presented at American Society for Legal History, October 22, 1983).

10. Ibid.

11. George Gallup, "Majority in Poll Votes against Married Women Having Jobs," *The National Weekly Poll of Public Opinion*, 15 November 1936, quoted in William H. Chafe, *The American Woman: Her Changing Social, Economic, and Political Roles, 1920–1970* (New York: Oxford University Press, 1972), 108.

12. Ruth Milkman, "Women's Work and the Economic Crisis," *Review of Radical Political Economics* 8 (Spring 1976): 73–97; Lois Scharf,

To Work and to Wed: Female Employment, Feminism, and the Great Depression (Westport, Conn.: Greenwood Press, 1980), chap. 5.

13. Meridel LeSueur, "Women on the Breadlines," in Swados, *The American Writer and the Great Depression,* 187.

14. Ibid., p. 185.

15. Margaret J. Hagood, *Mothers of the South: Portraiture of the White Tenant Farm Woman* (1939; reprint, New York: Norton, 1977), 100.

16. Rosalinda M. Gonzalez, "Chicanas and Mexican Immigrant Families: 1920–1940," in *Decades of Discontent,* ed. Lois Scharf and Joan M. Jensen (Westport, Conn.: Greenwood Press, 1983), 59–84; Vicki L. Ruiz, *Cannery Women, Cannery Lives: Mexican Women, Unionization, and the California Food Processing Industry, 1930–1950* (Albuquerque: University of New Mexico Press, 1987).

17. Winifred Wandersee, "The Economics of Middle-Income Family Life: Working Women during the Great Depression," *Journal of American History* 65 (June 1978): 60–74; Alice Kessler-Harris, *Out to Work* (New York: Oxford University Press, 1982), chap. 8.

18. This analysis draws heavily on Susan Ware, *Beyond Suffrage: Women in the New Deal* (Cambridge, Mass.: Harvard University Press, 1981), chaps. 1–2; on the origins of the female reform network see also Kathryn Kish Sklar, "Hull House in the 1890s: A Community of Women Reformers," *Signs* 10 (Summer 1985): 658–77, and Blanche Wiesen Cook, "Female Support Networks and Political Activism: Lillian Wald, Crystal Eastman, Emma Goldman," *Crysalis* 3 (1977): 43–61.

19. Mary McLeod Bethune, "Faith That Moved a Dump Heap," *Who, The Magazine About People* 1, no. 3 (June 1941): 54, quoted in Lerner, *Black Women in White America,* 143.

20. Alison Bernstein, "A Mixed Record: The Political Enfranchisement of American Indian Women during the Indian New Deal," *Journal of the West* 23 (July 1984): 13–20, quote from 16.

21. Ibid., quote from 17.

22. Ware, *Beyond Suffrage.*

23. This section on the Southern Women's Campaign Against Lynching draws on Jacquelyn Dowd Hall, *Revolt Against Chivalry: Jessie Daniel Ames and the Women's Campaign Against Lynching* (New York: Columbia University Press, 1979).

24. Sharon H. Strom, "Challenging 'Woman's Place': Feminism, the Left and Industrial Unionism in the 1930s," *Feminist Studies* 9 (Summer 1983): 359–86; see also Vera Buch Weisbord, *A Radical Life* (Bloomington: Indiana University Press, 1977); and Peggy Dennis, *The Autobiography of an American Communist: A Personal View of Political Life* (Berkeley, Calif.: Lawrence Hall, 1977).

25. Peggy Dennis, "A Response to Ellen Kay Trimberger's Essay, 'Women in the Old and New Left,'" *Feminist Studies* 5 (Fall 1979): 453; see also Weisbord, *A Radical Life.*

26. Meridel LeSueur, "What Happens in a Strike," *American Mercury* 33 (November 1934): 329–35, quote on 331.

27. Temma Kaplan refers to such attitudes as a "female consciousness" in contrast to a "feminist consciousness." See Temma Kaplan, "Female Consciousness and Collective Action: The Case of Barcelona, 1910–1918," *Signs* 7 (Spring 1982): 545–66.

28. Marjorie Penn Lasky, " 'Where I Was a Person': The Ladies Auxiliary in the 1934 Minneapolis Teamsters' Strikes," in *Women, Work and Protest: A Century of U.S. Women's Labor History,* ed. Ruth Milkman (Boston: Routledge & Kegan Paul, 1985), 181–205.

29. One of the best sources on the Women's Emergency Brigade is the documentary film *With Babies and Banners,* directed by Lorraine Gray, produced by Anne Bohlen, Lyn Goldfarb, and Lorraine Gray (New Day Films); see also Jean Westin, *Making Do: How Women Survived the '30s* (Chicago: Follett Publishing, 1976).

30. Chafe, *American Woman,* 83–85.

31. Ruth Milkman, *Gender at Work: The Dynamics of Job Segregation by Sex during World War II* (Urbana: University of Illinois Press, 1987), 34.

32. Quote from Kessler-Harris, *Out to Work,* 269; see also Milkman, *Gender at Work,* chap. 3.

33. See Rosalyn Terborg Penn, "Survival Strategies among African-American Women Workers: A Continuing Process," in Milkman, *Women, Work and Protest,* 141–47.

34. Gonzalez, "Chicanas and Mexican Immigrant Families, 1920–1940," in Scharf and Jensen, *Decades of Discontent,* 59–84; Vicki Ruiz, *Cannery Workers, Cannery Lives* (Albuquerque: University of New Mexico Press, 1987).

35. Dolores Janiewski, *Sisterhood Denied: Race, Gender, and Class in a New South Community* (Philadelphia: Temple University Press, 1985).

36. Joshua Freeman, "Catholics, Communists, and Republicans: Irish Workers and the Organization of the Transport Workers Union," in Michael H. Frisch and Daniel J. Walkowitz, *Working-Class America* (Urbana: University of Illinois Press, 1983), 256–83.

37. Ruth Milkman, "Redefining 'Women's Work': The Sexual Division of Labor in the Auto Industry During World War II," *Feminist Studies* 8 (Summer 1982): 337–72, and *Gender at Work,* chap. 3; Nancy Gabin, "Women and the United Automobile Workers in the 1950s," in Milkman, *Women, Work and Protest,* 259–79.

38. Sharon Hartman Strom, "We're No Kitty Foyles: Organizing Office Workers for the Conference of Industrial Organizations, 1937–50," in Milkman, *Women, Work and Protest*, 206–34.
39. Ibid.

10 / Women at War

1. Historians have puzzled over the long-term consequences of these changes, particularly the entry of 6 million new women into the paid labor force within only four years. William Chafe argues on the one hand that World War II constituted a "turning point in the history of American women" while Leila Rupp asserts that "the temporary lowering of barriers made no permanent impact on women's opportunities or status in society." These and other authors tend to agree on the facts, but differ sharply in their interpretations. The interpretations, in turn, depend in part on a broader frame of reference. William H. Chafe, *The American Woman* (New York: Oxford University Press, 1972), chap. 6, quote, 183–84; Leila J. Rupp, *Mobilizing Women for War: German and American Propaganda, 1939–1978* (Princeton, N.J.: Princeton University Press, 1978), quote on 177.
2. Harriet Arnow, *The Dollmaker* (New York: Macmillan, 1954).
3. Karen Anderson, *Wartime Women: Sex Roles, Family Relations, and the Status of Women during World War II* (Westport, Conn.: Greenwood Press, 1981), 76–77.
4. Susan M. Hartmann, *The Homefront and Beyond: American Women in the 1940s* (Boston: Twayne Publishers, 1982), 22; Chafe, *American Woman*, 138.
5. "USES Reports Changing Employer Attitudes," *Employment Security Review* 9, no. 12 (December 1942): 12–13.
6. Ruth Milkman, *Gender at Work* (Urbana: University of Illinois Press, 1987), 67–70; Hartmann, *Homefront*, 192.
7. "The Margin Now Is Womanpower," *Fortune* 27 (February 1943): 99, 100.
8. Ibid., 100.
9. Quoted in Ruth Milkman, "Redefining 'Women's Work,'" *Feminist Studies* 8 (Summer 1982): 341.
10. *Saturday Evening Post* 215 (June 12, 1943): 55.
11. In Carol Wald, *Myth America: Picturing Women 1865–1945* (New York: Pantheon Books, 1975), 168.
12. Hartmann, *Homefront*, 88.
13. Personal communication from Anne Firor Scott. According to Scott,

in the 1980s some of these groups have had reunions in Washington. "There is," she says, "a fascinating article waiting to be written about this phenomenon."

14. Mary Schweitzer, "World War II and Female Labor Force Participation Rates," *Journal of Economic History* 40 (March 1980), 93.

15. Nelson Lichtenstein, *Labor's War at Home: The CIO in World War II* (Cambridge: Cambridge University Press, 1982), 124.

16. Anderson, *Wartime Women*, 162–64.

17. Alice Kessler-Harris, *Out to Work* (New York: Oxford University Press, 1982), 279; Jacqueline Jones, *Labor of Love, Labor of Sorrow* (New York: Basic Books, 1985), chap. 7.

18. "The Margin Now Is Womanpower," 224.

19. Katherine Archibald, "Women in the Shipyard," *Radical America* 9 (July–August 1975): 139–45, quote on 142–43.

20. Minneapolis *Tribune*, 25 August 1942.

21. *Saturday Evening Post*, 9 January 1943.

22. Milkman, *Gender at Work*, 67–70.

23. Archibald, "Women in the Shipyard," 143.

24. Milkman, *Gender at Work*, 85.

25. Maureen Honey, "The Working-Class Woman and Recruitment Propaganda during World War II: Class Differences in the Portrayal of War Work," *Signs* 8 (Summer 1983): 672–87.

26. Anderson, *Wartime Women*, 83.

27. Honey, "The Working-Class Woman," 672–87, quote on 679.

28. "Smart Stuff," *True Romances*, May 1942.

29. See Hartmann, *Homefront*, 125–26.

30. Linda Gordon, *Woman's Body, Woman's Right* (New York: Grossman, 1976), chap. 12.

31. Quotes from John D'Emilio and Estelle B. Freedman, *Intimate Matters* (New York: Harper & Row, 1988), 260.

32. John D'Emilio, *Sexual Politics, Sexual Communities: The Making of a Homosexual Minority in the United States: 1940–1970* (Chicago: University of Chicago Press, 1983), 24.

33. Ibid., 28–29.

34. Ibid., chap. 2; and D'Emilio and Freedman, *Intimate Matters*, chap. 12.

35. See Sonya Michel, "American Women and the Discourse of the Democratic Family in World War II," in *Behind the Lines: Gender and the Two World Wars*, ed. M. R. Higonnet, et al. (New Haven, Conn.: Yale University Press, 1987), 154–67.

36. Margaret Mead, "The Women in the War," in *While You Were Gone: A Report on Wartime Life in the United States,* ed. Jack Goodman (New York: Simon & Schuster, 1946), 278, 274.

37. Quotes from Hartmann, *Homefront,* 169.

38. A. G. Mezerik, "Getting Rid of the Women," *Atlantic Monthly* 175 (June 1945): 79.

39. "Women Union Leaders Speak," U.S. Women's Bureau Union Conference, April 18–19, 1945 (Washington, D.C.: U.S. Department of Labor, 1945).

40. See Milkman, *Gender at Work,* 80–83, 129–30.

41. Lucy Greenbaum, "The Women Who 'Need' to Work," *New York Times Magazine,* 29 April 1945, 16.

42. Hartmann, *Homefront,* 92.

43. "Women Union Leaders Speak," 14; also Will Jones, "Women Workers Spurn Peace Jobs," *Minneapolis Tribune,* 15 September 1947, 7.

44. Mary Smith in Ruth Young and Catherine Filene Shouse, "The Woman Worker Speaks," *Independent Woman* 24 (October 1945): 274.

45. Margaret Barnard Pickel, "How Come No Jobs for Women?" *New York Times Magazine,* 27 January 1946, 46–47.

46. Anne Stein, "Post-War Consumer Boycotts," *Radical America* 9 (July–August 1975): 156–61.

47. Lillian Hatcher quoted in Nancy Gabin, "Women and the United Auto Workers in the 1950s," in *Women, Work and Protest,* ed. Ruth Milkman (Boston: Routledge & Kegan Paul, 1985), 262.

48. Ibid., 263–64; see also Nancy Gabin, "Women Workers and the UAW in the Post–World War II Period: 1945–1954," *Labor History* 21 (Winter 1979–80): 5–30; and " 'They Have Placed a Penalty on Womanhood': The Protest Actions of Women Auto Workers in Detroit-Area UAW Locals, 1945–1947," *Feminist Studies* 8, no. 2 (Summer 1982): 373–98.

49. Hartmann, *Homefront,* 148. Even the most supportive white women's organizations, however, had failed to support the National Council of Negro Women's wartime concerns regarding child care and other needs of black children and working women.

50. Philip Wylie, *Generation of Vipers* (New York: Holt, Rinehart & Winston, 1955), 194–217, quote from 215.

51. Edward A. Strecker, *Their Mothers' Sons,* quoted in Hartmann, *Homefront,* 177.

52. Mirra Komarovsky, "Cultural Contradictions and Sex Roles," *Ameri-*

can Journal of Sociology 52 (November 1946): 182–89; Margaret Mead, "What Women Want," *Fortune* 34 (December 1946): 173.

53. Della D. Cyrus, "Why Mothers Fail," *Atlantic Monthly* 179 (March 1947): 57, 58, 60; Rhona Ryan Wilber, "Home and the War Wife," *Atlantic Monthly* 179 (May 1947): 39.

54. "American Woman's Dilemma," *Life,* 16 June 1947, 105–7.

55. "The Fortune Survey: Women in America," *Fortune* 34 (August 1946): 5–14.

56. William H. Chafe, *The Unfinished Journey: American since World War II* (New York: Oxford University Press, 1986), 101–5; Elaine Tyler May, *Homeward Bound: American Families in the Cold War Era* (New York: Basic Books, 1988).

57. Betty Friedan, *The Feminine Mystique* (New York: W. W. Norton, 1963; New York: Dell, 1974), 174.

58. Bureau of the Census, *Historical Statistics of the United States,* pt. 1 (Washington, D.C.: U.S. Government Printing Office, 1975), Series B 214–15.

59. Marynia Farnham and Ferdinand Lundberg, *The Modern Woman: The Lost Sex* (New York: Harper & Brothers, 1947), 114, 355–77.

60. Ibid., 71, 265.

61. See Elaine Tyler May, *Homeward Bound: American Families in the Cold War Era* (New York: Basic Books, 1988), chaps. 4–5.

62. See Sara M. Evans and Barbara J. Nelson, *Wage Justice: Comparable Worth and the Paradox of Technocratic Reform* (Chicago: University of Chicago Press, 1988), chap. 2.

11 / The Cold War and the "Feminine Mystique"

1. Elaine Tyler May, *Homeward Bound* (New York: Basic Books, 1988), chap. 4.

2. Ronald Lora, "Education: Schools as Crucibles in Cold War America," in *Reshaping America: Society and Institutions, 1945–1960,* ed. Robert H. Bremner and Gary W. Reichard (Columbus: Ohio State University Press, 1986), 228.

3. John D'Emilio, *Sexual Politics, Sexual Communities* (Chicago: University of Chicago Press, 1983), 41, 42, 43.

4. May, *Homeward Bound,* 92–93.

5. Agnes E. Meyer, "Women Aren't Men," *Atlantic Monthly* 186 (1950): 32.

6. Alice Thompson, *Seventeen* (July 1951), no. 76: 106 in *The Adolescent: A Book of Readings,* ed. Jerome M. Seidman (Hinesdale, Ill.: Dryden Press, 1953).

7. Walter Dean Burnham, "The Eclipse of the Democratic Party," *Democracy* 2 (July 1982): 11.

8. William E. Leuchtenburg, *A Troubled Feast: American Society since 1945* (Boston: Little, Brown, 1973), 11, Seymour Martin Lipset quoted on 4.

9. The "feminine mystique" was named in 1963 by Betty Friedan in her book *The Feminine Mystique* (New York: Norton, 1963).

10. Susan M. Hartmann, *The Homefront and Beyond* (Boston: Twayne, 1982), 155–56; Eleanor Roosevelt and Lorena A. Hickok, *Women of Courage* (New York: G. P. Putnam's Sons, 1954), 29–34.

11. Cynthia Harrison, "A New Frontier for Women," *Journal of American History* 6 (Dec. 1980): 630–35.

12. Marynia Farnham and Ferdinand Lundberg, *Modern Woman: The Lost Sex* (New York: Harper & Bros., 1947), 264–65. See also Helene Deutsch, *The Psychology of Women: A Psychoanalytic Interpretation* (New York: Grune and Stratton, 1944).

13. *McCall's,* October 1950.

14. Anais Nin, *The Diary of Anais Nin, 1939–1944,* ed. Gunther Stuhlmann (New York: Harcourt, Brace and World, 1969), 214.

15. See Linda Gordon, *Woman's Body, Woman's Right* (New York: Grossman, 1976), 374–79 on group sex therapy in 1940s.

16. See Alfred C. Kinsey, Wardell Pomeroy, and C. E. Martin, *Sexual Behavior in the Human Female* (Philadelphia: W. B. Saunders, 1953); John D'Emilio and Estelle B. Freedman, *Intimate Matters* (New York: Harper & Row, 1988), chap. 11.

17. *Look* 20 (October 16, 1956): 35, 40.

18. Ibid., 38.

19. *Life* 41 (December 24, 1956): 41–46, quote on 46.

20. *Ladies Home Journal,* January 1959, and *Good Housekeeping,* January 1959.

21. Quote from Seymour Martin Lipset in William H. Chafe, *The Unfinished Journey: America since World War II* (New York: Oxford University Press, 1986), p. 141.

22. Lynn Weiner, *From Working Girl to Working Mother* (Chapel Hill: University of North Carolina Press, 1985), 89–96, see table on 89.

23. Valerie Kincade Oppenheimer, "Demographic Influence on Female Employment and the Status of Women," in *Changing Women in a Changing Society,* ed. Joan Huber (Chicago: University of Chicago Press, 1983), 184–99.

24. Barbara Melosh, *The Physician's Hand: Work, Culture, and Conflict in American Nursing* (Philadelphia: Temple University Press, 1982), chap. 5.

25. Oppenheimer, "Demographic Influence," 194–95; Weiner, *From Working Girl to Working Mother*, 89–94.

26. Weiner, *From Working Girl to Working Mother*, 93.

27. Mirra Komarovsky with Jane H. Phillips, *Blue-Collar Marriage* (1962; reprint, New Haven, Conn.: Yale University Press, 1987), chap. 3; Lillian B. Rubin, *Worlds of Pain: Life in the Working-Class Family* (New York: Basic Books, 1976), chap. 9.

28. *Look*, October 16, 1956, 35.

29. *Life* 41 (December 24, 1956), 30–35.

30. Friedan, *Feminine Mystique*, 53, 54.

31. Leila Rupp, "The Survival of American Feminism: The Women's Movement in the Postwar Period," in *Reshaping America*, ed. Robert H. Bremner and Gary W. Reichard (Columbus: Ohio State University Press, 1982), 33–66. For more detail see Leila Rupp and Verta Taylor, *Survival in the Doldrums: The American Women's Rights Movement, 1945 to the 1960s* (New York: Oxford University Press, 1987).

32. *Salt of the Earth;* Screenplay (Old Westbury, N.Y.: Feminist Press, 1978).

33. Nancy Gabin, "Women and the UAW in the 1950s," in *Women, Work and Protest*, ed. Ruth Milkman (Boston: Routledge & Kegan Paul, 1985), 259–79.

34. Daughters of Bilitis circular quoted in John D'Emilio, *Sexual Politics, Sexual Communities* (Chicago: University of Chicago Press, 1983), 104.

35. D'Emilio, *Sexual Politics*, chap. 6.

36. In addition to the examples cited below, see William H. Chafe, *Civilities and Civil Rights: Greensboro, North Carolina, and the Black Struggle for Freedom* (New York: Oxford University Press, 1980).

37. David J. Garrow, ed., *The Montgomery Bus Boycott and the Women Who Started It: The Memoir of JoAnn Gibson Robinson* (Knoxville: University of Tennessee Press, 1987); William H. Chafe, "The Civil Rights Revolution, 1945–1969: The Gods Bring Threads to Webs Begun," in Bremner and Reichard, *Reshaping America*, 90–91; J. Mills Thornton III, "Challenge and Response in the Montgomery Bus Boycott of 1955–56," *Alabama Review* 33 (July 1980); see also Howell Raines, *My Soul Is Rested: Movement Days in the Deep South Remembered* (New York: Putnam, 1977).

38. Aldon Morris, *The Origins of the Civil Rights Movement: Black Communities Organizing for Change* (New York: Free Press, 1984), 103–4, 112; Ella Baker, "Developing Community Leadership," in *Black Women in White America*, ed. Gerda Lerner (New York: Vintage, 1973), 349.

39. Daisy Bates, *The Long Shadow of Little Rock: A Memoir* (New York: David McKay, 1963).

40. Quoted in David Riesman, "The Found Generation," *American Scholar* 25, no. 4 (1956): 431–32.

41. Barbara Ehrenreich, *The Hearts of Men: American Dreams and the Flight from Commitment* (Garden City, N.Y.: Anchor/Doubleday, 1983).

42. Katherine Hamill, "Women as Bosses," *Fortune* 53, no. 6 (June 3, 1956), 106–7, 219.

12 / Decade of Discovery

1. Amy Swerdlow, "Ladies Day at the Capitol: Women Strike for Peace Versus HUAC," *Feminist Studies* 8 (Fall 1982): 493–520.

2. This description draws on the account by Mary McGrory quoted in Swerdlow, "Ladies Day at the Capitol," 508.

3. *Newsweek* 55 (March 7, 1960): 57–60.

4. Sara Evans, *Personal Politics* (New York: Alfred A. Knopf, 1979), 15–16.

5. See Alva Myrdal and Viola Klein, *Women's Two Roles: Home and Work* (London: Routledge & Kegan Paul, 1956); Robert W. Smuts, *Women and Work in America* (1959; reprint, New York: Schocken Books, 1971); National Manpower Council Reports, *Womanpower: A Statement with Chapters by the Council Staff* (New York: Columbia University Press, 1957–58); National Manpower Council Reports, *Work in the Lives of Married Women: Proceedings of a Conference on Womanpower Held October 20–25, 1957* (New York: Columbia University Press, 1957–58).

6. See James Putnam O'Brien, "The Development of a New Left in the United States, 1960–65" (Ph.D. diss., University of Wisconsin, 1971), 83–84, 214–22.

7. Michael Harrington, *The Other America: Poverty in the U.S.* (New York: Macmillan, 1962).

8. Helena Z. Lopata, *Occupation: Housewife* (New York: Oxford University Press, 1971), 362–76.

9. Ibid., 31–41.

10. Divorce had soared in the immediate postwar years and declined during the 1950s. Divorce rates increased steadily through the 1960s, presaging a more dramatic acceleration in the 1970s. U.S. Bureau of the Census, *Historical Statistics of the United States: Colonial Times to 1970*, pt. 1 (Washington, D.C.: U.S. Government Printing Office, 1975), 64; Figure 1, "Marital Status and Living Arrangements: March 1984," U.S. Bureau of the Census, *Current Population Reports: Population Characteristics*, series p-20, no. 299, p. 3.

11. Swerdlow, "Ladies Day at the Capitol, 493–520, quote on 510.

12. Quote from Lopata, *Occupation: Housewife*, 376.

13. Lopata, *Occupation: Housewife;* Lillian Breslow Rubin, *Worlds of Pain: Life in the Working-Class Family* (New York: Basic Books, 1976), quotes on 181–82.

14. Lopata, *Occupation: Housewife,* quotes on 122, 128.

15. See Reynolds Farley, *Growth of the Black Population: A Study of Demographic Trends* (Chicago: Markham Publishing Co., 1970), 145–47.

16. Daniel Patrick Moynihan, *The Negro Family: The Case for National Action* (Washington, D.C.: U.S. Government Printing Office, 1965).

17. Carol Stack, *All Our Kin: Strategies for Survival in a Black Community* (New York: Harper & Row, 1974), 42.

18. Lopata, *Occupation: Housewife,* 291–94, 340.

19. Fannie Lou Hamer, *To Praise Our Bridges: An Autobiography of Mrs. Fannie Lou Hamer* (Jackson, Miss.: KIPCO, 1967), excerpted in *Eyes on the Prize: America's Civil Rights Years: A Reader and Guide,* ed. Clayborne Carson, et al. (New York: Penguin Books, 1987), pp. 133–34.

20. Quoted in Tracy Sugarman, *Stranger at the Gates: A Summer in Mississippi* (New York: Hill & Wang, 1966), 115.

21. See Evans, *Personal Politics,* chaps. 2–4.

22. Stanley Wise quoted in Bernice Johnson Reagon, "Rubye Doris Smith Robinson," in *Notable American Women: The Modern Period* (Cambridge, Mass.: The Belknap Press, 1980), 586.

23. Jacqueline Jones, *Labor of Love, Labor of Sorrow* (New York: Basic Books, 1985), 302; Bureau of the Census, *Black Population: Historical View,* 74.

24. See J. Craig Jenkins, "The Transformation of a Constituency into a Movement: Farmworker Organizing in California," in *Social Movements of the Sixties and Seventies,* ed. Jo Freeman (New York: Longman, 1983), 52–70; Ronald B. Taylor, *Chavez and the Farm Workers* (Boston: Beacon Press, 1975); Dick Meister and Anne Loftis, *A Long Time Coming: The Struggle to Unionize America's Farm Workers* (New York: Macmillan, 1977).

25. Ellen Cantarow with Susan Gushee O'Malley and Sharon Hartman Strom, *Moving the Mountain: Women Working for Social Change* (Old Westbury, N.Y.: Feminist Press, 1980), 94–151, quote on 134.

26. Cynthia E. Harrison, "A 'New Frontier' for Women: The Public Policy of the Kennedy Administration," *Journal of American History* 67 (December 1980), 630–46; quote 640.

27. Ibid., 641–642.

28. Harrison, "New Frontier," 642.

29. Jo Freeman, *The Politics of Women's Liberation: A Case Study of an*

Emerging Social Movement and Its Relation to the Policy Process (New York: David McKay, 1975), 52–53.

30. Quotes from Friedan Manuscript Collection, Schlesinger Library Manuscript Collections, Radcliffe College, Cambridge, Mass., quoted in Elaine Tyler May, *Homeward Bound* (New York: Basic Books, 1988), 209, 210, 212.

31. Leila Rupp and Verta Taylor, *Survival in the Doldrums* (New York: Oxford University Press, 1987), chap. 8, esp. 176–79.

32. *New York Times,* "Editorial," 21 August 1965.

33. Judith Hole and Ellen Levine, *Rebirth of Feminism* (New York: Quadrangle Books, 1971), 84.

34. Ibid.

35. Freeman, *Politics of Women's Liberation,* 74.

36. Ibid., 73.

37. "A Work of One's Own," in *Working It Out: 23 Women Writers, Artists, Scientists, and Scholars Talk about Their Lives and Work,* ed. Sara Ruddick and Pamela Daniels (New York: Pantheon Books, 1977), 128–46, quote 129.

38. "Contradictions," in Ruddick and Daniels, *Working It Out,* 213–27, quote 223.

39. "A Work of One's Own," in Ruddick and Daniels, *Working It Out,* 145.

40. Ibid., 223. This section draws primarily on Sara Evans, *Personal Politics* (New York: Knopf, 1979).

41. Elizabeth Sutherland, ed., *Letters from Mississippi* (New York: McGraw-Hill, 1965), 22–23. On the experiences of summer volunteers see also Mary Aiken Rothschild, *A Case of Black and White: Northern Volunteers and the Southern "Freedom Summers"* (Westport, Conn.: Greenwood Press, 1982), and Doug McAdam, *Freedom Summer* (New York: Oxford University Press, 1988).

42. Arvonne S. Fraser, "Insiders and Outsiders: Women in the Political Arena," in *Women in Washington: Advocates for Public Policy,* ed. Irene Tinker (Beverly Hills, Calif.: Sage Publications, 1983), 122.

43. Ibid.

44. John D'Emilio, *Sexual Politics, Sexual Communities* (Chicago: University of Chicago Press, 1983), 236.

13 / The Politicization of Personal Life

1. Jo Freeman, *The Politics of Women's Liberation* (New York: David McKay, 1975), 148.

2. *New York Times,* 31 January 1970, 1.

3. Winifred D. Wandersee, *On the Move: American Women in the 1970s* (Boston: Twayne Publishers, 1988), chap. 6.

4. *New York Times*, 19 March 1970, 51; *Ladies Home Journal* 87 (August 1970), 63–71.

5. See *New York Times*, 27 August 1970; see also Ethel Klein, *Gender Politics: From Consciousness to Mass Politics* (Cambridge, Mass.: Harvard University Press, 1984), 1; Freeman, *Politics of Women's Liberation*, 84–85.

6. Freeman, *Politics of Women's Liberation*, 150.

7. Sophy Burnham, "Women's Lib: The Idea You Can't Ignore," *Redbook* 135 (September 1970): 188, 191.

8. See, for example, "The New Woman, 1972: A *Time* Special Issue," *Time* 99 (March 20, 1972); "How Bosses Feel About Women's Lib," *Business Week* 2140 (September 5, 1970): 18–19; Betty Rollin, "What's Women's Lib Doing to the Family? Plenty!" *Look* 35 (January 26, 1971): 40; Joyce Brothers, "Women's Lib Backlash," *Good Housekeeping* 175 (September 1972).

9. Wandersee, *On the Move*, 150–54; see also Billie Jean King, with Kim Chapin, *Billie Jean* (New York: Harper & Row, 1974), and Bud Collins, "Billie Jean King Evens the Score," *Ms.*, July 1973, 37–43.

10. Ethel Klein, *Gender Politics: From Consciousness to Mass Politics* (Cambridge, Mass.: Harvard University Press, 1984), 12, Fig. 1.1.

11. Mary Ann Milsap, "Sex Equity in Education," in *Women in Washington*, ed. Irene Tinker (Beverly Hills: Sage Publications, 1983), 93–94; see also Klein, *Gender Politics*, 25–26.

12. See Byron E. Shafer, *Quiet Revolution: The Struggle for the Democratic Party and the Shaping of Post-Reform Politics* (New York: Russell Sage Foundation, 1983), chap. 17; Wandersee, *On the Move*, chap. 2.

13. Wandersee, *On the Move*, chap. 2.

14. *Roe v. Wade*, Supreme Court of the United States, 1973, 410 U.S. 113, 93 S.Ct. 756, 35 L.Ed.2d 147; *New York Times*, 24 January 1973, 40.

15. Joseph Adelson, "Is Women's Lib a Passing Fad?" *New York Times Magazine*, 19 March 1972, 26.

16. Susan Griffin, "Rape—the All-American Crime," *Ramparts* (September 1971), republished as "The Politics of Rape," in *Made from This Earth: An Anthology of Writings* (New York: Harper & Row, 1982), 39–58; see also Susan Brownmiller, *Against Our Will: Men, Women, and Rape* (New York: Simon & Schuster, 1975).

17. Pauline Bart and Melinda Bart Schlesinger, "Collective Work and Self-Identity: The Effect of Working in a Feminist Illegal Abortion

Collective," in *Workplace Democracy and Social Change*, ed. Frank Lindenfeld and Joyce Rothschild-Whitt (Boston: Porter Sargent, 1980), 139–53.

18. Charlotte Bunch, *Passionate Politics: Feminist Theory in Action* (New York: St. Martin's Press, 1987), 183.

19. Radicalesbians, *The Woman-Identified Woman*, New York, 1970.

20. Bunch, *Passionate Politics*, 184.

21. See Bunch, *Passionate Politics*, 159–214, for a description of one key activist's journey through this dimension of the women's movement.

22. Freeman, *Politics of Women's Liberation*, 121.

23. Klein, *Gender Politics*, 31.

24. See Heather Huyck, "To Celebrate a Whole Priesthood: The History of Women's Ordination in the Episcopal Church" (Ph.D. diss., University of Minnesota, 1981).

25. Mary Daly, *Beyond God the Father* (Boston: Beacon Press, 1973) and *Gynecology* (Boston: Beacon Press, 1978); Rosemary Radford Reuther, *Sexism and God Talk: Toward a Feminist Theology* (Boston: Beacon Press, 1983).

26. Interview with Jan Schakowsky by Harry C. Boyte, Evanston, Ill., April 30, 1977. See also Harry C. Boyte, *The Backyard Revolution: Understanding the New Citizen Movement* (Philadelphia: Temple University Press, 1980), 77–78.

27. Quotes from Paula Giddings, *When and Where I Enter* (New York: Bantam Books, 1984), 309, 308.

28. See Brownmiller, *Against Our Will*.

29. Giddings, *When and Where I Enter*, 315.

30. Ibid., 319.

31. Ibid., 345.

32. Quoted in ibid., 339.

33. Harry C. Boyte, *Community Is Possible: Repairing America's Roots* (New York: Harper & Row, 1984), chap. 4.

34. Johanna Von Gottfred, "Diary from the Fresno County Farm," *America* 129 (October 13, 1973): 262–66; J. V. Chavez, "Women of the Mexican-American Movement," *Mademoiselle* 74 (April 1972): 82 ff.

35. See, for example, Paula Gunn Allen, *The Sacred Hoop: Recovering the Feminine in American Indian Traditions* (Boston: Beacon Press, 1986); Audre Lorde, *Sister Outsider: Essays and Speeches* (New York: Crossing Press, 1984).

36. Interview with Day Piercy, Chicago, Ill., July 19, 1981.

37. Chicago *Sun-Times*, 4 February 1977, 1.

38. Sara M. Evans and Harry C. Boyte, *Free Spaces: Sources of Democratic Change in America* (New York: Harper & Row, 1986), 147–48.

39. Interviews with Olga Madar, Detroit, December 10, 1982; Dorothy Haener, Detroit, January 21, 1983; Addie Wyatt, Chicago, June 15, 1983; Joyce Miller, New York City, February 7, 1983. *New York Times*, 25 March 1974, 27.

40. Joan M. Goodin, "Working Women: The Pros and Cons of Unions," in Tinker, *Women in Washington*, 140–47.

41. Wandersee, *On the Move*, 120.

42. Wandersee, *On the Move*, chap. 6.

43. See, for example, Ellen Carol Dubois, Gail Paradise Kelly, Elizabeth Lapovsky Kennedy, Carolyn W. Korsmeyer, and Lillian S. Robinson, *Feminist Scholarship: Kindling in the Groves of Academe* (Urbana: University of Illinois Press, 1985).

44. Nancy Barrett, "Women and the Economy," in *The American Woman 1987–88: A Report in Depth,* ed. Sara E. Rix (New York: W. W. Norton, 1987), 107, table 3.1.

45. Claudia Goldin, "The Earnings Gap between Male and Female Workers: A Historical Perspective," Working Paper No. 1888, National Bureau of Economic Research, Inc., Working Paper Series, Cambridge, Mass., 1986, 22.

46. See Joseph Pleck, *Working Wives/Working Husbands* (Beverly Hills, Calif.: Sage Publications, 1985).

47. See U.S. Bureau of the Census, *Current Population Reports*, Series P-20, No. 399 (Washington, D.C.: U.S. Government Printing Office, 1985), table A.

48. See ibid., table C.

49. Lenore J. Weitzman, *The Divorce Revolution: The Unexpected Social and Economic Consequences for Women and Children in America* (New York: Free Press, 1985), chap. 10.

50. See Mary Jo Bane, "Household Composition and Poverty," in *Fighting Poverty: What Works and What Doesn't,* ed. Sheldon H. Danziger and Daniel H. Weinberg (Cambridge, Mass.: Harvard University Press, 1986).

51. Andrew Cherlin, "Women and the Family," in Rix, *The American Woman, 1987–88,* 77; see also table 6, "Births to Unmarried Teenage Mothers by Race, 1984," 295.

52. Cherlin, "Women and Family," 96.

53. See Diana Pearce, "The Feminization of Poverty: Women, Work, and Welfare," *Urban and Social Change Review* 11 (February 1978): 28–36.

54. U.S. Department of Labor, *1975 Handbook on Women Workers*, Wom-

en's Bureau Bulletin 197 (Washington, D.C.: U.S. Government Printing Office, 1975), table 38. See also Barbara Bergmann, *The Economic Emergence of Women* (New York: Basic Books, 1986).

55. Richard McGahey and John M. Jeffries, "Equity, Growth and Socioeconomic Change: Anti-Discrimination Policy in an Era of Economic Transformation," *New York University Review of Law and Social Change* 13, no. 2 (1984): 233–80.

56. Ibid., 250.

57. Quotes in Edith Mayo and Jerry K. Frye, "The ERA: Postmortem of a Failure in Political Communication," in *Rights of Passage: The Past and Future of the ERA*, ed. Joan Hoff-Wilson (Bloomington: Indiana University Press, 1986), 85.

58. See Jane J. Mansbridge, *Why We Lost the ERA* (Chicago: University of Chicago Press, 1986), chaps. 7 and 8, for a discussion of feminist attitudes regarding the draft. She argues that ERA supporters harmed their cause by accepting the necessity of a female draft under the ERA without attention to the strategic consequences of this position (and the fact that other positions were equally supportable).

59. See Jane DeHart-Mathews and Donald Mathews, "The Cultural Politics of the ERA's Defeat," in Hoff-Wilson, *Rights of Passage*, 44–53.

60. *Phyllis Schlafly Report* 5 (February 1972), quoted in Mansbridge, *Why We Lost the ERA*, 104.

61. Wandersee, *On the Move*, 182–85.

62. See Linda Gordon and Allen Hunter, "Sex, Family, and the New Right: Anti-Feminism as a Political Force," *Radical America* 11–12 (November 1977–February 1978): 9–25; Rosalind Pollack Petchesky, *Abortion and Women's Choice: The State, Sexuality, and Reproductive Freedom* (New York: Longman, 1984); Alan Crawford, *Thunder on the Right: The "New Right" and the Politics of Appeasement* (New York: Pantheon Books, 1980); Carol Virginia Pohli, "Church Closets and Back Doors: A Feminist View of Moral Majority Women," *Feminist Studies* 9 (Fall 1983): 529–58; Faye Ginsberg, "The Symbolic Function of Abortion in Activists' Life Stories," in *Interpreting Women's Lives: Feminist Theory and Personal Narratives*, ed. The Personal Narratives Group (Bloomington: Indiana University Press, forthcoming 1989).

63. Wandersee, *On the Move*, 49–53.

64. Freeman, *Politics of Women's Liberation*, 39; Mansbridge, *Why We Lost the ERA*, chap. 2.

65. Alice Rossi, *Feminists in Politics: A Panel Analysis of the First National Women's Conference* (New York: Academic Press, 1982), 58–59, table 2.3.

66. Quotes from Rossi, *Feminists in Politics,* 178, 179.

67. Wandersee, *On the Move,* 145. Full-time housewives in the 1960s spent 44 hours per week on housework. A decade later they spent 30. Employed women decreased their hours of housework in the same time from 26 to 21 hours per week.

68. Boyte, *Community Is Possible,* chap. 5, quote on 135.

69. Quotes from Evans and Boyte, *Free Spaces,* 199; and Boyte, *Community Is Possible,* 128.

70. Sara M. Evans and Barbara J. Nelson, *Wage Justice: Comparable Worth and the Paradox of Technocratic Reform* (Chicago: University of Chicago Press, 1989).

71. See M. Wilhelm, "Grieving Angry Mother Charges That Drunken Drivers Are Getting Away with Murder," *People* 15 (June 29, 1981): 24–26; Norma Phillips and Rep. James M. Jeffords, "Should the Government Withhold Funds from States That Refuse to Raise Their Minimum Drinking Age to 21 by October 1?" *New York Times,* 5 June 1986, sec. B, 8; M. B. Selinger, "Already the Conscience of a Nation, Candy Lightner Prods Congress into Action Against Drunk Drivers," *People Weekly* 22 (July 9, 1984): 102.

72. Klein, *Gender Politics,* 30. See also Ruth B. Mandel, "The Political Woman," in *The American Woman 1988–89: A Status Report,* ed. Sara Rix (New York: W. W. Norton, 1988): 78–122.

73. For one view see Phyllis Chesler, *Sacred Bond: The Legacy of Baby M* (New York: Times Books, 1988).

74. *Newsweek,* 4 January 1988, 40–48.

75. Robert Bellah, et al., *Habits of the Heart: Individualism and Commitment in American Life* (Berkeley: University of California Press, 1985).

Further Reading

Readers interested in pursuing specific points will find in the notes a fairly complete listing of the sources I have drawn on in writing *Born for Liberty*. For those who would like suggestions for further reading, I have listed below some of the major works that could serve as starting points.

Several subjects already have their own specialized histories covering the colonial period to the present. Alice Kessler-Harris has chronicled women's wage labor in *Out to Work: A History of Wage-Earning Women in the United States* (New York: Oxford University Press, 1982) whereas Susan Strasser's *Never Done: A History of American Housework* (New York: Pantheon, 1982) and Ruth Schwartz Cowan's *More Work for Mother: The Ironies of Household Technology from the Open Hearth to the Microwave* (New York: Basic Books, 1983) analyzed work within the home. The literature on black women remains relatively scarce; however, two major histories offer contrasting emphases: Jacqueline Jones, *Labor of Love, Labor of Sorrow: Black Women, Work, and the Family from Slavery to the Present* (New York: Basic Books, 1985), emphasizes work and family especially among poor and rural blacks, whereas Paula Giddings, *When and Where I Enter: The Impact of Black Women on Race and Sex in America* (New York: William Morrow, 1984), focuses on middle-class black women's organized, public activities. The history of sexuality has also recently received a major treatment in John D'Emilio and Estelle B. Freedman, *Intimate Matters: A History of Sexuality in America* (New York: Harper & Row, 1988). See also Carl Degler, *At Odds: Women and the Family in America from the Revolution to the Present* (New York: Oxford University Press, 1980), and Lois Banner, *American Beauty* (New York: Alfred A. Knopf, 1983). Most writings in women's history, however, cover more specialized time periods and topics.

As is noted in chapter 1, early writings by American Indian women do not exist. Indeed, the richest vein of writing consists of recent works

367

such as Carolyn Niethammer, *Daughters of the Earth: The Lives and Legends of American Indian Women* (New York: Collier Books, 1977). Two excellent collections of recent scholarship on Indian women are Patricia Albers and Beatrice Medicine, eds., *The Hidden Half: Studies of Plains Indian Women* (Washington, D.C.: University Press of America, 1983), and Mona Etienne and Eleanor Leacock, eds., *Women and Colonization: Anthropological Perspectives* (New York: Praeger, 1980). Canadian scholars have led the exploration of women's roles in fur trade society; for example, Sylvia Van Kirk, *"Many Tender Ties": Women in Fur Trade Society in Western Canada, 1700–1850* (Winnipeg: Watson & Dwyer, 1980).

Seventeenth-century New England colonial women come vividly to life in Lauren Thatcher Ulrich, *Good Wives: Image and Reality in the Lives of Women in Northern New England, 1650–1750* (New York: Alfred A. Knopf, 1982); Carol F. Karlsen, *The Devil in the Shape of a Woman: Witchcraft in Colonial New England* (New York: W. W. Norton, 1987); and John Demos, *A Little Commonwealth: Family Life in Plymouth Colony* (New York: Oxford University Press, 1970). Women's legal status is explored in Marylynn Salmon, *Women and the Law of Property in Early America* (Chapel Hill: University of North Carolina Press, 1986). European women in the middle and southern colonies have been less studied. See, for example, Lois Green Carr and Lorena S. Walsh, "The Planter's Wife: The Experience of White Women in Seventeenth-Century Maryland," *William and Mary Quarterly,* 3rd series, 34 (1077): 542–571, and the classic study by Julia Cherry Spruill, *Women's Life and Work in the Southern Colonies* (New York: W. W. Norton, 1972). African women and the beginnings of slavery are described in Deborah White, *Ar'n't I A Woman: Female Slaves in the Plantation South* (New York: W. W. Norton, 1985), as well as numerous articles cited in the notes. For firsthand accounts see the documents in Gerda Lerner, ed., *Black Women in White America: A Documentary History* (New York: Vintage, 1973).

Two key books provide overviews of women in the era of the American Revolution: Linda Kerber, *Women of the Republic: Intellect and Ideology in Revolutionary America* (Chapel Hill: University of North Carolina Press, 1980), and Mary Beth Norton, *Liberty's Daughters: The Revolutionary Experience of American Women, 1750–1800* (Boston: Little, Brown, 1980). See also Joan Jensen, *Loosening the Bonds: Mid-Atlantic Farm Women, 1750–1850* (New Haven, Conn.: Yale University Press, 1986), and Nancy Cott's classic exploration of the emergence of "woman's sphere" in the postrevolutionary era, *The Bonds of Womanhood: "Woman's Sphere" in New England, 1780–1835* (New Haven, Conn.: Yale University Press, 1977).

An excellent and wonderfully readable monograph that describes the processes of urbanization and modernization in the first half of the nineteenth century from the perspective of white and free black women in a southern city is Suzanne Lebsock, *The Free Women of Petersburg:*

Status and Culture in a Southern Town, 1784–1860 (New York: W. W. Norton, 1984). Among the best studies of working-class women in early-nineteenth-century mills and cities are Thomas Dublin, *Women at Work: The Transformation of Work and Community in Lowell, Massachusetts, 1826–1860* (New York: Columbia University Press, 1979), and Christine Stansell, *City of Women: Sex and Class in New York, 1789–1860* (New York: Alfred A. Knopf, 1986).

The rise of female voluntary associations, their relationship to changing economic and class dynamics of the first half of the nineteenth century, and their links to the early women's rights movement are explored in two subtly argued community studies, Mary Ryan, *Cradle of the Middle Class: The Family in Oneida County, New York, 1790–1865* (Cambridge, Mass.: Cambridge University Press, 1981), and Nancy A. Hewitt, *Women's Activism and Social Change: Rochester, New York, 1822–1872* (Ithaca, N.Y.: Cornell University Press, 1984). On married women's property laws and women's changing legal position see Norma Basch, *In the Eyes of the Law: Women, Marriage, and Property in Nineteenth-Century New York* (Ithaca: Cornell University Press, 1982).

Biographies that place women in their broader social context provide a vivid look at social reform movements and the intersections of private and public life in the early nineteenth century. Among the best are Gerda Lerner, *The Grimke Sisters from South Carolina: Pioneers for Woman's Rights and Abolition* (New York: Schocken, 1966), Kathryn Kish Sklar, *Catharine Beecher: A Study in American Domesticity* (New Haven: Yale University Press, 1973), and Celia Eckhardt, *Fanny Wright: Rebel in America* (Cambridge, Mass.: Harvard University Press, 1984). Ellen Carol Dubois explores the emergence of the suffrage movement in *Feminism and Suffrage: The Emergence of an Independent Women's Movement in America, 1848–1869* (Ithaca, N.Y.: Cornell University Press, 1978), which builds on Eleanor Flexner's classic study, *Century of Struggle: The Woman's Rights Movement in the United States* (1959; rev. ed., Cambridge, Mass.: The Belknap Press, 1975). To read the speeches and stories of the women themselves see Mari Jo Buhle and Paul Buhle, eds., *The Concise History of Woman Suffrage: Selections from the Classic Work of Stanton, Anthony, Gage, and Harper* (Urbana: University of Illinois Press, 1978).

The experience of black women under slavery is still relatively unexplored, although there are many studies of the black family and black culture which touch on women's lives. Deborah White, *Ar'n't I A Woman*, cited earlier, provides the best introduction to this subject. On southern white women see Anne Firor Scott, *The Southern Lady: From Pedestal to Politics, 1830–1930* (Chicago: University of Chicago Press, 1970), and Elizabeth Fox-Genovese, *Within the Plantation Household: Black and White Women of the Old South* (Chapel Hill: University of North Carolina Press, 1988).

On the emergence of Victorian culture and the ways in which women responded to, appropriated, and resisted its strictures see the collected articles of three pioneering historians of women: Gerda Lerner, *The Majority Finds Its Past: Placing Women in History* (New York: Oxford University Press, 1979); Carroll Smith-Rosenberg, *Disorderly Conduct: Visions of Gender in Victorian America* (New York: Oxford University Press, 1985); and Barbara Welter, *Dimity Convictions: The American Woman in the Nineteenth Century* (Athens: Ohio University Press, 1976).

The impact of Victorian gender ideology on those who moved west is a key thread in Johnny Mack Faragher, *Women and Men on the Overland Trail* (New Haven, Conn.: Yale University Press, 1979). Additional sources on women's experience in the west include Elizabeth Hampsten, *Read This Only to Yourself: The Private Writings of Midwestern Women, 1880–1910* (Bloomington: Indiana University Press, 1982), and Sandra L. Myers, *Westering Women and the Frontier Experience: 1800–1915* (Albuquerque: University of New Mexico Press, 1982).

Histories of the post–Civil War women's reform movements include Ruth Bordin, *Woman and Temperance: The Quest for Power and Liberty, 1873–1900* (Philadelphia: Temple University Press, 1980); Barbara Epstein, *The Politics of Domesticity: Women, Evangelism, and Temperance in Nineteenth-Century America* (Middletown, Conn.: Wesleyan University Press, 1981); Estelle B. Freedman, *Their Sisters' Keepers: Women's Prison Reform in America, 1830–1930* (Ann Arbor: University of Michigan Press, 1981); Mari Jo Buhle, *Women and American Socialism, 1870–1920* (Urbana: University of Illinois Press, 1981); and Linda Gordon, *Woman's Body: Woman's Right: A Social History of Birth Control in America* (New York: Grossman, 1976). The reemergence and final triumph of the woman suffrage movement is chronicled in Flexner, *Century of Struggle,* and Buhle and Buhle, *Concise History of Woman Suffrage,* cited earlier. Paula Giddings' *When and Where I Enter* explores the growing self-organization of black women and the ongoing realities of segregation and racism within the white women's movement.

The background to these movements lay in the rapid growth of the educated middle class and of women's professions in the late nineteenth century. See, for example, Barbara Solomon, *In the Company of Educated Women: A History of Women and Higher Education in America* (New Haven, Conn.: Yale University Press, 1985); Barbara Melosh, *The Physician's Hand: Work, Culture, and Conflict in American Nursing* (Philadelphia: Temple University Press, 1982); Regina Morantz-Sanchez, *Sympathy and Science: Women Physicians in American Medicine* (New York: Oxford University Press, 1985); and Jane Addams, *Twenty Years at Hull House* (New York: Macmillan, 1911). Dolores Hayden in *The Grand Domestic Revolution: A History of Feminist Designs for American Homes, Neighborhoods, and Cities* (Cambridge, Mass.: MIT Press, 1981) explores some of the more radical feminist visions for rearranging social life in the interests of sexual equality. And Peter Filene examines the implications of changing definitions of womanliness and manliness on both sexes in *Him/Her Self: Sex Roles in Modern America*, 2d ed. (Baltimore: Johns Hopkins University Press, 1986).

Changes in women's work outside the home and women's organized responses can be traced in the following (in addition to Alice Kessler-Harris cited earlier): David Katzman, *Seven Days a Week: Women and Domestic Service in Industrializing America* (Urbana: University of Illinois Press, 1981); Margery W. Davies, *Woman's Place Is At the Typewriter: Office Work and Office Workers, 1870–1930* (Philadelphia: Temple University Press, 1982); Meredith Tax, *The Rising of the Women* (New York: Monthly Review Press, 1980); Lynn Y. Weiner, *From Working Girl to Working Mother: The Female Labor Force in the United States, 1820–1980* (Chapel Hill: University of North Carolina Press, 1985); and Susan Porter Benson, *Counter Cultures: Saleswomen, Managers, and Customers in American Department Stores: 1890–1940* (Urbana: University of Illinois Press, 1986).

William H. Chafe, *The American Woman: Her Changing Social, Economic, and Political Roles, 1920–1970* (New York: Oxford University Press, 1972), laid the groundwork for subsequent studies of twentieth-century women. On the middle class see Sheila Rothman, *Woman's Proper Place: A History of Changing Ideals and Practices, 1870 to the Present* (New York: Basic Books, 1978), and Filene, *Him/Her Self,* cited earlier. The latter explores the changing dynamics of gender for both women and men in the twentieth century.

Numerous studies are beginning to explore the story of women's changing labor force participation in the twentieth century, with its complexities of class, race, and relationship to the labor movement. See Alice Kessler-Harris, *Out to Work,* and Margery W. Davies, *Woman's Place Is At the Typewriter,* cited earlier. On Mexican-American women see Sara Deutsch, *No Separate Refuge: Culture, Class, and Gender on an Anglo-Hispanic Frontier in the American Southwest, 1880–1940* (New York: Oxford University Press, 1987), and Vicki L. Ruiz, *Cannery Women, Cannery Lives: Mexican Women, Unionization, and the California Food Processing Industry, 1930–1950* (Albuquerque: University of New Mexico Press, 1987). On black women see Dolores Janiewski, *Sisterhood Denied: Race, Gender, and Class in a New South Community* (Philadelphia: Temple University Press, 1985), and Carol Stack, *All Our Kin: Strategies for Survival in a Black Community* (New York: Harper & Row, 1974). Ruth Milkman, *Gender at Work: The Dynamics of Job Segregation by Sex during World War II* (Urbana: University of Illinois Press, 1987), chronicles critical changes during World War II. A broader overview of the forties is Susan Hartmann, *The Homefront and Beyond: American Women in the 1940s* (Boston: Twayne, 1982). On the cold-war era see Elaine Tyler May, *Homeward Bound: American Families in the Cold War Era* (New York: Basic Books, 1988).

Histories examining the profound impact of organized women on American public life—in feminism, social movements, and politics—are also beginning to appear. See especially Nancy F. Cott, *The Grounding of Modern Feminism* (New Haven, Conn.: Yale University Press, 1987); Jacquelyn Dowd Hall, *Revolt Against Chivalry: Jessie Daniel Ames and the Women's Campaign Against Lynching* (New York: Columbia University Press, 1979); Susan Ware, *Beyond Suffrage: Women in the New Deal* (Cambridge: Harvard University Press, 1981); David Garrow, ed., *The Montgomery Bus Boycott and the Women Who Started It: The Memoir of JoAnn Gibson Robinson* (Knoxville: University of Tennessee Press, 1987); and Sara Evans, *Personal Politics: The Roots of Women's Liberation in the Civil Rights Movement and the New Left* (New York: Knopf, 1979). For the most recent descriptions of women's status in all aspects of American life see the series sponsored by the Women's Research and Education Institute in Washington, D.C.: Sara Rix, ed., *The American Woman 1987–88: A Report in Depth* (New York: W. W. Norton, 1987) and *The American Woman 1988–89: A Status Report* (New York: W. W. Norton, 1988). Subsequent editions are scheduled on a yearly basis.

INDEX

Abbott, Grace, 207–208
Abolition movement, 75, 79
  women's participation in, 75, 79–81
  and women's rights, 80–81, 101, 104, 122–23
Abortion, 85, 143, 293–94
  controversy over, 278, 291–92, 298, 305, 307, 312
Abzug, Bella, 291, 306
Actresses, motion-picture, 176, 179, 197–98, 248
Adams, Abigail, 54, 56
Adams, John, 47, 55, 56
Addams, Jane, 139, 148, 149, 153–54, 171, 180, 311
Advertising, 201, 248, 251
Ah Choi, 106
Aid to Dependent Children, 210
AIDS epidemic, 313
Air, Martha, 42–43
Alabama, 114, 116
Alimony, 302
Allen, Florence, 209
Allen, Ruth, 185
Alliances, cross-class, 149–52, 169, 188, 191–94, 256; see also Women's Trade Union League
Amalgamated Clothing Workers, 160
American Association of University Women, 191, 234, 277, 290–291, 295–96
American Federation of Labor (AFL), 157, 158–59, 202

American Federation of State, County, and Municipal Employees (AFSCME), 310
American Female Moral Reform Society, 74
American Revolution, 2, 4, 52–53, 54–55, 239
  contradictory images of women in, 47–48
  women in, 45–46, 48–52, 53–54, 59
American Woman Suffrage Association (AWSA), 124
Ames, Jessie Daniel, 211, 212
Anderson, Mary, 205, 207–208
Angel, Mary, 42–43
Anthony, Susan B., 103, 122, 123–24, 153, 156, 168
Antidiscrimination laws, 77, 272, 276–78, 303; see also Equal Rights Amendment
Antifeminism, 292, 304–307, 311
Antislavery movement. See Abolition movement
Antiwar movements. See Peace groups, women's
Appleton, Elizabeth Rogers, 21
Archibald, Katherine, 225
Arendt, Hannah, 2
Arizona, 166
Arkansas, 170
Armstrong, Mary, 119
Arnow, Harriet, 220
Arthur, T. S., 69

373

Index

Asian-American women, 106, 227, 307
Association of Collegiate Alumnae (ACA), 140
Association of Southern Women for the Prevention of Lynchings (ASWPL), 211–13
Athletics, women's, 178, 289, 291
Atlanta, Georgia, 130, 152, 170
Atlantic Monthly, 236, 245
Auto industry, 231, 257; *see also* United Auto Workers (UAW)

"Baby M," 312–13
Bagley, Sarah, 84
Baker, Ella, 258–59, 271
Bakker, Tammy Faye, 308
Barry, Leonora, 137
Bates, Daisy, 260
Beard, Mary, 5
Beatniks, 266–67
Beecher, Catharine, 70, 71–72, 81, 96, 105, 139, 141, 155
Beecher, Lyman, 73
Berkshire Conference on the History of Women, 301
Bethune, Mary McLeod, 208, 211, 233
Birth control, 200, 248
  advocacy of, 78, 162, 177, 227–28
  pill used for, 265–66, 281–82
Birth Control Federation of America, 227
Birthrates, 63–64, 200, 220, 237–38, 246, 265
Black women, 223, 258–59, 269–70, 297–98, 302; *see also* Slave women
  in civil rights movement, 258–60, 270–72, 280
  families of, 112–13, 119–21, 132, 269–70: under slavery, 38, 60, 90, 108–109
  and field labor, 29, 38, 60, 120–21
  jobs open to, 90, 134, 199, 225, 272
  and late-twentieth-century women's movement, 272–73, 297
  middle-class, 89, 151–52
  in the south, after emancipation, 119–22, 152–56, 259–60, 270–72
  and white women's organizations, 187, 188–89, 211, 145, 155–56

Blacks, 117–22, 132, 251; *see also* Black women; Civil rights movement; Slavery
Blackwell, Alice Stone, 153
Blackwell, Antoinette Brown, 103
Blackwell, Elizabeth, 105, 106
Blackwell, Henry, 103, 122, 123, 124
Bloomer, Amelia, 103–104
Bloor, "Mother," 214
Boarders, 131–32
Boardinghouses, 83, 84, 141, 149
Boston, 99–100, 140, 156, 165, 293, 299
  in colonial period, 24–25, 42–43, 49
Bow, Clara, 161, 179
Boycotts, 49–50, 62, 232, 259, 296
Bradstreet, Anne Dudley, 24–25
Bromley, Dorothy Dunbar, 194–95
Brown, Charlotte Hawkins, 141, 188–89
Brown, Minnijean, 260
Brown v. *Board of Education*, 260
Bryn Mawr Summer School for Women Workers, 191–92, 274
Buckminster, Joseph, 65
Buffalo, New York, 132, 150
Bunch, Charlotte, 294
Burnham, Sophy, 288–89
Burns, Lucy, 166
Bushnell, Horace, 96
Business and Professional Women, 232, 234, 290

California, 106, 156, 165
Capitalism. *See* Economy, changes in the
Career women, 142, 147–48, 182
Carmichael, Stokely, 282
Carter, Jimmy, 306
Carter, John Mack, 288
Catholic Church, 305
Catholics, 129, 298, 306
Catt, Carrie Chapman, 171, 172, 173, 187–88, 190
  and woman suffrage movement, 165, 168–69, 170, 171
Charities, 99–100
Charleston, South Carolina, 28, 156
Chase, Lucy, 118
Chicago, 130, 150, 169, 267, 293–94, 299; *see also* Hull House
Chicanas, 204, 256–57, 272–73

374

Index

Child care, 78, 224, 291
Child rearing, 74, 92, 95, 181, 238
Childbirth, 30, 190
Children's Bureau of the Department of Labor, 160, 189, 194, 205, 207–208, 210
Chinese women, 106
Chisholm, Shirley, 274, 291, 297
Church, Mary (Mary Church Terrell), 147
Churches
  black, 120, 259, 270
  women in, 36–37, 56–57, 74, 259, 270: as ministers, 103, 111, 296; *see also* Religion, role of women in
CIO (Congress of Industrial Organizations), 215, 217, 237
Citizenship, 19, 48; *see also* Public life; Republican motherhood
  active, 3, 4, 6
  legal, 173
  women's, 57, 95, 143
Civil Rights Act of 1964, 272, 276
Civil rights movement, 264–65, 270, 272
  women's role in, 258–60, 270–72, 280
Civil War, 112–18, 141
Clark, Septima, 271
Class differentiation, 60–61, 85, 101, 151, 158, 191, 226–27, 251–52; *see also* Alliances, cross-class
  in colonial period, 34, 35
  in the south, 36–37, 88
Clerical workers, female, 171, 223, 224, 253, 272
  in nineteenth century, 115, 134–35
  organizations of, 216, 217, 299–300
  public perceptions of, 115, 182–84
Cleveland, Grover, 154
Clothing. *See* Dress
Coalition of Labor Union Women (CLUW), 300, 310
Cochran Gardens, 298
Cold war, 234, 236–37, 243–44
College Equal Suffrage League, 164
Colleges. *See* Higher education for women
Colonial period
  demographic imbalance in, 24, 26, 27, 33

families in, 3, 38, 41–42
increasing segregation of women during, 21, 37, 40
informal power exercised by women in, 3–4, 33–34, 42–43
marriage in, 22, 26, 34–35, 42–43
motherhood in, 29–31
sexual behavior in, 35
slavery in, 26–27, 29, 34, 37–40
tension during, between spiritual equality and female subordination, 31–34
women in religion during, 25, 31–32, 36–37, 40–41
work done by women in, 27–29, 35–38
Common law, 22, 64, 76–77, 193
Communist party, 213–14, 264
Communities Organized for Public Service (COPS), 309–10
Community, female, 70, 74, 96–97, 107, 173, 179, 188, 210, 261
  erosion of, 145, 173, 178, 179, 195, 210, 217–18
Companionate marriage, 63, 177, 179, 180
Comparable worth, 230–31, 310
Congress of Industrial Organizations (CIO), 215, 217, 237
Congressional Union, 166–67, 169
Consciousness-raising, 282–83, 289–90, 293
Consumer boycotts, 49–50, 62, 232, 259, 296
Consumerism, 195–96, 229, 250
Consumers' Leagues, 151; *see also* National Consumers' League
Contract motherhood, 312–13
"Cooperative commonwealth," 130, 137
Cooperatives, 136–37
Co-ordinating Committee for Building Better Race Relations, 223–224
Cortez, Beatrice, 309
Cotton, Dorothy, 271
Cotton, John, 25, 31, 32
Council for Interracial Cooperation (CIC), 188–89
Counterculture, 281
Crawford, Joan, 197, 248
Crocker, Hannah Mather, 67

Crowds. *See* Riots, women in
Culture, female. *See* Community, female
Cyrus, Della, 235–36

Dalton, Lucinda Lee, 107
Daly, Mary, 296
Dance halls, 160, 161, 184
Daughters of the American Revolution (DAR), 190
Daughters of Bilitis (DOB), 258, 283
Daughters of Liberty, 49
Daughters of St. Crispin, 136
Davidson, Hannah, 110
Davis, Angela, 298
Davis, Bette, 197
Day, Doris, 248
Day, Dorothy, 214
Day care, 78, 224, 291
Dell, Floyd, 182
Democratic party, 167, 169, 207, 217, 247, 291, 311
    Women's Division of, 247
Dennis, Peggy, 213
Department stores, 135, 151
Depressions
    of 1893–94, 149, 158
    of 1930s, 197, 198–204
Detroit, 220, 224, 231
Dewson, Molly, 205, 207, 209
Dietrich, Marlene, 197
Diseases, 12, 25, 26, 30, 51
Divorce, 42–43, 267–68, 302
    among native Americans, 11
    effect of, on women's standard of living, 267–68, 302
    laws governing, 143, 312
    rates of, 63, 267, 302
Dix, Dorothea, 114
Dollmaker, The (Arnow), 220
Domestic science movement, 162–63
Domestic servants, 121, 132, 133–34, 157, 180–81, 199, 215
    black women as, 134, 199, 225, 272
    immigrant women as, 133–34, 185–86
Domesticity, 57, 67, 87, 95–96, 101; *see also* Republican motherhood
    as basis for reforming zeal, 76, 95–96, 137, 143, 153, 154
    and education, 71–72

narrowly defined, as ideology confining women to the home, 93, 107, 124, 240, 262, 268–69
    and working-class women, 86–87, 98–99
Dorr, Rheta Childe, 167
Douglass, Frederick, 104, 122
Dress, 161, 227, 243, 247–48
Dress reform, 103–104
Dudley, Anne. *See* Bradstreet, Anne Dudley

Eastman, Crystal, 167–68, 191
Eckford, Elizabeth, 260
Economy, changes in the, 68, 73, 125, 137, 145–46
    effect of, on women's status, 42, 43, 62, 68–69, 73–74, 76–77, 81–84, 125, 146, 195–96, 255
Edenton, North Carolina, 49–50
Ederle, Gertrude, 178
Education for women, 28, 42, 58, 61, 65, 70–72; *see also* Higher education for women
Edwards, India, 247
Elizabethton, Tennessee, 184
Ellis, Havelock, 162
Elstain, Jean Bethke, 2–3
England, suffrage movement in, 165–68
Enlightenment thought, 54–55, 63, 65, 88, 153
    place of women in, 54–56, 63
Equal Employment Opportunity Commission (EEOC), 276, 277, 278, 291, 310
Equal Opportunity Act of 1972, 291
Equal Pay Act of 1963, 275, 291
Equal pay for equal work, 224, 240, 275, 291
Equal Rights Amendment (ERA), 187, 290–91, 297, 305, 306, 307
    before the 1970s, 187, 193–94, 232, 256, 274–75, 278
    conservative opposition to, 306
    traditional opposition of female reformers to, 193–94, 274–75
    unions and, 256, 278, 291
Europe, beliefs about women held in, 22–23
Executive Order 11375, 278

Index

Factories, women workers in, 61, 81–84, 99, 115, 132–33, 134, 136, 157, 221
  during World War II, 221–22, 223
Fall River, Massachusetts, 130
Families, 63, 200–201, 240; *see also* Marriage
  black, 112–13, 119–21, 132, 269–70: under slavery, 38, 60, 90, 108–109
  middle-class, 68–70, 128, 177–78
  working-class, 86–87, 98–100, 199–200, 254
Family planning, 64, 143; *see also* Birth control
"Family wage," 136
Farenthold, Sissy, 291
Farnham, Marynia, 238–39, 248, 261
Fashion, 243, 247–48
Female Anti-Slavery Society, 75
Female community. *See* Community, female
Female culture. *See* Community, female
Female-headed households, 251–52, 269
Female reform tradition, 153, 187–89, 193–94
  decline of, 186–88, 190–95, 256
  influence of, on modern welfare state, 196, 205–10
Female solidarity. *See* Community, female
"Feminine mystique," 246–50, 255
Feminine Mystique, The (Friedan), 275
Feminism, 194–95, 310, 312; *see also* Equal Rights Amendment; National Women's Party
  emergence of, in early twentieth century, 167–68
  and higher education, 300–301
  legislative and judicial victories of, 290–92, 310
  nonwhite women and, 296–98, 306–307
  opposition to, 292, 304–307, 311-
  radical, 287–88, 292–95
  reemergence of, in 1960s and 1970s, 273–85, 287–92, 295–96, 301
  working-class women and, 299–300, 304
Feminist Studies, 301

"Feminization of poverty," 303
Ferraro, Geraldine, 311
Fertility, 14, 29–30, 34, 90, 138, 143, 200, 312
  restriction of, 15, 64, 143; *see also* Birth control
Fifteenth Amendment, 122, 123, 124
Firestone, Shulamith, 282
Fisher, Sally Logan, 54
Fitzgerald, Zelda, 175–76, 179
Flappers, 161, 175–76, 178, 184, 197, 200
Flint, Michigan, sit-down strike, 214–15
Flynn, Elizabeth Gurley, 167, 214
Fortune, 183, 221, 236
Fourteenth Amendment, 122, 124, 274
Fraser, Arvonne, 283
Freeman, Jo, 295
Freudianism, 177, 248
Friedan, Betty, 237, 275–76, 276–77, 291
Frontier, women on the, 29, 60, 96–98, 106
Furies, the, 294

Galloway, Abigail, 42–43
Garbo, Greta, 197
Garlic, Delia, 110
Garment industry, 115–16, 132, 159–60
Gay liberation, 284
Gay men, 228, 284; *see also* Homosexuality
General Federation of Women's Clubs (GFWC), 150, 152, 157–58, 168, 191, 208, 232
Gesell, Arnold, 238
Gibson girl, 147, 161
Giddings, Paula, 297
Gilkey, Bertha, 298
Gilman, Charlotte Perkins, 154–55, 162, 167, 195
Girl Scouts, 295
Godey's Lady's Book, 96, 105
Goldman, Emma, 162, 173, 177
Good Housekeeping, 138–39
Great Awakening, 41, 47, 56, 57
Great Awakening, second, 65, 72–74, 95
Great Depression, 197, 198–204
Greeley, Horace, 143

Index

Greenbaum, Lucy, 231
Greenwich Village, 161–62, 280
Griffin, Susan, 293
Griffiths, Martha, 276
Grimke, Angelina, 79–81, 87–88, 89, 92
Grimke, Sarah, 79–81, 87–88, 92

Haener, Dorothy, 300
Hagood, Margaret, 203, 204
Hall, Radclyffe, 180
Hamer, Fannie Lou, 270–71, 274
Harper, Frances, 145
Hatcher, Lillian, 233
Health reformers, 105
Hefner, Hugh, 261
Height, Dorothy, 273, 297
Hepburn, Katharine, 197, 248
Hernandez, Aileen, 274
Hernandez, Sonia, 309–10
Heterodoxy, 167, 280
Hicksite Quakers, 79, 93–94, 101
Higher education for women, 105–106, 139, 141, 147, 176–77, 261, 265, 287, 300–301
Hillsboro, Ohio, 126
Hispanic women, 298; see also Mexican-Americans
History, women's, 1–2, 5–6, 301
Home, the; see also Domestic servants; Home work; Housework; Housing
cultural meanings of, 62, 88, 100, 239
separation of, from work, 61–62, 68–69, 88, 125, 236; see also Public and private spheres, distinction between
Home economists, 163, 181
"Home Protection Ballot," 127–28
Home work, 115, 132; see also "Putting-out" system
Homeless women, 203
Homophobia, 245, 294, 313
Homosexuality, 178, 228, 258, 284; see also Homophobia; Lesbians
House Un-American Activities Committee (HUAC), 244, 263–64
Housework, 27–29, 137, 138–39, 155, 162–63, 180, 236, 251, 302; see also Domestic servants
effect on, of new technology, 138, 180–81, 204, 251, 308

Housing, 138, 149, 157, 198, 199–200, 224, 249
in boardinghouses, 83, 84, 141, 149
Houston, Texas, 306–307
Howe, Julia Ward, 128
Hull House, 148, 149, 157–58
Hutchinson, Anne, 25, 30, 31–32, 33, 41

Illegitimacy, 75, 269, 302
Illinois, 149, 157–58, 166, 296; see also Chicago
Illinois Women's Alliance, 149, 157–58
Immigrants, 85, 99, 130–32, 133–34, 156, 158, 186, 216
during colonial period, 23–24
Indentured servants, 25–26
Indian Reorganization Act (IRA), 208–209
Indians; see Native Americans; Native-American women
Individualism, 120, 153
as threat to female community, 146–47, 173, 187, 195, 278
Infant mortality, 30, 189
Infanticide, 30–31, 42, 85–86
International Ladies Garment Workers Union (ILGWU), 159, 160, 215
International Woman Suffrage Alliance, 165, 168
International Women's Congress, 171
International Women's Year, 306–307
Interracial cooperation, 188–89, 211, 233–34
Ipswich, Massachusetts, 21, 49
Irish women, 99–100, 117, 131, 133, 135
Iroquois, 7, 8, 9, 13, 19, 53, 317n.11
women's power among, 3–4, 11–12, 18
Italian women, 132, 161

Jackson, Mary, 116
Jane Club, 149
Japanese-Americans, 227
Jay, Sarah, 48
Jeannette Rankin Brigade, 284
Jeffrey, Mildred, 233

378

Jewish women, 131, 160–61, 306
Johnson, Carrie Parks, 189

Kansas, 123, 130, 166
Kearney, Belle, 155
Kelley, Florence, 149, 151, 171
Kelly, Lavinia, 69
Kennedy, John Fitzgerald, 265, 274
Kenney, Mary, 149
King, Billie Jean, 289
King, Martin Luther, Jr., 259, 271
Kinsey, Alfred, 249
Knights of Labor, 136–38, 154, 160
Knights of St. Crispin, 136
Knox, Lucy Flucker, 54
Komarovsky, Mirra, 235
Ku Klux Klan, 121, 185, 186, 244

Labor force participation, 156, 182,
    240, 252, 301–302, 303
  of black women, 157, 269
  of married women, 156, 157, 202,
    204, 225, 234, 252–54
  of middle-class women, 236, 252
Labor movement, women in, 135–38;
    see also Unions, women in
Ladies Home Journal, 138–39, 181,
    283, 288
Lady's Magazine, 63
Laney, Lucy, 141
Lathrop, Julia, 160
Lawrence, D. H., 248–49
League of Women Voters (LWV),
    191, 205, 211, 234, 247, 268
  origins of, 187
  and women's rights, 232, 277, 290,
    296
Lease, Mary Elizabeth, 130
Lee, Mother Ann, 73, 78
Lemlich, Clara, 159
Lesbians, 228–29, 249, 258, 283–84,
    294, 299, 307
  discrimination against, 233, 245
  before World War II, 179–80
LeSueur, Meridel, 200, 203, 214
Librarians, 142, 202
Life, 236, 250, 254–55
Literacy, 25, 42, 46, 61, 65, 72, 108
Little Rock, Arkansas, 260
Livy, Caroline, 71
Locke, John, 77
Long Island, 49, 51
Look, 249, 249–50, 254

Lopata, Helena, 267
Lopez de la Cruz, Jesse, 272–73
Lorde, Audre, 298
Los Angeles, black women's organiza-
    tions in, 156
Lowell, Massachusetts, 82–84
Lowell Female Reform Association,
    84
Lucas, Eliza (Eliza Lucas Pinckney),
    37
Lucy, Authurine, 260
Lundberg, Ferdinand, 238–39, 248,
    261–62
Lynching, 212, 297
  crusade against, 152, 211–13
Lynd, Helen, 181
Lynd, Robert, 181
Lynn, Massachusetts, 98–99, 135–36
Lyon, Mary, 70, 72
Lyon, Phyllis, 258

McCall's, 247
McCarthyism. See Red scares
McClintock, Mary Ann, 93, 94
McDowell, Mary, 148
McWeeney, Marjorie, 236
Madar, Olga, 300
Marriage, 69–70
  age of, 29–30, 34, 133, 177, 237,
    246, 253, 265, 302, 308
  changing conceptions of, 62–63,
    68, 69, 178
  companionate, 63, 177, 179, 180
  control over choice of partners for,
    34–35, 42, 62
  legal status of women in, 22
  in middle classes, 68–70, 128, 177–
    78
  native-American women and, 11,
    12–15
  women's property rights in, 22, 42,
    64, 76–77, 94, 102–103, 193
"Marriage market," 177–78
Marriage rates, 200, 220, 237, 246
Martin, Del, 258, 283
Maryland, 50, 111–12
Massachusetts, 21, 31–34, 50–51, 70,
    84, 130, 164, 168; see also Bos-
    ton; Salem witchcraft trials
Maternal Associations, 74
"Maternal commonwealth," 127, 141,
    143, 146, 154, 188, 210
Maternity leave, 312

Index

Mead, Margaret, 230, 235
Medical education for women, 105–106, 141–42
Memphis, Tennessee, 152, 156
Merson, Ruth, 227
Methodist Women's Missionary Council, 212
Metis, 15
Mexican-Americans, 185–86, 204, 256–57, 272–73
Meyer, Agnes E., 245
Michigan, 166, 214–15; *see also* Detroit
Middle class, 145, 146, 155, 177, 252, 279; *see also* Middle-class women
  in early nineteenth century, 67
  polarized gender roles within, 128
  prejudices of, 85, 95, 155, 172
Middle-class women, 73, 138–42, 172, 250–51
  attempts by, to help working-class women, 135, 140–41, 148–52; *see also* Women's Trade Union League
  black, 88, 151–52
  as bulwark of many voluntary associations, 124, 126–27, 139–41, 148–51
  labor force participation of, 252–54
  and marriage, 68–70, 128, 177–78
  and temperance, 126–27
Midwives, 30, 105, 142, 190
Military, women in the, 51–52, 222–23, 228, 304
Milton, John, 22, 41
Minneapolis, 203, 214
Minnesota, 97–98, 203, 214
Miss America Beauty Pageant, 178–79, 283
Mississippi, 122, 270–71
Modern Woman, The (Farnham and Lundberg), 238–39
"Momism," 235
Monroe, Marilyn, 248
Montgomery bus boycott, 259, 270
Moore, Colleen, 176
Moore, Eileen, 250
Moral superiority, women's supposed, 71–72
Moreno, Luisa, 215–16
Mormons, 107
Morrison, Toni, 298

Motherhood, 92, 143, 181, 234–36; *see also* Birthrates; Child rearing; Republican motherhood
Mothers Against Drunk Driving (MADD), 311
"Mother's pensions," 150, 164
Mott, James, 95
Mott, Lucretia, 81, 93
Mount Holyoke Seminary, 72
Movies, 176, 179, 182–83, 197–98, 222, 248, 257, 308
Moynihan, Daniel Patrick, 269, 297
"Ms.," 290
Ms. magazine, 296, 305
Muncie, Indiana, 181
Murray, Judith Sargent, 58, 63
Murray, Pauli, 273
Music teachers, 142

National American Woman Suffrage Association (NAWSA), 153–56, 166–71, 187
National Association of Colored Women (NACW), 152
National Conference on the Cause and Cure of War, 190–91
National Consumers' League, 148, 151, 187, 188, 205
National Council of Jewish Women, 212
National Council of Negro Women, 233, 297
National Organization for Women (NOW), 277–78, 283, 287, 288, 296, 300, 305–306
National Right to Life Committee, 305
National Woman Suffrage Association (NWSA), 123–24
National Woman's Party (NWP), 187, 193, 261, 274, 276, 295
  and Equal Rights Amendment, 187, 274
  narrow base of, 232, 255–56, 295
  and woman suffrage, 167, 168, 169–70, 172
National Women's Political Caucus (NWPC), 291, 296, 297
National Women's Studies Association, 301
Native Americans, 59–60; *see also* Native-American women
  diversity of, 7–8

380

effects of European domination on, 12–18, 25, 53, 90–91, 98
marriage and divorce among, 11
misunderstanding of, by whites, 18–19, 98
sexual division of labor among, 8–9, 16–18, 19, 97
in twentieth century, 208–209, 298–99, 307
Native-American women, 59–60, 91–92, 97–98, 208–209, 298–99, 307
intermarriage of, with Europeans, 12–15
political power of, 3–4, 11–12, 18–19, 208–209, 317n.11
in religious myths and rituals, 7, 10, 17
work done by, 8–10, 13–14, 16, 19, 97, 99, 317n.4
New Deal, 199, 204–205, 208–209
women in, 204–10
New Hampshire, 69
New Jersey, 50, 51, 168, 306
New Mexico, 256–57
New Orleans, black women's organizations in, 156
"New woman," 146–52, 154, 161–62
New York Children's Aid Society, 100, 101
New York City, 101, 131–32, 137, 161–62, 165, 216
in Civil War, 114, 115, 117
in colonial period, 36, 45
organizations of women in, 137, 150–51, 159–60
poverty in, 61, 85–86, 100, 115, 135, 203
New York Moral Reform Society, 74–75
New York State, 72, 93–95, 103, 168–69, 170, 306; see also Buffalo; Long Island; New York City; Utica
New York Times, 276, 287, 292
Newsweek, 265, 288
Nin, Anais, 248–49
Nineteenth Amendment, 172, 288
Nine-to-Five, 299–300, 310
North Carolina, 49–50, 64, 116
Norton, Eleanor Holmes, 310
NOW. See National Organization for Women
Noyes, John, 78

Nurses, 52, 114, 141–42, 189, 253, 303
training schools for, 141–42
Nurses aides, 253

Office holders, proportion of women among, 247, 311
Ohio, 126, 166; see also Toledo, Ohio
Oneida Community, 78
Oregon, 166
Orgasm, 248–49
Our Bodies, Ourselves, 293
"Outwork," 86
Owen, Ruth Bryan, 209

Pacifism, 170–71; see also Peace groups, women's
Pankhurst, Emmaline, 165–66
Parent/teacher associations, 247, 268
Parks, Rosa, 259
Paul, Alice, 166–67, 168, 169, 187
Peace groups, women's, 170–71, 190–91, 284, 311
Women Strike for Peace, 263–64, 267, 268, 278, 284, 311
Pennsylvania, 64, 168; see also Philadelphia; Pittsburgh
Perkins, Frances, 205, 207–208
"Personal is political, the," 280, 284–85
Petersburg, Virginia, 65, 70, 90, 101
Peterson, Esther, 274
Petition campaigns by women, 75, 84, 103, 117
Phelps, Aurora, 134
Philadelphia, 36, 50, 75, 130, 135
Phillips, Dorothy, 179
Physicians, 105, 141, 189–90
female, 105–106, 114
Pickel, Margaret, 231–32
Pickford, Mary, 161
Pinckney, Eliza Lucas, 37
Pittsburgh, 130, 132
Plains Indians, 8, 9, 15–18
Planned Parenthood Federation of America, 227–28
"Playboy philosophy," 261
Polish women, 131
Polygamy, 16, 107
Populists, 129–30
Pornography, 311, 312
Porter, Lavinia, 96–97
Posner, Blanche, 263

Post, Lydia Mintern, 51
Poverty, 149, 269–70, 312
    efforts to alleviate, 61, 148–50,
        201, 210
    and prostitution, 61, 100
    women's special vulnerability to,
        61, 85–86, 99–100, 202–203,
        251–52, 303, 308–309, 312
    of women wage earners, 115, 135
Presidential Commission on the Sta-
    tus of Women, 274–75
Pressman, Sonia, 297
Prison reform, 128
Prisoners, female, 128, 141
Private domain. See Public and pri-
    vate spheres, distinction between
Professionals, female, 173, 202, 261–
    62, 274, 278–79
    in female professions, 4, 141–42,
        202, 303
    in traditionally male professions,
        105–106, 114, 262, 300–301
Property rights, women's, 22, 42, 64,
    76–77, 94, 102–103, 193
Prostitution, 61, 74–75, 100, 106
Protective legislation, 192–94, 210
Providence, Rhode Island, 49
PTAs, 247, 268
Public and private spheres, distinc-
    tion between, 3, 15–17, 47, 48,
        61–62, 68–69, 138
    in American Revolution, 2–3, 4
    challenge to, by women, 4–5, 76,
        94–95, 279, 290, 313–14
    erosion of, 255
    sharpening of, by European con-
        quest, 15, 19
    in the south, 88, 89
Public life
    broadened understanding of, 19,
        59, 295
    exclusion of women from, 1, 4, 21,
        43, 45–46
    middle-class women's critical per-
        spective on, 141
    women's, 3–4, 67–70, 74, 92, 160–
        62, 240, 293–95
    women's impact in changing the
        meaning of, 3, 4–5, 59, 217, 295,
        313
Puritans, 21, 22, 24–25, 31–34, 40,
    42–43, 57
"Putting-out" system, 60, 98–99

Quakers, 19, 24, 25, 36, 64, 79, 81,
    94

Radcliffe College, 139
Rankin, Jeannette, 171, 284
Rape, 39, 51, 109–10, 198, 293
    as issue for women's groups, 293,
        297
Rawalt, Marguerite, 275
Reagan administration, 307, 308, 310
Reconstruction, 121–22, 125
Red scares
    after World War I, 190–91
    after World War II, 243–45, 257
Reed, James, 194
Relief, public, 61, 210
Religion, women's role in, 10, 17, 31–
    32, 40–41, 296; see also
    Churches, women in; Revivals
Republican motherhood, 62, 95, 154,
    234, 239
    as bond between women, 60, 66
    defined, 57, 67
    as impetus to community participa-
        tion by women, 58–59, 64–66,
        142–43
    modernized version of, 246–47
    reshaping of, by women, 67, 95
    and women's education, 58, 255
Republican party, 122, 124, 169, 247,
    291, 305
Republicanism, 2, 55–56, 68; see also
    Citizenship; Republican mother-
    hood
    entrepreneurial version of, 68
Reuther, Rosemary Radford, 296
Revivals, religious, 41, 47, 73
    women in, 41, 56, 57, 65, 72–74,
        95
Revolution. See American Revolution
Reynolds, Debbie, 248
Richmond, Virginia, 116, 120
Riggs, Bobby, 289
Riggs, Mary Ann Longley, 97, 117
Riots, women in, 46, 54, 116, 117,
    186
Rivera, Iris, 299
Robinson, Joanne, 259
Robinson, Marie, 248, 249
Robinson, Rubye Doris Smith, 271–
    72
Rodgers, Elizabeth, 137
Roe v. Wade, 291–92, 305

Index

Romantic love, 63, 69
Rome, Georgia, 71
Roosevelt, Eleanor, 205, 206–207, 217, 232, 240–41, 274
Roosevelt, Franklin D., 204, 205, 227
Rose, Ernestine, 103
"Rosie the Riveter," 222
Ross, Betsy, 1
Rousseau, Jean-Jacques, 55–56
Rubin, Lillian, 269
Ruddick, Sara, 279
Rush, Benjamin, 58

Salem withcraft trials, 4, 32, 35
Saleswomen, retail, 134, 135, 151, 185, 272
Salt of the Earth (film), 257
Sampson, Deborah, 52
San Antonio, Texas, 309–10
Sandford, Mrs. John, 68
Sanger, Margaret, 162, 177, 227–28
Sanitary Commission, 114, 124
Saturday Evening Post, 226, 250
Savvy, 308
Scandinavian women, 99–100, 133
Schakowsky, Jan, 296
Schlafly, Phyllis, 304–307, 311
Schroeder, Patricia, 311–12
Science, 146, 164, 173, 181
Scudder, Vida, 148
Secretaries' Day, 299–300
Sedgwick, Catharine, 69
Seneca Falls convention, 94–95, 104
Servants. *See* Domestic servants; Indentured servants
Service Employees International Union, 300
Settlement houses, 148–50, 160, 162
in black community, 152
professionalization of, 163–64, 191
Seventeen, 245–46
"Sex radicals," 164, 167
Sexual experimentation, 161–62, 176–77, 228, 266–67, 281–82
Sexuality, female, 11, 47, 109, 161–62, 177–78, 197, 200, 245–46, 248, 281–82
Shakers, 73, 78
Shaw, Anna Howard, 171–72
Sheppard-Towner Act, 189, 194, 210
Shoemaking, 98–99, 135–36
Signs, 301

Single women, 35–36, 133, 140–41, 142, 147, 156, 161–62, 302
as parents, 251–52, 302
Slave women, 26–27, 89–90
in colonial period, 37–40
family ties of, 38, 60, 90, 108–109
sexual abuse of, by masters, 39–40, 88, 109–10
work done by, 29, 38, 60
Slavery, 26–27, 52, 72, 108–13; *see also* Abolition movement; Slave women
immediate aftermath of ending of, 117–25
sexual division of labor under, 28, 38, 109
and southern white women, 36–37, 40, 87, 88, 89, 92
Smeal, Eleanor, 306
Smith, Hilda, 191
Smith, Howard, 276
Smith, Margaret Chase, 276
Smith, Mary, 25
Smith, Mary Rozet, 180
Smith, Sarah, 128
Smith, Sophia, 139
Smith College, 139, 255
Socialists, 129, 151, 155, 158, 160, 162, 167
Social work, 142, 148, 163–64, 202, 209, 313
Solidarity, female. *See* Community, female
Sororities, 178
Sorosis, 139, 139–40
South, the, 52–53, 117–22, 146, 203–204; *see also* Slavery
black women in, 119–22, 152, 156, 188–89, 259–60, 270–72; *see also* Slave women
class differentiation in, 36–37, 88
interracial cooperation in, 188–89, 211–13
white women in, 36–37, 87–89, 92, 107–108, 116–17, 132–33, 155, 184, 188–89, 212
woman suffrage in, 155–56, 170
women's voluntary associations in, 87, 88, 156, 188–89, 211–13
South Carolina, 29, 37, 39, 64, 112, 121; *see also* Charleston, South Carolina

Index

Southern Christian Leadership Conference (SCLC), 259
Southern Methodist Women's Missionary Council, 188
Spencer, Anna Garlin, 153
Spock, Benjamin, 238
St. Louis, black women's organizations in, 156
Stanlaws, Penrhyn, 179
Stanton, Elizabeth Cady, 77, 81, 93, 102–103, 122, 123–24, 153, 170–71
Starr, Ellen Gates, 148
Stein, Gertrude, 180
Steinem, Gloria, 296
Stephens, Christine, 309
Stevenson, Adlai, 255
Stone, Lucy, 72, 103, 122, 123, 124
STOP ERA, 304
Stowe, Harriet Beecher, 155
Strecker, Edward A., 235
Strikes, 99, 135, 159–60, 214–15, 216, 256–57
  by farm workers, 186, 273
  in textile industry, 83, 184, 216
Student movement of the 1960s, 264, 279–80
  women within, 280–83
Student Nonviolent Coordinating Committee (SNCC), 271–72, 280
Students for a Democratic Society (SDS), 280–81
Suburbs, 145, 246, 247, 249, 250
  housewives in, 250–51, 267–68
Suffrage
  black male, 122, 124–25
  white male, 76
  woman. See Woman suffrage
Summer Schools for Women Workers, 191–92
Surrogate motherhood. See Contract motherhood
Sutton, Marjorie, 250
Swanson, Gloria, 179

Tanguay, Eva, 161
Tanner, Aletha, 53
Teachers, 61, 70–72, 106, 140, 141, 202, 244, 303, 313
  black, 259
  Catharine Beecher's ideas about, 71–72, 105, 141
  married women as, 223, 253

Television, 246, 252
Temperance movement, 75, 103, 125–30, 137
Terrell, Mary Church, 147, 152, 156
Textile industry, 60–61, 81–84, 132–33, 184, 216
Thomas, M. Carey, 191
Title VII of the 1964 Civil Rights Act, 276, 278
Title IX of the Higher Education Act, 291
Tocqueville, Alexis de, 67–68
"Togetherness," 247, 249
Toledo, Ohio, 137, 198
Train, George, 123
Trask, Sarah, 98–99
Travelers' Aid societies, 140–41
Triangle Shirtwaist Fire, 160, 207
Troy, New York, 70, 135
Troy Seminary, 71
Truman administration, 237, 240
Truth, Sojourner, 104, 122
Tubman, Harriet, 111–12, 113
Tucker, Mary Orne, 63
Tuskegee, Alabama, black women's organizations in, 156

Unemployment, 198
  of women, 199, 202–203
Unions, 236–37, 256, 272; see also United Auto Workers
  championing of women workers' interests by, 223–24, 225, 226
  and Equal Rights Amendment, 256, 278, 291
  hostility or indifference of, to women workers, 136, 158–59, 192, 215, 216–17, 226, 256
  women in, 157–60, 191–92, 215–17, 226, 256, 273
United Auto Workers (UAW), 215, 216, 225, 277, 278, 291, 300
  Women's Bureau of, 230, 233, 241, 257–58, 277
United Electrical Workers, 233
United Farm Workers' Union, 273, 298
Universities. See Higher education for women
Urosova, Natalya, 159–60
Utica, New York, 75
Utopian communities, 77–78

Index

Van Horne, Edith, 300
Vassar College, 139
Victorian values, 67, 92, 138
Virginia, 36–37, 50, 52, 87
Voluntary associations, women's, 3, 67, 101, 247
  among blacks, 120, 152
  class background of, 139–41, 146–52
  creation of new public spaces for women by, 3, 4–5, 66, 67–68, 92, 313
  and emergence of a distinctive women's perspective, 66, 68
  and religion, 56–57, 65–66, 237
  in suburbs, 237, 267
Vorse, Mary Heaton, 167, 168
Vote, right to. *See* Suffrage; Woman suffrage

WACs, 222, 223
Wages, 203
  gap between men's and women's, 61, 99, 272, 310
  women's, 135, 265, 272, 303
Walker, Alice, 298
Walker, Margaret, 111, 121
Wallin, Madeleine, 147
War Labor Board, 221–22, 226
Warren, Mercy Otis, 58
Wars; *see also* American Revolution; Civil War; World War I; World War II
  women in the military during, 51–52, 222–23, 228
  women's assumption of men's traditional tasks during, 53–54, 59, 114–15, 171–72, 221–22, 223–27
  women's efforts to prevent, 170–71, 190–91, 284, 311; *see also* Women Strike for Peace
  women's voluntary activities during, 114, 171–72, 220–21
Washington, D.C., 53, 224, 294
Washington Court House, Ohio, 126
Washington State, 165
WAVES, 222, 223
Wear, Magdalen, 29
Weisbord, Vera Buch, 214
Welfare state, 5, 196, 205
Well of Loneliness, The (Hall), 180
Wellesley College, 139
Wells-Barnett, Ida B., 152, 212

West, women in the, 106–107, 142, 146
Westward migration, 90, 107
  women in, 59–60, 91, 96–97
Wheatley, Phyllis, 53
White-collar work, 134; *see also* Clerical workers; Professionals, female; Saleswomen, retail
Whitehead, Mary Beth, 312–13
Widows, 22, 26, 35, 77, 303
Wilber, Rhona Ryan, 236
Willard, Emma, 70–71
Willard, Frances, 126, 127, 128–29, 311
Wills, Helen, 178
Wilson, Dagmar, 263–64, 268
Wilson, Woodrow, 166, 169
Winthrop, John, 22, 32
Wisconsin, 166
Witchcraft, 32
  trials for, in Salem, Massachusetts, 4, 32, 35
Woman suffrage movement, 103, 122–25, 152–56, 164–72, 173, 187
  class and race prejudices within, 155–56
Woman Suffrage Party of Greater New York, 169
Woman's Journal, 124, 165
Woman's Peace Party, 171, 190
Women Against Military Madness (WAMM), 311
Women Employed, 299–300, 310
Women Strike for Peace (WSP), 263–64, 267, 268, 278, 284, 311
Women workers; *see also* Clerical workers; Domestic servants; Saleswomen, retail; Strikes; Unions
  gender segregation of jobs for, 194, 216, 231, 252–53, 303, 310
  male workers' attitudes toward, 136, 215, 221, 225, 226
  married, 15, 201–202, 236, 240, 253
  public perceptions of, 115, 171, 182, 201–202, 221–22, 225–27, 231–32, 236, 253, 254–55, 262
  in textile industry, 60–61, 81–84, 132–33, 184, 216

Women workers *cont.*
   wages of, 135, 265, 272, 303; compared with men's, 99, 272, 310
   after World War II, 229–32, 240
Women's Bureau of the Department of Labor, 191, 192–93, 205, 207–208, 224, 274
Women's Christian Temperance Union (WCTU), 127–30, 137, 141, 154, 165, 191, 212, 268, 280, 311
Women's clubs, 139–40, 150, 160, 188, 247
   as middle-class phenomenon, 150
Women's Equity Action League (WEAL), 278, 283, 287, 300
[*Women's*] *Home Companion,* 138–39
Women's Home Journal, 138–39
Women's International League for Peace and Freedom (WILPF), 190
Women's Joint Congressional Committee, 190
"Women's lib," 287, 292, 305
Women's liberation movement, 279–85, 287, 295; *see also* Feminism
Women's National Loyal League, 117
Women's Peace Party, 311
Women's rights movement, 101–105
   during Civil War, 117
   roots of, 95
"Women's sphere," 71, 142–43; *see also* Public and private spheres, distinction between
Women's Strike for Equality, 288
Women's studies, 300–301
Women's Trade Union League (WTUL), 158–60, 188, 191, 192, 205, 232, 234, 237
Woodhull, Victoria, 124

Work, separation of from the home, 61–62, 68–69, 88, 125, 236
Worker education, 191–92
Working-class families, 86–87, 98–100, 254
Working-class women, 81–87, 107, 130–38, 184, 226, 256, 268–69, 309–10; *see also* Unions; Women workers
   in cross-class alliances, 149–52, 188, 191–94, 256; *see also* Women's Trade Union League
   and feminism, 299–300, 304
"Working girl, the," 146–47, 156–60, 161, 173, 182
Working Woman, 308
Working women. *See* Professionals, female; Women workers
World War I, 170, 185
   expansion of women's roles during, 171–72
World War II, 219, 221–27, 239–41
   women's employment during, 221–22, 223–27
   women's voluntary activities in, 220–21
World's Congress of Representative Women, 145
Wright, Fanny, 78–79, 92
Wright, Martha, 93
Wyatt, Addie, 274, 300
Wylie, Philip, 235

Young, Marilyn, 279
Young Women's Christian Association (YWCA), 135, 140–41, 188, 191, 208, 247, 261, 296
   and nonwhite women, 188, 208, 234, 241, 270
   and women's rights, 233, 290, 296